Industrial Structure and Policy in Less Developed Countries

Industrial Structure and Policy in Less Developed Countries

C. H. Kirkpatrick, N. Lee and F. I. Nixson

University of Manchester

London
GEORGE ALLEN & UNWIN
Boston   Sydney

George Allen & Unwin (Publishers) Ltd,
40 Museum Street, London WC1A 1LU, UK

George Allen & Unwin (Publishers) Ltd,
Park Lane, Hemel Hempstead, Herts HP2 4TE, UK

Allen & Unwin Inc.,
Fifty Cross Street, Winchester, Mass. 01890, USA

George Allen & Unwin Australia Pty Ltd,
8 Napier Street, North Sydney, NSW 2060, Australia

First published in 1984

British Library Cataloguing in Publication Data

Kirkpatrick, C. H.
  Industrial structure and policy in less
developed countries.
1. Developing countries—Industries
I. Title. II. Lee, N. III. Nixson, F. I.
338′.09172′4   HC59.7
ISBN 0-04-338115-4
ISBN 0-04-338116-2 Pbk

Library of Congress Cataloging in Publication Data

Kirkpatrick, C. H. (Colin, H.), 1944–
  Industrial structure and policy in less developed
countries.
Bibliography: p.
Includes indexes.
1. Industry and state—Developing countries.
2. Developing countries—Industries. 3. Economic
development. 4. International business enterprises.
I. Lee, Norman, 1936–   . II. Nixson, F. I.
III. Title.
HD3616.D44K57   1984   338.9′009172′4   84-14493
ISBN 0-04-338115-4
ISBN 0-04-338116-2 (pbk.)

Set in 10 on 11 point Times by Preface Ltd, Salisbury
and printed in Great Britain by Mackays of Chatham

Contents

Tables

Figures

List of abbreviations

cif	cost, insurance, freight
DAC	Development Assistance Committee (of the OECD)
DC	developed country
DFI	direct foreign investment
DRC	domestic resource cost
EOI	export-oriented industrialisation
GFCF	gross fixed capital formation
GDP	gross domestic product
GNP	gross national product
ILO	International Labour Office/Organisation
ISI	import-substituting industrialisation
ISIC	International Standard Industrial Classification
LDC	less developed country
MES	minimum efficient scale
MVA	manufacturing value added
NIC	newly industrialising country
OECD	Organisation for Economic Co-operation and Development
OPEC	Organisation of Petroleum Exporting Countries
PE	public enterprise
R&D	research and development
RBP	restrictive business practices
SITC	Standard International Trade Classification
SOE	state-owned enterprises
S–P	structure–performance
TFP	total factor productivity
TNC	transnational corporation
UN	United Nations
UNCTAD	United Nations Conference on Trade and Development
UNIDO	United Nations Industrial Development Organisation

Acknowledgements

We are grateful to the following publishers for permission to reprint various tables reproduced in this book: North-Holland Publishing Company (table 3.8); Institut für Weltwirtschaft (table 6.1); Basil Blackwell Publisher Ltd. (table 3.9); OECD (tables 2.9 and 4.3); Oxford University Press (tables 2.1, 2.2, 2.13, 5.1, 5.2 and 5.3).

Preface

Industrialisation plays a critical role in the process of economic development and is a fundamental policy objective in most less developed countries (LDCs). The purpose of this textbook is to analyse, at both aggregate and microeconomic levels, the industrial conditions prevailing in Third World countries and to relate these to the process of economic and structural transformation that they are undergoing. It combines the analytical approaches of two previously separate branches of economics – development economics and industrial economics. Development economics has a long-standing interest in the industrialisation process in LDCs but, to a considerable degree, it has confined its main attention to the aggregate and sectoral levels of analysis. Industrial economics, by contrast, has been mainly preoccupied with analyses at the industry, market or enterprise level – and primarily in the developed country (DC) rather than the LDC context. In our view, these two approaches can usefully complement each other and this is what has been attempted in this case.

The book is written for students who have previously studied economics at first-year university level or its equivalent, but it does not assume any prior knowledge of development or industrial economics. It is primarily intended to be used as a textbook on development and industrial economics courses in both developed and developing countries. However, it should also be of interest to other readers concerned with the problems and policies of industrial development in the Third World.

It is written in a form that is intended to encourage a careful, analytical approach to the study of industrial problems and policies in LDCs. It draws together a wide range of source material that would not otherwise be readily accessible to most students and each chapter includes guidance on further reading, which may be augmented from the full list of references at the end of the text.

The authorship of each chapter is shown in the contents; although there has been a great deal of collaboration in the preparation of the book, each contributor's responsibility is limited to the particular chapters of which he is an author. We wish to express our appreciation to our colleagues in the Economics Department at the University of Manchester and to a number of former colleagues and other economists in Third World countries for their advice and encouragement, although absolving them from responsibility for any errors that remain. We are also grateful to Jean Ashton, Julie Owen, Julie Gorton, Linda Cooper and Tracy Holehouse for their invaluable help in typing successive drafts of the manuscript.

C. H. K.   N. L.   F. I. N.
February 1984
University of Manchester

1 Introduction

1.1 INDUSTRY AND DEVELOPMENT

For the great majority of LDCs[1], industrialisation remains a fundamental objective of economic development. In such countries industrial development is considered necessary to achieve high rates of economic growth, to provide for the basic needs of the population, to create more employment opportunities, to lead to an increasingly diversified economy and to give rise to desirable social, psychological and institutional changes (UNIDO, 1979a, chs I and IV). Consequently, development economists have shown considerable interest in analysing, *at the more aggregate level*, the relationship between industrialisation and the development process in LDCs. Far less attention has been paid to the analysis of industrial structure, behaviour and policy in LDCs at the *microeconomic level*. Although there are a number of well-established textbooks in industrial economics that focus on the microeconomic level of industrial activity and policy, without exception they confine their analysis to developed economies, notably the United States and the United Kingdom.

The purpose of this text is to analyse, at both aggregate and microeconomic levels, the industrial conditions prevailing within a range of LDCs and to relate these to the process of development taking place within them. It draws upon the literature from two previously separate branches of economics – industrial economics and development economics. Drawing upon these two distinct sources of economic analysis has important implications for the structure, content and methodological approach adopted in the book.

First, industrial economics has traditionally been more concerned with analysis at the level of the individual establishment, firm, market and industry, whereas development economics has focused primarily upon industry's sectoral relationships within the development process as a whole. In bringing these two elements together it is possible to achieve a more comprehensive and more fully integrated treatment of the different levels of industrial analysis in less developed economies.

Second, industrial economics has typically focused upon issues of central concern to mature industrial economies serving large domestic markets: the structure of those markets, their competitiveness, the transmission of new knowledge into new products and processes, the levels of technical and allocative efficiency that are achieved. Development economics has focused upon a different range of industrial issues: structural change in industrial production and foreign trade during the development process, the role of foreign-owned corporations in the industrialisation and development process, the appropriateness of the technology transferred from DCs to LDCs, the adoption of broad industrial strategies and policies. Again, in drawing upon both branches of the subject, a more balanced treatment of industrial issues relevant to LDCs is possible.

Third, both industrial economics and development economics have their own methodological traditions but in neither case is one single methodological approach dominant. In industrial economics, the neoclassical tradition exists alongside a more inductive form of analysis based upon the use of case studies and institutionally based forms of analysis, as well as the more formal methods of statistical analysis used in hypothesis testing (Devine *et al.*, 1979, ch. 1). Similarly, in development economics, neoclassical analysis exists alongside Marxist and more inductive and institutional forms of analysis (Todaro, 1981, chs 1 and 3). By drawing upon these different approaches a better understanding can often be obtained through uncovering implicit assumptions in the analysis, introducing new kinds of evidence, raising wider issues or offering new interpretations of the existing evidence.

1.2   CLASSIFICATION OF INDUSTRIAL ACTIVITIES

An industrial classification system is a device for grouping similar production activities into industries and is therefore basic to the study of the industrial structure of any economy. However, there are a number of different criteria that could be used to determine 'similarity'; for example, activities might be grouped according to the main material that they use, the type of product (or service) that they make, or the production process that they use. In order to promote uniformity and comparability in official industrial statistics relating to their own economy, many countries have developed their own standard industrial classification (SIC). In turn, to assist in comparisons of industrial structure between different economies, the United Nations has prepared an International Standard Industrial Classification (ISIC). This is the main industrial classification used in this text. The ISIC groups production activities at four levels of aggregation. In descending order of size, these are: *major divisions* (identified by a one-digit code), *divisions* (two-digit code), *major groups* (three-digit code) and *groups* (four-digit code) (United Nations, 1971).

At the highest level of aggregation, production activities are grouped into nine major divisions as follows:

1   Agriculture, hunting, forestry and fishing
2   Mining and quarrying
3   Manufacturing
4   Electricity, gas and water
5   Construction
6   Wholesale and retail trade and restaurants and hotels
7   Transport, storage and communications
8   Financing, insurance, real estate and business services
9   Community, social and personal services

Each major division is divided into a number of two-digit divisions; for example, major division 3 (Manufacturing) is divided into:

31 Food, beverages and tobacco
32 Textile, wearing apparel and leather industries
33 Wood and wood products, including furniture
34 Paper and paper products, printing and publishing
35 Chemicals and chemical, petroleum, coal, rubber and plastic products
36 Non-metallic mineral products, except products of petroleum and coal
37 Basic metal industries
38 Fabricated metal products, machinery and equipment
39 Other manufacturing industries

In turn, each division is divided into a number of three-digit major groups and most major groups are further subdivided into four-digit groups. For example, division 31 is divided into major groups 311–12 food manufacturing, 313 beverage industries and 314 tobacco manufacturing. Similarly, major group 313 is divided into groups 3131 distilling of spirits, 3132 wine industries, 3133 malt liquors and malt, and 3134 soft drinks and carbonated waters industries.

The term *industry* is used in a variety of different ways in the economic literature and it is necessary to clarify its meaning to avoid subsequent confusion. As in this text, 'industry' normally refers to any of the major divisions listed above *or* to any of the divisions, major groups or groups that are subdivisions of these (the main exceptions arise from the somewhat different classification of international trade flows, which is described below). In most cases it should be clear from the context which level and type of industrial aggregation is being used. However, it should be noted that some writers restrict the term 'industry' to groupings of particular types of activities, although there is no general agreement on the types of activities to which the term should be limited: some restrict it to activities contained within major divisions 2–4, some also include major division 5 and/or exclude major division 2, others limit it to activities within major division 3 alone. In this text, the term 'industry' is not restricted to particular types of economic activity but industries are, for certain forms of analysis, grouped into *sectors*: for example, the agricultural sector (major division 1), the industrial sector (major divisions 2–5) and the services sector (major divisions 6–9).

In assigning economic activities to particular industries, the basic statistical unit that is most commonly used is the *establishment*, although in a minority of countries other units are used. The establishment may be defined as a workplace under one ownership at a single physical location. It is allocated to a particular industry according to the nature of the principal economic activity that is carried on there. Therefore, the output, employment, etc., of an industry (whatever its level of aggregation) are obtained by adding together the output, employment, etc., levels of all of those establishments whose principal activity falls within the boundaries of the industry in question. A *firm* (sometimes referred to as an enterprise) is a unit of ownership and control of economic activities. A firm may own two or more establishments, which will 'belong' to different industries if the principal activities carried on within them are sufficiently dissimilar. For this reason the output, employment, etc., levels of industries cannot be reliably obtained by adding together output, etc., measures for individual firms. In common usage, the terms 'industry', 'firm' and 'establishment' are frequently interchangeable but, because of the confusion that this can cause, this should be avoided wherever possible.

International trade flows are expressed in terms of gross value and are classified using the Standard International Trade Classification (SITC) system. The SITC groups merchandise exports and imports at four levels of aggregation. The major *sections* (identified by one-digit code) are:

0   Food and live animals chiefly for food
1   Beverages and tobacco
2   Crude materials, inedible, except fuels
3   Mineral fuels, lubricants and related materials
4   Animal and vegetable oils, fats and waxes
5   Chemicals and related products (not elsewhere specified)
6   Manufactured goods classified chiefly by material
7   Machinery and transport equipment
8   Miscellaneous manufactured articles
9   Commodities and transactions not classified elsewhere

Each section is disaggregated into *divisions* (identified by a two-digit code), which are in turn disaggregated into three- and four-digit codes.

Since the SITC and ISIC systems are not identical, trade and industrial data cannot be directly compared with each other. For comparative purposes it is common practice to select a definition of trade in manufactures that roughly matches the range of activities commonly identified with manufacturing in the ISIC framework. For example, manufactures is normally defined as SITC sections 5–8 (in some cases SITC 68, non-ferrous metals, is excluded).

1.3   AVAILABILITY AND RELIABILITY OF DATA

Although most LDCs have established systems for the collection and publication of industrial statistics, few of these are fully developed yet. LDCs also often suffer from insufficient skilled manpower and financial resources for data collection and processing. It is therefore important to be aware of the possible limitations in the data currently available and to take these into consideration when analysing the data and drawing conclusions (Fessey, 1981). These limitations are briefly outlined below.

A prerequisite for the collection of industrial data in any country is a list of business enterprises and establishments, which ideally should be as comprehensive and up-to-date as possible. However, because the preparation of such lists is time consuming and expensive, they may be updated only at long intervals. This may mean that enterprises and establishments created since the last listing are ignored, unless other means of identification are available (e.g. tax records).

A further difficulty arises where production is carried on within large numbers of very small establishments or domestic residences. Because of the practical difficulties involved, most LDCs limit their listings, and the surveys based upon these, to establishments above a certain threshold size, ranging usually (according to country) from five to twenty employees. The listing therefore provides very inadequate coverage, if any, of what is referred to as the 'informal', 'traditional' or 'non-modern' sector of economic activities. Estimates of the size of this sector have to draw upon such other less satisfactory sources as might be available and may be subject to a wide margin of error.

On the basis of the businesses list available, estimates of output, employment, investment, etc., are sought at intervals using postal questionnaires and interviews. Again, because of the time involved, the intervals may be considerable and for the intervening period estimates may be prepared on the basis of extrapolations from the last survey and such other industrial information as may be available. Where surveys are carried out, errors may occur through both inaccurate reporting and non-response.

Finally, once the raw data have been collected they have to be processed and, particularly where there are insufficient skilled personnel for the task, errors may occur through assigning establishments to the wrong industrial categories, through mistakes in transposing and aggregating data and through using unsuitable methods to deal with problems of non-response and incomplete coverage.

In view of these kinds of difficulties, it is advisable that:

- wherever possible the source of any statistical data being used should be identified and the following should be checked: Are the data based upon an estimate or an actual survey? What is the coverage in terms of establishment size? How up-to-date are the businesses and establishments lists? What steps have been taken to deal with incomplete coverage?
- any conclusions drawn should take into account the likely margin of error in the data upon which they have been based.
- particular care should be taken in making comparisons of industrial conditions between countries because the difficulties mentioned above are compounded through the lack of strict comparability between the industrial statistics collected from different countries (despite the use of the ISIC system).

1.4   INDUSTRIAL CHARACTERISTICS OF LDCs

Although LDCs that are the subject of this study are superficially similar, they differ greatly in their economic and industrial structures. The differences are often as great as those existing between groups of LDCs and DCs. In order to illustrate their diversity, the values of a number of economic indicators are reported in Table 1.1 for each of thirty LDCs, and the range between the lowest and highest value for each indicator is shown in Table 1.2. The values recorded for two DCs (UK and USA) are also shown for comparative purposes.

LDCs differ enormously in size (measured in terms of both area and

Table 1.1 *Selected economic indicators for thirty LDCs and two DCs*

Country	Population size (mid-1981) m.	Population density (mid-1981) m. persons/ '000 sq. km	GNP per capita (1981) $US	Share of gross domestic product (1981) Industry %	Manufacturing %
Low-income economies (per capita GNP not more than $US 400):					
Bangladesh	90.7	0.63	140	14	8
Malawi	6.2	0.05	200	20	13
India	690.2	0.21	260	26	18
Tanzania	19.1	0.02	280	15	9
China	991.3	0.10	300	46	N.A.
Sri Lanka	15.0	0.23	300	28	16
Pakistan	84.5	0.11	350	26	17
Sudan	19.2	0.008	380	14	6
Ghana	11.8	0.05	400	12	7
Lower middle-income economies (per capita GNP $US 400–1,700):					
Kenya	17.4	0.03	420	21	13
Indonesia	149.5	0.08	530	42	12
Zambia	5.8	0.008	600	32	18
Egypt	43.3	0.04	650	38	32
Thailand	48.0	0.09	770	28	20
Philippines	49.6	0.17	790	37	25
Nigeria	87.6	0.09	870	37	6
Zimbabwe	7.2	0.02	870	37	27
Peru	17.0	0.01	1,170	41	25
Jamaica	2.2	0.2	1,180	37	15
Turkey	45.5	0.06	1,540	32	23
Jordan	3.4	0.03	1,620	30	14
Upper middle-income economies (per capita GNP $US 1,700–6,000):					
Korea, Rep. of	38.9	0.40	1,700	39	28
Malaysia	14.2	0.04	1,840	36	18
Algeria	19.6	0.008	2,140	55	11
Brazil	120.5	0.01	2,220	34	27
Mexico	71.2	0.04	2,250	37	22
Argentina	28.2	0.01	2,560	38	25
Chile	11.3	0.01	2,560	35	22
Hong Kong	5.2	5.2	5,100	N.A.	27
Singapore	2.4	2.4	5,240	41	30
Industrial market economies:					
United Kingdom	56.0	0.23	9,110	33	20
United States of America	229.8	0.02	12,820	34	23

Notes:
1 All data relate to the year(s) stated or to the nearest year for which data were available.

Share of manufactured exports in total merchandise exports (1980) %	% of labour force employed in industrial sector 1960	% of labour force employed in industrial sector 1980	Average annual growth rate (1970–81) in total population %	Average annual growth rate (1970–81) in urban population %	GNP per capita annual growth rate (1960–81) %	Average annual growth rate in production (1970–81) Industry %	Average annual growth rate in production (1970–81) Manufacturing %
66	3	11	2.6	6.5	0.3	9.0	11.2
10	3	5	3.0	7.0	2.7	N.A.	N.A.
59	11	13	2.1	3.7	1.4	4.4	5.0
16	4	6	3.4	8.6	1.9	2.2	2.9
49	N.A.	19	1.5	N.A.	5.0	8.3	N.A.
19	14	14	1.7	3.6	2.5	4.2	2.1
50	18	20	3.0	4.3	2.8	5.5	4.4
3	6	10	3.1	7.1	−0.3	3.2	1.5
N.A.	14	20	3.0	5.0	−1.1	−2.2	−1.0
16	5	10	4.0	7.3	2.9	8.5	9.5
2	8	15	2.3	4.0	4.1	11.2	13.9
N.A.	7	11	3.1	6.5	0.0	−0.4	0.3
11	12	30	2.5	2.9	3.5	7.6	8.7
29	4	9	2.5	3.4	4.6	9.9	10.3
37	15	17	2.7	3.7	2.8	8.4	6.9
1	10	19	2.5	4.8	3.5	6.0	12.4
N.A.	11	15	3.2	6.3	1.0	N.A.	N.A.
16	20	18	2.6	3.5	1.0	3.4	2.9
63	25	25	1.5	2.5	0.8	−3.6	−2.6
27	11	13	2.3	4.1	3.5	6.1	5.5
36	26	20	3.7	4.7	N.A.	N.A.	N.A.
90	9	29	1.7	4.6	6.9	14.4	15.6
19	12	16	2.5	3.3	4.3	9.3	11.1
1	12	25	3.3	5.6	3.2	7.6	11.6
39	15	24	2.1	3.9	5.1	9.1	8.7
39	20	26	3.1	4.2	3.8	7.4	7.1
23	36	28	1.6	2.0	1.9	1.4	0.7
20	20	19	1.7	2.4	0.7	0.7	0.0
93	52	57	2.4	2.5	6.9	N.A.	9.3
54	23	39	1.5	1.5	7.4	9.0	9.7
74	48	42	0.1	0.3	2.1	0.4	−0.5
68	36	32	1.0	1.5	2.3	2.3	2.9

2   N.A. = not available.
Source: World Bank (1983).

Table 1.2 *Range in values of selected economic indicators for thirty LDCs and corresponding values for the United Kingdom and United States*

Indicator	Lowest LDC value (country in brackets)	Highest LDC value (country in brackets)	UK	USA
Population size (1981, millions)	2.2 (Jamaica)	991.3 (China)	56.0	229.8
Population density (1981, million persons/1,000 sq. km)	0.008 (Algeria, Sudan, Zambia)	5.2 (Hong Kong)	0.23	0.02
GNP per capita (1981, $US)	140 (Bangladesh)	5,240 (Singapore)	9,110	12,820
Industrial sector's contribution to gross domestic product (1981, % share)	12 (Ghana)	55 (Algeria)	33	34
Manufacturing sector's contribution to gross domestic product (1981, % share)	6 (Nigeria, Sudan)	32 (Egypt)	20	23
Manufactured exports as share of total merchandise exports (1981, %)	1 (Algeria, Nigeria)	93 (Hong Kong)	74	68
Proportion of labour force employed in industrial sector (1980, %)	5 (Malawi)	57 (Hong Kong)	42	32
Average annual growth rate in total population (1970–81, %)	1.5 (China, Jamaica, Singapore)	4.0 (Kenya)	0.1	1.0
Average annual growth rate in urban population (1970–81, %)	1.5 (Singapore)	8.6 (Tanzania)	0.3	1.5
Average annual growth rate in GNP per capita (1960–81, %)	−1.1 (Ghana)	7.4 (Singapore)	2.1	2.3
Average annual growth rate in industrial production (1970–81, %)	−3.6 (Jamaica)	14.4 (Korea, Rep. of)	0.4	2.3
Average annual growth rate in manufacturing production (1970–81, %)	−2.6 (Jamaica)	15.6 (Korea, Rep. of)	−0.5	2.9

Source: Table 1.1.

population), resources and material living standards. Jamaica and Singapore have populations little in excess of 2 million, whereas China has nearly 1,000 million inhabitants. Countries such as Nigeria, Algeria, Indonesia and Zambia are rich in oil or other mineral resources, while others, such as Hong Kong, possess limited natural resources of most forms. Annual per capita incomes were less than $US200 in Bangladesh in 1981, but in excess of $US5,000 in both Hong Kong and Singapore in the same year. LDCs also differ greatly in their social and political systems and, therefore, in the development objectives and industrialisation strategies that they adopt (Donges, 1976).

All of these factors contribute to the diversity among LDCs in their basic industrial characteristics. For example, Ghana's industrial sector contributes only 12 per cent of its gross domestic product, whereas the same sector is responsible for 55 per cent of GDP in Algeria. The proportion of the labour force employed in the industrial sector ranges between 5 per cent (in Malawi) to over 55 per cent (in Hong Kong). Manufacturing industry accounts for only 6 per cent of GDP in Nigeria and Sudan but for 32 per cent in Egypt and 27 per cent in Hong Kong. These differences are reflected in the composition of their overseas trade. Only 1 per cent of the merchandise exports of Algeria and Nigeria are in the form of manufactured goods but over 90 per cent of Hong Kong's merchandise exports are in this category.

LDC economies also differ in their rate and pattern of change over time. Their populations are generally increasing at a faster rate than in DCs, but the actual annual rate of population increase varies between the quite wide limits of 1.5 per cent (China, Jamaica, Singapore) and 4 per cent (Kenya). The annual rate of growth in the urban population in LDCs tends to be much higher again, but varies between 1.5 per cent (Singapore) and nearly 9 per cent (Tanzania). Average annual growth rates in GNP per capita diverge sharply between those LDCs that experienced negative growth rates over the period 1960–81 (Ghana, Sudan) and the higher growth economies of Korea, Hong Kong and Singapore, which recorded per capita growth rates of 7 per cent per annum over the same period. The industrial and manufacturing sectors are frequently amongst the most rapidly expanding, although this is often from a very low base line. Between 1970 and 1981, seven LDCs in the sample (Bangladesh, Indonesia, Thailand, Nigeria, Republic of Korea, Malaysia, Algeria) achieved annual growth rates in production in their manufacturing sector in excess of 10 per cent; at the other extreme, Jamaica and Ghana experienced negative growth rates. The percentage of the labour force employed in the industrial sector increased in most LDCs over the period 1960–80, most dramatically in Republic of Korea (from 9 to 29 per cent) and in Singapore (from 23 to 39 per cent). However, in a minority of cases this proportion has actually fallen (Peru, Jordan, Argentina, Chile).

Such is the diversity in the industrial characteristics and industrial experience among LDCs that only in the case of two out of the twelve indicators used in Table 1.2 (namely, GNP per capita and population growth) do the values recorded for both the UK and USA fall outside the limits recorded within the LDC group.[2] This high degree of diversity is a factor that must be continuously borne in mind both in the analysis of the industrialisation process and in the formulation of industrial policies for the Third World.

1.5   STRUCTURE OF THE BOOK

The structure of the remainder of this text reflects the combined use of the tools of industrial and development economics in the analysis of industrial structure and policy in LDCs. Chapter 2 examines, at the sectoral level, the relationships between industrial structure and different stages of development in LDCs, paying particular attention to whether or not there is a common 'pattern' to the industrialisation process by which development takes place in different LDCs. The relationship between industrialisation and the pattern of LDCs' international trade is also considered. In Chapter 3 the analysis switches from the level of the industrial sector to the individual enterprise and market. The main types of enterprise operating within the LDC industrial sector, and their relative importance, are examined. The levels of overall concentration and of concentration in individual markets are assessed and their relationship to the levels of performance achieved within the industrial sector evaluated. In Chapter 4 the focus of analysis is the behaviour of privately owned enterprises within the LDC industrial sector. The major emphasis is on the behaviour and performance of transnational corporations (TNCs), but the chapter also contains an examination of the less well-documented subject of the conduct and performance of large- and small-scale indigenous enterprises. Chapter 5 contains a parallel analysis of the behaviour and performance of publicly owned enterprises within the LDC industrial sector. It pays particular attention to their financial results, pricing policies and factor productivity performance.

The various analyses in chapters 2–5 expose a wide range of industrial policy issues, which are then critically evaluated in Chapter 6. For this purpose, the issues are grouped into eight major policy areas: industrial trade policies, industrial planning, industrial concentration and competition policies, regulation of TNCs, technology policy, policies towards small-scale enterprises, public enterprise regulation, and location of industry policies. The chapter concludes with summary findings on the formulation and implementation of industrial policies in LDCs and with recommendations for the strengthening of economic analysis of industrial structure and policy in the Third World.

FURTHER READING

In order to provide further guidance to students, each chapter in the book concludes with advice on further reading, which can be supplemented by consulting the detailed references cited within each chapter. As supplementary reading to this introductory chapter, students should find it helpful to consult three types of reference. First, a general text in industrial economics (for example, Devine *et al.*, 1979; George and Joll, 1981) will provide further guidance on the methods of analysis used in industrial economics, including the analysis of industrial and market structures, and on different theories of business behaviour. Second, it is advisable to consult one of the more recently published reviews of the industrialisation process in LDCs (for example, Kirkpatrick and Nixson, 1983; Cody *et al.*, 1980; UNIDO, 1979a) to provide the Third World perspective that is missing from most existing texts in industrial economics. Finally, students should familiarise themselves with the more accessible international sources of LDC industrial statistics (for example, the annual series published by the World Bank and by the United Nations) and with the uses and limitations of these data sources.

NOTES

1   LDCs are defined as countries within the Caribbean area, Central and South America, Africa (other than South Africa), the Asian Middle East (other than Israel) and East and South-East Asia (other than Japan).
2   Both the UK and USA have per capita incomes that are higher, and rates of population growth that are lower, than those in all of the LDCs listed in Table 1.1.

2 Industrial Structure, International Trade and Development

2.1 INTRODUCTION

While the industrial characteristics of individual less developed countries differ greatly (see Chapter 1, section 1.4), the analysis of a particular country's industrialisation experience is often enriched by considering that experience in a broader, comparative framework. This chapter is intended, therefore, to prove an overview of the pattern of industrialisation and structural change in the less developed countries.

Section 2.2 provides a mainly statistical account of the industrial structure of LDCs, at the sectoral and industry level, using output and employment data. Section 2.3 begins with an examination of the cross-sectional evidence on the relationship between industrialisation and the structure of imports and exports. The remaining part of this section is concerned with LDCs' trade in manufactured exports: the changes that have occurred in the commodity composition of manufactured exports are identified, and alternative explanations of these trends are considered. Section 2.4 analyses the relationship between changes in industrial structure and economic growth in LDCs and, in particular, evaluates the attempts that have been made to identify a standard pattern of industrial growth. Section 2.5 summarises the main conclusions reached in the chapter and briefly reviews future prospects for further industrial development in the Third World.

2.2 INDUSTRIAL STRUCTURE IN LDCs

Industrial structure can be defined as 'the relative importance of individual industries or groups of industries within an economy' (Devine et al., 1979, p.26). This section describes the crosss-country characteristics of LDCs' industrial structure at the sectoral and industry level, using output and employment data.

SECTORAL LEVEL

Table 2.1 shows the sectoral division of GDP for three groups of developing countries, classified according to per capita income levels.[1] The data show considerable variation between different per capita income groups. Agriculture shows the greatest variation, ranging from 10 per cent in the upper middle-income economies to 45 per cent of GDP in the low income economies (excluding India and China) in 1981. Although it accounts for a

Table 2.1   *Distribution of GDP by sector^a in LDCs, 1960 and 1981^b*

Income group	Agriculture		Industry		(Manufacturing)		Services	
	1960 %	*1981* %	*1960* %	*1981* %	*1960* %	*1981* %	*1960* %	*1981* %
Low-income economies[c] (excluding India and China)	48	37	25	34	11	16	27	29
	(48)	(45)	(12)	(17)	(9)	(10)	(40)	(38)
Lower middle-income economies[d]	36	22	25	35	15	17	39	43
Upper middle-income economies[e]	18	10	33	39	23	24	49	51

Notes:

a   The agricultural sector comprises agriculture, forestry, hunting and fishing. The industrial sector comprises mining, manufacturing, construction, and electricity, water and gas. All other branches of economic activity are categorised as services.

b   All figures are weighted averages.

c   LDCs with per capita GNP less than $410 in 1981.

d   LDCs with per capita GNP $410–$1,700 in 1981.

e   LDCs with per capita GNP $1,700–$4,000 in 1981.

Source: World Bank (1983), Annex, Table 3.

smaller share of GDP, industry also shows wide variation across country groups, being more than twice as large (39 per cent) in the upper middle-income countries than in the low-income economies (17 per cent). The data show a declining share of agriculture over time for all income groups, and a corresponding increase in the share of the industrial sector and, to a less marked extent, in the share of the manufacturing sub-sector.

The sectoral division of the labour force is shown in Table 2.2 The data should be treated with caution, as most of the figures for 1980 are based on geometric extrapolations of earlier estimates by the International Labour

Table 2.2   *Distribution of labour force^a by sector in LDCs, 1960 and 1980*

	Percentage of labour force in:					
	Agriculture		Industry		Services	
	1960	*1980*	*1960*	*1980*	*1960*	*1980*
Low-income economies (excluding India and China)	77 (82)	70 (73)	9 (7)	15 (11)	14 (11)	15 (16)
Lower middle-income economies	71	55	11	17	18	28
Upper middle-income economies	49	30	20	28	31	42

Notes:

As for Table 2.1.

a   The labour force comprises economically active persons aged 10 years and over, including the armed forces and the unemployed, but excludes housewives, students and other economically inactive groups.

Source: World Bank (1983), Annex, Table 21.

Table 2.3 *Distribution of LDCs' total manufacturing value added (MVA) by income group, 1960–75*

Income group	GNP per capita (1975 dollars) [a]	Group population (% of total)	Constant annual growth rate of MVA for the group %	Share in LDCs' total MVA (in 1970 dollars) [b] 1960 %	Share in LDCs' total MVA (in 1970 dollars) [b] 1975 %
Low-income	<265	56.7	5.2	20.6	16.2
Lower middle-income	265–520	16.4	7.1	10.0	10.3
Intermediate middle-income	521–1,075	17.3	8.6	33.4	39.3
Upper middle-income	1,076–2,000	7.9	7.3	29.5	28.2
High-income	>2,000	1.6	8.3	5.3	5.8

Notes:
a Where GNP per capita was not available, GDP per capita was used to classify countries.
b Shares do not total 100 due to rounding errors.
Sources: UNIDO (1979a), Table II.5 and Figure III.

Table 2.4 *The LDCs with largest manufacturing value added at current prices, 1980*

Country[a]	Share of MVA in GDP %	Share in MVA of all LDCs %
Brazil	26.6	18.67
Argentina	32.6	12.42
Mexico	24.6	12.25
India	17.8	8.42
Republic of Korea	29.3	5.14
Iran	19.2	4.62
Turkey	20.1	3.43
Philippines	25.6	2.68
Venezuela	13.9	2.46
Colombia	22.6	2.19
		Total 72.28

Note:
a Countries are ranked according to the absolute level of their MVA.
  Source: UNIDO (1983b), Tables 2 and 4.

Organisation (ILO) for 1960. Nevertheless, the figures do serve to illustrate the point that a rather different picture of structural composition and changes can emerge from using alternative measures of each sector's relative importance. This is most evident in the much lower share of the agriculture sector in total production (Table 2.1) than in the total labour force (Table 2.2), reflecting the concentration of underemployed, low-productivity labour in this sector.

The distribution of total manufacturing activity between LDCs is very uneven. Table 2.3 shows that countries in the intermediate middle-income and upper middle-income range ($521–$2,000) account for much of LDCs' total manufacturing value added (MVA), their share increasing from 63 per cent in 1960 to 67 per cent in 1975.[2] In the low-income countries, in contrast, within which 57 per cent of total LDC population is concentrated, the manufacturing sector has grown at a rate below that achieved by the LDCs as a whole, and their share of LDC total MVA fell from 21 per cent in 1960 to 16 per cent in 1975.

Futher evidence of the concentration in Third World manufactured production within a small number of LDCs is contained in Table 2.4, which shows that the ten developing countries with the largest manufacturing value added between them accounted for 72 per cent of all LDC MVA in 1980. The figures '. . . testify to limited participation of many developing countries in the process of industrial growth of the economic group as a whole' (UNIDO, 1979a, p. 42).

INDUSTRY LEVEL

Following the procedure originally adopted by Hoffman (1958), the commodity composition of MVA can be classified into two broad categories,

Table 2.5 *Structure of LDCs' manufacturing value added at constant (1975) prices, 1963, 1973, 1979*[a]

Branch	ISIC	1963 %	1973 %	1979 %
Light industry[b]				
Food products	311/12	17.7	13.7	13.1
Beverages	313	3.1	2.7	3.3
Tobacco	314	3.4	2.4	2.3
Textiles	321	13.4	10.1	8.8
Wearing apparel	322	3.4	2.5	2.3
Leather and fur products	323	0.8	0.5	0.5
Footwear	324	1.3	0.9	0.8
Wood and wood products	331	2.5	2.1	2.0
Furniture and fixtures excluding metal	332	1.3	1.1	0.9
Printing and publishing	342	2.8	2.4	1.9
Rubber products	355	1.6	1.9	1.9
Plastic products	356	0.8	1.4	1.3
Other manufactures	390	1.8	1.4	1.3
Light industry total		53.9	43.1	40.4
Heavy industry[b]				
Paper and paper products	341	2.3	2.4	2.3
Industrial chemicals	351	2.4	3.9	4.2
Other chemicals	352	4.8	5.9	6.5
Petroleum refineries	353	10.7	10.5	8.9
Miscellaneous products of petroleum and coal	354	0.3	0.5	0.5
Pottery, china and earthenware	361	0.7	0.7	0.7
Glass	362	0.7	1.0	1.0
Other non-metallic mineral products	369	3.0	3.4	3.9
Iron and steel	371	4.3	4.9	5.6
Non-ferrous metals	372	1.8	1.9	2.0
Metal products, excluding machinery	381	4.0	4.5	5.0
Non-electrical machinery	382	2.7	5.4	5.4
Electrical machinery	383	2.9	4.4	6.0
Transport equipment	384	5.0	7.2	7.2
Professional and scientific equipment, photographic and optical goods	385	0.3	0.4	0.4
Heavy industry total		45.9	57.0	59.6
All manufacturing total	300	100.0	100.0	100.0

Notes:

a   The data for 1963 cover 59 countries which, in 1975, accounted for 95 per cent of the manufacturing value added of all LDCs; the data for 1973 and 1979 cover 50 countries which, in 1975, accounted for 88 per cent of the MVA of all LDCs. Therefore, although the structures for all years are probably representative of LDCs as a whole, the variation in country composition should be noted.

b   Light and heavy industry are defined in note 4 to this chapter.

Source: UNIDO (1983b), Table 10.

'light' and 'heavy' industry.[3] Light industry production consists mainly of basic consumer goods, and heavy industry is made up of the production of industrial supplies, producers' goods and advanced consumer goods.[4] The figures in Table 2.5 show a steady decline in light industry's share of total manufacturing activity in the LDCs, from 54 per cent in 1963 to 40 per cent in 1979. As income has grown, the need for heavy industries producing industrial intermediates and capital goods has increased. Table 2.5 provides further information on the commodity composition of LDCs' MVA at the major group level. Using data on value added in individual manufacturing groups summed over the countries in the sample and then expressed as a percentage of total MVA as a measure of relative importance, the figures show that in 1979 only the food products branch (major group) had a share of more than 10 per cent. This branch, together with petroleum refineries, textiles, transport equipment and other chemicals, accounted for almost 45 per cent of LDCs' total MVA in 1979. A comparison of the composition of MVA in 1963 and 1979 indicates that most branches of light industry declined in relative importance over this period, with the corresponding gains in the share of heavy industry occurring mainly in industrial chemicals, non-electrical and electrical machinery and transport equipment.

The share of manufacturing sector employment in total employment varies considerably between LDCs. Estimates for countries with per capita income

Table 2.6 *Manufacturing employment by branch of industry in LDCs, 1968–75*

Branch	ISIC	Annual growth rate in employment %	Contribution to the total increase of manufacturing employment %
Food, beverages and tobacco	31	4.8	13.34
Textiles	321	5.1	16.77
Wearing apparel, leather, footwear	322–324	8.7	16.18
Wood and wood products, incl. furniture	33	8.1	9.86
Paper and paper products, printing and publishing	34	6.3	2.96
Chemicals	35	8.9	8.39
Non-metallic minerals	36	7.9	7.52
Basic metals	37	14.4	5.27
Metal products, machinery and equipment	38	9.5	16.66
Light manufacturing		6.2	65.17
Heavy manufacturing		9.2	34.83
Total manufacturing		7.0	100.00

Source: UNIDO (1979a), Tables VII.5 and VII.6.

levels greater than $400 (in 1978 prices) suggest that the manufacturing sector's share in total employment rose from 17 per cent in 1960 to 23 per cent in 1978, while over the same period the sector's share in GDP increased from 31 to 34 per cent. For LDCs with per capita income levels below $400, the share of manufacturing in total employment rose from 9 per cent in 1960 to 11 per cent in 1978, whereas the sector's share in GDP increased from 17 per cent in 1960 to 24 per cent in 1978 (UNIDO, 1981a, p. 40).

Although employment in the heavy manufacturing activities has grown more rapidly than employment in light manufacturing, the major part of manufacturing sector employment is provided in the more labour-intensive light manufacturing sector. Over the period 1968–75, the traditional activities of food, textiles and wearing apparel together accounted for almost half of the total increase in manufacturing employment (Table 2.6).[5]

SUMMARY

The use of cross-sectional aggregated data for groups of LDCs to analyse industrial structure patterns in the Third World is subject to two important limitations: first, it disguises the variation between the individual country observations; second, it fails to reveal the process of change that occurs over time within them. Subject to these reservations, the evidence presented in this section on LDCs' structural characteristics can be summarized as follows:

- The share of the agricultural sector in GDP is inversely related to the level of per capita income, and the share of industry tends to increase as per capita income levels rise (Table 2.1).
- The proportion of the total labour force in the industrial sector increases as per capita income rises, but is lower than the share of the industrial sector's output in total GDP (Table 2.2).
- The manufacturing production activities in LDCs are heavily concentrated in a limited number of large, middle-income countries (Tables 2.3 and 2.4).
- The share of light industry branches in total manufacturing activity has declined over time, with a corresponding increase in such heavy industry activities as industrial chemicals, non-electrical and electrical equipment and transport equipment (Table 2.5).
- The share of manufacturing sector employment in total employment varies widely between LDCs. While employment in heavy industry has grown proportionately more rapidly, light industry accounts for a larger share of the absolute growth in total manufacturing employment (Table 2.6).

2.3   TRADE STRUCTURE AND INDUSTRIALISATION

THE STRUCTURE OF EXPORTS AND IMPORTS

The growing importance of LDCs' industrial activities is reflected in the changes that have occurred in the structure of their imports and exports. The

Table 2.7 *Commodity composition of LDCs' exports and imports, 1965 and 1979*

Commodity group	SITC	Exports		Imports	
		1965 %	1979 %	1965 %	1979 %
Primary commodities, excluding fuels	0+1+2+4+68	53.7	22.9	23.4	17.7
– food and beverages	0+1	28.2	12.4	15.6	10.9
– raw materials	2+4+68	25.5	10.5	7.8	6.8
Fuels	3	31.4	56.6	8.9	15.4
Manufactures	5+6+7+8+9 less 68	14.9	20.5	67.7	66.9
Total	0–9	100.0	100.0	100.0	100.0

Source: UNCTAD (1981a), Table A.5, p. 117.

share of manufactures in total LDC exports has risen from 15 per cent in 1965 to 21 per cent in 1979 (Table 2.7): if oil exports are excluded, manufactures accounted for almost half of total LDC non-oil merchandise exports in 1979. Changes in the structure of imports are less evident, with the exception of fuels, which have almost doubled their share of total imports over the same period.

The differences in the statistical procedures used to record production and trade activities (see Chapter 1, section 1.2) make it difficult to compare export manufacturing data directly with manufacturing output figures. However, studies that have attempted to reconcile these two types of data suggest that exports of manufactures do not account for a significant

Table 2.8 *Ratios of manufactured exports to gross value of manufacturing and of manufacturing value added to GDP, by selected groups of LDCs, 1970*

Groups of countries	Ratio of manufactured exports to gross value of manufacturing %	Ratio of manufacturing value added to GDP %
Largest exporters[a]	12.4	19.5
Primary-oriented exporters[b]	10.2	10.9
Others[c]	12.0	14.2
Average	11.5	14.9

Notes:
a   The countries included as the largest exporters are: Brazil, India, Republic of Korea, Singapore and Thailand.
b   Primary-oriented exporters (countries where exports of manufactures were less than 10 per cent of their total exports) include: Chile, Ethiopia, Honduras, Indonesia, Iran, Kuwait, Libya, Nigeria, Panama, Sudan, Tanzania, Zambia.
c   Other countries are: Barbados, Colombia, Congo, Egypt, Fiji, Ghana, Guatemala, Kenya, Madagascar, Malawi, Mauritius, Peru, Philippines, Somalia, Sri Lanka, Tunisia and Turkey.
Source: UNIDO (1979a), Table V.5, p. 152.

proportion of total manufacturing output in most LDCs. Table 2.8 shows that, for a sample of thirty-four developing countries, exports averaged 11.5 per cent of total manufacturing output in 1970. Keesing (1979a) estimated the average share for LDCs to have been 10 per cent in 1973, and pointed out that even in the highly export-oriented economies the share seldom exceeded 30 per cent.

A large proportion of total LDC manufactured exports is supplied by a limited number of countries, with the six largest exporters (Republic of Korea, Hong Kong, Brazil, Singapore, India, Argentina) accounting for almost 55 per cent of all LDC manufactured exports in 1977 (UNIDO, 1981a).[6]

COMMODITY COMPOSITION OF MANUFACTURED EXPORTS

Information on the commodity composition of LDCs' manufactured exports is given in Table 2.9. From this, it appears that the established LDC exporters (the so-called 'newly industrialising countries' – NICs) have a higher proportion of exports of more advanced, technologically mature products in the machinery and transport equipment category, and a correspondingly lower proportion of crudely processed raw materials (basic chemicals and other basic manufactures). Indeed, the variation between different stages of industrial development may be even greater than the figures in Table 2.9 suggest, since a significant proportion of the exports under machinery and transport equipment (SITC 7) and clothing (SITC 84) from the 'second-tier' LDCs consists of labour-intensive, subcontracted assembly and processing activities based on imported inputs. A similar shift in commodity composition is observed over time, with a general decrease in the share of processed raw materials, and an offsetting rise in finished manufactures taking place. The share of finished manufactures (SITC 7 and 8) rose in the NICs from 57 per cent in 1970 to 64 per cent in 1979.

The broad shifts in commodity composition shown in Table 2.9 disguise the variation in growth rates of different products and the widening range of items exported by LDCs. Table 2.10 shows, at the four-digit level, the twelve products recording the fastest rates of growth over the 1970–6 period. The figures reveal rapid increases in the LDCs' share of the developed countries' total imports of both labour-intensive fashion products (leather and fur clothing, silk threads) and high-technology products (telecommunications, accounting machinery, electric power machinery).

EXPLANATIONS OF COMMODITY COMPOSITION

Economic theory offers a number of explanations of the pattern of trade in manufactures between developed and less developed countries. The orthodox Heckscher–Ohlin theory of comparative advantage predicts that exchange between two countries will be determined by the relative factor endowments, each country exporting commodities that use intensively the factors with which it is relatively well endowed. In a simple, two-factor model, this would imply that LDCs will be more competitive in products that are intensive in the

Table 2.9 Product composition of LDCs' manufactured exports,[a] 1970 and 1979

| | Manufactured products as share of total manufactured exports | | | | | |
| | Newly-industrialising countries (NICs) | | 'Second-tier' LDC manufacturing exporters | | Other LDCs | |
Products	1970 %	1979 %	1970 %	1979 %	1970 %	1979 %
Chemicals (SITC 5)	8	5	16	14	14	20
Basic manufactures (SITC 6 less 68)	34	31	54	31	75c	70c
(of which: textiles (SITC 65))	(16)	(14)	(16)	(12)	(22)	(7)
Machinery and transport equipment (SITC 7)	21	32	12	22	10	9
Miscellaneous manufactures (SITC 8)	36	32	18	33	N.A.	N.A.
(of which: clothing (SITC 84))	(20)b	(17)b	(11)	(22)	(7)	(8)
Total manufactures as share of total exports (%)	53	67	7	17	11	8

Notes:
a Excluding fuels.
b Excludes Taiwan owing to lack of data on Taiwan's clothing exports.
c Includes SITC 8.
Source: OECD (1982a), Table XII-2, p. 130.

Table 2.10   *LDC exports with high growth rates*

Product	Growth rate (1976 as multiple of 1970)	Value of increment $m.	Share of total developed countries' imports 1970 %	1976 %
Telecommunication equipment	9.5	444	3	9
Leather clothes	9.7	411	22	46
Watches, movements, cases	34.6	290	2	22
Motor vehicle parts	10.8	207	0	1
Switchgear	11.1	200	1	6
Piston engines, non-air	9.7	184	1	3
Accounting machines	26.2	184	1	15
Electric power machinery	9.3	182	2	7
Sound recorders	40.8	166	0	7
Domestic electrical equipment	14.7	134	1	4
Fur clothes	18.3	122	7	25
Silk yarn and threads	52.7	94	10	66

Source: Extracted from UNCTAD (1978a), as reported in Lall (1981b), p. 183.

use of labour, and less competitive in products that are capital intensive. Alternative theories have attempted to provide a more realistic explanation of international trade flows by relaxing some of the restrictive conditions of the comparative cost theory – in particular, the assumptions that all economies have equal access to technology, and that factors of production are immobile internationally.[7]

The closely related 'technological gap' and 'product cycle' views of international trade argue that technological developments have an important influence on the pattern of trade and international competitiveness.[8] Technology is not a freely, instantaneously and universally available good, and countries that innovate first have an initial competitive advantage in new products. But, as technology becomes internationally diffused and the production process becomes standardised, competitive advantage shifts to countries with lower-cost, unskilled labour supply.

The source of technological innovation is frequently the transnational corporation (TNC), which transfers this knowledge through the process of international investment (see Chapter 4, section 4.8). The international mobility of capital through the medium of the TNC emphasises the interrelationship between international flows of trade, investment and technology, and provides the basis for a third approach to explaining LDCs' export patterns. This approach stresses the growing internationalisation of production through the activities of the TNCs so that, contrary to the traditional theory's assumption that international exchange represents market transactions between independent economic agents, an increasing proportion of international trade occurs on an intra-firm basis.[9] The TNC's decision to establish production in a particular LDC is then based upon the comparative advantage associated with the location of a part of the internationally integrated production structure, rather than with the characteristics of the final product (see Chapter 4, sections 4.3 and 4.4).

This summary of alternative theories of international specialisation suggests a range of factors that will influence the composition of LDCs' manufactured exports. Traditional comparative cost theory implies that labour intensity, in particular unskilled labour requirements, will be an important characteristic of LDC manufactured exports. The product cycle and technology diffusion approaches emphasise the dynamic nature of competitive advantage, and suggest that LDCs will have an increasing advantage in the production of standardised, fairly capital-intensive products based on a mature technology (for example, steel, shipbuilding, certain engineering products, motor vehicles). The internationalisation of production through the activities of the TNCs implies that the 'sourcing' of productive activities will be determined by the comparative costs of different processes in the production cycle, rather than by the characteristics of the final products (see Chapter 4, section 4.11). The availability of low-cost labour will influence the relocation of labour-intensive subcontracting and assembly activities in LDCs; in other instances, preferential tariff provisions by developed countries for imports from certain LDCs, or fiscal incentives offered by the LDCs themselves, may determine the TNCs' location decisions (Helleiner, 1973; Sharpston, 1975; Kirkpatrick and Yamin, 1981).

It is beyond the scope of this chapter to provide an exhaustive review of the numerous empirical tests of the hypotheses outlined above. (A useful summary is provided by Stern, 1975.) Instead, the results of a study by UNIDO (1981a, Ch. II), which provides cross-sectional evidence on the various characteristics discussed in the preceding paragraphs, are summarised. The study used two developing country samples.[10] The first consisted of seven NICs, all of which had a minimum per capita income of $1,100 and a share of MVA equal to at least 20 per cent of GDP, in 1978. The second sample was composed of a further ten LDCs for which detailed export data were available.

Export commodities (at the three-digit level) were classified by three different criteria: factor intensity – labour intensive or capital intensive; skill intensity – high skill intensive or low skill intensive; product development – high or low rates of product development, measured by the number of items within a given SITC group or subgroup that appeared or disappeared over a given time period.[11]

The product cycle hypothesis was examined by distinguishing between 'new' and 'mature' products. New products are still in the early phase of their product life cycle and are therefore likely to require relatively large amounts of skilled labour, whereas mature products will have more limited requirements for skilled labour. The technological gap view of trade was tested by distinguishing between 'standardised' and 'unstandardised' products, the former being characterised by a low rate of product development. In both cases, the factor intensity of each product group was also identified.

The final stage of the analysis was to identify the export commodities in which the sample countries appeared to have a competitive advantage. This was measured in terms of export performance ratios – a commodity's share in a given country's total manufactured exports as a ratio of the share of world exports of that commodity in total world manufactured exports. The higher the export performance ratio's value is above the 'normal' value of unity, the greater is the country's competitiveness in that particular export product.

The product characteristics of manufactured exports in which the sample countries had a pronounced competitive advantage (i.e. high export performance ratio) are shown in Table 2.11. When classified in terms of the product cycle argument, the results show that both the NICs' and other LDCs' manufactured exports are heavily concentrated in labour-intensive, mature products. There were, however, significant differences between individual countries. For example, the share of Singapore's 'new' industries was 21 per cent, consisting mainly of electrical machinery, tele-communications apparatus, office machines and pharmaceutical products. The share of 'mature' industries was highest in Hong Kong, accounting for 67 per cent of all manufactured exports covered in the study. A similar pattern was apparent when industries were arranged according to their rate of

Table 2.11 *LDCs' manufactured exports, by type of industry, 1975–6*

Type of industry	Manufactured exports by type of industry % of total manufactured exports[a]	
	NICs[b]	LDCs
Mature industries:		
Labour-intensive	32.5	22.6
Capital-intensive	1.8	1.7
Total[c]	34.3	24.6
New industries:		
Labour-intensive	5.3	0.6
Capital-intensive	0.1	0.4
Total[c]	5.4	1.0
Standardised industries:		
Labour-intensive	34.6	20.3
Capital-intensive	0.7	1.5
Total[c]	35.3	21.8
Unstandardised industries:		
Labour-intensive	3.2	2.9
Capital-intensive	1.2	0.6
Total[c]	4.4	3.8

Notes:
a   Only industries for which the share of the sample countries' exports in their total manufactured exports exceeds the world average are included.
b   Figures in this column are an average of the individual country data in the original source, as reported in Ballance *et al.* (1982), p. 151.
c   The 'total' share may include industries for which the classification 'labour-intensive' or 'capital-intensive' was inappropriate.
Source: UNIDO (1981a), Table II.5.

product development, with the sample countries' exports concentrated in the labour-intensive, standardised products. This is particularly evident in the case of NICs, with 35 per cent of the total manufactured exports covered by the study falling in this category. Overall, the results show that the developing countries' competitive advantage is concentrated in mature and/or standardised products (standardised products are not necessarily the same as mature products: product differentiation by means of advertising can result in rapid product development while the technology remains largely unaltered). Also, in accordance with the notion of factor proportions, these exports are overwhelmingly labour intensive in character.

SUMMARY

The purpose of this section has been to describe the structural characteristics of the LDCs' international trade sector, and to examine the changing pattern of their manufactured exports. The main findings can be summarised as follows.

First, the growth of manufacturing activities in the Third World has resulted in significant changes in the structure of LDCs' exports and imports: the share of manufactures in total exports increased to more than 20 per cent by 1980; if oil exports are excluded, the share rises to almost 50 per cent. The most significant change in the structure of imports has been the large increase in the share of fuels (Table 2.7).

Secondly, a small number of LDCs account for a large share of total LDC manufactured exports, but, even in the most export-oriented economies, manufactured exports normally account for a small proportion of total manufacturing sector output (Table 2.8).

Thirdly, there is considerable variation in the commodity composition of individual LDCs' manufactured exports, with some evidence to suggest that more advanced technologically mature products account for a larger share of manufactured exports in the NICs. A similar shift in commodity composition can be observed over time, with a decline in the share of basic manufactures and an offsetting rise in finished manufactures (Table 2.9).

Fourthly, a number of different factors have been proposed in the theoretical literature as possible explanations of the pattern of LDCs' manufactured exports trade. These include factor endowments, the life cycle of a product, and the internationalisation of production through intra-firm trade. An examination of the characteristics of LDCs' exports suggests that each of these considerations influences the composition of LDCs' manufactured exports, which are predominantly labour-intensive, mature and/or standardised products (Table 2.11).

2.4 PATTERNS OF STRUCTURAL CHANGE AND INDUSTRIALISATION

INTRODUCTION

Many attempts have been made to identify and analyse in quantitative terms the structural changes that occur in the process of growth and development, and, in the case of industrial development in particular, the objective has often been to identify a 'normal' or 'standard' pattern of industrial growth. The basic hypothesis is that, as per capita income rises, 'industrialisation occurs with a sufficient degree of uniformity across countries to produce consistent patterns of change in resource allocation, factor use and related phenomena' (Ballance *et al.*, 1982, p. 109).

It was the early quantitative work of Simon Kuznets that first drew attention to the consistent patterns of structural change observed as per capita income increased.[12] Using data from mainly developed countries (at least initially), Kuznets grouped countries according to per capita income and demonstrated that, as per capita national income rose, there was:

- a consistent decline in the share of agriculture in national product;
- a consistent increase in the share of the industrial sector in national output; and
- no clear pattern in the share of the services sector.

With respect to the share of the labour force employed in the different sectors, the following patterns emerged:

- there was a decline in the proportion of the labour force engaged in the agricultural sector;
- for most countries, the share of the industrial sector in the total labour force rose, but this rise was less consistent and less pronounced than the rise in its share of national output;
- there was a rise in the share of services sector employment in the total labour force, with the share of transportation and trade in particular rising most consistently.[13]

Since the publication of Kuznets' work, a large number of empirical studies have produced results that in general are consistent with his findings. The earlier work is summarised in Sutcliffe (1971, ch. 2) and the more recent analyses can be found in UNIDO (1979a, ch. II, section B), Ballance *et al.* (1982, ch. III), Ballance and Sinclair (1983, chs 4 and 5) and Batchelor *et al.* (1980a). The following sections examine in some detail the work of Chenery and his associates and of UNIDO, and attempt to assess critically the value of such studies and their relevance to policy formulation in LDCs.

Chenery (1960, p. 624; 1979, p. 6) and his associates (Chenery and Syrquin, 1975, p. 5) have argued that a number of factors give rise to considerable uniformity in the transition from a 'traditional' to a 'developed' economy in all economies over a given period. These include:

- similar variations in the composition of consumer demand with rising per capita income, characterised by a fall in the share of basic foodstuffs and a rise in the share of manufactured goods in total domestic spending;
- the accumulation of capital, both physical and human, at a rate exceeding the growth of the labour force, in order to increase per capita output;
- access of all countries to similar technology; and
- access to international trade and capital inflows.

It is recognised that a number of factors can be expected to produce different patterns of structural change – for example, differences in social objectives and policy choices, variations in natural resource endowments, differences in the size of countries, differences in access to foreign capital and changes in the so-called 'uniform factors' over time (technology, human wants, etc.). Chenery (1979, p. 7) is of the opinion, however, that in a given historical period the factors making for uniformity in the pattern of structural change tend to predominate.

INDIVIDUAL STUDIES

Chenery (1960)
Chenery argued that the close relationship between levels of income and industrial output was more pronounced than would be predicted from changes in demand alone. His basic objective, therefore, was to incorporate changes in both demand and supply conditions (overall increase in the stock of capital per worker and the increase in education and skills of all kinds) into a general explanation of the growth of individual sectors of production in order to explain observed patterns of industrial growth. With data from thirty-eight countries (both developed and less developed, for years mainly between 1950 and 1956), he estimated a linear logarithmic regression equation in which per capita value added depended on per capita income and population.

$$\log V_i = \log B_{i0} + B_{i1} \log Y + B_{i2} \log N$$

where

V_i = per capita value added in industry or sector i
Y = per capita national income
N = population
B_{i0} = value of value added at per capita income of \$100 and population of 10 million
B_{i1} = income growth elasticity = $(dV_i/V_i)/(dY/Y)$
B_{i2} = population size elasticity = $(dV_i/V_i)/(dN/N)$

He also estimated a similar function for imports, with data from sixty-three countries based on an average for 1952–4.

Chenery argued that industrialisation involved a number of changes in economic structure, including:

• a rise in the relative importance of manufacturing industry;
• a change in the composition of industrial output;
• changes in production techniques and sources of supply for individual commodites.

The first two can be measured from the regression analysis, and an attempt is then made to determine the relative importance of demand and supply in causing the growth of each industrial sector.

Chenery's results indicated what he called a 'contemporary pattern of growth' (p. 635). At an income level of US$100, the share of industrial output (manufacturing, construction, electric power, handicrafts) in national output was predicted to be 17 per cent (12 per cent for manufacturing alone), rising to 38 per cent (33 per cent for manufacturing alone) at an income level of $1,000. The share of transportation and communication in national output also doubled over this per capita income range, while the share of primary production in national output was estimated to decline from 45 per cent to 15 per cent. Hardly any countries deviated in per capita value added in industry by more than 50 per cent from the 'normal' relation that he established between income level and industrial output.

With respect to composition of industrial output, industries were classified according to the nature of the demand for their products, namely, investment and related products, intermediate goods and consumer goods. The difference in growth elasticities between investment goods and consumer goods was almost as great as the difference between agriculture and industry. At an income level of US$100, 68 per cent of manufacturing output was predicted to consist of consumer goods and only 12 per cent of investment goods. At an income level of $600, the respective shares were 43 per cent and 35 per cent. Intermediate goods maintained a fairly constant share of total manufacturing output at different income levels. The regression of sub-sector value added on per capita income and population gave a reasonably good statistical fit for almost all of the sub-sectors identified. The import regression, too, confirmed the existence of a fairly uniform pattern of change in the import of industrial products as income per capita rose (p. 639).

Chenery also considered the 'causes' of industrialisation, which he identified as:

- the substitution of domestic production for imports;
- the growth in the final use of industrial products; and
- the growth in intermediate demand arising from the first two factors.

Chenery then attempted to explain the causes of the positive deviation from proportional growth for each industry by calculating the deviation from proportional growth for each sector and by using the sector growth function to explain the source of this deviation.[14] The regression analysis showed that import substitution as defined by Chenery (the increased share of domestic production in total supply) accounted for 50 per cent of the total deviation from proportionality between per capita income levels of $100 and $600. The growth in final demand accounted for 22 per cent of the deviation from proportionality, or 32 per cent if the intermediate demand deriving from the growth in final demand was added. A residual of 18 per cent was attributed to price changes, estimation errors and the possible net substitution of manufactured goods for other goods and services (handicraft products, for example).

Chenery argued that his results contradicted the assumption usually made that changes in the composition of demand were the main cause of industrial growth. Rather:

changes in supply conditions, resulting from a change in relative factor costs as income rises, cause a substitution of domestic production for imports and, to a lesser extent, of factory goods for handicraft goods and services. These supply changes are more important in explaining the growth of industry than are the changes in demand. (Chenery, 1960, p. 644)

Differences in income level alone accounted for 70 per cent of the variation in the levels of total industrial output among countries. Other factors that were of importance included:

- *Effects of market size*: economies of scale were important in many industries (for example, paper, rubber, petroleum products, metals and textiles). Industries that had significant scale effects produced about 40 per cent of manufacturing output at an income level of $300 and 57 per cent at $600 (p. 645); an increase in population from 2 to 50 million caused manufacturing output per capita nearly to double and the sectors having significant scale economies to more than triple in size.
- *Effects of income distribution*: these were not estimated quantitatively, but Chenery believed that they explained significant positive deviations from proportionality when income distributions were highly unequal.
- *Factor proportions*: the expectation was that countries lacking natural resources would turn to manufacturing at an earlier stage in their development in order to compensate for their lack of primary products for export and domestic use (see Chenery and Taylor, 1968, below).
- *Regional differences*: there were variations between different developed and less developed regions. Industrial output was higher in Europe than predicted by the model, but lower overall in Asia; Africa exhibited 'normality of industrial output' (p. 650); 'colonial policies and cultural factors' were suggested as possible explanations of 'under-achievement'.

Chenery's overall conclusions can be summarised as follows. First, the association between industrialisation and rising income does not explain the rise in income itself. The analysis does indicate, however, the change in the pattern of resource allocation that normally accompanies a rise in income, and growth can thus be accelerated by anticipating desirable changes in resource use. Second, after allowing for variations in the size of the country, there is a well-defined pattern of growth for individual sectors of the economy. Deviations from this normal pattern are smallest for services, agriculture and most manufactured consumer goods. The greatest variations in output shares are to be found in industries producing machinery, transport equipment and intermediate goods where economies of scale are most important. Third, industrial growth in the twentieth century differs from that of the nineteenth century in so far as, during the present century, industrialisation based on import substitution is of greater relative importance than industrialisation based on the export of manufactured goods. Fourth, the analysis focuses on similarities in patterns of growth, but there are also substantial variations between countries and the separation of 'particular' from 'universal' factors is of importance (see below for a discussion of Chenery's 'universal' factors).

Chenery and Taylor (1968)

To test the hypothesis that there were uniform patterns of change in the structure of production as income levels rose, Chenery and Taylor brought together evidence from historical studies of advanced, industrialised economies, comparisons among countries at different income levels and time series data from LDCs. Their statistical procedure was designed to test for several types of uniformity in development patterns:

> . . . similarities between the production relations estimated from time-series and cross-section data, systematic shifts in these relations over time, and improvements in the estimates that may come from grouping countries in accordance with *a priori* criteria. The remaining variation in production is attributed to forces specific to each country. (Chenery and Taylor, 1968, p. 392)

Data were taken from fifty-four countries, both developed and less developed over the period 1950–63. The dependent variables in the regression equations were the share of primary production (mining and agriculture), the share of industry (manufacturing and construction) and the share of services (all other sectors). The independent or explanatory variables were: per capita GNP (in 1960 dollars), population, share of gross fixed capital formation in GNP, share of primary exports in GNP and share of manufactured exports in GNP. A non-linear term (the square of income per capita) was also included in the regressions to allow for the decline in elasticities with rising income and to avoid the necessity of subdividing the sample of countries by income level.

The sample countries were divided between:

- large countries (population greater than 15 million);
- small countries, which were further subdivided, on the basis of an index of trade orientation, between
  - industry-oriented countries,
  - primary-oriented countries.

This division gave better statistical results than the pooled regression, and three patterns of development emerged:

- *Large-country patterns.* The share of industry in GNP rose rapidly from 16 per cent at $100 per capita income to 32 per cent at $400; it then rose less rapidly to reach a peak of 37 per cent at $1,000 per capita income. The share of primary production in GNP fell steadily and, at a per capita income of $280, the shares of primary production and industry were equal at 27 per cent. There were few significant deviations from this pattern – Nigeria and Korea had less industry than predicted, and Burma and India had a higher share than predicted.
- *Small, industry-oriented country patterns.* The variation in production

shares with income was similar to the large country pattern. As was to be expected, however, changes in the composition of exports between primary products and manufactured goods made a significant difference to the composition of output as a whole.

- *Small, primary-oriented country patterns.* The development pattern exhibited by these countries was different from the first two types. Primary production declined more slowly and its share of GNP exceeded that of industry up to a per capita income level of $800. Rich natural resource endowments produced significant deviations from the average and variations in trade patterns had a greater effect on the share of industry than was the case in the small industry-oriented country sample. Once a per capita income of $1,000 was exceeded, primary resources appeared to have less effect on the share of industry and the three patterns converged (p. 400).

When the industrial sector was disaggregated, the explanations of development patterns were improved and the differences between the three patterns were sharpened. The sector was divided into industries classified according to the stage of development at which they made their main contribution to industrialisation. Three groups of industries were thus identified:

- *Early industries.* These supplied the essential demands of the poorest countries, utilised relatively simple technologies and increased their share of GNP relatively little above per capita income levels of approximately $200. They had relatively low income elasticities of demand (1.0 or less), and their potential for import substitution or export growth was exhausted at fairly low income levels. Examples of 'early' industries included food, leather goods and textiles.
- *Middle industries.* These industries initially doubled their share of GNP as per capita income rose from very low levels, but their share grew relatively little above per capita income levels of $400–500. They exhausted their import substitution potential at fairly low income levels. They had income elasticities of demand of 1.2–1.5. Examples of these industries included non-metallic minerals, rubber products, wood products, chemicals and petroleum refining.
- *Late industries.* These industries continued to grow faster than GNP up to the highest income levels, and they typically doubled their share of GNP in the later stages of industrialisation (above $300 per capita). This group included clothing, printing, basic metals, paper and metal products as well as consumer durables with high income elasticities.

These observations relate to the large-country sample. In the small industry-oriented countries, a given level of demand was reached at a higher per capita income (a delay of $300 or more), with the most pronounced scale effects shown by basic metals, printing, rubber products, chemicals, textiles and non-metallic minerals. In the small primary-oriented countries, the scale and resource effects worked together to lower the share of industry and, although industrialisation took place in most sectors, in some industries it could be postponed indefinitely (p. 145).

Chenery (1979)
In his later work, Chenery, with his associates (for example, Chenery and Syrquin, 1975), developed more complex models to simulate the evolution of the structure of production with rising income and to identify the sources of observed differences in development patterns. Industrialisation was seen as resulting from the interplay of rising demand for manufactured goods, changing factor proportions, trade policies and technological development. The models used an inter-industry framework in which domestic demand, trading patterns and technology were treated as functions of income levels and resource endowments.[15]

As in Chenery and Taylor (1968), sample countries were classified according to size and pattern of specialisation in international trade, with extreme cases (very large countries, small countries with extreme primary specialisation, small countries with high capital inflow) identified to indicate possible ranges of variation (Chenery, 1979, p. 92).

Export patterns accounted for much of the variation in overall patterns of industrial growth. At the middle-income level of $400 per capita, manufactured goods comprised 5 per cent of exports in the small primary-oriented countries, but were more than 50 per cent of exports in large countries and small industry-oriented countries (p. 92).

In large countries, the main characteristic of the development pattern was the relatively low level of international trade; the larger the country and the more inward-looking its policies, the closer it got to the extreme case of a closed economy. Domestic markets were larger, natural resources were more diversified and internal transport costs were higher than in small countries, and, together with deliberate government policies, there was a shift from external to internal markets and from foreign to domestic sources of supply.

In large countries, at a per capita income of $400, primary exports were lower than the normal level, but this was largely offset by lower manufactured imports. The effect of this was to reduce primary output by 20 per cent below the average pattern and to increase heavy industry output by 50 per cent above. The greater economies of scale and capital requirements of heavy industry favoured its earlier introduction in larger economies. Light industry was less sensitive to differences in trading patterns at a per capita income level of $400, largely because import substitution was virtually complete. For very large, semi-closed economies, there was a further reduction in primary exports and production; to offset the reduction in foreign exchange availability, there was further import substitution in heavy industry.

In small countries, the benefits arising from external trade were greater because of their smaller markets and less diversified resources. Foreign capital was also more available to small countries, and it played a more significant role in financing investment and imports than it did in large countries.

For small primary-oriented countries, at a per capita income of $400, primary exports were approximately 50 per cent higher than in the normal case and primary output was 25 per cent higher. Almost all manufacturing, apart from food processing, was lower than average because of lower manufactured exports and smaller intermediate demand. To continue to grow beyond middle-income levels, these countries needed to diversify their exports (with the exception of the oil exporters), and a number of them have experienced difficulties in achieving this (for example, Chile and Uruguay). Chenery (1979, pp. 102–3) considered this lag in transforming the export pattern so common that it could be considered a typical feature of the small primary-oriented pattern of development, although he argued that it could be avoided by the implementation of suitable economic policies.

Small industry-oriented countries were characterised by limited natural resources, adequate skilled labour supplies and access to substantial amounts of foreign capital, both private and public. In the typical case, capital inflows replaced the foreign exchange normally earned from primary exports for a period sufficient for industry to establish itself and develop the ability to export. At a per capita income of $400, light industries (textiles and clothing in particular) were of special importance, and both primary output and heavy industry were below normal.

There were similarities in the expansion of the industrial sector in all the patterns identified, but there were also important differences with respect to timing and sectoral composition. The growth of each sector can be decomposed into four elements:

- domestic demand effects;
- export expansion effects;
- import substitution effects;
- effects of technological change.

Depending on the method of decomposition selected (for the technical details, see Chenery, 1979, pp. 108–15), various estimates of the quantitative importance of these four sources of growth were obtained. For example, defining the four elements so that they accounted for the total increase in the output of each sector gave the results shown in Table 2.12.

When the deviation from proportional growth was estimated, however, to

Table 2.12 *Sources of sector growth – average pattern*

Sector	Domestic demand %	Export expansion %	Import substitution %	Technological change %
Primary (agriculture and mining)	60	56	−10	−6
Light industry (including food)	73	18	3	6
Heavy industry (including machinery)	51	26	16	8

Source: Chenery (1979), Table 3-10, p. 112.

focus on the causes of change in the composition of output, the importance of demand as a cause of structural change was reduced and the importance of import substitution and technical change increased. Import substitution now accounted for 38 per cent of the increased share of heavy industry, for 18 per cent in light industry and for 20 per cent in the primary sector (Chenery, 1979, Table 3–10, p. 112). These estimates of the importance of import substitution are closer to those of Chenery (1960), but quite clearly the quantitative significance of both the sources of sectoral growth and the sources of change in the composition of output and resource allocation depend crucially on the methodologies and techniques utilised for their estimation.

In the analysis of the sources of sector growth for the large-country pattern, import substitution and export expansion had smaller effects than is the case in the average pattern in Table 2.12. Increases in domestic demand accounted for 65 per cent or more of the explanation of growth of each sector. Trade still played an important role, however, and the changing composition of exports could add substantially to the growth of both heavy and light industry. Import substitution was of importance in the earlier stages of industrialisation (especially in heavy industry) but was of relatively little significance in later periods.

In the small primary-oriented country pattern, primary exports continued to provide the main source of the increase in exports and in primary output; industrialisation took place later in the transition of the economy and was due more to import substitution than to export promotion. The small manufacturing-oriented countries resembled the small primary-oriented countries in terms of the importance of trade, but were closer to the large countries in terms of the overall composition of their exports. Both small-country patterns showed a later development of heavy industry than that in large countries.

UNIDO (1979a)
The UNIDO analysis covered the period 1960–75 and provided further evidence for the existence of a systematic relationship between the level of per capita income and structural change affecting the manufacturing sector. Structural change appears to be more rapid at intermediate-income levels than at higher-income levels, with the most rapid phase of structural change occurring between income levels of $265 and $1,075 (UNIDO, 1979a, p. 44). At higher-income levels (above $1,000 per capita), although the manufacturing sector's share continued to grow, it did so at a slower rate. The growth path exhibiting these features is described as an S-shaped curve (a logistic curve), and is illustrated in Figure 2.1.

As in the studies discussed above, countries were grouped according to their similarities in resource endowment, domestic or export market orientation and primary or manufacturing production orientation. Four country groups were thus identified:

- large countries;
- small countries with modest resources;

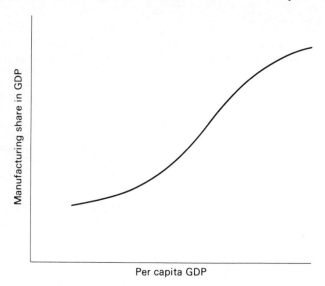

Figure 2.1 Hypothesised growth path of manufacturing sector's share in GDP.
Source: UNIDO (1979a), Fig. V, p. 45.

- small countries with ample resources and oriented to primary production;
- small countries with ample resources and oriented to industrial production.

In contrast to the earlier studies, the share of manufacturing value added in the non-services component of GDP (referred to as commodity GDP) was estimated and used in the analysis (UNIDO, 1979a, p. 46).

Figure 2.2 illustrates the estimated growth path for each of the four country groups. At all levels of per capita income, the share of manufacturing in commodity GDP is higher for the large country group than for other country groups. This is most marked at lower levels of per capita income. At higher levels of per capita income, however, the share in small countries (except those with a primary orientation) begins to approach that of the large countries. The growth in domestic demand in these countries, alongside the increase in manufactured goods exports, enables them to begin to exploit economies of scale not previously available to them.

The UNIDO study (1979a, p. 49) concluded that:

... the typical growth paths of each country group show a wide range of industrial structures at lower levels of per capita income. As the pace of structural change accelerates, the differences between the groups are reduced (with the possible exception of countries having a primary orientation). At higher per capita incomes, the average share of manufacturing in commodity GDP approaches similar levels, although via different development paths.

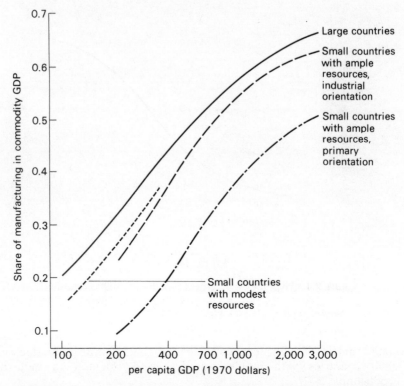

Figure 2.2   Estimated growth paths of manufacturing for four country groups

Notes
1   The curves are plots of a logistic function with the population variable held
     constant at the average value for each group.
2   The number of observations at higher-income levels was insufficient to extend the
     curve for small countries with modest resources beyond $400 per capita income.
     Source: UNIDO (1979a), Fig. VI, p. 47.

PATTERNS OF INDUSTRIALISATION: AN EVALUATION

Opinions differ as to the value and relevance of statistical analyses that
attempt to identify 'normal' patterns of development and industrialisation.
On the one hand, it is argued that such analyses more clearly highlight the
salient features of historical patterns of development and provide useful
guidelines for policy-makers and planners in contemporary LDCs. On the
other hand, there are those who argue that the statistical evidence is not as
unambiguous as is sometimes suggested, and that great care should be
exercised in drawing conclusions from these analyses. Both of these positions
will be considered briefly in turn.

For the supporters of 'normal' patterns analyses,

... studies of industrial growth have produced an impressive body of
evidence revealing important similarities in the development patterns of

most countries. Cultural, economic, political and social phenomena all serve to individualise the development process. However, the evidence suggests that some key economic measures . . . grow in a similar fashion during the process of transition from a developing to a developed country. (UNIDO, 1979a, p. 43)

From this perspective, Chenery and Syrquin (1975, p. 135) have argued that the notion of a dichotomy between developed and less developed countries can be replaced by the concept of a transition from one state or structure of development to another:

The transition from a traditional to a developed economy can be defined in general terms as the set of changes in the economic structure required to sustain a continued increase in income and social welfare. (Chenery, 1979, p. 6)

If a standard or 'normal' pattern of industrial growth can be identified, it will indicate the types of economic changes that are expected to result from industrialisation and also suggest some of the causes and consequences of deviations from it (Sutcliffe, 1971, p. 33). Such an exercise could, in principle, have important implications for economic policy formulation and planning in LDCs. Indeed, Chenery has argued that development policy should increasingly be concerned with the management of structural change and with 'the development of feasible combinations of market forces and government intervention that make this task possible' (Chenery, 1979, p. 2).

The critics of 'normal' patterns analyses have tended to focus on the assumptions that underlie these exercises and point to the data limitations and statistical problems associated with them. Increasingly, they question the relevance and usefulness of the conclusions that can be drawn from them to policy formation in contemporary LDCs. For the sake of clarity and simplicity, these criticisms are listed and briefly discussed below.

(1) In his 1960 article, Chenery argued that the expectation of some degree of uniformity in patterns of growth was based on the existence of certain similarities in supply and demand conditions in all countries. The so-called 'universal factors' thus identified were (Chenery, 1960, p.626):

- common technical knowledge;
- similar human wants;
- access to the same markets for imports and exports;
- the accumulation of capital as the level of income increases;
- the increase in skills as the level of income increases.

It is not obvious that it can be assumed that the first three conditions hold, even approximately, for all LDCs. Access to technology and the ability to make use of the technology acquired differ widely between different LDCs (see Chapter 4, section 4.8). The issues relating to human wants are also of some complexity – for example, how are wants generated? what is the role of the TNC in want creation via the transfer of tastes? (see Chapter 4, section

4.8). Some of Chenery's 'universal factors' may thus be rather more particular than 'normal' patterns theorists assume and the 'universality' assumptions underlying these analyses should be questioned.

(2)   Data limitations, classification and definitional problems and the special limitations of cross-section data are rarely explicitly mentioned. Chenery's 1960 model was re-run using time series data and the results obtained were inconsistent with the 'normal' pattern (see Steuer and Voivodas, 1965). The definition of import substitution used by Chenery in the 1960 model has been subjected to significant criticisms (summarised in Ballance *et al.*, 1982, ch. II; Colman and Nixson, 1978, ch. 8), and it is of interest to note that Chenery's later (1979) estimates of the quantitative importance of import substitution as a cause of industrial growth were significantly below the 1960 estimates (with no reasons explicitly advanced to explain the 'discrepancy').

Chenery and Taylor (1968) argued that the time series data supported the results based on cross-country data. Recent work by Jameson (1982), however, casts considerable doubt on such assertions. Jameson argued that the re-evaluation of the data in Chenery and Syrquin (1975) showed that time series for countries in the postwar period did not show the correspondence claimed and could not be used as evidence favouring the existence of patterns of development (Jameson, 1982, p. 432). Further (p. 444):

> The direct implication is that the claims for patterns should be limited to cross sections which are the result of an historical process which has generated the observed variations across countries. It cannot be expanded to a claim about changes in given countries over time.

These are serious assertions, which will undoubtedly generate further debate. The general point relevant to this discussion is that it should not be assumed that any cross-country data will necessarily indicate a pattern that an individual economy will follow over time.

(3)   With respect to the relevance of these statistical exercises to policy formulation and planning in contemporary LDCs, a number of points need to be kept in mind:

●   The distribution of income within the individual LDC is likely to influence both the rate and characteristics of the process of economic growth and development. Chenery (1960) explicitly discussed income distribution, but it is not elsewhere formally incorporated into the models underlying the statistical analyses.
●   The extent and nature of government intervention or involvement in the development process will vary between different LDCs and over time for individual LDCs. Active government intervention may well cause deviations from the standard pattern, in a planned economy in particular, raising the relative share of industry in general in total output and raising the share of heavy industry in particular. Sutcliffe (1971, p. 54) argued that 'cross-section data, especially with planned economies excluded, can be of little if any use to economic planners'.

- The 'normal', 'standard' or 'average' pattern all too often assumes a normative value or significance that it does not merit. Normal patterns are neither necessarily desirable nor even possible for all LDCs, and deviations from the normal pattern in themselves are neither good nor bad, neither a sign of success nor failure. As Sutcliffe (1971, p. 62) has argued:

> Cross section or even comparative time series regression analysis of the pattern of industrial growth is an important tool of description. But it is a producer of useful yardsticks for classification rather than a guide to policy and planning. Typical patterns are neither necessary patterns nor predictable patterns.

Clearly, the pattern of development and industrialisation of each individual country will be influenced by its own economic and political history, its relationships with other countries, especially the industrialised, developed economies, and by changes in the external environment. With these important qualifications in mind, the identification of normal patterns of structural change and industrialisation can be of use for policy-makers and planners in LDCs, not in the sense that they provide rigid guidelines about what 'should' be done but rather in the sense that they raise important issues relating to the nature and consequences of structural change and permit a more informed discussion of those issues.

Given the complexities of the issues involved, the data limitations and the less than complete knowledge that exists to explain how and why economies evolve over time, the balanced assessment of Batchelor *et al.* (1980b, pp. 55–6) is worth quoting:

> Belief in the futility of a search for laws of growth applicable to every corner of the world economy need not rule out the existence of identifiable groups of countries for which valid generalisations can be found and common models constructed. But the many doubts about uniform growth patterns suggest that countries must be similar in many ways before the simple model can be applied, and the number of categories to which they might belong multiplies rapidly with increases in the number of criteria by which they are classified.

2.5   CONCLUSIONS: PAST EXPERIENCE AND FUTURE PROSPECTS

PAST EXPERIENCE

This chapter began with a description of the structural characteristics of the industrial sector in Third World countries. Using cross-country evidence covering the period 1960–80, the growing share of the manufacturing sector in both total output and employment was identified. The examination of the composition of the manufacturing sector's output showed the increasing importance of heavy industrial activities. Section 2.3 indicated the major changes taking place in the structure of LDCs' trade, and examined in some detail the trends in Third World countries' exports of manufactures.

These changes in the structure of LDCs' manufacturing production and trade were then considered from a more analytical perspective. The various attempts that have been made to identify a 'pattern' of structural change and, in particular, to discover a systematic relationship between the level of per capita income and the share of the manufacturing sector in GDP were reviewed in some detail in section 2.4. In evaluating this type of analysis, it was emphasised that the 'normal' pattern identified from cross-sectional data ought not to be interpreted in normative terms. Active government intervention can cause deviations from the standard pattern, and such deviations in themselves are neither good nor bad, neither a sign of success nor failure. The changing composition of LDCs' manufactured exports was analysed in the second part of section 2.3, with attention being drawn to the varying influence exerted by a country's factor endowment, the international diffusion of technology, and the involvement of the TNCs in intra-firm trade and production location decisions.

The structural changes in the industrial and trade sectors of the LDCs have had a significant impact on world industrial production and trade. Between 1960 and 1980, the LDCs' share of world manufacturing value added rose steadily from 8 to 11 per cent (UNIDO, 1981a, Table 1.1) (a continuation of the past rate of increase would not be sufficient, however, to realise the LDCs' target of 25 per cent of world MVA by the year 2000 – the so-called 'Lima Target'[16]). The share of LDCs in world exports of manufactures (SITC 5–8 less 68) increased from 3.9 per cent in 1960 to 9.0 per cent in 1980 (UNIDO, 1981a, Fig. III).

FUTURE PROSPECTS

Having identified the major structural changes taking place in industrial production and trade both within the LDCs themselves and at the global level, the purpose of this section is to consider some of the possible consequences and implications of these changes. Section 2.4 cautioned against the mechanistic use of past trends and patterns to predict the future direction of structural change. National and international policy decisions will have a major influence on the pattern of further industrial development and the discussion in this section should be interpreted, therefore, as no more than an attempt to indicate the possible direction of future structural change.

The growth of LDCs' manufactured exports depends heavily on market conditions in the advanced industrial economies, which at present absorb over three-fifths of total LDC manufactured exports. A slowdown in demand in the industrial countries has an immediate impact on the export of manufactures from LDCs.[17] Since the mid-1970s, the LDCs' exports of manufactures to developed countries have faced increasing protectionism (Sampson, 1980; UNCTAD, 1983). This 'new protectionism' has been applied in a variety of forms – 'voluntary' export restraints, orderly market arrangements, restrictive health and quality regulations, subsidies to domestic producers – and has often been imposed on specific products imported from specified countries. These discriminatory protectionist measures have affected particularly the low-cost, labour-intensive or mature manufactured goods in which LDCs have a competitive advantage, the most seriously affected products being textiles and clothing, footwear, steel, transport equipment and mechanical engineering goods (UNCTAD, 1983).

The increase in restrictions against manufactured exports from LDCs has been, in part, the result of the developing countries' earlier success in expanding their manufactured exports. Imports from the developing countries have been seen by the developed economies as a serious 'threat' to domestic industry and as a major cause of unemployment. The nature and dimensions of the LDC 'threat' can, however, be exaggerated. Although DC imports from LDCs have risen steadily since the mid-1960s, their share of total DC imports of manufactures is only 13 per cent, and represents less than 4 per cent of the developed countries' total consumption of manufactures (Table 2.13).[18] Furthermore, research into the causes of unemployment in industries where imports from NICs have risen significantly suggests that shifts in demand and increasing productivity, rather than the displacement of domestic production by imports, account for the major share of the decline in employment (OECD, 1979c; Foreign and Commonwealth Office, 1979; Krueger, 1980; Cable, 1983).

More fundamentally, the growth of protectionism can be interpreted as

Table 2.13 *Share of LDCs' manufactured exports in industrial countries' imports and consumption of manufactures*

	1970 %	*1980* %
Imports of manufactures from LDCs as percentage of industrial countries' total imports of manufactures	6.8	13.1
Imports of manufactures from LDCs as percentage of industrial countries' total consumption of manufactures	1.7	3.4
Imports of selected manufactures from LDCs as percentage of industrial countries' total consumption of that good:		
Food	3.5	3.7
Clothing	4.0	16.3
Textiles	2.3	5.4
Footwear	2.6	16.3
Leather products	6.2	17.3
Wood products	1.9	3.6
Paper	0.2	0.5
Chemicals	2.0	3.8
Non-metallic minerals	0.3	1.1
Base metals	3.5	4.1
Cutlery and handtools	0.8	3.3
Metal furniture	0.6	1.6
Radios, televisions and the like	1.1	6.7
Other	4.0	8.0

Source: World Bank (1982), Table 2.4 and World Bank (1983), Table 2.7.

symptomatic of the difficulties that confront the developed countries in adjusting to the changing international pattern of industrial production and trade. The process of 'industrial restructuring' is neither instantaneous nor frictionless. It creates major economic, political and social problems for the advanced economies, and the LDCs are likely, therefore, to continue to face protectionist constraints upon their efforts to increase further their share of the developed economies' market for manufactures.[19]

These prospects have important implications for the future development of industrial production and trade in the LDCs. First, if LDCs' manufactured exports are to continue to expand, markets other than those in the developed economies will need to increase in relative importance. An expansion of trade between LDCs ('South–South' trade) is one way of achieving this. Although South–South trade is a small fraction of total world trade, it grew rapidly during the 1970s, increasing its share of their exports from 20 per cent in 1973 to 24 per cent in 1980.[20] This expansion in inter-LDC trade took a number of different forms. In Latin America, regional trading arrangements encouraged trade diversion, with trade mainly in relatively capital-intensive and high-cost goods, rather than in exports that reflected the comparative advantage of Latin American countries (Diaz-Alejandro, 1974). In East Asia, on the other hand, regional trade encouraged a more efficient division of production (World Bank, 1983, p. 15). The newly industrialising countries increased their demand for raw materials, and at the same time began to export more sophisticated goods and services, some of which went to countries within the region. This in turn created opportunities for the region's primary producers and for those countries in the region specialising in cheaper, less advanced manufactures.

A second implication of the experience of the late 1970s–early 1980s is that the pattern of rapid 'export-led' industrial growth based on expanding markets in the advanced economies and subject to few trade restraints that was experienced by the NICs in the 1960s and early 1970s will not be replicated by the majority of the remaining LDCs (Cline, 1982). In turn, this suggests that the uncritical advocacy by many economists of an export-led strategy of industrialisation and the rejection of industrialisation based on import substitution has been injudicious, and that further industrial development in the LDCs will require an effective combination of policies of both export promotion and import substitution.[21] These alternative industrialisation strategies are discussed in detail in Chapter 6, section 6.2.

FURTHER READING

The United Nations Industrial Development Organization's (UNIDO) biennial *Development Surveys* contain detailed analysis of the trends in industrial structure in LDCs. The same organization's periodical *Industry and Development* publishes articles relating to various aspects of industrialisation in developing countries. The literature on patterns of industrialisation is reviewed in Sutcliffe (1971), ch. 2 and Ballance *et al*. (1982), ch. 3. The relationship between industrialisation and international trade is explored in

Batchelor *et al.* (1980a) and Ballance *et al.* (1982), ch. 4. Ballance and Sinclair (1983) provide a useful introduction to the issue of industrial restructuring in the international context.

NOTES

1 The weighted cross-country averages shown in Table 2.1 are based on a larger sample of countries than those listed in Table 1.1.

2 Note that the remaining tables in the section are taken from UNIDO sources, and differ in their country coverage from the World Bank estimates reported in Tables 2.1–2.2.

3 This paragraph draws heavily on Ballance and Sinclair (1983), pp. 67–70.

4 Light industry is defined in terms of the following ISIC divisions and major groups: food, beverages and tobacco (31); textiles, wearing apparel and leather (32); wood and wood products including furniture (33); printing, publishing and allied industries (342); rubber products (355); plastic products (356); and other manufactures (39). Heavy industry consists of the following: paper and paper products (341); industrial chemicals (351); other chemical products (352); petroleum refineries (353); miscellaneous products of petroleum and coal (354); non-metallic mineral products except products of petroleum and coal (36); basic metals (37); and fabricated metal products, machinery and equipment (38). A classification of greater analytical usefulness is the separation of activities by end use into consumer, intermediate and capital goods. For a classification of ISIC (and SITC) codes into these categories, see UNIDO (1979a), p. 172.

5 Data on manufacturing employment, as previously stated (Chapter 1, section 1.3), are often unreliable. The statistical coverage of manufacturing employment is usually limited to enterprises above a certain minimum size, thus excluding small-scale concerns. While these latter activities may account for only a small part of total manufacturing output, they are an important source of manufacturing employment in many LDCs, accounting in some countries for more than 75 per cent of manufacturing jobs (UNIDO, 1979a, p. 223). The recorded growth in manufacturing employment will be exaggerated, therefore, if modern sector growth occurs partly by displacing informal sector activities, or if a more comprehensive statistical coverage is adopted.

6 In recent years, a growing number of developing countries have emerged as 'second-tier' exporters of manufactures. Thus, the number of LDCs exporting more than $100 million worth of manufactured exports (at 1975 prices) increased from 18 in 1965 to 47 in 1979 (OECD, 1982a; also Havrylyshyn and Alikhani, 1982).

7 A further limitation of the orthodox theory is the assumption that international trade is in dissimilar products. However, recent empirical evidence indicates that intra-industry trade, defined as the simultaneous export and import of products belonging to the same industry, is a significant element in international trade. Intra-industry trade occurs largely between the advanced industrial economies, being based on product differentiation and specialisation in narrow product ranges, which is associated with advanced stages of industrialisation. For a detailed study on intra-industry trade in relation to LDCs, see Laird (1981).

8 For a useful summary of the product cycle theory, see Wells (1972). Hirsch (1974) also provides a review of alternative theories.

9 A comprehensive discussion of intra-firm trade is contained in Helleiner (1981b).

10 A third group of developed countries included in the original study has been omitted.

11 For details of the procedures used to classify commodities into these three groups, see UNIDO (1981a), appendix to ch. II, pp. 103–8. This study also contains an analysis of resource-based exports.

12 Kuznets' work was initially published under the general title of 'Quantitative aspects of the economic growth of nations' as ten papers in various issues of *Economic Development and Cultural Change* between October 1956 and January 1967. The first three papers (relating to aggregate growth and to shares of production sectors in product and labour force) have been revised and extended and published as Kuznets (1971). See also Kuznets (1965, 1966 and 1982). Clark (1957) had earlier attempted to identify patterns of structural change with respect to the proportion of the working population engaged in different economic sectors.

13   More recently, Kuznets (1982) has surveyed the statistical evidence on the shift of the male labour force from agriculture to the industrial and service sectors for both developed and less developed countries for the period 1950–70, utilising International Labour Office data. He found that the absolute size of the declines in the labour force share in agriculture was quite small for highly agricultural countries with initial high shares in the agricultural sector, widened significantly among the more industrialised of the LDCs and then narrowed in the industrialised, more developed countries with lower initial shares in the agricultural sector. The different levels of shares of the labour force in agriculture were significantly and negatively associated with levels of product per capita or per worker. Among the LDCs, the poorer and more agricultural economies showed a smaller shift out of agriculture and a lower growth rate of per capita product. The middle- and upper-income LDCs experienced a greater shift of labour out of agriculture and higher growth rates of per capita product (Kuznets, 1982, pp. 58–9).

Sutcliffe (1971, ch. 2) has questioned whether contemporary LDCs will experience the historical pattern of a decline in the share of their labour force in agriculture:

> Economic stagnation, expecially when it has been combined with population growth, has sometimes quite considerable effects upon the sectoral structure of output and of the labour force. . . . For a number of reasons the search for a pattern of structural change of the labour force, applicable to different countries at different times, seems on the face of it more vain than the search for a pattern of structural change in output. (Sutcliffe, 1971, pp. 29–30 and p. 31).

14   The following expression was derived in order to calculate the deviation of the actual production level from proportionality:

$$dX = (X^1 - X^P) = (1 - u^0)(dW + dD + dE) + (u^0 - u^1)Z^1$$

where:

d = deviation from proportional growth in each case
X^1 = final level of output
X^P = proportional growth (the level of output in the final year if growth and production had been proportional to income)
W = intermediate demand
D = total domestic final use
E = domestic exports
Z^1 = total supplies of product in end period
$u^0 \& u^1$ = ratios of imports to total supplies in the first and last periods respectively.

The three 'causes' of non-proportional growth were thus:

- import substitution = $(u^0 - u^1)Z^1$, that is, the difference between the growth in output with no change in the import ratio and the actual growth;
- non-proportional increases in final demands = $(1 - u^0)(dD + dE) = (1 - u^0)(D^1 - D^P + E^1 - E^P)$;
- non-proportional increases in intermediate demand = $(1 - u^0)(dW)$.

15   The formal structure of the model consisted of five sets of equations that were solved in sequence to determine the pattern of output and factor use corresponding to any combination of exogenous variables. Three exogenous variables were identified: level of per capita income, population and inflow of capital. These three variables were used to estimate typical patterns of growth of the major aggregates over the income range $100–1,500 (in 1964 dollars) per capita (or $200–3,000 per capita in 1976 prices), which were taken 'to represent the transition from an underdeveloped to a developed economic structure' (Chenery, 1979, pp. 33–4).

16   For a discussion of the Lima Target, see Singer (1979).

17 Singer (1983) estimates the multiplier between a slowdown in the industrial countries' growth and the exports of manufactures from LDCs to have been not less than 8.4:1 in recent years.

18 The level of import penetration is much higher, however, in certain narrowly defined products – see Table 2.10.

19 'Industrial restructuring' has been discussed extensively in various international forums in recent years. See, for example, OECD (1979a), UNCTAD (1982, Pt III; 1983), UNIDO (1981b). For a more analytical treatment, see Ballance *et al.* (1982), Ballance and Sinclair (1983) and Franko (1981).

20 The remainder of this paragraph draws heavily on World Bank (1983), p. 15.

21 This argument is developed in Kirkpatrick and Nixson (1983), section V.

3 Business Concentration in LDCs

3.1 INTRODUCTION

The industrialisation process in LDCs is taking place through the activities of a variety of different kinds of sizes of business enterprise, which operate within markets of varying structural characteristics. The standards of performance that these enterprises achieve is basic to the success of that industrialisation process.

Industrial economists who study the manufacturing sector commonly assume that the performance of business enterprises is strongly influenced by the structure of the markets within which they operate (Devine *et al.*, 1979, ch. 2). For this reason, business behaviour is frequently analysed within a *market structure–performance framework*. However, it is becoming increasingly clear that market performance is also affected by the *type and overall size* of the business enterprises that operate in particular markets. Section 3.2 therefore reviews entrepreneurship, the types of business enterprise engaged in manufacturing in LDCs (distinguishing between informal and formal sector, indigenous and foreign owned, privately and publicly owned enterprises) and, more specifically, the role of the small- and large-scale manufacturing enterprises in such economies. This is followed in section 3.3 by a description and evaluation of the structure–performance framework from the standpoint of its relevance and usefulness in examining business behaviour in LDCs. Section 3.4 then contains an empirical review and analysis of market structures and of their relationships to different measures of market performance in LDCs. Data for the reviews in sections 3.2 and 3.4 relate to a cross-section of LDCs consisting of Bangladesh, Brazil, India, Kenya, Malaysia, Mexico, Nigeria, Pakistan, Philippines and the Republic of Korea. Section 3.5 summarises the main findings of the chapter.

3.2 ENTREPRENEURSHIP AND BUSINESS ENTERPRISE

ENTREPRENEURSHIP IN LDCs

Entrepreneurship has a special place in the industrial development process. In its narrow sense it may be defined as perceiving market opportunities or needs and gaining command over resources to meet these. However, where the business is small or the immediate subordinates are not considered sufficiently competent or trustworthy, the entrepreneurial role may extend into such managerial activities as:

purchasing inputs; marketing of the product; dealing with the public bureaucracy; management of worker, customer and supplier relations;

financial management; production management; assembly of factories; industrial engineering; upgrading processes and product quality; introduction of new production techniques and products. (Kilby, 1971, pp. 27–8)

The development process depends upon an adequate supply of entrepreneurs, capable and willing to undertake these types of functions. At one time it was considered that deficiences in supply, particularly of indigenous entrepreneurs, would act as a serious bottleneck in the development process. This view is less strongly held today, but nevertheless supply constraints have probably been an important influence on the emerging pattern of business enterprise and on the rate of development in the manufacturing sector of LDCs (Leff, 1979a).

Various attempts have been made to identify the principal factors that may influence the supply of entrepreneurship in LDCs (Kilby, 1971, pp. 1–14). According to such writers as Schumpeter (1934), entrepreneurs are drawn from the sub-set of the community that possesses certain personal attributes – for example, the capacity for anticipatory thought, the energy to overcome fixed habits of thought, and a desire for power – and these occur randomly in any ethnically homogeneous population. Others (see below) have suggested that the supply of entrepreneurs will vary according to the cultural, religious and other social characteristics of the community concerned. The community characteristics particularly conducive to the development of entrepreneurship that have been identified in different studies include: acceptance of the Protestant ethic, child-rearing practices that stimulate achievement-oriented behaviour, dependence of higher social status on occupational performance, and presence of minority cultural groups. Such factors as these have been used to try to explain why particular types of social groups or communities within an LDC appear to participate more extensively in entrepreneurial activities than others: for example, the greater participation rate of minority cultural groups (the Lebanese in West Africa, the Chinese in South-East Asia, the Indians in East Africa) and of particular indigenous ethnic groups in Nigeria (Harris, 1971), Kenya (Marris and Somerset, 1971), India (Nafziger, 1971) and Pakistan (Papanek, 1971b). Similar kinds of factors have also been mentioned as obstacles to the industrialisation process in those communities where it is difficult in the short term to change socio-cultural systems that are not conducive to entrepreneurial development (Kilby, 1971).

These explanations are almost certainly incomplete, however, because they tend to ignore the ways in which economic and political forces may also have affected the development of entrepreneurial activities in these same groups or communities. For example, the ethnic groups that participate most fully in entrepreneurial activities may also be the best educated, have the closest links with government and have the greatest opportunities to accumulate surpluses in agriculture or trade. Further, whatever the initial reason for involvement in entrepreneurial activities, the subsequent accumulation of capital and business experience that it permitted, combined with the continuance of strong social ties within ethnic groups, would tend to consolidate the premier position of such groups in entrepreneurial activities during subsequent stages of economic development so long as the political climate was favourable. As will be shortly observed, however, the increasing concentration of entrepreneurial activity within particular social groups (whether indigenous or foreign based) in LDCs can lead to sharp changes in that political climate and so cause major changes in the pattern of entrepreneurial activities.

A simplified explanation of the growth of entrepreneurship in LDCs, which combines socio-cultural and economic determinants (but abstracts, initially, any strictly political variables), can be summarised in terms of Figures 3.1(a) and 3.1(b). DD, in Figure 3.1(a), represents the demand for entrepreneurial services in an LDC. It is a derived demand such that economic expansion creates new investment opportunities and increases the demand for entrepreneurial services (D_1D_1). S_1S_1 represents a perfectly inelastic supply function for entrepreneurial services, such as would apply if non-economic factors dominated suppy conditions. If such a supply function existed, then the entrepreneurial bottleneck would be a major obstacle to further economic development. S_ES_E is an alternative form of the entrepreneurial supply function: it acknowledges the influence of socio-cultural factors but also recognises that, within the constraints they impose, some extension in supply can take place in response to the economic incentive of a higher rate of return. Thus economic development induces an extension in the supply of entrepreneurial services – the extent of which depends upon the elasticity of the supply function – and this provides a less severe constraint to further development. In the longer term, as shown in Figure 3.1(b), the supply function as a whole may shift as the socio-cultural environment responds to the process of development that is taking place $(S_ES_E \rightarrow S_{E_1}S_{E_1})$.

Governmental intervention may affect these supply and demand variables in both the short and longer term. For example, import-substituting policies may raise the rate of return accruing to entrepreneurial services in the

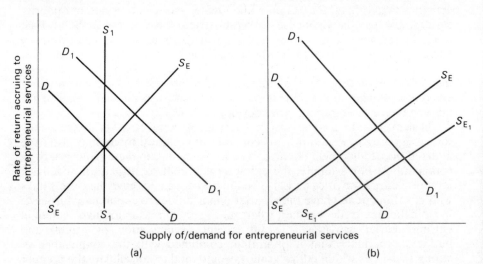

Supply of/demand for entrepreneurial services

(a)   (b)

Figure 3.1   The growth of entrepreneurship in LDCs

manufacturing sector and stimulate an extension in their supply, whereas price controls that reduce rates of return may have the opposite effect. Governmental policies towards TNCs and private indigenous enterprises may affect the level as well as the composition of entrepreneurial services that are supplied within an LDC. Similarly, governmental training and educational programmes may reinforce or retard the changes taking place in the socio-cultural environment and so contribute to the longer-term shift in the entrepreneurial supply function.

Given the differences among LDCs in the socio-cultural environment, in the development process and in the governmental role, it is to be expected that there will be a corresponding variation between them in the conditions of supply and demand for entrepreneurial services and in resulting patterns of business enterprises. Similarly, since these conditions tend to change over time to a greater degree in LDCs than in more industrially mature and stable DCs, a correspondingly greater variation over time is to be expected in the pattern of business enterprise within particular LDCs. A further examination of these and other issues relating to the development of entrepreneurship and management in LDCs is contained in Chapter 4, section 4.16.

THE INFORMAL SECTOR AND SMALL-SCALE ENTERPRISES

Small-scale enterprises are numerically very important in the manufacturing sector of all types of economy but are particularly so in most LDCs. In recent years the activities of these enterprises have been principally associated with the 'informal sector' of manufacturing, although it would be unwise to assume that all small-scale enterprises are engaged in the informal sector, especially as the terms 'small-scale' and 'informal sector' are both given variable and often vague definitions. According to UNIDO (1979a, p. 270), the manufacturing sector in most LDCs can be divided into three main components:

(a) a modern component, comprising the largest industrial enterprises, using comparatively modern technology and located mainly in urban areas;
(b) a modernising component, comprising mainly small to medium-sized enterprises, using various intermediate levels of technology and located primarily in urban areas, but also in some rural areas;
(c) a non-modern component, comprising small industrial enterprises and artisan workshops, using traditional and upgraded traditional technologies, located largely in rural areas but also in urban areas.

The informal sector is taken to comprise mainly (c) category activities but also some of the activities in transitional category (b). According to another view (Bromley, 1978), informal sector activities have the following common characteristics: ease of entry; reliance on indigenous resources; family ownership; small-scale operation; labour-intensive and traditional technology; skills acquired outside the formal school system; unregulated and competitive markets.

Where attempts have been made to estimate the size of the informal manufacturing sector, it has usually been defined as comprising those manu-facturing establishments that employ less than a stated number of workers. This implies that all small-scale establishments are owned by small-scale enterprises, which is probably correct in the great majority of cases.

In most LDCs, censuses of industrial production exclude manufacturing establishments that employ less than a certain number of workers (the limit normally ranging from five to twenty workers according to country). There-fore estimates of the size of the informal sector are often based upon those small establishments that have been excluded, using estimates of production employed in constructing the national income accounts or special surveys of small-scale enterprises where these have been undertaken. In some countries the definition of the informal sector has been broadened to include some of the small establishments covered by the industrial production census, but, in practice, such coverage is often incomplete. This means that the data avail-able relating to small-scale enterprises and the informal sector have to be interpreted very cautiously because:

● the definition of a small-scale enterprise varies between LDCs and may not closely correspond to that of an enterprise engaged in the informal sector;
● the data available on small-scale enterprises within LDCs are very incomplete and subject to substantial margins of error.

Estimates of the relative importance of small-scale establishments within the informal sector of manufacturing in selected LDCs are summarised in Table 3.1. Depending upon the definition of 'small-scale' that is adopted, these suggest that between 5 per cent and 25 per cent of manufacturing *output* may take place within the informal sector. As might be expected, its relative importance appears to be greatest in those LDCs that are least industrialised and that have the lowest per capita incomes. In contrast, the proportion of total manufacturing *employment* in the informal sector ranges between 20 per cent and 95 per cent. These relatively high percentages reflect the labour-intensive nature of informal sector production and the extensive use of part-time and underemployed workers.

Special surveys within individual LDCs provide more reliable and detailed information on particular aspects of the operations of small-scale enterprises in the informal sector. In Nigeria, for example, a special regional survey in the early 1970s of small-scale enterprises with less than fifty employees and a maximum investment of ₦60,000 revealed the wide range of industrial activities in which informal sector enterprises are engaged:

bicyle repairing, baking, blacksmithing, bookmaking, brewing, brickmak-ing, carpentry, carving, dry cleaning, dyeing, electricals, furniture-making, gold-smithing, grain milling, knitting, leather, motor repairing, photo-graphy, pottery, printing, rubber processing, saw-milling, shoe-making, soap manufacture, tailoring, watch repairing, weaving, welding. (Industrial Research Unit, 1975, p. xiv)

Table 3.1 *Estimates of the relative importance of small-scale enterprises and of the informal sector in manufacturing in selected LDCs, various dates*

Country	Share of informal sector in total manufacturing output or manufacturing value added (%)	Share of informal sector in total manufacturing employment (%)
Bangladesh	In 1975, 26% of manufacturing value added was undertaken in establishments of less than 10 workers (UNIDO, 1979a).	In the 1970s, over 85% of total manufacturing employment was in small-scale and cottage industries (Ahmad, 1978).
Brazil	In the 1970s, establishments with less than 5 workers accounted for 10% of total industrial production (UNIDO, 1981a).	
India	In 1974, 21% of manufacturing value added was undertaken in establishments with less than 10 workers using power or less than 20 workers not using power (UNIDO, 1979a).	In 1971, 78% of total manufacturing employment was engaged in informal sector (UNIDO, 1979a).
Kenya	In 1975, 19% of manufacturing value added was undertaken in enterprises with less than 50 workers (UNIDO, 1979a).	In 1974, 61% of total manufacturing employment was in enterprises with less than 20 workers or with capital investment below a specified threshold (UNIDO, 1979a).
Mexico	In 1970, artisan and small-scale enterprises employing up to 25 employees accounted for at least 5% of total manufacturing output (World Bank, 1979a).	In 1970, artisan and small-scale enterprises accounted for at least 23% of total manufacturing employment (World Bank, 1979a). In the 1970s, 75% of total manufacturing employment could have been engaged in establishments with less than 5 workers (UNIDO, 1979a).
Nigeria		In the early 1970s, over 90% of manufacturing workers were engaged in establishments of less than 10 workers (Adejugbe, 1979).
Pakistan	In 1974/5, small-scale enterprises (excluding cottage industries) accounted for 16% of total manufacturing value added (UNIDO, 1979a).	In the 1970s, 95% of total manufacturing employment was engaged in establishments not using power or employing less than 20 workers (UNIDO, 1979a).
Philippines	In 1974, establishments with less than 5 workers accounted for 20% of total manufacturing value added (UNIDO, 1979a).	

Of these enterprises, 98 per cent were single proprietorships; only 10 per cent were officially registered businesses.

The pattern of relationships between enterprises in the informal and formal sectors is not yet fully understood but is of considerable significance from the standpoint both of industrial policy and of the development process as a whole. Producers within the informal manufacturing sector may obtain their supplies from within the sector, but in other cases (for example, when obtaining plastics, metals, machines) they may be dependent upon formal sector enterprises for their supplies. Sales by informal producers to formal sector enterprises appear to be relatively less important, except in the case of particular products (e.g. clothing). In some circumstances the expansion of the formal sector is at the expense of competing informal sector activities; in other cases it may indirectly create extra sources of supply and opportunities for increased sales within the informal sector. Whether, on balance, the relationships between the two sectors are 'benign' or 'exploitive' remains a matter of dispute (Tokman, 1978). Certain parts of industrial policy that may influence these relationships deserve closer examination; for example:

- Have government policies for industrialisation been more supportive of development in the large-scale formal sector than in the small-scale informal sector?
- Given the relatively high proportion of manufacturing employment supported, on a part- or full-time basis, in the informal sector, should employment policies for LDCs be more oriented towards job creation in this sector?

THE FORMAL SECTOR AND LARGE-SCALE ENTERPRISES

The formal sector of manufacturing activity can be subdivided according to type of ownership into citizen-owned private enterprises, foreign-owned enterprises, publicly owned enterprises and 'joint venture' enterprises. Sometimes a further category of expatriate-owned enterprises is added, which may be associated in statistical analyses with either citizen- or foreign-owned enterprises. These various distinctions are of economic as well as political significance, because the behaviour and performance of business enterprises may differ according to type of ownership. The relative importance of these different types of enterprise in a sample of LDCs is reviewed below. This is followed by an examination of the role of the large-scale enterprise within the formal manufacturing sector.

Reliable data are difficult to obtain on the relative importance of foreign-owned enterprises in the manufacturing sector in many LDCs, and this difficulty is compounded by the absence of a generally accepted definition of what constitutes a foreign-owned enterprise. For example, some studies define foreign-owned enterprises as those in which over 50 per cent of the equity is foreign owned, whereas others (Newfarmer and Mueller, 1975) adopt a 25 per cent ownership threshold. It is clear from the nature and variation in these definitions that the dividing line between different types of ownership can be drawn only approximately; a foreign-owned enterprise in one LDC might be

Table 3.2 *Estimates of the relative importance of foreign-owned enterprises in the manufacturing sector of selected LDCs, various dates*

Country	Share of foreign-owned enterprises in manufacturing sector
Brazil	In 1972, the share of total manufacturing sales was approx. 50% and had risen sharply over the previous decade; 59% of 100 largest manufacturing companies were foreign-owned (Newfarmer and Mueller, 1975).
India	In 1972–3, foreign-controlled enterprises accounted for 30% of the annual turnover of the private corporate sector (Kumar, 1982).
Kenya	In 1972, 63% of manufacturing output was produced in firms where 50%+ of equity was owned by non-residents (71% in 1967) (Swainson, 1980).
Malaysia	In 1972, foreign-owned establishments (i.e. 50% of equity held abroad) accounted for 52% of sales and 33% of employment in the manufacturing sector (Lall, 1979b).
Mexico	In 1970, foreign-owned enterprises accounted for 28% of total manufacturing sales (20% in 1962); in 1972, 61% of 100 largest manufacturing companies were foreign owned (Newfarmer and Mueller, 1975).
Nigeria	In 1969, 63% of all shares by nominal value of companies registered in Nigeria were held by expatriates. Expatriate board members had a majority of total board holdings in 63% of all registered companies (Teriba *et al.*, 1972).
Pakistan	In 1968, approximately 7% of manufacturing assets were controlled by foreign-owned enterprises (White, 1974b).
Philippines	No aggregate data are available, but a significant foreign-controlled share of the manufacturing sector in 1970 is reported (Lindsey, 1979).
Republic of Korea	No aggregate data are available, but evidence is reported of significant foreign-share ownership in particular manufacturing industries (UNIDO, 1981a).

classified as a joint venture or even a citizen- or publicly-owned enterprise in another LDC.

Some of the data available on the relative importance of foreign-owned enterprises in a selection of LDCs are summarised in Table 3.2. Even after allowance has been made for the limitations in the data, they clearly indicate the very great variation in the role of foreign enterprises between LDCs. During the late 1960s, less than 10 per cent of the manufacturing sector's assets were foreign owned in Pakistan, while 50–70 per cent of manufacturing sector activities (measured by assets or sales) were foreign owned in Brazil, Kenya, Malaysia and Nigeria. Time series data are very deficient, but they suggest that the relative importance of foreign enterprises in the manufacturing sector of many LDCs increased during the 1960s. Largely as a consequence of LDC government action in the late 1960s or 1970s, this trend was arrested or reversed in many cases during the 1970s.

For reasons discussed more fully in the next chapter, foreign-owned enterprises are normally associated with high-technology or capital-intensive manufacturing activities, and this is largely the case in the sample of LDCs that have been investigated. It is also clear, however, that the industrial composition of foreign enterprise activity varies considerably between LDCs, particularly if they are at different stages of development. Though such enterprises most commonly produce chemicals, metals manufacture and engineering products, in some LDCs they are also very prominent in food and drink manufacture and textile industries.

Table 3.3 contains an indication of those industries, in a selection of LDCs in the late 1970s, in which a significant participation by the public sector already existed or was planned. It shows that public sector involvement in the manufacturing sector was mainly concentrated in the 'basic industrial goods' category and, to a lesser and varying extent, in the capital goods industries. A smaller number of countries (for example, Bangladesh, India and Mexico) possessed public enterprises engaged in the manufacture of basic consumer goods, but only one country in the sample (Mexico) possessed extensive public sector interests in the 'other manufacturing' category.

For the reasons already stated, it is not possible to provide precise measures of the relative importance of publicly owned enterprises within LDCs or of how their relative importance has changed over time. However, on the basis of the data available (see Table 3.4) it is clear, first of all, that their relative importance varies greatly within the sample investigated between the extremes of Bangladesh (50 per cent of value added and 85 per cent of investment in industry) and the Republic of Korea (10 per cent of investment in manufacturing) in the mid 1970s. Secondly, as a response to the growing importance of foreign-owned enterprises and the existence of powerful, indigenous private enterprise groups within their own manufacturing sectors as well as from a desire to become more directly involved within the industrialisation process of their country, a number of LDC governments increased the public sector share in the manufacturing sector during the 1970s. For example, public sector investment in manufacturing rose from 15 per cent in 1971 to 50 per cent in 1974 in Mexico and from 47 per cent in 1965–70 to a planned 76 per cent in 1975–80 in Pakistan; in India, the public sector share in manufacture and mining output rose from 8 per cent in 1960 to 30 per cent in 1975/6. Data relating to other LDCs can also be found in Table 5.4 (Chapter 5).

The existence of major foreign-owned and publicly owned components alongside the indigenous, privately owned component in the manufacturing sector of most LDCs increases the potential complexity of industrial analysis and the evaluation of policy. The conduct and performance of enterprises may be affected by their type of ownership as well as by the type of markets in which they are operating. The type of ownership may affect choice of production technique, level of technical efficiency, export performance, profit rates, etc. In addition, the considerable changes that take place in the degree of foreign enterprise and public sector involvement mean that the structural

Table 3.3 *Manufacturing industries with significant existing or projected participation by the public sector in selected LDCs, late 1970s*

Country	Basic industrial goods	Basic consumer goods	Capital goods	Other manufacturing
Bangladesh	Fertilizers and pesticides; cement, lime and plastics; iron and steel.	Food, beverages and tobacco; textiles and clothing.	Machinery (misc.)	—
Brazil	Petrochemicals; petroleum refining; iron and steel.	—	—	—
India	Pulp and paper; petrochemicals; fertilizers and pesticides; petroleum refining; cement; iron and steel; copper.	Sugar refining; textiles and clothing.	Engines, agricultural and non-electrical machinery.	Misc. chemical products.
Mexico	Pulp and paper; petrochemicals; fertilizers and pesticides; petroleum refining; basic metals.	Food, beverages and tobacco; textiles.	Machinery and transport equipment; motor vehicles.	Wood and paper products; pharmaceuticals; rubber and other metal products.
Nigeria	Pulp and paper; petrochemicals; fertilizers and pesticides; petroleum refining; iron and steel.	Sugar refining.	Electrical machinery; motor vehicles.	—
Pakistan	Petrochemicals, fertilizers and pesticides; petroleum refining; non-metallic mineral products; cement; iron and steel.	—	Engines, agricultural and electrical machinery; motor vehicles.	—
Republic of Korea	Petrochemicals; fertilizers and pesticides; petroleum refining; basic metals.	—	Machinery and transport equipment; electronics	—

Source: UNIDO (1979a).

Table 3.4   *Estimates of the relative importance of publicly owned enterprises in the manufacturing sector of selected LDCs, various dates*

Country	*Share of publicly owned enterprises in manufacturing sector*
Bangladesh	In the mid-1970s, 85% of the assets of the industrial sector were held by the public sector, which also accounted for 50% of industrial value added output (UNIDO, 1979a; Ahmad, 1978).
Brazil	In 1972, approx. 30% of registered capital in the group of 300 largest manufacturing enterprises was state-owned (Newfarmer and Mueller, 1975).
India	The share of the public sector in the output of manufacturing and mining industry rose from 8% in 1960 to 30% in 1975/6; the public sector's share of industrial investment averaged approx. 60%, 1965–75 (UNIDO, 1979a).
Kenya	Prior to the 1970s, state involvement in the manufacturing sector was small, but by 1976 there was some degree of governmental participation in most major industrial sectors either through wholly owned companies or through those in which it had a controlling or minority interest (Swainson, 1980).
Mexico	In 1972, approx. 8% of manufacturing output took place in the public sector, but thereafter this percentage grew rapidly. Public sector share of total manufacturing investment rose from 15% to nearly 50%, 1971–4 (UNIDO, 1979a; World Bank, 1979a).
Nigeria	Public sector share of total manufacturing investment was 18%, 1970–4 (UNIDO, 1979a).
Pakistan	The government-owned sector of manufacturing increased rapidly after 1972. The public sector share of total manufacturing investment rose from 47% (1965–70) to a planned 76% (1975–80) (UNIDO, 1979a).
Republic of Korea	Public sector share of total manufacturing investment was 10%, 1972–6 (UNIDO, 1979a).

characteristics of manufacturing markets in LDCs are unlikely to be stable over time. It is for this reason that market structure–performance analyses cannot be safely isolated from the ownership characteristics of the enterprises operating within the markets being investigated (see sections 3.3 and 3.4).

The detailed analysis of the conduct of these different types of enterprise is contained in Chapter 4 (foreign-owned and indigenous private enterprises) and Chapter 5 (publicly owned enterprises). However, one related feature, to be examined at this stage, is the dominant position of a relatively small number of large-scale enterprises within the formal manufacturing sector of many LDCs. Many of these enterprises are multi-product, multi-market organisations in their own right or belong to a parent company, corporation or group that is such an organisation. Their existence points to a form of economic concentration and business conduct based upon the overall size and scale of an enterprise's operations and not only upon its share of production and sales of a given product within a particular market. This underlines the need to take account of both the type *and* scale of operations of enterprises as well as of the structural characteristics of individual markets when analysing business conduct and performance.

Determining the level of overall economic concentration in the formal manufacturing sector is also a difficult task. For some LDCs it is possible to estimate the proportion of the output, assets or employment of the sector that is attributable to the largest companies or corporations, although in some of these cases a less comprehensive measure has to be used. However, all of these measures tend to understate the degree of economic concentration because they ignore the links that exist both between legally autonomous companies and corporations within the manufacturing sector and between such enterprises in the manufacturing sector and those in other sectors or based overseas. In some cases there is a clearly defined (though not necessarily easily identified) link – for example, where an enterprise is a wholly owned subsidiary of a large parent company. In other cases, the links may be less obvious – for example, where one enterprise has a minority shareholding in another; where companies are connected through interlocking directorates; or where separate enterprises are controlled by different members of the same extended family.

Some of the limited information available on the relative importance of large-scale enterprises and on the overall level of economic concentration in the formal manufacturing sector in a sample of LDCs is summarised in Table 3.5. It shows that large-scale organisations are to be found in each of the types of enterprise that have been previously identified – foreign, domestic and publicly owned – as well as in joint ventures between them. Large-scale, foreign-owned enterprises are frequently linked to TNCs and therefore often form part of much larger economic organisations of a multi-product, multi-market nature. Such organisations are particularly prominent in economies with a substantial foreign manufacturing sector (for example, Brazil, Mexico, Kenya, Nigeria, Malaysia, Philippines). In such countries they are frequently major producers in a range of different industries within the manufacturing sector.

In many LDCs a significant proportion of the indigenous, privately owned component of the formal manufacturing sector is controlled by a relatively small number of economic groups, each of which encompasses a considerable number of different business enterprises. Such groups exist in many Latin American, Asian and African countries and have the following common characteristics:

First, the group draws its capital and its high-level managers from sources which transcend a single family. The capital and the managers may come from a number of wealthy families, but they remain within the group as a single economic unit. The group's owner–managers typically include some (but by no means all) members of the family within which the group's activity orginated. ... Participants are people linked by relations of interpersonal trust, on the basis of a similar personal, ethnic, or communal background. Second, ... groups invest and produce in several product

Table 3.5   *The role of large-scale organisations in the manufacturing sector of selected LDCs*

Country	Degree of concentration in manufacturing sector
Brazil	In 1972, TNCs owned 59 of the largest manufacturing enterprises and were responsible for 50% of manufacturing output. Foreign affiliates were generally the leading firms in the more oligopolistic markets. Large-scale state-owned enterprises engaged in iron and steel, chemicals, petroleum refining (Newfarmer and Mueller, 1975). In 1962, 29 indigenous groups each controlled in excess of 21 companies (Leff, 1978).
India	In 1951–75, 20 groups controlled approx. 25–30% of private corporate assets (Chandra, 1979). See also Sharma (1973) and Ito (1978) for further details.
Kenya	Lonrho, believed to be the largest TNC operating in Kenya, by 1975 had interests in printing, brick manufacture, vehicle assembly, office equipment, wattle production and textiles as well as in non-manufacturing sectors (primary production, transport, urban development). Increasingly involved in joint ventures with Kenyan government. Large Asian groups: Chandaria family owned 14 industrial concerns by 1975 (aluminium, steel rolling, matches, nails, wire manufacture); Khimasia family owned 6 industrial concerns mainly in food production and clothing; Madhvani family was mainly engaged in glass, rayon, sugar and steel manufacture. Karume, who became chairman of the Gema Holdings Corporation, was director of 36 firms by 1974 (Swainson, 1980).
Malaysia	In 1972, the largest 98 companies owned 65% of total assets of all companies and were responsible for 50% of gross output of all companies, partnerships and sole proprietors. 75% of share value of these companies was in large shareholdings of $800,000 or more, and institutional shareholdings from other sectors or foreign-based companies were very high (Ling, 1979, 1980).
Mexico	In 1972, half of the 300 largest manufacturing firms were owned by TNC affiliates and produced 28% of total manufacturing sales. These affiliates were among the leading firms in the majority of the more oligopolistic markets. In the public sector, the 5 largest enterprises each had fixed assets above $100m; their principal interests were in steel, fertilizers, motor vehicles and railway equipment (Newfarmer and Mueller, 1975). Indigenous economic groups also played a significant role in the economy (Derossi, 1972).
Nigeria	Of 1.285 companies registered by 1969, only 100 had a share capital in excess of ₦200,000. Of these, 21 were owned by governmental institutions, 11 were joint ventures in which Nigerians owned at least 40% of the shares; all of the remainder had a majority foreign share-holding (Teriba *et al.*, 1972). These proportions have subsequently changed as a result of the indigenisation decrees implemented during the 1970s.

Table 3.5 – *cont.*

Country	Degree of concentration in manufacturing sector
Pakistan	In 1968, 50 groups controlled almost 50% of all manufacturing assets in the formal sector, the indigenous groups controlling 42% of the total. 7 enterprises were under foreign control and 40 groups were associated with particular families. The main investments of the indigenous groups were in textiles, chemicals and sugar, but they also extended into petroleum, cement, steel, paper, vehicle assembly and other foodstuffs. 'The major industrial families and entrepreneurs were no strangers to each other . . . Members of the familes tended to sit on each other's boards of directors. They also sat on the boards of companies outside of the groups that have been analysed' (White, 1974b, p. 81). 31 large firms were nationalised in 1972.
Philippines	In 1970, 60 largest manufacturing firms owned 54% of the total assets of the whole manufacturing sector and the largest 5 of these accounted for 32% of the assets of the 60 largest firms. A number of these were linked to other Philippines enterprises or to TNCs. 'There would seem to be little doubt that the turnover in firms (1960–70) in the ranks of the 60 largest has resulted in an increasing concentration of industrial resources in the hands of foreign and already powerful domestic capitalists' (Lindsey, 1979, p. 138; see also Yoshihara, 1971).
Republic of Korea	In 1974, 20 groups accounted for 32% of the output of South Korean industry. Between them they produced nearly 400 different products: in the great majority of these product lines there were fewer than 4 producing firms (Leff, 1979b).

markets rather than in a single product line. These product markets may be quite diverse, ranging, for example, from consumer durables to chemicals to steel-rolling. . . . Large groups have also established banks and other financial intermediaries to tap capital from sources outside the immediate members of the group. Finally, the groups usually exercise a considerable degree of market power in the activities in which they operate. (Leff, 1978, pp. 663–4)

There is evidence of the importance of large indigenous economic groups for Brazil, Mexico, India, Pakistan, Kenya, Korea and the Philippines, at some point in their industrial development. Such groups are particularly significant where foreign penetration is slight and where only a small proportion of the manufacturing sector is in public ownership (for example, Pakistan during the late 1960s).

In a number of LDCs, some of the publicly owned enterprises are large-scale organisations in their own right but they also form part of a much larger, though not necessarily closely co-ordinated, group of wider public sector manufacturing activities. The importance of large-scale public sector enterprises and joint ventures grew considerably during the 1970s in many of the countries in the sample (for example, Bangladesh, India, Pakistan, Mexico, Kenya, Nigeria, Malaysia) as governments took measures to restrain or reduce the degree of overall economic concentration of TNCs or large indigenous groups. This has probably altered the relative importance of the different types of large-scale enterprise but has not diminished their overall importance in the manufacturing sector.

In summary, the pattern of ownership control in the manufacturing sector in LDCs is, in many respects, more diverse and therefore analytically more complex than its counterpart in the market economies of the developed world. This arises from the fact that there is probably greater variability in the 'mix' of types and scale of operations in the business enterprises in LDC economies. Very small-scale enterprises using more traditional, labour-intensive techniques are active in a wide range of industries and, collectively, are of considerable importance, particularly in those LDCs that are least industrialised and that have low per capita incomes. In many cases, this 'informal' sector serves separate markets from those supplied by the more modernised, formal manufacturing sector, but in some product areas (textiles, clothing, food and drink manufacture) their markets overlap. Small-scale enterprises have received relatively little attention in industrial development programmes, although this is now being partially remedied (see Chapter 6, section 6.6). At the other extreme of the size spectrum, the role of the large-scale enterprise and the overall level of economic concentration in the formal manufacturing sector in many LDCs are at least as great as, and in some cases considerably greater than, in some of the market economies of the West (Chandra, 1979). In certain cases this high level of concentration reflects the primacy of a small number of indigenous economic groups in the privately owned domestic sector of manufacturing activity, but in many LDCs – those with substantial foreign and publicly owned sectors of manufacturing – it also reflects the important role of large-scale TNCs and publicly owned enterprises and the formal (joint venture) and informal (interlocking directorates, etc.) links between them.

The primacy of different kinds of large-scale enterprises and the high level of overall economic concentration with which it is associated in LDCs have been analysed less extensively than the growth of large firms in the developed world. However, the potential significance of large-scale enterprises for business conduct and performance and for industrial policy is broadly similar in both types of economy (George and Joll, 1981, chs 4 and 5). Their prominence within the industrial sector raises a number of analytical and policy questions that are examined in greater detail at later stages in this book. For example, who controls the policies and operations of these enterprises and in what ways does that control affect their objectives and resulting conduct and performance (Chapter 4)? Do different kinds of large-scale enterprise – private domestic, public, foreign-owned, joint venture – behave in discernibly different ways, and does this result in different patterns of resource allocation (Chapters 4 and 5)? Does the possession of business interests in many different markets enable large-scale enterprises to exercise greater economic power than if their operations were confined to a single market (Chapter 3, section 3.3)? Do large-scale enterprises, by virtue of their size, confer benefits on host LDCs that may offset the adverse effects of the concentration of economic power in their hands (Chapter 3, section

3.4)? Should industrial policy contain special measures for the regulation of large-scale enterprises, whether or not these possess monopoly power in particular markets, as an integral part of an LDC's industrial development strategy (Chapter 6, section 6.4)?

3.3   MARKET STRUCTURE–PERFORMANCE ANALYSIS

THE FRAMEWORK FOR ANALYSIS

It is commonly assumed that the performance of business enterprises (that is the efficiency with which they use scarce resources) is strongly influenced by the structure of the markets in which they operate. The market structure–performance (S–P) framework that is used to analyse these relationships is derived from the traditional theory of the firm, which distinguishes different types of market structures (for example, perfect competition and monopoly) and deduces the ways in which firms will behave and perform within the constraints of these different structures (Devine *et al.*, 1979, ch. 2). Four main structural features of a market are usually identified:

- *seller concentration*: the number and size distribution of sellers within the market;
- *buyer concentration*: the number and size distribution of buyers within the market;
- *entry barriers*: the ease with which new sellers may enter the market;
- *product differentiation*: the extent to which the products sold within the market are close substitutes for each other.

In the theoretical limiting case of a perfectly competitive market, there are a very low level of seller and buyer concentration and no entry barriers or product differentiation. At the other theoretical extreme of the single-firm monopoly there are very high seller concentration and very high entry barriers. In the former type of market, firms are predicted to achieve a high level of performance because in order to survive in the long run they must be technically progressive and cost-efficient, they must utilise resources in a way that is consistent with the optimal allocation of resources[1] and they are prevented from earning more than normal profits. By contrast, the single-firm monopolist is predicted to be a less satisfactory performer because it need not be technically progressive or cost-efficient to survive, it is likely to make price and output decisions that lead to a misallocation of resources and, unless there is the countervailing influence of high buyer concentration within the market, it is expected to obtain super-normal levels of profit (Devine *et al.*, 1979, ch. 8).

In the real world, firms operate in markets that lie at varying points between these two theoretical extremes, and whose relationships between structure and performance are less clearly understood and less precisely defined (because of their greater complexity). In such circumstances it is often the practice to identify the relationships that are expected to exist by extrapolating between the two theoretical limiting cases outlined above. This has been most frequently attempted by hypothesising a relationship between market structure and profit margins (which acts as one indicator of performance[2]) along the following lines:

- profit margins tend to be higher in those markets where (other things being equal) seller concentration is higher;
- profit margins tend to be higher in those markets where (other things being equal) entry barriers are higher;
- profit margins tend to be higher in those markets where (other things being equal) buyer concentration is lower.

Less frequently, and more controversially, it is hypothesised that technical progressiveness and cost efficiency are lower in those markets in which seller concentration and entry barriers are higher (Devine *et al.*, 1979, chs 2, 5 and 8).

An analytical framework incorporating these kinds of relationships has been extensively used in empirical studies of industries and markets in developed economies and it is now being increasingly used for similar purposes in LDCs. Such an analytical framework may be useful in the following ways:

- to describe and classify those characteristics of individual industries and markets that are believed to be economically significant, in the sense that they are important influences on the behaviour and performance of firms operating within those industries and markets;
- to explain the observed behaviour and performance of firms operating within these industries and markets;
- to identify public policy measures that may improve overall industrial performance by modifying the existing structural characteristics of industries and markets, and to predict the size of the impact on performance they are likely to have.

Potentially, the structure–performance framework is a very important tool in industrial analysis. However, there are limitations to its practical usefulness and dangers of incorrect use if it is applied in an over-simplistic way. A number of these limitations have been identified through the many structure–performance empirical studies that have been completed in developed economies. There are additional difficulties that may arise when conducting such studies in the different and much more variable circumstances that prevail in LDCs. These general and more LDC-specific limitations and difficulties are reviewed below.

A CRITIQUE OF THE S–P FRAMEWORK AND ITS USE

General difficulties
A basic difficulty in constructing structure–performance investigations is the absence of a generally accepted body of theory that satisfactorily explains the

behaviour and performance of large firms in terms of the actual oligopolistic market structures that are the subject matter of most empirical studies. Attempts have been made to construct S–P models that are more closely derived from oligopoly theory itself, but these are usually based upon fairly simple notions of oligopolistic objectives and interdependence (Hay and Morris, 1979, ch. 7). The aspects of actual market practice that tend to be ignored or treated inadequately in S–P studies include the following:

- Each market is analysed as though it is independent of all other markets. However, large firms typically produce in many industries and sell in many markets, as indicated in the preceding section of this chapter. Therefore their power to influence behaviour and performance in a given market may be seriously underestimated by simply measuring firms' share of production or sales within that particular market. For similar reasons the behaviour and performance of a large firm in one market may influence its behaviour and performance in another market.

- In the typical S–P model, the structural characteristics of the market are taken to be the predetermined, causal determinants of market behaviour and performance. However, the large firms operating within a given market may possess sufficient overall power to change the structure of that market where they consider their own commercial performance to be unsatisfactory. In other words, in such markets there may not be a simple line of causality running from structure through behaviour to performance; in certain circumstances, the line of causality may be reversed.

- Each market tends to be analysed as if it is in long-run equilibrium – that is, the profit margin (or other measures of performance used) observed at a given period of time is assumed to reflect the market structure that exists at the same period of time. However, in more realistic dynamic market conditions, responses to change are continuous and non-instantaneous and in such conditions simple forms of comparative static analysis are less appropriate.

In addition, a number of empirical difficulties arise as a result of lack of suitable data when carrying out S–P studies. The response to these difficulties is often a further simplification of the S–P model to make use of such data as are available and this tends to reinforce the existing theoretical weaknesses of the model. The most common empirical difficulties are as follows:

- Data are mainly derived from censuses of production, which contain measures of national production in individual industries rather than of sales and purchases in individual markets. Industrial production data often cover a range of products, not all of which are sold in a single market, and ignore the existence of imports and exports and the presence of regional and local markets for certain products. Therefore, the 'market' definition that has to be used in empirical studies does not closely correspond to the theoretically ideal definition.

- Data often do not exist to estimate all of the structural characteristics of markets. For this reason most studies have excluded buyer concentration from their analyses.
- Lack of appropriate data often means that some structural characteristics have to be defined and measured more crudely than is theoretically desirable. This has frequently been the case in measuring seller concentration, entry barriers and product differentiation.
- Corresponding deficiencies in the data available for the measurement of performance indicators have meant that a relatively narrow range of performance indicators has been used in S–P studies. The analysis in most studies is limited to the profit indicator of performance and in only relatively few cases have technical progressiveness and cost efficiency been investigated. Furthermore the measures of profit performance that are available often do not correspond closely to the measures that are ideal for the purpose.

Additional difficulties in LDC studies

The theoretical and empirical difficulties in S–P studies that have been described so far are common to all types of economy, developed and developing. However, there are reasons for believing that these difficulties are likely to be more severe in LDC economies. In part, this is because the data available in most LDCs are less extensive and reliable than in the DCs. At a more fundamental level, however, it is because LDCs possess characteristics that make them less suitable candidates for the simpler forms of S–P analysis.

The S–P analytical framework was initially developed for use in the United States economy, and it can be argued that it is best suited to analyse business behaviour in economic systems that display similar characteristics. The US economy contains a relatively large and mature manufacturing sector, many of its domestic markets are mainly supplied from its own industries, which operate within a largely free-enterprise system in which the profit measure is a relevant indicator of success. These conditions do not apply widely in most LDCs, so if the S–P model is to be useful in the Third World context, it may need to be fairly extensively modified and extended to take such differences adequately into account.

First, industrialisation is a fairly recent development in most LDCs, and consequently both the relative importance and the composition of the manufacturing sector are changing considerably, even over the short and medium term. Market structures are not yet stabilised to the degree that is found in mature industrial economies. It is therefore all the more important to analyse S–P relationships over time rather than rely exclusively upon 'snapshot' analyses of relationships at a given point in time.

Secondly, in most LDCs a significant proportion of manufacturing production takes place in the small-scale, informal sector (see section 3.2). Because of data deficiencies, the role of the informal sector tends to be ignored in S–P studies. However, to ignore the informal sector where it is competing in the same market as formal sector businesses leads to an upward bias in measures of seller concentration and entry barriers. Therefore attempts should be made to take some account of informal sector activities in those markets in which they have a significant presence.

Thirdly, LDCs are substantially less self-sufficient in manufacturing than the USA. In these countries, imports and foreign trade regulations are a much more important influence on market structures and therefore should be taken into account when estimating seller concentration and entry barriers.

Fourthly, the large-scale, privately owned enterprise plays an equally large (and often larger) role in the manufacturing sector in many LDCs as it does in more mature economies (section 3.2). These enterprises are of two main kinds – indigenous and foreign owned; the later in particular is often of much greater relative importance in LDCs than in most DCs. Therefore there is, if anything, a stronger argument in the case of LDCs for extending S–P studies to take explicit account of the overall scale and types of large-scale enterprise operating within particular markets.

Finally, public sector involvement in the manufacturing sector is far more extensive in many LDCs than it is in the United States economy (see section 3.2) and the S–P model needs to be modified to take this into account. For example, the profit objective is less relevant to publicly owned than to privately owned enterprises. Similarly, governmental regulations play a much more important role, in addition to that of market structure, in determining market conduct and performance in certain LDCs.

The conclusion to be drawn from this critical review is *not* that the S–P framework is an inappropriate tool of industrial analysis in LDCs but that the simple S–P model needs to be modified to make it more relevant to LDC conditions. The practical dilemma that this raises is that a modified model will almost certainly require more data, which the statistical services departments of most LDC governments would find difficult to satisfy.

3.4 MARKET STRUCTURE–PERFORMANCE STUDIES

INTRODUCTION

A large number of structure–performance studies have been carried out for the manufacturing sector in developed economies, especially the USA and UK, and the findings of these studies have been collected and evaluated in a number of publications (Devine *et al.*, 1979; George and Joll, 1981; Scherer, 1980). The majority of these studies have sought to determine whether differences in profit levels between markets could be explained by differences in their structural characteristics (notably seller concentration and entry barriers) and in other market characteristics (for example, the capital intensity of production and the growth rate in market demand). However, the actual variables included in the S–P model used, and the ways in which these have been defined and measured, vary considerably between individual studies and this complicates comparisons between their findings. What they tend to show, however, are, first, considerable variability in levels of seller concentration and entry barriers between markets but with the majority of markets showing oligopolistic characteristics. Second, although the findings of studies are not unanimous, the weight of evidence supports the hypothesis that increasing

Table 3.6 *Selected studies of industrial or market concentration in LDCs*

Country	Study	Data (Year)	Number of industries	Concentration measure	Treatment of imports and exports
India	Bain (1966)	(a) 1956 (b) 1960–1	16 16	Number of largest plants accounting for 50% of total employment in industry. % of output or capacity of industry controlled by 1–4 largest firms.	None
India	Gupta (1968)	1958	29	4-plant employment concentration ratio.	None
India	Sawhney & Sawhney (1973)	1958	25	8-plant employment concentration ratio.	None
India	Walgreen (1971)	1958	29	4-plant employment concentration ratio.	None
India	Ghosh (1975)	1948, 1953, 1958, 1963, 1968	22	4- and 8-firm asset concentration ratios (also estimates Gini ratios and Herfindahl measures).	None
India	Katrak (1980)	1963	55	4-plant asset concentration ratio	Treated as separate variables in structure–performance regression analysis.
Pakistan	White (1974b)	1967–8	23 (all Pakistan) 59 (W. Pakistan)	4-firm output or capacity concentration ratio.	Import protection level treated as a separate variable.
Pakistan (W.)	Amjad (1977)	1968	25 (W. Pakistan)	4-firm output or sales concentration ratio.	Imports treated as a separate variable.
Pakistan	Sharwani (1976)	1967, 1968, 1970, 1973	27	2-firm sales concentration ratio.	Imports treated as a separate variable.
Malaysia	Gan & Tham (1977)	1968–71	42	8-plant output concentration ratios.	Import protection level treated as a separate variable.
Malaysia	Gan (1978)	1968–71	42	4- and 8-plant output concentration ratios.	Ratios adjusted for imports.

Country	Author (year)	Year(s)	No.	Concentration measure	Notes
Malaysia	Lall (1979b)	1972	46	4-plant employment concentration ratios.	None
Philippines	Sicat & Villarroel (1974)	1960	18	Large number of different measures used based on fixed assets, employment and value added plant data.	None
Philippines	Lindsey (1977)	1970	18	3-plant employment and value added concentration ratios.	Imports treated as a separate variable.
Korea (S.)	Nam (1975)	1966–9	234	4- and 8-firm output and employment concentration ratios.	Deliberately ignores imports because very small in this period.
Kenya	House (1973)	1963	31	3-establishment employment concentration ratio, adjusted for exports and imports.	Concentration measure adjusted for exports and imports.
Kenya	House (1976)	1967	25	As above.	As above.
Brazil	Newfarmer & Mueller (1975)	1968	302	4-plant output concentration ratio.	None
Brazil	Evans (1977a)	1961, 1965, 1967, 1968	1	4-, 8-, 20-, 50-firm output concentration ratios.	None
Mexico	Newfarmer & Mueller (1975)	1970	230	4-plant output concentration ratio.	None
Argentina, Chile, Colombia, Costa Rica, Ecuador, Mexico, Paraguay, Peru, Uruguay, Venezuela	Meller (1978)	Various years, 1963–8	18	Entropy index based on plant employment ratio.	None

levels of seller concentration and high entry barriers are associated with higher profit margins. Thirdly, in many studies these market structure variables explain only a minor proportion of the variation in profit between markets. This suggests that either the variables in the S–P model have not been correctly defined or measured and/or the model needs to be extended to include other variables that may be contributing to these profit differences.

A minority of other studies have examined the relationship between market structure and other measures of performance such as cost efficiency and technical progressiveness. The conclusions that can be drawn here are much more tentative. There is nevertheless some support for the view that very high levels of seller concentration are associated with lower levels of cost efficiency (Primeaux, 1977) but that technical progressiveness is probably greater at intermediate, rather than very low or very high, levels of seller concentration (Devine *et al.*, 1979, ch. 5).

By contrast, there have been far fewer S–P studies carried out for the manufacturing sector in LDCs, although their numbers are growing. Here, too, the majority of studies attempt to explain differences in profit levels between markets in relation to differences in their structural and other market characteristics. In general, however, they use simpler S–P models than those employed in the DC studies and focus to a greater degree upon the measurement and influence on profitability of the seller concentration variable. The following review of S–P studies is divided into two parts:

(i)   the measurement of seller concentration in LDCs and its determinants, and the types of industries within the manufacturing sector in which seller concentration tends to be the highest;
(ii) the relationship between seller concentration (and other market characteristics) and profit levels in different LDC manufacturing markets.

The studies that are reviewed mainly relate to the sample of LDCs that have been investigated throughout this chapter, but studies of broader scope are also examined where they shed light on the topics being explored.

SELLER CONCENTRATION IN LDCs

Table 3.6 summarises the main features of the studies that have attempted to measure levels of seller concentration in the sample of LDCs investigated. A major feature is the multiplicity of ways in which seller concentration has been measured. The main differences observed are of the following kinds:

Differences in the definition of the market. In all cases data relate to *industries* rather than *markets*; in only a minority of cases are imports taken into account. The breadth of the industrial categories varies greatly and where each industry covers a very wide range of products the level of seller concentration is likely to be seriously underestimated.

Concentration measures based upon firms or establishments. Ideally, seller concentration measures should be based upon the market shares of the largest *firms* rather than of the largest *establishments*. However, because of the problem of confidentiality, only establishment data are available in most LDCs. Nevertheless, one study of Belgian industries found a very high correlation between establishment and firm concentration measures (Vanlommel *et al.*, 1977). This may suggest that the former may be used as a proxy for the latter, although it will tend to systematically *understate* the true level of seller concentration in LDC markets because the largest plants will tend to be owned by multi-plant enterprises.

Units of measurement of market share. The relative importance of an establishment in a market or industry has been measured according to its share of sales, value added, output, production capacity or value of assets. In general one would expect a high correlation to exist between these different measures and therefore it is not of crucial importance which is used. Share of sales or valued added is probably the best measure; measures based upon employment or capital assets tend, respectively, to underestimate or overestimate the level of seller concentration in a market because large establishments are often more capital intensive than small establishments.

Concentration measure. The simplest and most commonly used measure is the concentration ratio, which measures the share of the output, sales, etc., of the total industry or market that is accounted for by a given number of the largest establishments or firms in the industry or market. The most common number of establishments or firms for this purpose is four but, as Table 3.6 shows, the actual number used in the studies reviewed varied between one and fifty. There are reasons for arguing, however, that performance may be affected by the total number as well as the size distribution of sellers in a market and two measures that have been used in single studies and capture both of these elements are the Herfindahl index and the entropy index.[3]

The diversity of measures reported in Table 3.6 means that considerable care is needed in making comparisons between the findings of the different studies. It is intended first of all, to examine the basic determinants of seller concentration and then to identify the differences in concentration that might be expected between (a) developed countries and less developed countries, (b) different-sized countries within the LDC group, and (c) different industries within the LDC group, using the findings of the above studies and related evidence as illustrative material.

Determinants of seller concentration
The level of seller concentration depends upon three factors: the size of the establishment, the number of establishments owned by each firm in a given market, and the total size of the market. As mentioned earlier in this section, most S–P studies in LDCs base their measures of seller concentration on the establishment rather than the firm and use industry-based data to measure the size of the market. Therefore the critical determinant of most measures of seller concentration in LDCs is likely to be the relationship between the minimum efficient scale (MES)[4] of establishments in a given industry relative

to the total size of its domestic production, adjusted for overseas trade transactions where these are of significance.

The MES of establishments depends primarily on the state of technology and relative factor prices. If all economies possessed the same technological knowledge and faced the same relative factor prices, then the MES for a given industry would be of the same order of magnitude in all economies. In these simplified circumstances one might expect, in long-term equilibrium, that the typical plant size in a given industry would be similar in all economies. Therefore, since markets in a given industry vary considerably in size between countries, 'smaller markets will . . . contain fewer plants, and other things being equal, will display a higher degree of concentration' (Merhav, 1969, p. 41). As LDCs typically have much smaller markets than DCs, this means that LDCs will tend to have higher levels of seller concentration than DCs and that the highest levels of seller concentration will occur in those LDCs with the smallest markets.

In practice, however, the typical plant size (measured by employment level) in an industry tends to be smaller in LDCs than in DCs (Banerji, 1978). There are various possible reasons for this. In the larger markets of DCs, establishments may have grown beyond their MES because there is no significant cost penalty in doing so – this would be likely if cost functions are L-shaped rather than U-shaped. Establishment sizes may also be smaller in LDCs because more plants use an older technology with a lower MES or because differences in relative factor prices make an alternative technology with a lower MES more appropriate (see Chapter 4, section 4.8 for a discussion of technological access in LDCs). Finally, it has been suggested that foreign-owned enterprises may operate smaller establishments in LDCs than in their base economies because they prefer to have some production capability within such limited-sized markets rather than relinquish them entirely to their international competitors. In other words, the 'small replica' establishment is a defensive competitive device characteristic of international oligopolistic rivalry (Evans, 1977a).

Seller concentration levels
Though establishment sizes are typically smaller in LDCs than in DCs, the general level of seller concentration will still be higher in LDCs than in DCs (as hypothesised above), provided that the markets they serve are proportionately smaller still. The general weight of evidence seems to suggest that this is the case (Bain, 1966; Merhav, 1969; White, 1974b; Lall, 1979b). Table 3.7 contains some comparative data for Pakistan and the United States and for Malaysia and the United Kingdom to illustrate this. However, in a comparative study of the pharmaceuticals industry in Brazil and the United States, Evans (1977a) has identified one situation where oligopolistic rivalry may have led to the opposite effect. On the other hand, Meller's (1978) comparative study of ten Latin American countries supports the view that LDCs with smaller domestic markets (for example, Costa Rica, Uruguay and Peru) tend to have higher levels of seller concentration than LDCs with larger domestic markets (for example, Argentina, Mexico and Venezuela).

The MES of establishments is expected to differ between industries and

Table 3.7 *Comparison of seller concentration in selected industries, Pakistan and United States, 1967/8, and Malaysia and United Kingdom, 1972*

Four-firm seller concentration ratio			*Four-establishment seller concentration ratio*		
Industry	Pakistan %	United States %	*Industry*	Malaysia %	United Kingdom %
Fertilizer	100	33	Soap	94	52
Sulphuric acid	100	54	Ice-cream	87	73
Paper	100	26	Tobacco	76	23
Nylon yarn	100	91	Bicycles	72	61
Cigarettes	92	81	Cement	69	48
Cement	86	28	Chemical fertilizers	63	38
Jute textiles	37	70	Printing	19	4
Cotton textiles	25	30	Plastic products	18	3
Dyeing, bleaching and finishing	10	42	Furniture	18	10
Unweighted average (51 industries)	66	49	Unweighted average (28 industries)	35	24

Sources: Pakistan and United States – White (1974b); Malaysia and United Kingdom – Lall (1979b).

thereby cause differences in the average size of establishments between industries. Those industries that have the highest MES are expected to be ranked highest in terms of the typical size of their establishments. In turn, these industrial rankings are likely to be similar in all countries to the extent that their determinants (e.g. MES) are also similar in the same countries. It follows that, if the sizes of the market served by individual industries are ranked in a similar order in each country, the rankings of industries according to the level of seller concentration will also be similar in the same countries. These two hypotheses are tested below against the available evidence.

A number of comparative studies have been completed on the size distribution of establishments for individual industries across a wide range of DCs and LDCs (Teitel, 1975; Banerji, 1978). Although the results vary to some degree according to their coverage, definition of industries and measures of size used, their conclusions are broadly similar. They indicate that there is considerable similarity in the rankings of industries according to average establishment size between DCs and LDCs, with, as might be expected, a higher level of association (as measured by the concordance coefficient, see Table 3.8) within the DC group than within the LDC group. The average rankings obtained for relatively broad industrial categories in Banerji's (1978) study are also given in Table 3.8. He shows, for example, that in most economies there tend to be larger establishments in the production of tobacco, basic materials, chemicals, textiles and paper products than in the wood products, furniture and clothing industries. Teitel's study shows a higher ranking for petroleum products and beverages and a

Table 3.8 *Average rank ordering of industries according to average employment size of establishments, various dates*

Industry	Rank		
	All countries	High-income countries	Middle- and low-income countries
Tobacco	1	1	2
Basic metals	2	2	1
Chemicals	3	4	5
Paper and pulp	4	6	4
Textiles	5	8	3
Petroleum	6	3	10
Electrical machinery	7	5	9
Rubber	8	10	6
Non-electrical machinery	9	9	8
Transport equipment	10	7	12
Non-metallic minerals	11	12	11
Printing and publishing	12	18	7
Beverages	13	11	16
Leather products	14	13	13
Food processing	15	15	15
Fabricated metal	16	16	14
Miscellaneous industries	17	19	17
Clothing	18	14	18
Furniture	19	17	19
Wood	20	20	20
Coefficient of concordance[a]	0.40	0.52	0.39

Note:

a The coefficient measures the relationship between the industry rankings in the countries comprising the sample. In each case it is significant at the 1% level. However, the coefficient is higher for high-income than for middle–lower-income countries, indicating that the rank ordering of industries is closer within the DC group.

Source: Banerji (1978).

somewhat lower ranking for textiles and printing in LDCs (Teitel, 1975). More detailed data would probably show that the MES and average plant size also varied between different branches within certain of these industries (for example, chemicals and textiles).

Because of the different ways in which seller concentration ratios have been calculated there are only a limited number of opportunities to compare the rankings of industries between countries according to their levels of seller concentration. Meller's (1978) study enables such a comparision to be made between ten Latin American countries. It shows that each of these countries has a similar seller concentration hierarchy among its industries: the industries that have high concentration levels in one country tend to have high concentration levels in the other nine countries (this is reflected in the value of the concordance coefficient in Table 3.9). Further, the average ranking of industries by level of seller concentration in Table 3.9 bears similarities to the

seller concentration in individual industries or markets and the levels of overall concentration in the manufacturing sector or economy as a whole. In the case of large-scale indigenous enterprises, Leff (1978) has made the general observation that the economic groups possess a considerable degree of market power in many of the different activities in which they operate. White (1974b), in his study of Pakistan, shows that in the late 1960s one or more of the forty-three leading groups were among the four largest sellers in a number of the more highly concentrated industries such as artificial fibres, paper, petroleum refining and cement. However, they were also very prominent in industries that had a much lower level of concentration, notably cotton and jute textiles. In the case of foreign-owned enterprises, it has frequently been observed that TNCs are prominent in the more highly concentrated industries. According to the study by Newfarmer and Mueller (1975), 61 per cent of TNC production in Mexico in 1970 was sold in markets where the largest four plants accounted for half or more of the markets' total sales. A similar positive relationship between TNC penetration and level of industrial concentration has been identified in Brazil by the same authors (Newfarmer and Mueller, 1975). Particularly in the case of TNCs, attempts have been made to identify the causal relationship between oligopolistic markets and the presence of large-scale enterprises. One view is that the technical characteristics of oligopolistic markets – such as higher than average MES, capital and technological requirements – mean that large-scale enterprises will have a competitive advantage over smaller firms in such markets and that for this reason they will tend to be more oligopolistic. An alternative view is that the actions of the TNC cause the market to be more oligopolistic than its technical characteristics require. Lall's (1979b) study of Malaysia lends support to the second of these views, whereas Evans' (1977a) 'small replica' hypothesis points in the opposite direction. A further examination of this issue is contained in Chapter 4, section 4.6. Further investigations are needed before a confident conclusion can be reached on this point.

Another matter of importance is how levels of seller concentration in LDCs are changing over time. There are a number of variables to consider: changes over time in the size of the market, in the size of establishments, in the number of establishments controlled by the same enterprise, and in government policy towards public ownership and the regulation of foreign competition. One of the very few studies of the longer-term changes taking place in levels of seller concentration in LDCs relates to India over the period 1948–68 (Ghosh, 1975). This records a considerable decline in the four-firm concentration ratio in a number of industries, and this is principally explained by the expansion of the market and governmental regulation of large 'management agency' groups. However, this trend in India is not necessarily typical of LDCs as a whole. Where large-scale indigenous groups and TNCs were able to expand their scale of operations during the 1960s, under the protective wing of an import-substitution policy, the reverse trend in concentration may have occurred. Similarly, the effects on seller concentration of an extension of public ownership in a number of LDCs during the 1970s may have intensified the oligopolistic features of certain markets. Better time series data are needed to determine the direction and extent of the considerable changes taking place in seller concentration and other elements of market structure in LDCs.

Summary
Although the detailed picture is very incomplete, many of the main features of seller concentration in LDCs are now reasonably clear. In general, the levels of *establishment* and *firm* concentration measures tend to be higher in LDCs than in DCs. This means that LDC markets are typically more oligopolistic in structure than DC markets. As the manufacturing sector in LDCs expands, concentration measures might be expected to decline as a consequence of the expansion of domestic markets. However, the influence of other variables on these measures is uncertain, and there is no guarantee that a decline in seller concentration will occur unless specific governmental measures are taken to promote it.

The ranking of industries according to average plant size shows a number of similarities both between DCs and LDCs and within the LDC group of countries. In many cases this also broadly corresponds to the ranking of industries according to seller concentration. This means that it is largely the same kinds of industries that experience the higher levels of concentration, irrespective of the country concerned. These are frequently the same industries in which large-scale enterprises are prominent sellers. In part this occurs because the technical characteristics of these industries place the large-scale enterprise at a competitive advantage, but it could also be that the entry and subsequent behaviour of these enterprises have themselves contributed to the oligopolistic structure of these industries.

SELLER CONCENTRATION AND BUSINESS PERFORMANCE

It is frequently suggested that the existence of high levels of seller concentration in an industry or market, particularly if associated with high entry barriers, may increase price–cost margins, raise the level of unit costs and adversely affect the quality and range of products produced and other aspects of business performance in the manufacturing sector (see section 3.3). The great majority of empirical structure–performance studies in LDCs have explored the effects of seller concentration only on price–cost margins or some other measure of business profitability, and this is the main relationship that is examined below. However, the effects of seller concentration on other aspects of business performance may be of equal or greater welfare significance and these are explored more briefly towards the end of this sub-section.

The main empirical studies that have been carried out on seller concentration–profit margin relationships in the sample of LDCs investigated in this chapter are listed in Table 3.10. The following features of these studies should be noted when interpreting their findings.

First, in the majority of studies, the profit measure is recorded only for a single year or for a small number of years. Since the industries concerned are unlikely to have been in long-run equilibrium at the time when the profit measure was taken, part of the profit recorded is likely to result from

Table 3.10 *Studies of the relationship between industrial/market concentration and profitability in LDCs*

Study	Country	Profit measure	Explanatory variables	Concentration–profitability relationship
Gupta (1968)	India	One year's profit rate (definition not given).	Three measures of entry barriers and concentration ratio.	Positive but not statistically significant (test of significance not defined).
Sawhney & Sawhney (1973)	India	Gross and net price–cost margins averaged over 5 years.	Concentration ratio, capital–output ratio, rate of capacity utilisation.	Positive and significant at 5% level or better. Non-linear formulation gives better results.
Walgreen (1971)	India	Same as Gupta.	Concentration ratio and economies of scale variable.	Average profit rate higher in industries where concentration ratio >50% than where ratio <50%, but difference is not statistically significant.
White (1974b)	Pakistan	Pre-tax profit on net worth by industry (2 years).	Concentration ratio, import restriction and capacity utilisation variables.	Positive; dummy variable dividing the concentration ratio at 33.3% is significant at 5% level.
Amjad (1977)	Pakistan (W.)	Net price–cost margin (1965–7, single years and average for period).	Concentration ratio, capital–output ratio, foreign competition variables, capacity utilisation.	Positive and consistently significant at 5% level or better.
Sharwani (1976)	Pakistan	Two alternative measures of rate of return on capital (data for 4 years).	Concentration ratio, presence of TNC, presence of govt-regulated firm, import penetration, capacity utilisation.	Positive and significant at 5% level of better.
Gan (1978)	Malaysia	Gross price–cost margins (average 1968–71).	Concentration ratios, capital–output ratios.	Positive and significant correlation at 10% or better in case of both 4-plant concentration ratio (CR4) and 8-plant concentration ratio (CR8) (continuous and discontinuous versions). Threshold levels are CR4:55%, CR8:85%.
Gan & Tham (1977)	Malaysia	Gross price–cost margin (average 1968–71).	Concentration ratio, economies of scale, absolute capital requirement, advertising–sales ratio, effective tariff protection, presence of foreign-owned enterprise,	Positive and significant correlation at 10% level dependent upon other explanatory variables included.

Author (year)	Country	Dependent variable (measure)	Independent variables	Results
Lindsey (1977)	Philippines	Gross price–cost margin (1970).	growth of market demand, administrative controls, capital–output ratio, export–output ratio. Value added concentration ratio is only variable.	Positive and significant at 5% level.
Nam (1975)	Korea (S.)	Net profit–gross capital ratio, net profit–net sales ratio, 1967–9 (single years and average for period).	Concentration ratio is only variable.	Higher profits and greater under-utilisation of capacity among industries with seller concentration ratio above 70% (no significance test reported).
House (1973)	Kenya	Gross and net price–cost margin (1963).	Concentration index, capital–output ratio, proportion of industry's output exported.	Positive and significant at 5% level or better where 'hybrid' concentration index is used (both 'continuous' relationship and 'distinct break' when index exceeds 40%).
House (1976)	Kenya	Gross and net price–cost margin (1967).	Similar variables as in House (1973).	Similar results to those in House (1973); 'hybrid' concentration measure positive and significant at 20% level or better.
Newfarmer & Mueller (1975)	Brazil	As below (1972).	As below.	Where market share exceeds 25%, broad earnings ratio is three times greater than where share is less than 10%.
Newfarmer & Mueller (1975)	Mexico	'Broad earnings' (inc. technology fees) of US manufacturing affiliates as % of their equity (1972).	Market share of affiliate (NB seller concentration ratio for industry not used).	Where market share exceeds 50%, broad earnings ratio is two-thirds higher than where share is less than 10%.
Connor & Mueller (1982)	Brazil	Two measures, 'simple' profits and 'broad' profits, as % of stockholder equity for TNC affiliates (1972).	4-firm concentration ratio, relative market share of affiliate, advertising–sales ratio, financial leverage, industry growth rate, firm size, trade intensity, % affiliate stock owned by parent TNC.	Both the concentration ratio and the relative market share of the affiliate have a positive and significant correlation with profit levels at the 5% level.
Connor & Mueller (1982)	Mexico	As above.	As above.	As above.

short-run market conditions unconnected to the structure of the industries or markets involved.

Second, the actual measure of profit used also varies between studies. Some use a rate of return on capital (which may be equity capital or the net worth of the enterprise), whereas others use a price–cost margin (gross, or net of depreciation, interest, etc.). Where, for example, gross price–cost margins are used, part of the profit recorded is likely to be due to the capital intensity of the industry concerned as well as to its structure.

Third, in the majority of the studies, the number of market structure and other variables used to explain profit levels is quite small. The more recent studies tend to be more sophisticated and to include a greater number of control variables. All studies include a seller concentration variable, sometimes adjusted to take account of foreign competition, although in some other cases this is treated as a separate variable. Other variables that are included in certain of the studies are capital–output ratios (measuring capital intensity but sometimes also used as an indicator of entry barriers facing new entrants), economies of scale (an alternative indicator of entry barriers), advertising–sales ratios, capacity utilisation and types of firm operating within the industry concerned.

It should be appreciated that a number of the theoretical and empirical difficulties that often arise in structure–performance studies (see section 3.3) are also to be found in these particular investigations, whose results need to be cautiously interpreted because of this.

The principal finding that emerges from these studies is that, in most cases, there is a statistically significant positive association between seller concentration and the profitability measure used. In some studies it is shown that the profit measure is considerably higher in those industries or markets where seller concentration exceeds a certain threshold level than where it is below the threshold. In one of the Kenyan studies, for example, the average net price–cost margin in the first group of industries was almost double the level prevailing in the second group (House, 1973). However, more frequently the relationship between seller concentration and profitability is a continuous one: typically, profit levels are progressively higher in those industries with the higher concentration levels. Exceptionally, in two Indian studies, profit levels appear to fall again at the highest levels of concentration – a feature that may reflect the influence of anti-monopoly policies in that country (Sawhney and Sawhney, 1973; Katrak, 1980).

Where the calculation of the seller concentration measure takes account of imports and exports as well as domestic production, its association with profit levels is usually stronger than where these items are ignored (House, 1973, 1976). On the other hand, where overseas trade values are included as separate variables in the S–P model they usually have a statistically significant relationship with the profit measure (that is, a negative relationship in the case of imports). A Nigerian study of differences in industrial profitability also found that those industries that enjoyed the greatest degree of import protection were generally those that were achieving the highest profit rates (Packard, 1969). Similar results have been obtained by Kemal (1978) for Pakistan. Hence import protection measures appear, in these cases at least, to have reinforced the effects of high levels of seller concentration in raising profit margins.

The capital–output ratio usually has a statistically significant positive association with gross price–cost margins but performs less satisfactorily when correlated with net price–cost margins. This suggests that it is useful in capturing the effect of the capital intensity of production on gross margins but is not a good indicator of the height of entry barriers when explaining net margins. In general, these studies are not particularly successful in determining the influence of entry barriers on profits, exceptions being Gan and Tham (1977) and Connor and Mueller (1982). However, given the association between seller concentration and the typical size of plants in a number of industries, it is possible that seller concentration and certain measures of entry barrier levels are themselves correlated. If so, the seller concentration measure may already be capturing some of the influence of entry barriers on profit levels.

The use of the capacity utilisation variable in certain of these studies creates a problem of interpretation because its relationship to profit levels is ambiguous. If seller concentration is high, firms may both enjoy high rates of return and under-utilise their productive capacity. On the other hand, a short-run increase in demand is likely to lead to an increase in capacity utilisation and an increase in profit margins. A positive association between under-utilisation and profits would be expected in the former case, whereas a negative association would be anticipated in the latter case. One study of Korean industry found some support for the former hypothesis, and studies relating to India and Pakistan lend support to the latter view (Nam, 1975; Sawhney and Sawhney, 1973; Amjad, 1977).

Two studies attempt to establish whether the types of firm operating within an industry may have an influence, additional to that of the structure of the industry, upon profit levels (Sharwani, 1976; Gan and Tham, 1977). Sharwani found that profit levels were higher in those industries where a transnational enterprise is a leading producer, and lower where a government-regulated firm is a leading producer, than the level of concentration in those industries would otherwise suggest. The possible reasons for these differences are various: TNCs may be operating in more capital-intensive, faster growing industries; they may operate in an environment in which the pursuit of profit is more politically acceptable; or they may be more commercially efficient in their production and marketing operations. Gan and Tham also found that the presence of foreign enterprise was associated with higher profit margins in the consumer goods industries but not in the producer goods industries of Malaysia. This issue is examined further in Chapter 4, section 4.13, but more extensive and detailed investigations are needed to shed further light on the subject.

Effects of increased profit margins
The likely impacts of increased profit margins on an LDC economy can be analysed with the aid of Figure 3.2 (see also George and Joll, 1981, ch. 11). The most immediate, direct impacts from raising profit margins (by PP_1) above their normal level (and assuming, for the moment, that $MC_1 = AC_1$

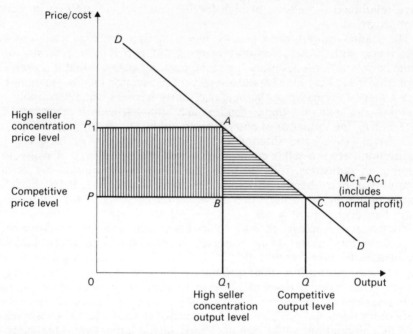

Figure 3.2   The consequences of high levels of seller concentration – I (unit costs remain unchanged)

remains unchanged) are:

- a loss of welfare to the economy as a whole through the restriction of output below its competitive level, equal to the triangle ABC; and
- a redistribution of income from consumers to producers, equal to the rectangle PP_1AB.

The size of the welfare loss depends upon the extent of the increase in price–cost margins and the price elasticity of demand for the goods being produced. Estimates of these losses in developed economies range widely between, in the case of the United Kingdom, less than 1 per cent and over 7 per cent of national output (Sawyer, 1981, ch. 14). No corresponding estimates are yet available for LDCs. As Figure 3.2 shows, the magnitudes involved in the redistribution of income that results from increased profit margins are much greater than those associated with the welfare loss. To the extent that large-scale private sector enterprises are the major recipients of these producer surpluses, they will tend to be associated with increased inequalities in wealth and income, unless compensating fiscal and redistributive public policy measures are enforced.

Taking a longer-term, more dynamic, viewpoint however, it is also necessary to consider how these increased producer surpluses might be used. At one extreme, they may be repatriated by TNCs or used by the owners of the indigenous groups and their families to purchase imported luxury consumer goods. At the other extreme, they may be reinvested in the further development of the LDCs' manufacturing sector. Again, more reliable information is needed before the full consequences of the increased profits resulting from high seller concentration on such key variables as investment levels, imports and the pace of development can be determined. An attempt to analyse certain of these longer-term indirect effects on the economy of Pakistan has been made by Kemal (1978).

Other impacts on LDC economies
However, high profit margins may not be the most important consequence of higher levels of seller concentration. Protection from the full force of competition may cause changes in the level of productive efficiency[5] in an industry and, as a consequence, in the general level of costs of production (Devine *et al.*, 1979, ch. 8). Although in certain cases, where there are economies of large-scale production to be obtained, increases in seller concentration (e.g. through mergers) may be associated with cost reductions and welfare gains to society (for example, if the $MC_1 = AC_1$ line in Figure 3.2 *falls*), reductions in competitive pressures can also lead to losses of efficiency and increases in unit costs. The measurement of productive efficiency and its association with different types of market structure in LDCs is still in its infancy. One of the few studies carried out suggests, in the context of Pakistan, that high levels of concentration may have led to a fall in productive efficiency such that indigenous firms in more highly concentrated markets appear to have 'indulged' in more capital-intensive methods of production than firms facing more competition (White, 1976). If this is the case then market structure may be an influence on the appropriateness of the technology used in LDCs as well as on the general level of productive efficiency. A correlation between high levels of seller concentration, import protection and lower productive efficiency has also been detected by Kemal in a number of Pakistan industries, although import protection appears to have been the stronger influence on efficiency levels (Kemal, 1978).

The welfare effects of a rise in unit costs that results from reduced competitive pressures within industry are illustrated in Figure 3.3. Suppose that an increase in seller concentration leads to a rise in unit costs from AC_1 to AC_2 but that price is maintained at OP_1 by government regulation. Then only normal profit margins are earned but a welfare loss of PP_1AC results from the fall in productive efficiency.

In addition, further changes in welfare may result over the longer term if changes in seller concentration affect the rate of technical progress and innovation in an industry or industry's capacity to manufacture and market its products. It is noteworthy, in this context, that in a number of LDCs large-scale indigenous or foreign-owned enterprises are seen as playing a key role in the innovative and international marketing processes within particular industrial sectors. In these circumstances, high levels of overall and market concentration may be tolerated so that technical and marketing benefits can be realised. The tensions between curbing high concentration levels on the one hand and retaining the potential benefits of large-scale enterprise on the

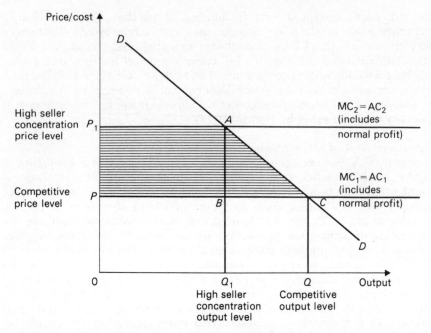

Figure 3.3 The consequences of high levels of seller concentration – II (unit costs increase because of reduced competition)

other are well illustrated by Indian experience in implementing industrial licensing and monopoly control legislation (Paranjape, 1980, 1982).

In view of the multiplicity of these welfare and distributive effects, it is desirable to use a wider range of performance indicators than those that are based solely on profits and to pay greater attention to the longer-term indirect impacts of higher seller concentration on the development process. However, real progress in this direction will be slow until better quality data become available.

3.5 CONCLUSIONS

The main purpose of this chapter has been to explore the industrialisation process taking place in LDCs at the level of the business enterprise and the industries and markets in which it operates. It is a level of analysis that is still relatively underdeveloped in the LDC context, and the forms of industrial analysis that are used cannot simply be transposed from the DC situation in which they have been mainly applied in the past.

The study of business enterprises during the early stages of industrialisation is, at its most basic level, concerned with the growth of entrepreneurship. This is determined by the interaction of three groups of factors – the socio-cultural environment, the development process itself, and the political system and policies of the LDCs concerned. These factors operate differently between countries and explain why there is a diversity in the patterns of business enterprise within the developing world and why these patterns are themselves changing, often rapidly, over time.

Although the overall picture of the industrialisation process at the level of enterprise, industry and market is one of considerable diversity and change, there are a number of common themes, which have been identified and highlighted in this chapter despite the severe limitations of data available. Typically, the manufacturing sector of most LDCs comprises an informal sector and a formal sector, although the dividing line between the two cannot be sharply drawn. The informal sector consists mainly of very small, labour-intensive enterprises, using largely traditional techniques of production. In the sample of LDCs that have been investigated, the informal sector accounted for 5–25 per cent of manufacturing production but for a much higher percentage of combined full- and part-time manufacturing employment. In general, the relative importance of the informal sector is greatest in the least developed countries. Within the formal sector, large-scale enterprises using relatively modern, more capital-intensive production methods are at least as prominent as, and often more prominent than, their counterpart enterprises engaged in manufacturing in DCs. They occur in four main forms: indigenous groups and expatriate enterprises; subsidiaries of TNCs; publicly owned enterprises; and 'hybrid' enterprises comprising two or more of the foregoing types of enterprise. The relative importance of these different types of enterprise varies considerably between LDCs and is changing considerably over time within individual LDCs, particularly in response to changes in government policy. These large-scale enterprises operate within a number of different industries and markets and typically occupy a dominant position in more than one of these. Hence in many LDCs there are important linkages between the level of business concentration in the manufacturing sector as a whole and the level of seller concentration within particular industries and markets.

The rankings of industries according to their level of seller concentration follow broadly the same pattern in most countries and appear to reflect the major differences in the technology of production between industries. However, the general level of seller concentration in industry tends to be higher in LDCs than in DCs and this difference is most pronounced in the case of the smaller LDCs, which possess smaller domestic markets. Particularly where this is associated with restrictions on foreign competition in the domestic economy, concentrated oligopoly is probably the most common market form. In turn, as the various market structure–performance studies have shown, high levels of seller concentration appear to be associated with high profit margins. More speculatively, high levels of seller concentration are also thought to influence other aspects of market performance such as choice of production techniques and levels of productive efficiency.

The welfare effects that may result from the combination of high levels of seller concentration and high levels of overall concentration in the manufacturing sector are of a multiple character and, in aggregate, could be very considerable in magnitude. However, insufficient information is yet available to determine with confidence the direction, let alone the magnitude, of many of the welfare effects that are occurring. One viewpoint is that these forms of concentration are, on balance, beneficial to economic development. It is argued that a mix of large-scale groups, TNC subsidiaries and public enterprises operating within concentrated markets helps to overcome the imperfections in internal markets, increases accessibility to capital and technical knowledge, and provides the blend of market stability and commercial inducement that is needed to stimulate entrepreneurial activity and economic expansion. An alternative view is that high levels of concentration have had adverse effects on the well-being of LDCs by causing short-term welfare losses, promoting greater inequalities in wealth and income, restricting the domestic base from which entrepreneurship might be expanded, and reducing the competitive pressures that might mould technical change and innovation more closely to LDC needs. One can only conclude that more satisfactory data and more detailed and careful analyses are needed before it is possible to establish precisely where, between these two limits, the truth lies.

FURTHER READING

Those wishing to read further on the relationship between entrepreneurship and economic development should consult Leff (1979a). Literature on the informal sector and on the role of different types of large-scale enterprise within the formal sector is fragmentary and specialised, but useful general information can be obtained from UNIDO (1979a) and, more specifically on economic groups, from Leff (1978). More detailed information on the types and levels of concentration in particular countries can be obtained from White (1974b), Swainson (1980) and Newfarmer and Mueller (1975). A general critique of structure–performance studies can be found in a number of industrial economics texts including Devine *et al.* (1979), which may be supplemented, for LDC material, by Lall (1978). Those individual LDC structure–performance studies that may be usefully consulted are referenced in Tables 3.6 and 3.10. Finally, the methods used for estimating the likely welfare effects of high concentration are reviewed in George and Joll (1981).

NOTES

1   The concept of the optimal allocation of resources is discussed more fully in Chapter 5 and in Devine *et al.* (1979), ch. 8.
2   Performance is being assessed from the standpoint of the economy as a whole and not from that of the individual enterprise. Although the earning of long-term super-normal profits may be welcomed by the individual enterprise, it is likely to be associated with a misallocation of resources and unsatisfactory performance from the standpoint of the economy as a whole. See section 3.4 and Figure 3.2 for a more detailed analysis of this point.
3   The Herfindahl index is obtained by summating the squared shares (measured as fractions of 1) of each seller in the market; the entropy index is measured by summating the share of each seller, weighted by the logarithm of the reciprocal of the seller's share (George and Joll, 1981, ch. 6).

4   The minimum efficient scale (MES) of an establishment is that scale of output where average costs of production first reach their minimum level.

5   *Productive efficiency* comprises *technical* and *factor price* efficiency. The former measures the degree of economy in resource inputs used to produce a given output; the latter measures the degree to which the best combination of resource inputs is used, having regard to their relative opportunity costs. Where the same output is produced using the same production technology, but fewer resources, an increase in *X-efficiency* also occurs.

4 Business Behaviour in the Private Sector

4.1 INTRODUCTION

This chapter is concerned with the characteristics and behaviour of business enterprises in the private manufacturing sector of the LDC. The differentiation between transnational corporations (TNCs) and indigenously owned private enterprises within LDCs is made because of what has been called the 'distinctive nature' of the TNC (Dunning, 1981, ch. 1). The subsidiary or affiliate of the TNC located within the LDC is part of a larger organisation, and its characteristics, behaviour and performance must be evaluated with reference to that fact. Unlike the multi-location domestic enterprise, the TNC owns and controls income-generating assets in different nation states; unlike the national firm that exports all or part of its product, much of the TNC's trade takes place within the corporation, rather than between independent economic agents; and, unlike the national firm that exports part of its factor inputs (material or human capital), the TNC supplies such inputs as part of a 'package' and maintains control over the use that is made of them (Dunning, 1981, p. 7).

The TNC thus deserves special attention, and sections 4.2–4.15 of this chapter discuss various aspects of the important and almost unique role that the TNC plays in the process of growth and development. Sections 4.2 and 4.3 cover the definition and economic characteristics of TNCs. Section 4.4 deals briefly with the theory of direct foreign investment (DFI). Section 4.5 outlines the geographical and sectoral distribution of DFI. Sections 4.6 and 4.7 cover TNCs and industrial structure and linkage creation. Section 4.8 deals with various aspects of technological choice and technology transfer. Section 4.9 covers employment creation by TNCs. Sections 4.10–4.13 deal with issues relating to the balance of payments, the export of manufactured goods, transfer pricing and profitability. Section 4.14 briefly discusses the emergence of TNCs from LDCs. Section 4.15 presents some conclusions.

Indigenous (domestic) enterprises are also, of course, of vital importance to the development effort, but, as will become clear later in this chapter, less time and effort have been devoted to their study. An attempt is made to redress the imbalance in sections 4.16–4.18. Section 4.16 considers the problems of entrepreneurship and management in indigenous enterprises in LDCs, looking in particular at Nigeria, Kenya, the Lebanon, Pakistan and India. Section 4.17 discusses the development of small-scale manufacturing enterprises and their potential contribution to industrial development. Section 4.18 briefly covers some issues relating to finance for industrial development. Finally, section 4.19 raises a number of wider issues relating to the complex relationships between TNCs, indigenous enterprises and the state in LDCs.

4.2   THE TRANSNATIONAL CORPORATION: DEFINITION

The transnational corporation (TNC)[1] may be defined as an enterprise that owns or controls assets such as factories, mines, plantations and sales offices in two or more countries. On the basis of this definition, the United Nations (1979, Table 1, p. 8) has estimated that in 1977 there were 10,373 firms with at least one foreign affiliate.

If the possession of a minimum number (greater than one) of affiliates or operation in a minimum number of host countries is specified, the TNC population obviously falls. In 1977, for example, there were 5,586 firms that operated in two or more host countries and there were 2,050 firms that operated in six or more host countries. The introduction of these additional criteria affects the distribution by origin of TNCs. TNCs originating in the USA, for example, account for 26.8 per cent of all firms with one or more foreign affiliates operating in one or more host countries but 36.9 per cent of all firms operating in six or more host countries. These data partially illustrate the dominance, by virtue of their greater size, of American TNCs. As the size of the corporation increases, the share of American TNCs in the total TNC population rises. In 1976, eight of the largest ten TNCs were of American origin.

Various measures of foreign content (relating to, for example, exports, sales, assets, earnings or employment) can also be used in defining TNCs, as can criteria relating to organisational form, motivation and the structure of decision-making or control in the TNC. There are, therefore, a number of possible ways of defining the TNC, and various working definitions can be used for specific purposes.

4.3   THE ECONOMIC CHARACTERISTICS OF TNCs

SIZE

TNCs '. . . are among the most powerful economic institutions yet produced by the capitalist system' (Dunning, 1981, p. 3) and this power is partly a consequence of size. In 1976, there were 411 industrial firms based in developed market economies with sales of at least $1 billion, and 872 such firms with sales of $395 million or over (United Nations, 1979, Table 7, p. 14). The two largest TNCs, Exxon and General Motors, had annual sales in 1976 approaching $50 billion (United Nations, 1978, Table IV–1, p. 288). It should also be noted that there is a high degree of concentration in the TNC population, with perhaps 3–5 per cent of TNCs accounting for the major part of direct foreign investment and total sales.

Size is a relative concept: what is ranked as a medium- or small-sized enterprise among a number of firms in various sectors or countries may well rank large in any particular sector or country. In addition, many TNCs are conglomerates and are engaged in many different activities and product lines. For the evaluation of any particular industry, the size of the relevant line may be more significant than the size of overall activity.

OWNERSHIP

The United States of America and the United Kingdom have traditionally enjoyed a dominating position as far as direct foreign investment and international production are concerned. However, as the data in Table 4.1 illustrate, that position had been eroded by the late 1970s by the increased share in the stock of global DFI accounted for by the Federal Republic of Germany and Japan, and to a lesser extent by Switzerland and Holland.

In addition to the larger number of companies and countries engaging in international production, a growing number of companies from a number of semi-industrialised LDCs (for example, India, Argentina, Hong Kong, Mexico, Singapore and South Korea) are entering international production, a development that is discussed in greater detail in section 4.14 below.

MARKET STRUCTURE (see also Chapter 3, section 3.4, and section 4.3 below)

TNCs most commonly operate within oligopolistic market structures (markets effectively controlled by a few sellers or buyers) and TNC behaviour can most usefully be analysed within an oligopoly framework. Certain important characteristics of TNC behaviour – rapid process and product innovation, product differentiation and heavy advertising – are also characteristics of, and in turn reinforce, oligopolistic structures. In addition, the patterns of entry of TNCs into LDC markets show clear evidence of oligopolistic rivalry. Direct foreign investment in an important market by one TNC might well be seen as a rivalrous move by other firms in the industry, since their share of the market in that country, supplied through exports or a non-equity operation, might be put at risk. This perception will bring forth 'defensive' DFI by these firms, and thus DFI in individual economies by rival

Table 4.1 *Percentage share of developed market economies in global stock of direct foreign investment, 1967–76*

Country	1967 %	1976 %
USA	53.8	47.6
UK	16.6	11.2
France	5.7	4.1
Switzerland	4.8	6.5
Canada	3.5	3.9
Federal Republic of Germany	2.8	6.9
Holland	2.1	3.4
Italy	2.0	1.0
Belgium–Luxembourg	1.9	1.2
Sweden	1.6	1.7
Japan	1.4	6.7
All other developed market economies (estimate)	3.8	5.8

Source: United Nations (1978), Table III-32, p. 236.

firms tends to be bunched together. (For a discussion of the theoretical issues and an empirical study, see Yamin, 1983.)

GLOBAL ORGANISATION

A unique feature of TNCs is their ability to view the world as a single economic unit and consequently to plan, manage and organise their activities on a global scale. TNCs are both products of and contributors to technological developments that have reduced the problems posed by geographical distance. For example, the widespread use of computers for data pro-cessing, collection and transmission has enabled global operations and decision-making to become highly centralised. It is the parent company that determines global strategy, decides on the location of new investment, allocates export markets and research and development (R&D) programmes to various parts of the corporation and determines the prices that are charged on intra-corporate transactions (transfer prices). The importance of intra-firm trade continued to grow during the 1970s and European TNCs, like their US counterparts before them, have increasingly centralised their global operations. The United Nations (1978, p. 44) has noted that

> ... control can become embedded within the fabric of the firm without being readily apparent to the outside observer. The more national units become conditioned to indirect, harmonized control procedures, the more difficult it becomes for them to respond unilaterally to the needs of the local economy.

CORPORATE OBJECTIVES

Within the capitalist system, firms are embodiments of privately owned property, organised primarily for the purpose of earning and accumulating profit. Even though there is much debate in the literature over the precise objectives that modern, large-scale corporations (both national and transnational) pursue (see Devine *et al.*, 1979, ch. 3), Hood and Young (1979, p. 115), after an extensive review of the literature, concluded that:

> To be on safest ground it is probably wise to view [TNC] behaviour as a form of constrained profit maximisation, where financial, structural, environmental and general resource variables limit pursuit of maximum profits.[2]

TNCs will also, as far as possible, attempt to minimise the amount of tax that they pay and will also wish to minimise the risks that they face, although clearly such objectives may be mutually exclusive in many instances.

It is not always possible, however, to explain or predict the behaviour of individual affiliates along these lines. Given that the interests of any one part of the TNC are subordinate to the interests of the TNC as a whole, different affiliates may pursue various objectives, all of which may well be consistent, in the long run, with global profit maximisation (Hood and Young, 1979, p. 99).

To achieve the objective of global profit maximisation, TNCs have devised a variety of financial strategies and policies. Examples include: a heavy reliance on local borrowing and the reinvestment of profits to finance affiliate operations; the take-over of existing operations in the LDCs, rather than the establishment of new ones; and the manipulation of transfer prices. Transfer prices are the prices that are charged on transactions that take place within the corporation (intra-corporate transactions); given that such prices are determined by the TNC itself and not by market forces, they can deviate to a considerable extent from so-called 'arms-length' or market prices. This issue is discussed in greater detail in section 4.12 below.

4.4   WHY DO FIRMS ENGAGE IN INTERNATIONAL PRODUCTION?

The entry of a firm into international production can take any of three forms: the production of the same goods elsewhere (horizontal extension); developing a stage in the production process that comes earlier or later than the firm's principal processing activity (vertical extension); and conglomerate diversification (Caves, 1971).

A number of theories have been advanced in the attempt to explain the determinants of horizontal international production (these are well surveyed in Hood and Young, 1979, ch. 2). There is now general agreement in the literature that a necessary condition for a firm to invest directly in another country (rather than merely export to that country or license its technology to local producers) is that it must possess some advantage or asset (an ownership-specific advantage) not shared by its local competitors. Various ownership-specific advantages have been suggested as being of significance – technological advantages, the ability to differentiate products, marketing skills, superior organisational skills and management techniques – all of which have the characteristics of a public good (although public only within the firm, of course) in that the firm transferring and utilising them in a foreign market can do so at a zero or low opportunity cost.

However, it is not the possession of these advantages as such that is of significance. Rather it is the fact that certain transactions or activities can be organised and carried out at a lower cost *within* the firm (the *internalisation* of those activities) than through the market that confers on the TNC its unique advantages. Dunning (1981, ch. 2), in arguing for an eclectic, integrated approach to international economic involvement (incorporating both theories of international trade and international production), puts the point well (p. 34):

The eclectic approach would argue that it is not the possession of technology *per se* which gives an enterprise selling goods embodying that technology to foreign markets (irrespective of where they are produced) an edge over its competitors, but the advantage of internalising that technology, rather than selling it to a foreign producer for the production of those goods. It is not the orthodox type of monopoly advantages which give the enterprise an edge over its rivals – actual or potential – but the advantages which accrue through internalisation, for example, transfer price manipulation, security of supplies and markets, and control over use of intermediate goods. It is not surplus entrepreneurial resources *per se* which lead to foreign direct investment, but the ability of enterprises to combine these resources with others to take advantage of the economies of production of joint products.

To obtain a more complete explanation of international production, location-specific factors have also to be taken into account. These include relative costs of production, marketing factors, trade barriers and government policies in both the home and host economies. Clearly, the relative importance of such factors will vary according to the nature and objectives of each individual act of DFI.

Without the incentive to internalise, the firm may well prefer to sell its knowledge or license its technology, or merely export the final product. Where the rent-yielding advantage of the parent firms lies in a 'one-shot' innovation of technique or product (for example, a new method for making plate glass or the secret ingredient of a successful soft drink – Caves, 1971), licensing the technology may well be the option chosen. Location-specific factors are again of importance. Host-country government policies may well preclude DFI and thus force the TNC to enter into licensing arrangements. On the other hand, the absence of the necessary skills or resources among indigenous firms in the host LDC may well make DFI unavoidable.

The discussion so far has focused on horizontal direct foreign investment. In the case of vertical direct foreign investment, the evidence from the developed economies suggests that the avoidance of oligopolistic uncertainty and the erection of barriers to the entry of new rivals are important factors underlying the investment decision (Caves, 1971). For LDCs, however, it may simply be the case that no local firm, either private or state owned, has the capital, technology and expertise to exploit effectively and efficiently the country's natural resources (especially mineral resources) and thus, at the very least, a limited dependence on the vertically integrated extractive TNCs is unavoidable.

It should be noted that Japanese DFI does not fit neatly into the analytical model outlined above. Japan's manufacturing DFI is clustered in relatively labour-intensive or technologically standardised products (textiles, metal products, relatively unsophisticated electrical products and chemicals). It is largely small- and medium-sized manufacturers that are active investors in the LDCs, and they are more inclined to accept minority ownership than, for example, are American TNCs. 'Group' investment (where a number of Japanese firms, usually involving trading companies, participate in a given overseas venture as co-partners) is popular, and there is a heavy dependence on external sources of funds (from both government-affiliated financial institutions and private banks) (Ozawa, 1979). DFI in extractive ventures is also higher for Japan than for any other developed economy. Japanese DFI is thus directed mainly at exploiting natural resources in other countries or in manufacturing labour-intensive products in labour-abundant LDCs, exported either back to Japan or to third-country markets.

Japanese TNC investment in the extractive sector is a reflection of Japan's inadequate or non-existent domestic supplies of a number of strategic raw materials. Such investment is consistent with the model of internalisation outlined above, but it is also, in part, the result of the policy of the Japanese government aimed at restructuring the Japanese economy in line with changing world economic conditions. Japanese overseas investment in labour-intensive industries occurs when Japan is losing its competitiveness in that industry (because of changes in Japanese factor endowments) and it is one that can be successfully 'transplanted' in the LDC with the help of Japanese capital, technology and expertise. The more competitive is the industry (that is, the less monopolistic or oligopolistic it is), and the less technologically sophisticated the product, the greater is the need for Japanese industry to move to offshore production. Ozawa (1979, pp. 88–9) concluded that Japanese enterprises have been

> ... driven overseas by the *macroeconomic* forces of factor scarcities at home, growing environmental constraints, and increasing uncertainties of the supply of key industrial resources – rather than by the growth of their internal capacities to operate on a global scale. Indeed, the very weakness of their capacity to go overseas as individual units is leading in part to Japan's unique pattern of government-supported and group-oriented multi-firm investments overseas and to a heavy reliance on external funds, much of which are generated directly or indirectly by the government.

An alternative explanation of DFI is based on the product cycle hypothesis. This hypothesis, closely associated with the work of Vernon (1966, 1971, 1979), is an attempt to explain changes in locational and trading patterns over time as a product moves through its life cycle. It is argued by Vernon that, historically, US enterprises have developed and produced new products that were labour saving or designed to satisfy high-income wants. In the first stage of the product cycle, there were good reasons why production would be located in the USA: the availability of engineers and scientists with the requisite skills; close contact with prospective customers and suppliers; efficiency of communication between the research specialists themselves and the specialists and the parent company; low price elasticity of demand for the product reducing the importance of cost differentials at alternative locations. Foreign demand would therefore be met by exports from the USA. In its second stage, the product matures. Technology tends to become more standardised, competitors might appear and costs of production become more important. To serve better overseas markets (particularly those of Western Europe, in the original formulation of the hypothesis), the firm can either license a local producer or, more likely, establish its own production subsidiary overseas (if the marginal costs of producing in the USA for export, plus the cost of transport, are greater than the full cost of producing in a foreign subsidiary). With US subsidiary production overseas, the US increasingly becomes an importer of the product in question. In the final stage, the product becomes 'standardised', price competition becomes intensified and production might well be transferred to LDCs with lower labour costs.

Vernon recognised the specific characteristics and limitations of his hypothesis, noting that it was more applicable to firms that were expanding overseas for the first time but was less relevant to those firms with already established global networks (Vernon, 1971, ch. 3; 1979) where new products and processes could increasingly originate in any part of that global network. Vernon (1979) also recognised changes over time in the international environment, with the other developed economies 'catching up' with the USA in terms of per capita income and market characteristics. However, he still defended its application to LDCs and argued that the emergence of TNCs from LDCs was consistent with the model's predictions (see section 4.14 below).

Others have been more critical. Clark (1975) argued that TNCs often transfer technology and other resources at a much earlier stage in the 'life' of products than would be predicted by the theory, and that the increasingly important practice of locating relatively labour-intensive assembly or process activities in LDCs (see section 4.11) is not consistent with the product cycle hypothesis. He concluded that 'the product cycle theory, as it stands, is a rather unsatisfactory description of modern international techno-economic relations' (Clark, 1975, p. 7). Hood and Young (1979, p. 83) urged caution in using the hypothesis to explain the expansion paths of TNCs.

4.5   DIRECT FOREIGN INVESTMENT IN THE LDCs

GEOGRAPHICAL DISTRIBUTION

Table 4.2 presents information on the global stock of direct foreign investment and the share of the LDCs, by destination, in that total, for selected years between the mid-1960s and the early 1980s. The data should perhaps be regarded as indicating orders of magnitude only, but they do indicate that (i) most DFI is located in developed capitalist economies and (ii) very few LDCs account for the major part of DFI located in the Third World. The OPEC countries, the tax havens and ten other LDCs (Brazil, Mexico, India, Malaysia, Argentina, Singapore, Peru, Hong Kong, the Philippines and Trinidad and Tobago) accounted for 71.2 per cent of the total LDC stock of DFI in 1967 and 76.5 per cent in 1975.[3]

It was noted above that size is a relative concept, and even a relatively small amount of DFI will exert an influence beyond its purely quantitative significance if it is concentrated in strategic, rapidly growing, technologically advanced sectors. The TNC is often the 'market leader' in the oligopolised sectors of the host economy and, with the growth of so-called non-equity operations (the licensing of technology, management and technical agreements, the use of trade marks and brand names), the distinction between ownership and control is becoming of increasing importance. Data relating to the stock of DFI in LDCs are thus no longer adequate indicators of the extent of TNC activities and their influence in LDCs.

Table 4.2   *Stock of direct foreign investment: worldwide and share of LDCs, 1967–81*

Year	Worldwide $b.	Share in LDCs $b.	as % worldwide stock	OPEC countries[a] and tax havens[b] $b.	as % worldwide stock	as % of LDC stock
1967	105	32.8	31	11.4	10.8	34.7
1971	158	43.3	28	15.5	9.8	35.8
1975	259	68.2	26	24.5	9.5	35.9
1976	287					
1978		96 ⎫				
1979		110 ⎪ variously				
1980		120 ⎬ estimated				
1981		130[c] ⎭ as 25–33		22.3 (OPEC only)		

Notes:
a   Algeria, Ecuador, Gabon, Indonesia, Iran, Iraq, Kuwait, Libyan Arab Jamahiriya, Nigeria, Qatar, Saudi Arabia, United Arab Emirates and Venezuela.
b   Bahamas, Barbados, Bermuda, Cayman Islands, Netherlands Antilles and Panama.
c   OECD (1983), Table 5, p. 25, gives a figure of $137b. for 1981, which includes 'unallocated amounts' and Japanese official support for private investment.
Sources: Kirkpatrick and Nixson (1981), Table 1; OECD (1982a; 1983).

Table 4.3   *Geographical distribution of allocated direct investment flows (net) from major source countries, 1979–81[a] (%)*

Home country	LDC region Europe[c]	Africa	Latin America	Asia	Total	Share of individual home countries in net DFI flow to LDCs, 1981
France	33 (34)	23 (16)	39 (6)	5 (2)	100	7.8
Germany	21 (18)	5 (3)	59 (7)	15 (4)	100	9.2
Japan	1 (4)	9 (16)	29 (11)	61 (49)	100	16.6
UK[b]	10 (13)	30 (25)	36 (7)	24 (9)	100	8.3
USA	5 (31)	9 (40)	69 (69)	17 (36)	100	44.7

Notes:
a   Figures in brackets denote the home countries' share in the total DFI of the continent from the five source countries, including official support for private investment by the Japanese government.
b   Excluding investments in the oil industry.
c   Greece, Portugal, Spain, Yugoslavia.
Sources: OECD (1983), Table 1, p. 27; Table 2, p. 18.

Table 4.3 illustrates the geographical distribution pattern of direct investment flows from the major OECD Development Assistance Committee (DAC) countries. Geographical proximity and historical and trade relations are factors that play a major role in influencing the location of DFI, although Japanese TNC investment in Latin America is an exception to that generalisation.

The United Nations (1983, p. 284) has estimated that in 1980 there were 104,000 TNC affiliates in total, of which 27,000 were located in LDCs. Data on the geographical distribution of TNC affiliates (Table 4.4) demonstrate a pattern similar to that shown by the geographical distribution of DFI. The bracketed figures in Table 4.4 show that the USA accounted for 62 per cent of total TNC affiliates in Latin America, 37 per cent in West Asia, and 34 per cent in South and East Asia. The UK accounted for 40 per cent of total TNC affiliates located in Africa and 26 per cent of total affiliates in both West Asia and South and East Asia. Japan accounted for 13 per cent of total TNC affiliates located in South and East Asia.

SECTORAL COMPOSITION

Table 4.5 gives details of the stock of DFI in LDCs, broken down by region and industrial sector. The sectors in which DFI has traditionally played a dominant role – petroleum, and mining and smelting – still account for the major part of the total stock of DFI in LDCs but the relative importance of these 'traditional' sectors in the overall stock of DFI is likely to fall in the future, given the rapid growth of DFI in manufacturing and the services sectors characteristic of the 1960s and 1970s. TNCs will nevertheless continue to be of great importance in petroleum and in a variety of strategic minerals – for example, iron ore, copper and bauxite.

TNC investment in the manufacturing sector, with perhaps the exception of Japanese DFI referred to above (section 4.4), can be broadly divided into two sub-sections: (i) research-intensive, technologically advanced industrial activities (pharmaceuticals, chemicals, machinery and office equipment); (ii) industries where marketing power is of importance (foodstuffs, soft drinks, cigarettes, cosmetics, automobiles) and brand names, product differentiation and heavy advertising are characteristic features. This distinction cannot always be clearly made, as much research and development expenditure (R&D) is diverted towards minor product changes (in, for example, pharmaceuticals, foodstuffs and automobiles), rather than going into basic research or the development of major new products or processes.

Throughout the 1970s, TNC investment in the services sector expanded rapidly in banking, insurance, accounting, advertising, tourism and hotels and consultancy. In addition, in the agricultural sector, so-called agribusiness TNCs are becoming of increasing significance for a variety of products – for example, pineapples, sugar, vegetable oils, tea, soya beans and beef. Clearly, there is overlap between the different sectors: manufacturing TNCs provide inputs for the agricultural sector (fertilizers, pesticides, etc.) and service sector TNCs provide a variety of service inputs (advertising, technical assistance, feasibility studies, legal advice, etc.) (see Feder, 1977).

Table 4.4 Distribution among LDC regions of foreign affiliates of companies from selected home countries, 1980 (%)

Home country	% of total affiliates of individual home countries located in LDCs	Distribution among LDC regions				
		Latin America	Africa	West Asia	South and East Asia	Europe
France	30.5	7.7 (3.1)	18.7 (18.1)	1.1 (6.2)	2.9 (1.3)	0.1 (3.2)
Germany	17.6	9.2 (5.9)	3.0 (4.6)	0.8 (7.0)	4.4 (3.2)	0.2 (8.2)
Japan	58.2	13.4 (3.5)	2.2 (1.4)	0.8 (3.0)	41.7 (12.6)	—
UK	24.2	4.7 (10.1)	7.7 (40.2)	0.9 (26.8)	10.4 (25.6)	0.5 (56.4)
USA	34.7	21.4 (62.2)	2.3 (15.9)	0.9 (36.5)	10.0 (33.5)	0.1 (10.9)

Note: The figures in brackets show the percentage of total TNC affiliates in each region accounted for by the home countries listed.
Sources: United Nations (1983), Table 11.8, p. 34; bracketed figures from Table 11.9, p. 35.

Table 4.5 *Stock of DFI in LDCs, by region and industrial sector, end 1972*

Sector	Africa $b.	Africa %	Latin America & Caribbean $b.	Latin America & Caribbean %	Middle East $b.	Middle East %	Asia & Oceania $b.	Asia & Oceania %	Total all regions $b.	% of total
Petroleum	4.1	45.0	5.3	23.5	3.6	87.8	2.4	29.6	15.4	35.0
Mining and smelting	1.5	16.5	2.2	9.7	—	—	0.6	7.4	4.3	9.8
Manufacturing	1.6	17.6	8.9	39.4	0.3	7.3	2.5	30.9	13.3	30.3
Other	1.9	20.9	6.2	27.4	0.2	4.9	2.6	32.1	10.9	24.8
Total all sectors	9.1	100	22.6	100	4.1	100	8.1	100	43.9	100.0
Region's share of total		20.7		51.5		9.3		18.4		

Source: United Nations (1978), Table III-51, p. 260.

WHY DO LDCs WANT DFI?

Despite the reservations that LDCs might have about the role of foreign capital in the development process, it remains the case that competition between the LDCs for transnational involvement in their economies continues to be intense. Although no longer uncritically viewed as 'engines of development', TNCs nevertheless own, control or have access to vast resources of capital, technology and all kinds of expertise, and, of increasing importance, often provide access to export markets, all factors that are in short supply or absent in the LDCs. The main attraction of TNC direct investment, therefore, is that these resources are all part of the DFI 'package'.

This argument should, however, be qualified in two respects. First, DFI began to assume a relatively less important role in the economies of the LDCs in the 1970s. For LDCs as a group, foreign trade increased much faster than DFI, but, perhaps more significantly, domestic investment increased more rapidly than DFI (United Nations, 1983, p. 17). Comprehensive data on rates of change of domestic investment and DFI are not readily available, but for the majority of LDCs, *in purely quantitative terms*, DFI is of only marginal importance in total capital formation. The inflow of DFI as a percentage of domestic investment (annual average, 1978–80) for five major recipients of DFI was as follows: Argentina, 3.0 per cent; Brazil, 2.1 per cent; Mexico, 3.3 per cent; Singapore, 10.1 per cent; Malaysia, 2.0 per cent. With the exception of the tax havens, Liberia and Singapore, for no LDC for which data were available was the figure greater than 10 per cent, and for the great majority of LDCs the figure was significantly less than 5 per cent (all data from United Nations, 1983, Annex Table II.4, pp. 311–15).

Second, it is increasingly appreciated that the 'packaged' nature of the resource transfer makes it difficult, if not impossible, to quantify with any degree of accuracy the real cost of the individual factors being supplied in the 'package'. Emphasis is thus being placed on the 'unpackaging' of DFI (that is, separating the sources of finance, technology and expertise) or on the 'unbundling' of the actual technology, that is, the disaggregation of the individual components of the technology (policies relating to the TNC and technological development in LDCs are discussed in sections 6.5 and 6.7 of chapter 6).

Keeping these qualifications in mind, however, it will be assumed for the purposes of the present discussion that LDCs want TNC investment, and the attempt will be made to analyse various aspects of the relationship between that investment and process of growth and development.

4.6   TRANSNATIONAL CORPORATIONS AND INDUSTRIAL STRUCTURE

This section is concerned with the effects of foreign ownership on the level of industrial concentration in LDCs. Other things being equal, the expectation is that foreign penetration rates will be highest in the most concentrated industries, which include the most technically advanced and capital-intensive activities (United Nations, 1978, p. 61). The available empirical evidence does not, however, allow the conclusion to be drawn that TNCs actually *cause* higher levels of concentration, although it is possible that their entry speeds up the natural process of concentration and that the weakness of local competitors (excluding state enterprises) permits them to achieve a higher degree of market dominance than they would enjoy in the developed economies.

Two alternative hypotheses have been advanced to explain the level of industrial concentration in LDCs and the role of TNCs in influencing or determining industrial structure:

- The first focuses on the limited size of the domestic market in the majority of LDCs and their reliance on large-scale, capital-intensive imported technologies, which TNCs have access to and utilise in LDCs. It predicts higher levels of concentration in LDCs than in the developed economies, with the presence of foreign capital on a large scale strengthening the prediction.
- The second focuses on the competitive entry of TNCs into host country markets, and predicts that all the major international producers will follow one another into an important LDC market (see section 4.3), and thus produce a 'miniature replica' of that industry within the small domestic market of the LDC, leading to a lower level of concentration than would be the case without DFI.

The available evidence for each of these competing hypotheses is considered in turn, looking first at the structure of the Mexican and Brazilian industrial sectors and their penetration by TNCs and then turning to a case study of the Brazilian pharmaceutical industry.

In the Mexican manufacturing sector in 1972, one-half of the largest 300 firms were TNC affiliates (of which 97 were of US origin) and 61 of the top 100 firms (which accounted for over 75 per cent of the largest 300 firms' assets) were predominantly US controlled (Newfarmer and Mueller, 1975, ch. III). TNC ownership and control were particularly significant in non-electrical machinery, transportation, chemicals, electrical machinery and in the tobacco and rubber sectors. Because of its proximity to the US and lower labour costs, US TNC investment in the food sector was of particular importance in Mexico.[4]

The most concentrated industries in Mexico were foreign dominated. For manufacturing as a whole, 61 per cent of TNC production was sold in markets where the largest four plants accounted for half or more of the markets' total sales. In the most concentrated industries, where the top four plants accounted for more than three-quarters of production, TNCs accounted for 71 per cent of sales (Newfarmer and Mueller, 1975, p. 61). Overall, the share of TNCs in total manufacturing sales rose from 20 per cent in 1962 to 28 per cent in 1970.

In Brazil, TNCs in 1972 accounted for 158 of the largest 500 non-financial enterprises in all sectors, and in manufacturing in the same year they accounted for 147 of the 300 largest firms. Of the largest 100 corporations in the manufacturing sector, 59 were TNC affiliates. In certain industries – motor vehicles and parts, pharmaceuticals, electrical machinery, machinery, rubber and plastics – TNCs accounted for more than two-thirds of the assets of the leading firms.[5]

Manufacturing production in general was quite concentrated in Brazil. In 176 of 302 industries, the four leading plants produced more than 50 per cent of the value of production and TNCs owned three or four of the four leading plants in 32 industries, which accounted for 26 per cent of industrial production (Newfarmer and Mueller, 1975, ch. V). Overall, TNCs were rated as leaders in 66 industries, accounting for 44 per cent of manufacturing production, and were associated with higher than average levels of concentration than was the case with national firms, since TNCs operated more frequently in oligopolistic industries.

In both Mexico and Brazil, Newfarmer and Mueller (1975) argued that a process of denationalisation was evident. TNCs were becoming increasingly influential in these economies as a whole and TNC conduct was of crucial importance to their performance. The possibility of TNCs pursuing non-economic (that is, political) objectives in such economies was an ever-present danger.[6]

The alternative hypothesis concerned with the effects of TNCs on LDC market structures, the so-called 'miniature replica' hypothesis, is considered by Evans (1977a). In this case, it is assumed that TNCs will enter a market under conditions that would deter a local enterprise, and that they will remain in the market under conditions that would drive out the local competitor. For example, all major TNCs in any given industry are likely to enter an important LDC market, even if the result is inefficiency and low levels of capacity utilisation, for fear of being excluded from that market by their rivals (see section 4.3 above). In addition, the TNCs will, by definition, possess the technology and capital resources required for market entry (resources that potential local competitors may not have access to). TNC subsidiaries are also likely to have lower exit (or death) rates from any given industry than their usually smaller and hence more vulnerable local competitors (Evans, 1977a, p. 376).

The structure of the Brazilian pharmaceutical industry appears to be consistent with the predictions of the 'miniature replica' hypothesis. The size distribution of firms in the industry has been stable over time and significantly less concentrated than the American size distribution of firms (Evans, 1977a, p. 379). Data for Mexico and Argentina, cited by Evans, also indicate more dispersed size distributions for the pharmaceutical industry than are typical for developed capitalist economies.

Clearly, there is a need for caution when discussing the characteristics of size distributions of firms in various industries in LDCs and the underlying factors determining those distributions. The special features of the pharmaceutical sector may well favour lower levels of seller concentration, and generalisations should not be made on the basis of such limited evidence.

One further point deserves mention. As already noted above (section 4.4), explanations of the expansion and consolidation of TNC involvement in host economies have tended to focus on the superior efficiency of TNCs *vis-à-vis* their local competitors and/or on TNC ownership of 'firm-specific' advantages that are most effectively and profitably exploited by TNCs by being kept within the TNCs themselves (internalised').

Newfarmer's (1979b) study of the Brazilian electrical industry suggested, however, that the use of specific market and extra-market tactics by TNCs, which aim at controlling competitive forces, market conditions and market development, could prevent or retard the erosion of their monopolistic advantages and the deterioration of entry barriers confronting potential (especially domestic) competitors. He discussed seven forms of TNC conduct in this respect: interlocking directorships; mutual forbearance (a 'live and let live' strategy); control of supply channels; cross-subsidisation; formal and informal collusion; formal political ties; and acquisition behaviour.

TNC corporate behaviour 'feeds back' into the market structure. In 1960, TNCs controlled approximately 66 per cent of the assets of the 100 largest electrical firms in Brazil but their share had grown to nearly 80 per cent by 1976 (Newfarmer, 1979b, p. 108). Newfarmer estimated that takeovers accounted for over 90 per cent of the increase in the foreign share of this industry over the period studied and he concluded (p. 135):[7]

> TNCs exhibit strong propensities towards organising and preserving various forms of market power in host economies. These tactics are often based on the advantages of global financial strength (such as in the case of cross-subsidisation or acquisitions) or perceived international and local interdependence (such as with interlocking directorates, mutual forbearance or collusion). . . . Clearly, barriers to entry which protect the monopolistic advantage of TNCs are not solely based on superior technology, but include specific corporate practices designed to deter new entry.

Lall (1979b; reprinted in Lall, 1980a) attempted to overcome what he saw as the defects of the previous studies by an analysis of how TNC entry affects market concentration within a comprehensive model of the determinants of industrial structure. Without such a model, he argued (1980a, p. 65),

> ... it is impossible to assess whether foreign entry has an influence on market structure *independently* of the industrial variables which are commonly thought to determine it, whether it is merely *associated with* structural characteristics that are inherent in different industries, or it *speeds up* the process of structural change which may occur even in its absence.

Lall's analysis suggests that the two hypotheses outlined above need not be mutually exclusive. In the short run, TNC entry may reduce concentration if it increases the number of local suppliers (but see Newfarmer, 1979a) and if it induces competing TNCs to follow suit (as has already been suggested). In the longer run, however, TNC entry may increase concentration for two reasons: the attributes of TNCs (capital-intensive technologies, differentiated products, superior managerial and organisational skills, etc.) may raise barriers to entry for local firms; and TNC conduct may accelerate the process of concentration, via acquisition of local firms, etc.

This still does not solve the problem, however, of whether TNC entry raises concentration only by changing industrial parameters (capital intensity, advertising intensity) or whether it exercises an independent influence after all other factors have been accounted for.

Lall (1979b) tackled this problem using regression analysis to analyse data taken from the 1972 Malaysian Survey of Manufacturing Industries. He concluded that (a) the factors that influenced concentration in the developed industrialised economies also determined it in an economy such as Malaysia: barriers to entry resulting from scale economies, capital requirements and product differentiation were all significant in promoting concentration; market size was negatively correlated with concentration and market growth had a minor, ambiguous effect; (b) TNC investment raised concentration over and above the level accounted for by the other industrial variables but also worked through those variables by raising capital intensity and minimum capital requirements and, to a lesser extent, through local advertising; (c) TNC investment had a greater impact on concentration in non-consumer goods industries, where foreign entry was more related to capital intensity, although the introduction of new processes had a strong independent influence in the regression results.

On balance, the evidence discussed above would appear to lend greater support to the view that TNC involvement is likely to increase the level of industrial concentration in any given LDC. The 'miniature replica' hypothesis, although supported by some evidence, is perhaps more likely to be a short-run phenomenon; in a dynamic, longer-run context, higher levels of concentration are to be expected. Clearly, this is an area that requires far more research, utilising, wherever possible, time series data to overcome the problems associated with cross-section analysis. Such research also needs to take into account both the characteristics of technology and its role in the production process, TNC involvement in the industry and the structure and characteristics of the industry at the international level.

4.7   TNCs AND LINKAGE CREATION

TNCs can exert a significant influence on both the rate and characteristics of the process of growth and development through the creation of forward and backward linkages with the host economy. Forward linkages refer to the sale of the output of the TNC to domestic firms for use as inputs into their productive processes, and backward linkages refer to purchases by TNCs from domestic supplier firms.

It is usually argued that TNCs will establish few linkages with domestic firms. The highly centralised global structure of the TNC and the integrated nature of its global operations, its use of capital-intensive technologies and the nature of the final product (see section 4.8), taken together lead many economists to argue that TNCs create a virtual 'enclave' in the host economy, integrating the 'modern', TNC-dominated sectors of the host economy with the international economy. The Chilean economist, Osvaldo Sunkel, went so far as to characterise this process as one of transnational integration and national disintegration (Sunkel, 1973; Sunkel and Fuenzalida, 1979).

Langdon's study (Langdon, 1975) of the Kenyan soap and detergents industry provided support for the view that TNCs create fewer linkages with domestic firms than do indigenously owned firms in the same industry. This is because TNC soap production technology offered fewer linkage possibilities than local, especially non-mechanized, soap production, but product choice was also a factor. The inputs for the basic laundry soaps produced by indigenous firms were available locally, whereas TNC input requirements had no Kenyan source of supply. In addition, tie-in clauses that compel the subsidiary to buy from the parent or some other subsidiary approved by the parent were used in the industry to forestall the possibility of alternative supply sources developing. Capital equipment was also likely to be supplied by the parent company, thus preventing or retarding the development of an indigenous machine-making capacity that could supply basic, labour-intensive equipment. Where linkage possibilities did exist – in, for example, packaging and printing operations – it was more likely to be other TNC subsidiaries that were able to take advantage of these opportunities, rather than indigenous firms.

From the above discussion, it is clear that it is not only ownership as such that determines linkage possibilities in LDCs, but also (and perhaps more importantly) the nature of the technology utilised and the characteristics of the final product (the question of TNCs and technological choice is discussed in section 4.8).

A general survey of the literature on TNC linkage creation in LDCs was carried out by Lall (1978). His conclusions were:

● with respect to import-substituting TNCs, extensive linkages had been created in the larger, semi-industrialised LDCs (India, Mexico, Brazil, Argentina), largely as a result of government pressure, but probably at an excessively high cost; in smaller or industrially backward LDCs, TNCs had created relatively few linkages;

● with respect to export-oriented TNCs, Lall distinguished between (i) TNCs that had moved from import substitution to the export of manufactured goods, for example Volkswagen in Brazil, (ii) TNCs that produced and exported 'traditional' products (footwear, textiles, processed food, etc.), (iii) TNC investments in 'modern' industries specifically designed for export (the Philips and General Electric complexes in Singapore, for example), and (iv) TNC 'sourcing' investments where a particular (labour-intensive) process was transferred to the LDC, as had happened extensively in the electronics industry (this is discussed further in section 4.11 below). Lall concluded that (i) and (ii) were likely to create the most local linkages, (iii) rather less and (iv) virtually none at all.

Lall (1980b) carried out a further study of linkage creation, looking in detail at two Indian truck manufacturers, Ashok Leyland (AL), majority owned by British Leyland, and the Tata Engineering and Locomotive Company (TELCO), almost entirely owned by the Tata Group of Indian companies, and a sample of twenty-six supplier companies. He found that, initially, both companies produced for themselves certain parts and components that in a developed industrialised economy would have been subcontracted, but that, over time, and under government pressure, they increasingly 'farmed out' many of these tasks to independent suppliers (Lall, 1980b, p. 211). He concluded that buying out and subcontracting were flourishing in India and that, in general, the patterns observed in India were similar to those found in the industrialised economies and conformed with the practices of particular licensors or parent companies abroad.[8] Technical linkages in particular (the provision of technical assistance or the exchange of technical information to match needs with supplies, to control quality and to facilitate innovation) were widespread in the industry, especially between suppliers of similar technologies (that is, those based on a common scientific, engineering and production experience) (Lall, 1980b, pp. 206, 218).

Two main points emerge from this discussion. First, caution is required when generalising about TNC linkage creation in LDCs. In his study of AL and TELCO, Lall did not discover any discernible difference between the two companies that could be attributed to the transnationality of AL, largely because of the closed nature of the Indian economy and government control of various aspects of corporate behaviour (Lall, 1980b, p. 222). In addition to intra-industry considerations, there will also be inter-industry differences within the same country and significant inter-country variations. Secondly, and related to the latter point, government policy is extremely important in creating an environment that encourages linkage creation and in exerting pressure on individual firms to accelerate the development of a subcontracting network. Although such policies may be costly in the short run (in terms of the costs associated with 'inefficient' import-substituting industrialisation – see Chapter 6, section 6.2 – of which linkage creation is a part), in the longer run, the costs of linkage creation may not be significant (Lall, 1980b, p. 224). Lall (1978, p. 223) succinctly summarised the main point thus:

> The extent of linkages created in particular LDCs depends upon the stage
> of development of indigenous industry, the availability of local skills and
> technology, institutions and government policies, changes in demand and
> technology in world markets and their political attractiveness to TNCs.

4.8   TNCs AND THE TRANSFER OF TECHNOLOGY

INTRODUCTION

For the purposes of this section, the definition of technology given by Stewart
(1977, p. 1) is adopted: technology encompasses the 'skills, knowledge and
procedures for making, using and doing useful things' (for a discussion of
alternative definitions and classifications of technology, see Dunning, 1982).
Technology in this sense thus includes both process technology (how
something is made) and product technology (the nature and specification of
what is produced) as well as managerial, organisational, financial and
marketing skills, transferred not only through DFI but also through a variety
of non-equity arrangements (referred to in section 4.5 above).

The TNC is probably the most important of the channels through which
LDCs acquire proprietary technology, and its activities in this respect have
generated a great deal of controversy. Interest has focused in particular on
two aspects of TNC operations:

- the 'appropriateness' of the technology transferred to, and utilised within,
  LDCs by TNCs to the resources and developmental objectives of the host
  LDCs; and
- the actual cost to the LDCs of the technology transferred to them by
  TNCs.

This section first considers the factors underlying the choice of technologies
transferred by TNCs. It then surveys the empirical evidence from LDCs to
determine whether or not it can be concluded unambiguously that TNCs
systematically select technologies different from those used by their local
counterparts. There is a brief discussion of the question of taste transfer by
TNCs. Finally, the costs of technology transfer are indicated. The
employment implications of TNC technology transfer and utilisation are
considered in section 4.9. No direct reference is made to the controversy
surrounding the theory of the choice of technique, which has occupied a
central position in development economics for the past thirty years (for a
survey and discussion of the major theoretical contributions, see Colman and
Nixson, 1978, ch. 10). Different indices can be used to measure capital or
labour intensity, the most commonly used measure being the capital–labour
ratio (K/L). However, the measurement of capital poses a number of
problems and labour cannot be assumed to be homogeneous (see below). In

addition, the K/L ratio does not measure the efficiency of factor use; thus the capital–output ratio (K/O) and/or the labour–output ratio (L/O) are also used. The share of wages in value added can also be used as a measure of labour intensity.[9] It must be emphasised that all these measures pose both conceptual and measurement problems, but, despite such limitations, there is nevertheless general agreement that they are useful for planning and policy-making. A valuable survey of the limitations of the various measures is provided by Bhalla (1975b).

THE RATIONALE OF TNC TECHNOLOGY TRANSFER

The argument concerning the 'appropriateness' of the technology transferred to LDCs by TNCs relates to the disparity between the factor endowments of the LDCs and the factor requirements of TNC technologies. In this section, some of the major arguments concerning the determination of the choice of technique are briefly considered, keeping in mind, however, that many of these considerations are relevant to both national and transnational firms.

Given the relatively labour-abundant/capital-scarce resource endowment of most LDCs, and assuming that the market prices of the factors of production reflect social opportunity costs, it is argued that LDCs should select technologies that utilise most intensively their relatively abundant factor (labour) and economise on the scarce factor (capital). The TNC, on the other hand, is more likely to transfer a capital-intensive technology to the LDC, a technology that has been developed and perfected in the capital-abundant/labour-scarce developed economy. Such a technology, it is argued, does not create large-scale new employment opportunities, it often creates a long-run dependence on imported equipment and associated inputs, and it prevents or slows down the effective anchorage and assimilation of the transferred technology in the host LDC.

One explanation for the apparent inconsistency between relative factor endowment and technology choice is based on the argument that, in the majority of LDCs, market prices do not in fact reflect social opportunity costs. It is maintained that labour is too 'expensive' (because of government minimum wage legislation, the influence of powerful trade unions, etc.) and that capital is too 'cheap' (interest rates are often negative when measured in real terms, government subsidies and incentives reduce the price of capital, over-valued exchange rates encourage the importation of capital equipment, and so on). It is argued that technological choice is merely a reflection of the 'distortions' in the factor and product markets of the LDCs, and that, once such 'distortions' are removed and market prices correctly reflect relative scarcities, producers, both national and transnational, will substitute between factors in the direction of greater labour intensity. This is the orthodox neoclassical view of the determination of the choice of technique – well illustrated in, for example, the work of Little, Scitovsky and Scott (1970).

Another explanation of the allegedly high capital intensity of TNC manufacturing operations relates to the competitive environment in LDCs within which they operate. The majority of LDCs have pursued policies of import-substituting industrialisation (ISI), an important aspect of which has been the protection of domestic enterprises (both national and foreign owned) from foreign competition by a variety of protective devices. The absence of powerful competitive pressures has, it is argued, lessened the need for firms in LDCs to minimise costs and, other things being equal, has led to the selection of more capital-intensive techniques by both national and transnational firms (United Nations, 1974a, pp. 6–7).

A third explanation relates to technical rigidity, that is, the limited substitutability of factors in the production process. This hypothesis was first advanced by Eckaus (1955), and has more recently been extended and tested by Forsyth *et al.* (1980). The distinction is made between:

- the basic case in which, given the state of technical knowledge, there is only one (or at most a very small number of) manufacturing process(es) that is (are) capable of producing a particular commodity;
- technical rigidities related to the specifications of the commodity to be produced (see below); and,
- technical rigidities imposed by the availability of techniques; even if alternative techniques exist, LDCs may not have access to them.[10]

The empirical results and conclusions of this study are discussed below.

A fourth set of explanations concerned with the choice of technique relates to 'behavioural' considerations. It has been argued, for example, that it is 'engineering man', rather than 'economic man', who determines objectives and selects techniques. Engineers play an important role in the design of manufacturing plant and equipment; even if they themselves do not actually select the equipment to be used, they are still largely responsible for the range of commercially available equipment. Engineers may also have a preference for sophisticated modern equipment that gives a high-quality final product, which may not be justifiable from a purely economic point of view (Wells, 1973; United Nations, 1974a, ch. 1). Managers may also be 'satisficers' with respect to technological choice. That is, given that their objectives may be other than those of profit maximisation, the pressures to find a cost-minimising set of techniques will be correspondingly reduced and capital-intensive techniques therefore selected in relatively labour-abundant economies.

Focusing attention specifically on the transfer of technology by the TNC, a number of points (not necessarily in descending order of importance) need to be made.

(1) From the point of view of the TNC, it is factor availability at the global level that is important, not the availability of factors in any particular LDC. Given its access to international capital markets and other parts of the organisation, the TNC affiliate is unlikely to face a capital constraint and is thus not required to economise in the use of that factor.

(2) The factors of production are not homogeneous. It has been argued (Arrighi, 1970) that capital-intensive techniques are characterised by a pattern of employment in which semi-skilled labour and high-level manpower predominate, whereas labour-intensive techniques make greater use of both skilled and unskilled labour. In most LDCs, skilled labour (in particular,

supervisory personnel) is often in very short supply, and thus the need to economise on this scarce factor dictates the choice of capital-intensive technology.

Even Arrighi's qualification to the simple two-homogeneous-factor world may be an over-simplification. Robinson (1979b, p. 27) identified eleven inputs that could, in varying degrees, influence the choice of technology[11] and he concluded that: 'I stress this large variety of inputs because, to an industrial economist, a discussion which fastens exclusively on [unskilled labour and capital embodied in machinery] is in the great majority of cases barren.'

(3) Related to point 2 is the argument that TNCs in particular may well wish to minimise their contact with local labour, through the utilisation of capital-intensive technologies. Streeten (1972, p. 234) suggested that labour in the LDC might well be 'unskilled, underfed, unhealthy, unreliable, undisciplined and perhaps hostile'. Support for this view emerged from a study of the choice of technique by manufacturing firms in Nigeria (Winston, 1979). Under the heading 'Machines are easier to get along with than people', Winston reported that the reduction of general labour problems by the choice of more capital-intensive production methods, especially in multi-shift plants, was mentioned by a number of managers. In addition to this, 'machine-paced' flows of production could be achieved by capital-intensive technologies, and the problem of theft (very costly for some industries) could be reduced.

(4) TNCs are typically large-scale producers, and it is the scale of output that determines the efficient factor intensity (Helleiner, 1975, p. 168).

(5) In many LDCs, material inputs are often expensive and difficult to obtain because of foreign exchange controls, import restrictions, etc. It will pay producers to substitute other factor inputs for such materials wherever possible, and capital–material substitution (for example, storage facilities that reduce spoilage; mechanised materials handling that reduces breakage; electronically controlled equipment to ensure mix specification, etc.) offers greater opportunities in this respect than labour–material substitution (Helleiner, 1975, pp. 168–9).

(6) 'Ethnic pride' (Winston, 1979) and 'good citizenship' (Helleiner, 1975) are also advanced as reasons why, respectively, LDCs 'demand' capital-intensive technologies and TNCs 'bow' to such pressures.

(7) Owing largely to the work of Frances Stewart (1972, 1977), it is now generally accepted that the choice of product (product technology) raises issues perhaps more fundamental than the choice of technique (process technology) and is itself an important determinant of the factor intensity of the process technology selected. The more closely specified is the product, the fewer are the possibilities for labour–capital substitution in its production, and, as Stewart has argued, 'to produce identical physical products only one method may be possible' (Stewart, 1972, p. 111). This view adds weight to the technical rigidity arguments referred to above and also raises the question of 'appropriate products' for production in and consumption by LDCs (see below and Chapter 6, section 6.7, for a further discussion of this issue).

(8) Reference was made in section 4.4 to the ownership-specific advantage of TNCs and clearly the ownership and control of technology are two of the most important (if not *the* most important) of these advantages. It

would be strange indeed if TNCs did not utilise within the LDCs the product and process techniques that they themselves have developed and perfected elsewhere in the world. It is the very possession of advanced technology, combined in a profitable 'package' with organisational, financial and marketing factors, which can be applied elsewhere at little extra cost, that explains much of the transnationality of these firms. In addition, the limited domestic markets and the varying stages of development of the LDCs do not make them sufficiently attractive for TNCs to develop separate products/processes for every market within which they operate. As Lall (1978, p. 238) argued:

> Minor on-the-spot adaptations may be made to suit local conditions, to meet official requirements, or to save foreign exchange, but by their very nature TNCs do not specialize in the simple labour-intensive products which can be adapted to LDC factor endowments.

THE EMPIRICAL EVIDENCE ON TECHNOLOGICAL CHOICE OF TNCs

It would be useful if, at the very least, tentative answers could be given to the following questions:

- Do TNCs systematically employ more capital-intensive technologies than their local counterparts in LDCs?
- Have TNCs attempted to adapt the technologies they transfer to local conditions?
- If TNCs do adapt to local conditions, do they adapt more efficiently and/or effectively than their local counterparts?

As will quickly become evident, the available empirical evidence does not permit straightforward and unambiguous answers to these questions. None the less, the evidence presented in some of these studies will be considered to see if, in fact, any useful generalisations can be made at all.

Econometric estimates of factor substitutability

A number of studies (surveyed by Morawetz, 1976; Gaude, 1975) have attempted to measure the elasticity of substitution, that is, the ease with which two inputs (usually capital and labour) can be substituted for one another. A low (less than one) elasticity of substitution (technical fixity or rigidity) indi-cates that a fall in the price of, for example, labour will induce a less than proportional increase in the use of labour in the production process and will thus reduce labour's share in total output. A high (greater than one) elasticity of substitution, on the other hand, indicates that a fall in the price of labour will be accompanied by a more than proportional increase in the use of labour, thus increasing its share in total output. Other things being equal, the higher the elasticity of substitution, the greater is the potential growth of output, because the relatively fast-growing factor (labour) can be easily sub-stituted for the relatively slow-growing factor (capital). This has important policy implications for the governments of LDCs (Gaude, 1975).

The econometric results varied widely: in general, the estimates of elasticity of substitution based on time series data were less than unity and lower than the estimates based on cross-section data (Gaude, 1975, p. 41). Morawetz (1976) argued that the studies indicated that there is some scope for factor substitution and that the scope differs from industry to industry. However, on the basis of the available evidence, it is not possible to identify conclusively industries that have relatively high or relatively low substitution elasticities.

Both surveys point to the many problems associated with such studies, problems that relate to: aggregation and the definition of capital, labour and output; the assumption that there are only two factors of production; the use of data that cover only technologies actually being used (that is, the studies ignore those technologies still in existence but not being utilised); the assumption that the elasticity of substitution is constant and that all firms are on their production frontiers; and a number of other problems, including several important difficulties relating to econometric estimation (Morawetz, 1974; 1976).

The tentative conclusion that can be drawn (and is referred to again below) is that it cannot simply be assumed that the relative prices of capital and labour are the major determinants of the choice of technique and that changes in those relative prices will induce factor substitution. The neoclassical view that assumes a smooth production function, factor price flexibility and infinitely variable factor proportions is thus, to say the least, an over-simplification.

Case studies of technological choice
Agarwal (1976). This study was based on data for thirty-four industries in the large-scale manufacturing sector in India. Two measures of capital intensity were utilised – average productive capital (fixed and working capital) per employee, and average value added per employee. With respect to average productive capital per employee, foreign firms in twenty-two of the industries were more capital intensive than their domestic counterparts. When average value added per employee was the measure used, foreign firms were more capital intensive than their local counterparts in thirty-one out of the thirty-four industries studied. The following factors were given as the probable reasons for the greater capital intensity of foreign firms: higher wage costs per unit of labour employed (TNCs pay higher wages on grounds of social prestige and better access to the labour market); relatively easier access to capital markets, both domestic and foreign; greater indirect pressure on domestic firms to use relatively more labour-intensive methods of production; strong tendency for domestic firms to substitute labour for capital in peripheral or ancillary operations; TNCs usually spend more on buildings than their domestic counterparts.

Leipziger (1976). This study compared the production characteristics of domestic Indian manufacturing firms with those of US-owned manufacturing affiliates in India. The distinction was made between *ex ante* and *ex post* substitution – the former referring to the particular technology transferred (for example, plant design and equipment), and the latter referring to the way in which the plant is run, that is, any adaptations that may actually be made in the light of existing factor price ratios. Leipziger found that US firms imported a less capital-intensive technology *ex ante*, but used more fixed capital per man *ex post*, because they faced a higher wage–interest ratio than did Indian firms.

Courtney and Leipziger (1975). This study estimated and compared production functions for 1,484 foreign affiliates of US-owned TNCs located in both less developed and developed economies. Utilising the distinction referred to above between *ex ante* and *ex post* substitution, it was found that *ex ante* technologies exported by TNC parents to developed economy and LDC affiliates differed in a number of industries but not in a systematic manner. In nine out of eleven industries, however, given technologies were more labour-using in LDCs, as the TNC affiliates responded to the lower wage–interest ratios and employed more labour per unit of capital *ex post*. The authors concluded that TNCs do respond to factor price in their choice of technology.[12]

Mason (1973). This study was based on data collected for fourteen US subsidiaries and fourteen closely matched local counterparts – nine matched pairs of firms in the Philippines and five matched pairs in Mexico. Each pair of matched firms produced a similar product or product mix and the attempt was made to compare firms of roughly equal size. It was found that the US firms employed more buildings but not significantly more equipment per factory worker than their local counterparts. Because of their relatively heavier investment in buildings and inventories, however, they tended to use more capital per worker, whether capital per worker was defined as buildings and equipment per factory worker or as total capital per employee. In US firms, a larger proportion of total employment was in the factory (that is, there were fewer overhead salaried personnel) and their skill mix also differed from that of their local counterparts: US firms used relatively more executive, technical and semi- or unskilled workers, whereas local firms used more skilled workers and professionals (accountants, skilled clerical workers, etc.) (see Arrighi, 1970, above). Mason concluded that the TNC could not be singled out as a contributor to the factor proportions problem.

Willmore (1976). This study used data for thirty-three matched pairs of non-resident and resident firms in Costa Rica, matched as in Mason's study (Mason, 1973) with respect to size and product mix. It was found that the non-resident (that is, foreign) firms had lower capital–output ratios than their resident (that is, domestically owned) counterparts. This result implies that foreign firms must have a higher output–labour ratio or a lower capital–labour ratio (or both) than their local counterparts.[13] It was indeed discovered that non-resident firms were less capital intensive than resident firms when capital intensity was measured by equipment per factory worker, fixed assets per employee or total assets per employee, but that when capital intensity was measured by the ratio of fixed assets or total assets to value added it could not be concluded that non-resident firms were less capital intensive than their local counterparts.

Forsyth and Solomon (1977). This study was based on data for 154 firms in ten industries (sawn timber, wooden furniture, bread, biscuits, etc., footwear, shirts, concrete blocks, small metal fabrications, small plastic fabrications, blouses, plywood and veneers) in the manufacturing sector in Ghana. It distinguished between three categories of firm – the TNC (forty-three firms), the private Ghanaian (forty-two firms) and the resident expatriate (sixty-nine firms). The latter category consisted of firms owned by foreigners permanently resident in the 'host' country (mainly Lebanese and miscellaneous European nationals) and it was argued that the characteristics of such firms might be a combination of those of both TNCs and private Ghanaian firms. For example, resident expatriate firms might have good contacts with the outside world that, together with a reputation for successful business operation, might give them access to capital markets denied to private Ghanaian firms. On the other hand, their knowledge of the local labour market and labour practices, indigenous technologies, the workings of governments, etc., might well distinguish them from the TNC and ensure their greater adaptability to the local environment.

The results of the analysis showed that both TNCs and resident expatriate firms tended to be more capital intensive than private Ghanaian firms within given sectors, but that there were important inter-industry variations and it was not the case that TNCs were always more capital intensive. Private Ghanaian firms producing footwear, plywood and veneers, and blouses were significantly less capital intensive than firms in the other two categories, but for bread products, private Ghanaian firms were more capital intensive. Ghanaian firms were, however, more skill intensive than firms in the other two categories (especially in the footwear, bread, wooden furniture and concrete block industries) and they generally paid lower wages.

Overall, the resident expatriate firms tended to be more like the TNCs than like the private Ghanaian firms, although they tended to be slightly more capital intensive than the TNCs (but this latter difference is not statistically significant). The fact that some TNCs were less capital intensive than their Ghanaian counterparts suggested to the authors that TNCs might enjoy lower search or research and development costs in locating more 'appropriate' technologies. However, this view is not supported by evidence from Brazil, for example, where Morley and Smith (1977b) found that TNCs did not engage in extensive searches for alternative techniques when planning their Brazilian operations and that, where a move to more labour-intensive methods was observed, it was usually the result of the 'scaling down' of operations for the smaller Brazilian market (see also Morley and Smith 1977a).

Chung and Lee (1980). This study matched nine US–Korean pairs of firms in seven different industries (electronics, automobile assembly, chemical fertilizer, food canning, livestock feed, furniture and sanitary paper) and eight Japanese–Korean pairs of firms in five different industries (electronics, wristwatches, paint, synthetic fibre and textile clothing). The results showed that there were no statistically significant differences in production techniques selected by foreign and local firms in Korea.

Reuber (1973). This study analysed data on approximately eighty private foreign investment projects in LDCs initiated by US, European and Japanese TNCs. In fifty-seven out of the seventy-eight cases examined, no changes were made to the production technology introduced to the LDC, and in an additional nineteen cases the technology was introduced in an adapted form. In the area of quality control, the investing firm introduced its standard system without adaptation in forty-eight out of fifty-nine cases and with adaptation in an additional nine cases (Reuber, 1973, pp. 194–5). The reasons given for such adaptation as occurred related to the need to scale down plant and equipment to the smaller LDC market and to meet the requirements of that local market, as determined by local customs, demand characteristics and government regulations. There were 'relatively few instances of adaptation to take advantage of low labour cost or to make up for the absence of skilled labour in the host country' (p. 196), but it is of interest to note that 'adaptations are more frequent the higher the degree of local ownership and control and the greater the independence of the subsidiary from the parent company' (p. 196).

Forsyth, McBain and Solomon (1980). The authors of this study developed an 'index of technical rigidity', based on the study of the characteristics of manufacturing sub-processses in a large sample of industries, to provide an engineering-based assessment of the opportunities for substituting labour for capital. The advantage that they claimed for this approach was that it focused attention on feasible techniques, rather than on merely the available techniques actually in use. Analysing data from Ghana, the Philippines, Turkey and Malaysia, they concluded that it was unlikely that there was an 'intrinsic inflexibility' of factor proportions that caused low rates of labour absorption in LDC manufacturing. Indeed, there was a strong tendency to substitute labour for capital, that is, where feasible, labour-intensive technologies were usually selected. The fact that in general such 'appropriate' technologies had not created large-scale employment opportunities in the manufacturing sector must throw doubt on the ability of LDC governments, through 'appropriate' policies (removal of factor price 'distortions', legislation on technology choice by TNCs, etc.), to create significantly larger numbers of jobs. The latter would only come, the authors argued, through the creation of new, indigenous, labour-intensive methods of production.

Other studies. A number of other studies were surveyed by Lall (1978) and Baer (1976). In this final sub-section, brief reference will be made to a number of points that deserve mention. The ILO report on Kenya (International Labour Office, 1972) argued that in those manufacturing sectors containing both local and foreign capital the foreign firm would be more likely to use the labour-intensive technology because it would be able to recruit more easily, and perhaps use more productively, the supervisory personnel required for labour-intensive technologies. TNCs, however, dominated production in inherently capital-intensive sectors and there were signs that capital-intensive technical change generated by the TNCs and coupled with their superiority in product differentiation, use of brand names, etc. was leading increasingly to the use of TNC-dominated, capital-intensive, large-scale production technologies.

Langdon's study of the Kenyan soap and detergents industry (Langdon, 1975) found that TNC subsidiaries were more capital intensive than their local counterparts, partly because of the nature of the product produced. Kaplinsky (1978b) studied seven subsidiaries of British TNCs in Kenya and formed the impression that the subsidiaries had chosen both core and peripheral technology suited to local conditions and that differed in many instances from that used by the parent firms. Pack (1976) studied forty-two manufacturing plants in Kenya and found 'considerable variation in feasible efficient production methods, particularly in peripheral operations' (p. 58). He also argued that TNCs were more likely to carry out labour-intensive adaptations and were more willing to use older equipment.

A study of the Nigerian brewing industry (Akpakpan, 1983) indicated that it was the age of the plant and equipment and scale of output that determined the capital intensity of the production technology, not nationality of ownership. Biersteker (1978, ch. 7), in his study of TNCs in Nigeria, also questioned the argument that TNC subsidiaries were inevitably more capital intensive than their local counterparts. Gershenberg and Ryan (1978) found that, in Uganda, TNCs employed more capital-intensive technologies *ex ante* but were at the same time more responsive to factor price differentials *ex post* than local firms.

What conclusions can be drawn from the empirical evidence?
A number of studies relating to the choice of technique in manufacturing industry have been considered in some detail, and perhaps the most important conclusion that can be drawn from the survey is the lack of unanimity in the findings. The studies show that in some instances TNCs are more capital intensive than their local counterparts, in other cases they are more labour intensive, and in yet other cases that are no observable differences in factor intensity relative to nationality of ownership. Econometric estimates indicate that there is some scope for the substitution of labour for capital in all enterprises, but such estimates are open to serious criticisms. The main conclusions that can be safely drawn are as follows:

First, when the attempt is made to reach conclusions on factor intensity, every effort should be made to ensure that, as far as possible, like is being compared with like. That is, matched pairs of firms, as similar as possible with respect to product mix, scale of output, age of equipment and the market conditions that they face, should be compared. When comparing different studies, differences in the measures of capital (or labour) intensity used and the different methodologies employed – all of which may well be open to a number of criticisms – must be kept in mind.

Secondly, technological fixity is clearly in no sense absolute, and there is plenty of evidence that both TNCs and nationally owned firms do adapt in some measure to local conditions. Such adaptations are especially pro-nounced in ancillary or peripheral operations (transport, packing, handling and storage operations) where relative prices may play a role in determining the technique chosen. However, other considerations (quality, the appear-ance of the final product, etc.) may well offset factor price considerations and lead to the selection of capital-intensive, mechanised techniques even in ancil-lary operations.

Thirdly, where there are no clearly observable differences between TNCs and locally owned firms, this situation may be the result of the latters' need to become more like TNCs in order to survive the competitive struggle with them (as suggested by Langdon, 1975). Even in those cases where local firms use relatively more labour-intensive technologies than their TNC counter-parts, they may nevertheless still be using relatively more capital-intensive technologies than they would in the absence of TNCs and their associated technologies (Kirkpatrick and Nixson, 1981).

Fourthly, there may well be significant inter-industry variations in the degree of technological flexibility, with flexibility being greatest in estab-lished, basic industries (clothing, foodstuffs, household utensils, construction materials, etc.) with low income elasticities of demand, catering for the needs of the mass of the population. For the more technologically advanced, sophis-ticated durable consumer goods, technological choice is likely to be limited or non-existent, and given that TNCs dominate such production it is not surpris-ing that TNCs occupy the most capital-intensive sectors of the LDC economy (as noted in the ILO report, 1972, on Kenya). Choice of product is thus important, both in terms of inter-industry variations in the bundle of goods and services being produced, and in terms of the characteristics of the indi-vidual commodities being produced.

Finally, of perhaps greater importance than the characteristics of the exist-ing technologies utilised by LDCs is the fact that technological change originating largely in the developed industrialised economies is continuous, rapid and generally in the direction of greater capital intensity. Given that it is the TNCs that are responsible for the commercial development of these tech-nologies and their transfer to LDCs, it seems unlikely that TNCs will become major suppliers of 'appropriate' process or product technologies to LDCs. This development can only increase the urgency of the need for LDCs to develop their own technologies or at least acquire the capacity to adapt or modify imported technologies. The whole question of technology policy in LDCs is considered in Chapter 6, section 6.7.

TNCs AND THE TRANSFER OF TASTES

The UN report on TNCs (United Nations, 1978, p. 40) noted that TNCs 'seek out and flourish most in foreign markets that most closely resemble the home market for which they first developed their products and processes'. Logi-cally, it could be expected that TNCs will attempt to create, if they do not already exist, similar conditions in the more important LDC markets (Nixson and Yamin, 1980). TNCs thus play a key role in the creation and moulding of consumer tastes in LDCs, and some authors have even gone so far as to refer to the creation of a 'global shopping centre' and the diffusion of an 'ideology of consumption' throughout the world (Barnett and Müller, 1974, chs 2 and 6).

Product differentiation and innovation, heavy advertising (for a discussion of advertising in LDCs, see James and Lister, 1980) and the creation of new markets are all aspects of TNC global operations and are all becoming increasingly important in LDCs. TNCs, however, are not the only sources of influence on consumption patterns in LDCs. Indigenous firms and LDC governments themselves may well introduce and encourage 'inappropriate' products and consumption patterns; Biersteker (1978, ch. 7) points to the Nigerian government's decision to establish a colour television network as an example of the latter. As has already been argued however, such actions by indigenous firms may best be seen as a response to TNC competition, rather than as the exercise of initiative on their part. The complexity of the process of demand creation is perhaps not yet fully understood, but it is desirable that this aspect of TNC operations in LDCs be recognised as an important phenomenon that deserves further study.

THE COST OF TECHNOLOGY TRANSFER

It was noted above (section 4.5) that one of the major attractions of TNC direct investment is that it supplies a 'package' of inputs, including technology, that are not available, or are available only in limited quantities, in the host economy. It is the very fact that technology is part of the 'package' that makes it extremely difficult, if not impossible, to estimate with any degree of accuracy the actual cost of the technology supplied to the 'buyer' of the technology, that is, the host LDC. As will be argued in section 4.10, the TNC can utilise a number of channels through which income can be remitted from an LDC, and actual payments for technology may thus pass unnoticed or be greatly underestimated. As Stewart (1977, ch. 5) has noted, royalty payments and licence fees may cover only a small proportion of the total payment for technology, which should also include the elements of technology payments included in imports of machinery and equipment, intermediate goods imports, payments of fees and salaries to foreign personnel and the profits earned on the TNC investment (which in turn may be distorted because of the manipulation of transfer prices – see section 4.12).

As already noted in section 4.4, it is argued by many economists that the marginal cost to the TNC of using an already developed technology is zero.[14] From the point of view of the buyer (the LDC), however, the marginal cost of replicating that technology or developing an alternative technology may be huge. Vaitsos (1973) has argued that the process of technology commercialisation is best seen as a bargaining process in which the buyer of the technology (the LDC) is in a position of structural weakness *vis-à-vis* the seller of the technology (the TNC), because the item that the buyer needs to purchase (technology) is at the same time the information that is needed in order to make a rational decision to buy. It is also alleged that the patent system and the restrictive use of trademarks, brand names, etc., are also detrimental to the interests of the LDCs (for a discussion of trademarks in the

LDCs, see the special issue of *World Development*, vol. 7, no. 7, July 1979).

Keeping in mind the reservations noted above concerning the difficulty of actually measuring LDC payments for technology, some indication of the amounts involved can be given. It has been estimated (by UNCTAD, figures quoted in Stewart, 1977, ch. 5) that the direct costs to LDCs of technology transfer (in the form of patents, licences, trademarks, management and technical fees) were approximately $1.5 billion in 1968, which was the equivalent of 5 per cent of LDC-non-oil exports and about 0.5 per cent of their total GDP. Assuming a rate of growth of 20 per cent per annum, it was estimated that these payments would total $9 billion by 1980. The rate of growth predicted was perhaps an overestimate, but nevertheless it is clear that very large sums of money are involved in the transfer of technology to LDCs.

4.9   EMPLOYMENT CREATION BY TNCs

Estimates of the total numbers directly employed by TNCs globally range from 13 to 30 million. In the LDCs, TNCs employ between 2 and 4 million people, representing 0.3 per cent of total employment and 2 per cent of total industrial employment in the formal sector (figures quoted in UNIDO, 1981a, p. 238).

In some LDCs (such as Brazil, Mexico, Peru, the Republic of Korea and Singapore), TNC employment represents a relatively greater proportion of total industrial employment (perhaps as high as 20 per cent in some cases), with employment tending to be concentrated in the manufacturing sector. TNC employment is likely to be concentrated in those sectors where TNCs tend to predominate: in Mexico, for example, TNCs account for a high proportion of employment in chemicals, electrical machinery and transport equipment; in Korea, TNCs are significant employers in petroleum and electrical machinery (UNIDO, 1981a, Table V.I, p. 239).

Indirect employment may be created by TNCs via the development of backward and forward linkages within the host LDC economy (see section 4.7). Such indirect employment creation may be substantial in the manufacturing sector, but data are scarce. In the Republic of Korea, for example, it has been estimated that TNC investment has created 102,000 jobs through backward linkages with domestic producers (UNIDO, 1981a, p. 239). As was pointed out in section 4.7 however, the extent of linkage creation and its associated indirect employment effects will depend on a number of factors, and care should be exercised in generalising on the basis of the limited information available.

A further point relates to employment in the services sector of the LDC. Baer (1976) and Baer and Samuelson (1981) have highlighted the linkages between industrial modernisation and significant service sector employment, and have hypothesised that the proportion of service sector employment that represents disguised unemployment will fall over time. Baer has also maintained that the growth of capital-intensive, large-scale industrial units would be more likely to generate high rates of growth of service employment (repairs, marketing, finance, modern health and urban services) than would a labour-intensive industrial strategy (Baer, 1976, p. 130). Technology and employment policies are discussed in Chapter 6, section 6.7.

The strategy of industrialisation selected may affect the extent of TNC employment creation. Export-led industrialisation may well utilise relatively labour-intensive techniques and thus create more jobs than 'inward-looking' import-substituting industrialisation. However, it is also likely to be the case that export-oriented TNCs create fewer linkages with the host economy and thus indirect employment creation is likely to be limited.

4.10   TRANSNATIONAL INVESTMENT AND THE BALANCE OF PAYMENTS

This section discusses the overall impact of direct investment by the TNC on the host country's balance of payments, although it must be emphasised that it is difficult to quantify that impact with any degree of accuracy.

The initial act of direct investment will usually, but not always (see below), involve a capital inflow, which will appear as a credit item in the capital account of the balance of payments. Exports by the TNC will appear as a credit item in the current account. Offsetting these credit items, will be a number of debit items. The activities that the TNC engages in may be import intensive, that is, require the import of capital goods (machinery and equipment), and raw materials and intermediate goods. The TNC subsidiary is also likely to make a variety of payments to the parent company, including payments for technology (royalties, technical and managerial fees, etc.) and contributions to headquarters' overhead expenditure and research and development expenditure. In addition, if it is profitable, the TNC subsidiary will, of course, wish to remit all or part of its after-tax profits to the parent or some other part of the corporation.

The act of direct investment by the TNC is not always associated with a significant capital flow. Data from Latin America, for example, indicate that American TNCs financed over 80 per cent of their investments from local sources, either from the reinvestment of earnings or from local borrowing (or borrowing from third countries) (figures quoted in Colman and Nixson, 1978, ch. 9, section 9.4). For other areas of the less developed world, especially sub-Saharan Africa, the importance of domestic sources of finance is not likely to be so great, but the general point remains valid – that care must be taken when assessing the capital contribution of TNCs.

It is also relevant to note in this context that much TNC direct foreign investment involves the take-over of already existing, domestically owned enterprises (for an analysis of TNC take-overs in Brazil, and the perceived 'uneven' distribution of benefits, see Newfarmer, 1979a). Clearly, it is not uncommon for TNCs to use domestic financial resources to buy out local firms. It cannot be determined *a priori* whether or not TNCs will use such resources more efficiently than domestic firms (although there is a general presumption in the literature that they will in fact do so).[15] Nor is it known what the previous owners are likely to do with the proceeds from the sale of their enterprises, but clearly both these factors should, if possible, be taken into account in any analysis of the impact of TNCs on the host economy.

As noted above, TNC direct foreign investment is likely to be import intensive, although the extent of import intensity depends, in part at least, on the degree of linkage creation in the host economy (see section 4.7). In some cases, the local economy may not be capable of supplying the required inputs, in that it may not have the technical resources to produce the input at all or it may be unable to reach the technical or quality standards demanded by the TNC subsidiary. In other cases, tie-in clauses impose a legal obligation on the subsidiary to buy from the parent or some other part of the corporation. Such restrictions are commonplace (Long, 1981). Vaitsos (1974, ch. IV), when analysing technology commercialisation contracts for a number of Latin American economies (Bolivia, Ecuador and Peru), found that 67 per cent of the contracts with relevant information had tie-in clauses. In all the countries, the pharmaceutical industry usually had the highest percentage of tie-in arrangements (Vaitsos, 1974, p. 45). The extent of intra-firm trade clearly determines the scope for transfer price manipulation (see section 4.12 below).

Two important empirical studies found TNC investment to be in general highly import dependent. Lall and Streeten (1977, ch. 7) analysed a sample of 159 firms in six LDCs (Jamaica, India, Iran, Colombia, Malaysia and Kenya) and found that over half the sample firms (two-thirds, if India was excluded) imported goods worth over 30 per cent of their sales. It is of interest to note, however, that there were no significant differences between TNCs and non-TNCs in this respect; import dependence appeared to be determined by the characteristics of the industry, the nature of the host economy and government policies (Lall and Streeten, 1977, p. 145).

Reuber (1973, ch. 5) studied approximately eighty private foreign investment projects in LDCs. He found a significant degree of import dependence, especially in the case of import-substituting projects, where imports displaced by local production were more than offset by increases in imports of raw materials, components and complementary finished products.[16] The reasons given for the high import dependence support those already referred to above – locally produced goods either were not available or were of inferior quality and/or uncompetitively priced.

The balance between capital account inflows and current account outflows, both visible and invisible, will vary over time, both for individual TNC subsidiaries and with respect to the operations of all foreign direct investment located within a particular economy. Lall and Streeten's analysis concluded that the net impact of their sample firms' activities on the overall balance of payments was negative in five of the countries analysed (Jamaica, India, Iran, Colombia and Malaysia), but was positive in Kenya (attributed to the importance of exports by some of the sample firms to Uganda and Tanzania) (Lall and Streeten, 1977, ch. 7, p. 132). On the whole, the sample foreign firms seemed to be 'taking more out than they were putting in' (p. 142).

Much of this empirical evidence is consistent with the view that foreign capital 'decapitalises' the LDCs. In other words, by taking out more than they put in, TNCs reduce the potentially reinvestible surplus in LDCs. Econometric analysis (Bornschier, 1980) has suggested that the short-term association between TNC direct foreign investment and income growth is positive and that the long-term association between cumulated DFI and income growth is negative, that is, the repatriation of income by TNCs in the longer run reduces the rate of growth of the economies thus affected.

The case for 'decapitalisation' is by no means proven, however. Hood and Young (1979, ch. 5), after reviewing the available empirical evidence, remained agnostic as to the impact of manufacturing sector DFI on the balance of payments of the host economy. Vernon (1971, ch. 5) argued that the 'decapitalisation' thesis is based on highly simplistic assumptions and that, once it is recognised that the presence of a TNC subsidiary has an impact on every item in the balance of payments account, the overall effect of DFI on the balance of payments crucially depends on the assumptions we make concerning the import-substituting effect of DFI and the latter's overall impact on the industrialisation process in the LDC (Vernon, 1971, pp. 170–6).

It could be argued, however, that too much emphasis has been placed on this aspect of TNC direct foreign investment in the past, and that this has tended to obscure the wider impact of DFI on resource mobilisation and utilisation both within the economy as a whole and within the manufacturing sector in particular.

4.11   TNCs AND THE EXPORT OF MANUFACTURED GOODS

A relatively small number of LDCs (Hong Kong, Taiwan, Republic of Korea, Singapore, India, Brazil, Mexico, Argentina, Malaysia and Pakistan) account for a large proportion (over 80 per cent) of total exports of manufactured goods from LDCs. Not a great deal is known, however, about the role of TNCs in the export of manufactured goods from these LDCs. For the early 1970s, it has been estimated (Nayyar, 1978) that TNCs accounted for about 55 per cent of total LDC manufactured goods exports, and it was predicted that their share would rise.

Not surprisingly, there were significant inter-country variations. In Singapore, for example, it was estimated that TNCs accounted for nearly 70 per cent of manufactured exports. This was the exception, however; estimates for other LDCs were much lower: for example, Hong Kong, 10 per cent; India, 5 per cent; Brazil, 43 per cent; Pakistan, 5–10 per cent; Mexico, 25–30 per cent; Colombia, over 30 per cent; Taiwan, 20 per cent; Argentina, 30 per cent; Korea, 15 per cent (see Nayyar, 1978, Table 1, p. 62). In general, it appeared that TNCs in Latin America played a more important role in manufacturing for export than did TNCs in Asia, although it may well be the case that Nayyar's results underestimate the relative importance of TNC exports. Lall (1981b) quoted more recent estimates: South Korea – in 1974, TNC contribution to all exports was 28 per cent; Singapore – in 1975, 85 per cent of exports were accounted for by foreign majority-owned enterprises and another 7 per cent by foreign minority-owned enterprises; Brazil – in 1973, for 318 leading enterprises, which accounted for nearly two-thirds of total industrial exports, TNCs accounted for over one-half of the total; Mexico (data from Jenkins, 1979) – in 1974, foreign firms were responsible for 34 per cent of exports of manufactured goods.

For the sake of simplicity of analysis, TNC manufactured goods exports may be divided into three categories (Lall, 1978):

- *Capital-/technology-intensive goods*: included in this category are chemicals, iron and steel, light engineering goods and machinery and transport equipment. In some cases, the TNCs involved were initially import-substitutors and have gradually moved into the export market (Lall, 1978, quoted the example of the German automobile firm – Volkswagen – in Brazil).
- *Simple labour-intensive products*: these include clothing, toys, sports goods, wigs and plastic products, and a number of other non-traditional, light manufactured goods. The production of these goods is usually in the hands of indigenous entrepreneurs in such countries as Hong Kong, Taiwan and South Korea who sell to transnational buying groups, initially Japanese (the *zaibatsu*), but increasingly from the USA and UK (Hone, 1974). The technologies required in the production of these goods are standardized and accessible, but they are consumer goods designed for high-income markets where design, brand names and trademarks, and advertising are all important and where the buyer guarantees market access. Foreign participation is thus an important ingredient in the export success of these economies. (This point is emphasised in a study of manufactured goods exports from Colombia – see de la Torre, 1974.)
- *Labour-intensive component manufacture and assembly* (also referred to as 'footloose industries', 'export platforms' or 'worldwide sourcing'): the period since the late 1960s has seen the location and development in the LDCs of specialised, relatively labour-intensive activities or processes that are a part of vertically integrated manufacturing TNCs (Helleiner, 1973). TNCs identify specific, relatively labour-intensive activities within their overall manufacturing operations and transfer them to LDCs where the reduced costs of labour more than offset the transport costs incurred. This relocation of production and assembly has occurred on a large scale in electronics (semi-conductors, tuners, valves), automobile components, clothing, leather goods and, as an example of a service activity, data processing. Countries such as Hong Kong, Singpore, Taiwan, Mexico and parts of the Caribbean have been important locations for such activities and increasingly countries such as Thailand, Malaysia, the Philippines and Morocco are becoming of significance. If wage rates rise in one country, the TNC can move to a lower wage economy because of the footloose nature of the activity concerned.

The availability of large supplies of relatively cheap labour that can be easily trained to perform semi-skilled operations is an important factor in this process of relocation. Even though labour productivity may be lower in the LDCs than in the developed economies, productivity differentials do not offset the vast differentials in wages; in any case, empirical evidence increasingly suggests that, in many industries in a number of countries, productivity in the LDC may be equal to, or even higher than, productivity in the developed economy (examples are cited in Sharpston, 1975). However, in addition to cheap labour, such countries must offer the TNCs political stability and labour docility (strict control over trade unions, anti-strike legislation, etc.) (Nayyar, 1978, p. 77).

Government policy in both the developed and less developed economies is another factor that needs to be taken into account. The tariff provisions of the industrialised economies give preferential treatment to imports that incorporate domestically produced components; that is, the tariff is applied only to the value added in the assembly or manufacturing processes undertaken overseas. In the US tariff, items 807.00 and 806.30 provide for duty-free re-entry of components that do not alter their physical identity in the assembled article, and LDC exports to the USA under this provision have increased more rapidly than total manufactured exports. Other developed economies, for example the Netherlands and the Federal Republic of Germany, have similar provisions (Finger, 1975), as has the Lomé Convention between the European Economic Community and the ACP (African, Pacific and Caribbean) LDCs.

Government policy in the LDCs involves the granting of a variety of concessions to the TNCs, including tax holidays, subsidised credit and rents, direct and indirect export subsidies, freedom from import duties and exchange controls, etc. Such incentives and concessions are often very generous and are both a result of, and contribute to, the relatively weak bargaining position of the LDCs *vis-à-vis* the TNCs (for a case study of a processing industry in Kenya that emphasises the bargaining process, see Kaplinsky, 1979).

Export processing zones are of particular importance in an increasing number of LDCs. By 1980, there were fifty-three such zones employing almost 1 million persons (United Nations, 1983, p. 155), with the seven largest zones (in the Republic of Korea, Singapore, Mexico, Hong Kong, Malaysia, the Philippines and Brazil) accounting for almost three-quarters of that employment. The most important industries in these zones are those manufacturing electrical and electronic goods, textiles and wearing apparel, and TNCs are of particular significance in these industries. Export processing zones are often physically isolated from the surrounding economy, and the enclave-like nature of such developments has a more limited effect on the industrial environment of LDCs than other forms of TNC participation in their economies.

The final issue to be considered is the relative export performance of TNCs compared to their indigenously owned counterparts. The available empirical evidence suggests that TNCs do not, in general, export a greater proportion of their output than local firms. Lall and Streeten (1977, p. 135) concluded that 'transnationality does not appear to have been an important aid to exporting' and may even in certain cases inhibit exporting. Jenkins (1979) found that in Mexico, although TNC subsidiaries accounted for an important share of manufactured goods exports, their competitive advantages did not result in a better export performance than local firms. TNC exports had a larger import content and were likely to go to the regional market (and were more likely to be offset by imports from the region) than were the exports of local firms.

Cohen (1975) compared the export performance of foreign and local firms in Taiwan, Singapore and South Korea and concluded that foreign firms were more likely to export than local firms in South Korea, less likely in Singapore and tended to export about as much as local firms in Taiwan. Foreign firms had a greater propensity to import than local firms in South Korea, a lesser propensity to import in Taiwan and a similar propensity to import in Singapore (Cohen, 1975, p. 115). Jenkins (1979, p. 91) quoted a number of other studies that reached conflicting conclusions. It is clear that, as with so many other aspects of the operations of TNCs in LDCs, no clear-cut picture emerges and great caution must be exercised when generalisations are made. TNCs are important exporters from LDCs, their supply of inputs and technology and their market access do permit the establishment of export activities that would not otherwise be possible, but they do not, in general, significantly outperform local firms in all respects.

4.12   THE TNC AND TRANSFER PRICING

Transfer prices (sometimes referred to as accounting prices) are the prices that are charged on transactions that take place within the TNC. The prices that are charged on these intra-corporate transfers can clearly deviate from market prices (so-called 'arms-length' prices) because trade within the TNC may be transacted outside the sphere of market forces. Indeed, in many cases, a market price may not exist for the particular good or service (the TNC being the sole owner or producer of the good or service in question).

For a variety of reasons, the LDC government may wish to control the external transfer of funds by TNC subsidiaries located within its borders. The TNC, on the other hand, may wish to evade or avoid such restrictions and the parent can ensure transfer of funds out of a country by raising the price of the inputs that it sells to its subsidiary in that country and lowering the price of what it buys from its subsidiary. Such manipulation of transfer prices – that is, the deviation of transfer prices from arms-length prices – may have a number of objectives (Lall, 1973):

- the achievement of global profit maximisation, net of taxation, given the existence of international differentials in tax rates, import duties and export subsidies;
- the minimisation of exchange risks, or indeed of any other risks (the threat of nationalisation may lead a TNC to minimise its investment in a particular country);
- the avoidance of restrictions on profit repatriation and/or other income transfers;
- the avoidance of political and social pressures that might result if 'high' profits were declared by a TNC in a particular host economy – local workers might demand higher wages, governments might be tempted to increase taxes, local shareholders (if any) might demand higher dividends, etc.

The scope and effectiveness of transfer price manipulation by TNCs vary widely from industry to industry and from one firm to another. Three sets of factors account for this uneven incidence (Lall, 1979a):

(1) inter-industry variations in the trade component of TNC production;
(2) variations in the extent of intra-firm trade as a proportion of total trade by TNCs;
(3) variations in the possibilities for manipulating transfer prices.

Point 1 is self-explanatory. With respect to point 2, Lall (1979a, p. 62) argued that intra-firm trade was likely to be larger in those industries that are of a 'high' technology (including large R&D requirements, high level of skills, and firm-specific products, designs, etc.), have specific marketing requirements (for example, close co-ordination between production and selling) and where there is risk and uncertainty attached to open market transactions. Examples of such industries include office machines, plastics, computers, instruments and transport equipment. With respect to point 3, Lall (1979a, p. 63) argued that the more advanced and firm-specific was the level of technology embodied in a product, and the more discontinuous its supply, the greater was the scope for transfer pricing. Pharmaceuticals provide a major example of transfer price manipulation (see below).

The manipulation of transfer prices in a manner detrimental to the interests of host LDCs may be extremely difficult to identify and control. As noted above, a market price will not exist where the TNC is the sole owner or producer of a good or service, and the identification of the 'correct' transfer price will pose major problems (see Lall, 1979a, pp. 67–8). Product differentiation also complicates matters, and it is safe to assume that TNCs will not willingly co-operate in supplying information to LDC governments investigating their affairs. LDCs will probably not have the personnel with the abilities to deal with these problems, although this will change over time, given increased international co-operation in these matters and the provision of technical aid (from, for example, the UN Centre on Transnational Corporations).

Offsetting these problems to a certain extent is the fact, emphasised by Lall (1979a), that not all TNCs are able to practise massive transfer price manipulation. Presumably, those that possess this potential can be identified, and attention (and perhaps legislation) directed specifically at their activities. Other authors (for example, Reuber, 1973, ch. 5) have tried to argue that profit transfers via transfer price manipulation are not as important as has sometimes been suggested in the literature: for example, tax and customs authorities do provide some check on abuse, and affiliate management and local host-country partners may resist transfer price manipulation that is unfavourable to them.

The available empirical evidence does not lend support to Reuber's assertions. The pioneering work of Vaitsos in Latin America (Vaitsos, 1974, ch. 4) found massive over-pricing on products imported by TNC subsidiaries in the pharmaceutical industry in Colombia, Chile and Peru and in the electronics industry in Colombia and Ecuador. In the Colombian pharmaceutical industry, the weighted average over-pricing of products imported by TNC subsidiaries was 155 per cent (for local firms, the figure was 19 per cent). Put another way, of the effective returns of the pharmaceutical TNC subsidiaries, reported profits accounted for 3.4 per cent, royalties accounted for 14.0 per cent and over-pricing accounted for 82.6 per cent.[17]

Case studies by UNCTAD (1977), Braun (1983) on the Colombian pharmaceutical industry and Adikibi (1983) on the Nigerian automobile tyre industry confirmed the over-pricing of imported intermediate inputs by TNCs. Clearly this is a problem for all host nations, both developed and less developed. Its magnitude should not be underestimated but, on the other hand, it is something that host economies, both individually and in co-operation with one another, can attempt to do something about, and in the longer run it may well be a problem of declining importance.

4.13   THE PROFITABILITY OF TNCs IN LDCs

The allegation is often made in the literature on the impact of TNCs on the process of growth and development that TNC operations in LDCs are very (perhaps excessively) profitable, and that the repatriation of these profits by TNCs drains the LDCs of a large part of their potentially reinvestible surplus (see section 4.10 above).

Even if it were found to be the case that TNC subsidiaries in LDCs were highly profitable, either or both of the following explanations could be valid:

- high TNC subsidiary profitability might be the result of competent management, superior technology and the availability of inputs, both local and foreign, at low market prices; or
- high profitability could reflect the existence of high monopoly rents resulting from, for example, protection against foreign competition, practices that reduced domestic competition, and legal and other forms of protection against all competition (for example, patent laws) (Vaitsos, 1974, ch. 5).

In addition, the declared profits of TNCs in LDCs must be treated with great caution. The power of TNCs to manipulate transfer prices and the variety of channels that they have available to them through which they can remit funds from one country to another were noted in section 4.12 above. There are reasons for believing that TNCs under-declare their effective profitability in a number of LDCs, even when there are no limits on profit repatriation and even when the tax rates are lower than in the country to which profits are remitted.[18] Vaitsos (1974, p. 68) concluded that:

In the countries in which we undertook research [Colombia, Chile, Ecuador and Peru] all foreign subsidiaries in the samples studied under-declared, sometimes considerably, the effective profitability accruing to their parent firms from their operations in such countries. Reported profits by foreign subsidiaries in Latin America are quite often much lower than those appearing in the rest of the world for affiliates of the same parents or lower than average profitability of local firms in comparable industrial activities in the host countries.

Furthermore, note must be taken of the possibility that the goal of the TNC subsidiary is not necessarily one of profit maximisation (see section 4.3 above). Apparently 'unprofitable' subsidiaries may, in fact, be highly profitable for the TNC as a whole, and, to complicate matters even further, subsidiary objectives may well change over time. Data for a single year, or a limited number of years, may thus not capture the full complexity of the possibly changing relationships between the parent and any or all of its subsidiaries.

The study of Lall and Streeten (1977; Lall, 1976a) examined the profitability of fifty-three manufacturing firms in India and fifty-six in Colombia, both foreign and locally owned. It was found that profitability was not greatly influenced by the origin of control or transnationality of the investment (Lall and Streeten, 1977, p. 122). Variations in profitability between different firms would result from a variety of factors – monopoly power, protection, managerial efficiency, financing patterns, age of enterprise – which in some cases would be associated with transnationality (monopoly power and efficiency, for example), but transnationality on its own would not be sufficient to exclude the influence of these other factors.

A study of 254 manufacturing corporations in the Philippines, 88 of which were foreign owned (Yoshihara, 1971), found the following median rates of return (ratio of net income to net worth) for 1968 for four different ownership categories:[19]

Foreign subsidiary (the TNC)	21.5%
Foreign non-subsidiary (a corporation controlled by foreigners whose primary business is in the Philippines)	15.3%
Domestic Filipino	7.5%
Chinese–Filipino	8.9%

The calculation of the median rate of return to paid-in capital further emphasised the difference between foreign and domestic enterprises, raising the rate of return to TNC subsidiaries to nearly 33 per cent and that of Filipino enterprises to only 8.7 per cent. Whether these can be considered to be 'fair' or 'acceptable' rates of return must be open to debate, but clearly the figures for domestic enterprises appear to be on the low side. Two factors were advanced to account for this: the Filipino corporation was not a purely economic institution whose only aim was to maximise the rate of return; and there was significant under-reporting of earnings (Yoshihara, 1971, p. 282).

The final study considered is that of Reuber (1973, ch. 4), who found that planned rates of return partly depended on the type of investment that the TNC was considering. Export-oriented investment in LDCs had a planned minimum rate of return of 20 per cent per annum with a short planning horizon (on average seven years). Market-development DFI, on the other hand, had planned rates of return of 14 per cent per annum and a longer planning horizon (eleven–twelve years on average).

Given that these figures are likely to represent *minimum* acceptable rates of return, it is clear that TNCs expect to recover the capital that they invest in LDCs relatively quickly. Lall (1978) was rather more agnostic in his conclusions concerning TNC profitability in LDCs. He accepted that TNCs were 'fairly profitable' in LDCs and on average performed better than local firms, but he argued that this superior profit performance might reflect not greater efficiency but rather the fact that TNCs were concentrated in more profitable industries, resulting from high barriers to entry, greater risks, etc. (Lall, 1978, p. 233; see also Connor and Mueller, 1982). However, TNC entry itself may well change market structures (see section 4.6) and thus the profitability of different industries (see Chapter 3 section 3.4).

Other things being equal, the expectation is that TNC activities in LDCs are more profitable than those of local enterprises and that TNC behaviour is dominated by the anticipation of profit (section 4.3). Reuber (1973, ch. 4) argued that 'profitability is a fundamental determinant of investment' (p. 109) and that 'there is little doubt that prospective profit over the life of investments has a basic influence on the level of investment' (p. 133). Clearly this is yet another area where further research is required before generalisations can be made with any degree of confidence.

4.14   TNCs FROM LDCs

A phenomenon that dates largely, although not exclusively, from the late 1960s, is the emergence of TNCs based in a selected number of LDCs. Enterprises from Hong Kong, Singapore, South Korea, India, Brazil, Mexico and Argentina are not large compared to TNCs from the developed industrialised economies, but they are nevertheless becoming increasingly significant in the manufacturing (and to a lesser extent, service) sectors of a number of LDCs. Indian firms are to be found in Sri Lanka, Iran, Kenya and Nigeria in engineering products, textiles and garments, food processing, and chemicals and petrochemicals. Indian non-manufacturing sector investment – hotels, construction, consultancies – is also growing elsewhere. Hong Kong enterprises have important investments in Indonesia, Malaysia and Singapore and are apparently about to enter the EEC (Lall, 1982, p. 133). Argentinian enterprises began production in Uruguay, Brazil and Chile in the late 1920s (Diaz-Alejandro, 1977). Thailand, as a 'host' nation to TNCs from LDCs, has enterprises from Hong Kong, India, Taiwan, Singapore and Malaysia located within its borders (Wells, 1977; Lecraw, 1977).

What 'firm-specific' advantages do such enterprises possess that enable them to go 'transnational'? Lall (1982) has suggested that TNCs from LDCs have tended to specialise in labour-intensive, standardised technologies, usually adapted and scaled down to local conditions. In Thailand, for example, Lecraw (1977) found that LDC TNCs were significantly less capital intensive than either other foreign or local firms. In addition, it appears that

TNCs from LDCs are able to reduce the costs of management and engineering personnel (Wells 1977, p. 141). TNCs from LDCs do not, in general, possess advantages with respect to the ability to differentiate products, but they may well possess other marketing skills – for example, the ability of firms from Hong Kong and Singapore to keep abreast of fashion, to package their products attractively, to maintain quality and to sell to high-income, sophisticated markets (Lall, 1982, p. 130).

Lall (1982) looked in detail at the emergence of TNCs from India. He noted that the two largest industrial groups in the country – Birla and Tata – accounted for nearly 50 per cent of total Indian foreign equity, and that all the major foreign investors were large, diversified and long-established business houses, with substantial industrial experience, and, in addition, were important exporters of manufactured goods. Their managerial, technical and financial resources were considerable and, although they were not major innovators, they nevertheless had foreign investments that were large and technologically advanced, often using capital-intensive technologies and producing sophisticated products, backed by extensive advertising and after-sales service (Lall, 1982, p. 139).

A feature of Indian DFI is that it uses intensively Indian plant, equipment and components, reflecting India's comparative advantage in the manufacture of a range of capital and intermediate goods and the Indian firms' experience in setting up projects and operating the technologies (Lall, 1982, p. 140). This, in turn, is related to India's policy with regard to technological development. India has attempted to achieve a degree of technological self-reliance not found in many other LDCs and, as Lall (1982, p. 143) noted:

> While this has resulted in various inefficiencies and technological lags, it has also enabled its national enterprises to build up a very broad base of technological competence. They have acquired the 'know-why' (i.e. basic design capabilities) of many industries rather than simply the 'know-how' (production technology). . . . The success of many Indian enterprises . . . leads us to believe that there is a strong case to be made for the protection of 'infant technological learning' rather than only the classic protection of 'infant industry' (where production know-how is mastered).

The important questions of technological development in the LDCs and appropriate government policies are discussed in Chapter 6, section 6.7. However, the emergence of TNCs from LDCs – a 'dynamic and complex phenomenon' (Lall, 1982, p. 144) – raises a larger number of important questions that cannot at present be satisfactorily answered. Do the 'home' countries benefit from the development of their 'own' transnationals? Do 'host' countries obtain greater economic benefits from LDC TNCs than from developed economy TNCs (as Lecraw, 1977, seems to suggest)? What are the implications of these developments for the alleged technological dependency of the LDCs? What are the political implications of such developments? These are just some of the questions that will have to be investigated in the future before a more complete understanding of TNCs from LDCs will become possible.

4.15   THE TNC: CONCLUSIONS

In this concluding section, reference is made to a number of issues not touched on above and an attempt will be made to pull some of the strands of the discussion together. The policy issues that arise from an examination of the impact of TNCs on LDCs – especially policies with respect to indigenous technological development and employment creation and more general policies towards the TNCs themselves (codes of conduct) – are dealt with in Chapter 6, sections 6.5 and 6.7.

In Chapter 3, section 3.2, the question of entrepreneurship in LDCs was raised. Are transnational activities within an LDC likely to encourage or retard the emergence of a local entrepreneurial class? On the one hand, there are those who argue that the domination of an LDC by TNCs prevents the emergence of an entrepreneurial class, or destroys such a class where it already exists (referred to as 'denationalisation' – see section 4.19 below). Latin America is often quoted as an area where the combined power of the TNCs and public enterprises, which dominate the 'commanding heights' of Latin American economies, leaves only limited opportunities open to private entrepreneurship. Others argue, however, that there is a 'spin-off' effect from TNC involvement in the local economy. TNCs train local personnel who may well establish their own enterprises (often as suppliers of inputs to TNCs) on the basis of the knowledge and experience gained by employment in the TNCs. TNC technologies may become anchored and diffused throughout the LDC economy, encouraging adaptation and further development by local entrepreneurs. The public sector, too, both on its own and in conjunction with TNCs, may become a powerful entrepreneurial force. These issues are discussed at greater length in Colman and Nixson (1978, ch. 9, section 9.6).

Profound economic and political issues are raised by the large-scale presence of TNCs in LDCs. Hood and Young (1979, ch. 5) referred to these as the 'sovereignty and autonomy' effects of TNC involvement, and economic development specialists usually discuss them within the context of various theories of 'dependency' (Colman and Nixson, 1978, ch. 2, part C). On the one side there are those who see the TNC as making possible the most efficient use of global resources and its presence within LDCs as a vital force for growth and development. On the other side, there are those who view the operations of the TNC as the most important aspect of the imperialist penetration of the LDCs by the developed capitalist economies. Clearly, the assessment that is made of the impact of the TNC on the process of growth and development in the LDC will, to a great extent, depend on which of these opposed theoretical (and ideological) positions is adopted, either whole or in part, implicitly or explicitly.

What is less widely recognised in the literature on the TNC and economic development is that the pattern or type of economic development that emerges as a result of the presence of TNCs is in large part a consequence of the various and complex relationships between foreign interests on the one hand and domestic groups or classes and the host-country government on the other hand (Kirkpatrick and Nixson, 1981). For example TNCs may well benefit from an unequal distribution of income in an LDC, but they are not, in general, the *cause* of that unequal distribution; TNCs may concentrate in the major urban centres and exacerbate regional and rural–urban inequalities, but again they are not, in general, the cause of those inequalities. The causes of such inequalities must be looked for in the totality of relationships in the LDC which determine the nature and characteristics of the development process.

Clearly the interests of the TNC and particular host-country governments often conflict – obvious examples are the repatriation of profits and other income, import and export propensities, employment creation and choice of technology (see Chapter 6, section 6.5) – but it is not a simple and straightforward conflict between the TNC on the one hand and the host government as defender of the 'national interest' on the other hand. The TNC interacts with local capital and the various institutions of the state in a variety of ways, each group or class depending on the others to maintain and strengthen its own position (see section 4.19 below). Such relationships clearly require detailed investigation for a fuller understanding and appreciation of the impact of TNCs on economic development to be obtained, and such investigations in political economy must be high on future research agendas.

4.16   THE INDIGENOUS ENTERPRISE: ENTREPRENEURSHIP AND MANAGEMENT

INTRODUCTION

Indigenous (or domestic) enterprises are defined as enterprises that are owned or controlled by the nationals of the LDC in which they have their origins. They vary in size, ranging from the thousands of small-scale enterprises that constitute the informal sector of the urban areas (Chapter 3, section 3.2) to very large manufacturing, financial and commercial conglomerates, such as those of Tata and Birla in India. They exhibit a variety of ownership and organisational characteristics – one-man businesses, partnerships, family enterprises, managing agencies (unique to India), joint stock companies – and many have varying associations with both foreign and public capital (various forms of joint venture arrangements). In many countries (the example of Ghana is quoted in section 4.8 above), the firm may be resident in (that is, incorporated in) the LDC but be owned by non-citizens (the resident expatriate firm).

Much has been written about the problem of entrepreneurship in LDCs (see Chapter 3, section 3.2) but, with some notable exceptions, there are comparatively few studies of indigenous enterprises. Relatively little is known about their objectives, their decision-making structures and criteria, and their performance. Although there is controversy over the relative importance of foreign and indigenous capital in the development process, only a limited number of studies exist that analyse in detail the interrelationships between local and foreign capital and examine the ability of local capital to benefit from its association with foreign capital.

In the following sections, the attempt is made to throw light on some of these issues. The remainder of this section considers the emergence and development of industrial entrepreneurship and management in LDCs and discusses the problems that it faces. The discussion of small-scale industrial enterprise development in section 4.17 overlaps with that of entrepreneurship but raises a number of new problems. The question of finance for industrial development is of sufficient importance to be treated separately in section 4.18. In the final section (4.19), the attempt is made to draw some of the strands of the discussion together in considering, in broad outline, the complex interrelationships that exist between domestic capital, foreign capital and the state in LDCs.

ENTREPRENEURSHIP IN AN AFRICAN SETTING

Nigeria
The role of entrepreneurship in the economic development of LDCs has already been considered in general terms in Chapter 3, section 3.2. According to Kilby (1971, p. 29), the empirical evidence suggests that businessmen in LDCs are responsive to economic opportunities, are willing to risk their own capital in long-term ventures, are adept at marketing and, with some exceptions, maintain good relations with their staff, suppliers and the public bureaucracy. Entrepreneurial performance is least satisfactory in the areas of technology and production management, identified by many writers (for example, Kilby, 1971, p. 30) as the major constraint on indigenous industrial development.

Some writers (for example, Schatz, 1963) have adopted the view that there are few problems with entrepreneurial supply and that the difficulties reside mainly in market conditions external to the firm – lack of competitive pressures, inexperience, the scarcity of market supplied skill inputs. Others, including Kilby, take the view that these shortcomings derive from sociological variables on the supply side. The 'attitudes and behavioural characteristics' of Nigerian entrepreneurs that, according to Kilby (1969, 1971), are rooted in socio-cultural factors and that constrain indigenous industrial development include:

- unwillingness to provide continuous supervision of business operations;
- general lack of interest in productive efficiency and the possibility for improving quality;
- failure to maintain equipment regularly;
- disinclination to utilise written records for purposes of control;
- slowness of reaction when operations come up against problems;
- limited propensity to undertake innovations;
- the propensity of better-educated entrepreneurs to launch second or third business ventures, a dissipation of effect that results in lower levels of efficiency (Kilby, 1969, p. 338).

In his study of the Nigerian bakery industry, Kilby (1965) observed good entrepreneurial responses to perceived opportunities, but poor management and organisation meant that three-quarters of potential profit was lost owing to raw material wastage, the damaging of bread during baking and extensive employee pilferage.

A study of the Nigerian saw-milling industry (Harris and Rowe, 1966) also identified serious defects in technical and managerial competence. The low level of capacity utilisation observed was largely due to managerial deficiencies, especially the inability to delegate authority effectively and the limited efforts made to train managers and supervisors. Other problems identified included:

- the low general standard of financial management and control, in particular the misunderstanding of depreciation and break-even points, which contributed heavily to business failure;
- unwise employment practices;
- poor organisation and layout of the saw-milling yard.

As noted above, Schatz (1963) once held the view that it was the adverse environment that was the prime obstacle to indigenous entrepreneurial development. He has since modified that view and has more recently argued (Schatz, 1972b, 1977) that economic environment constitutes a major, but not the sole, barrier. He nevertheless maintained that special difficulties are encountered by an indigenous businessman in an economy such as Nigeria's, including, *inter alia*:

- the 'alien' economic and social network (see below also);
- 'probabilistic discrimination' against the African entrepreneur (foreign firms are unable to distinguish between inefficient and dishonest indigenous businessmen and those that run their business capably and carefully);
- severe indigenous competition (excessive entry puts pressure on all businessmen in the industry and competition becomes 'pathological' – Schatz, 1972b, p. 34);
- difficulties in acquiring capital goods, raw material supplies, ancillary equipment, spare parts, etc., and the high cost of installation, maintenance, etc.;
- problems regarding the availability of human resources;
- the attitudes of government personnel, which are often 'inaccommodating or impeditive';
- infrastructural deficiences;
- underdeveloped marketing networks impeding the expansion of indigenous firms.

Schatz (1972b, pp. 52–3) concluded by questioning the legitimacy of conceiving of the economic environment and entrepreneurship as being separate and distinct and he was also critical of analyses (for example, that of Harris, 1972) that see the problems purely in terms of supply and demand schedules (as outlined in Chapter 3, section 3.2 above). Supply and demand are not independent of one another and both are, at least in part, determined by the economic environment (Schatz, 1972b, p. 54).

Kenya

Entrepreneurship and economic development have also been studied intensively from a variety of theoretical perspectives in Kenya.

A major study of African businessmen in Kenya (Marris and Somerset, 1971; Marris, 1971) gathered information from eighty-seven African businesses that had received loans from the Kenyan Industrial and Commercial Development Corporation, together with information from a variety of other sources, including a survey of market centres in ten regions of Kenya.

The African businessman was typically 'intelligent, experienced and ambitious' but frustrated because of his awareness of the 'backwardness of his people', the exploitation by foreigners of opportunities that should be open to him and personal failings largely related to lack of schooling (Marris and Somerset, 1971, p. 225). The African business organisation emulated the European 'model' ('impersonal, contractual and governed by principles of rational efficiency' – p. 226) and the attempt was made to segregate business interests from family and social relationships and responsibilities. For example, nearly 50 per cent of those interviewed preferred to employ outsiders rather than have relations as employees or business associates, and family enterprises were generally avoided to minimise jealousy, insubordination, resentment of authority and difficulties with respect to the application of sanctions.[20]

A number of management problems were identified by the study. The businessmen interviewed felt unable to trust their employees and thus had to adopt a style of management that relied on close personal supervision and immediate sanctions against default. The manager thus became 'lonely, insecure and suspicious, unable to delegate responsibility' (Marris, 1971, p. 242); this in turn placed restrictions on the capacity of the enterprise for growth. Other problems included a perceived lack of access to capital, vulnerability to larger competitors and, above all else, 'the disparity between the scale of the economy in which they compete, and the range of relationships they know how to handle' (Marris, 1971, p. 242). The economic and social worlds of the African businessman did not 'fit':

They lack the personal contacts, the fluency of communication, the familiarity, assurance and conventional respectability to make their way easily in the commercial culture which dominates them. At the same time they have to compete in this system on its own terms, and as they assimilate its values their manner of business becomes estranged from the expectations of their family and friends. As they differentiate economic affairs from kinship and community, they are forced to segregate business explicitly from social relationships. They lack the freemasonry of commerce, the clubs, golf courses, convenient marriages which facilitate business dealings amongst their European or Asian counterparts. They assimilate the principles of businesslike efficiency so whole-heartedly that these principles become a wall which imprisons as well as protects. They are doubly isolated: the social world to which they belong does not fully understand or accept their conception of business, while the commercial world in which they operate excludes them socially. (Marris, 1971, p. 243.)

Two points can perhaps be made at this stage before the discussion of entrepreneurship is broadened and extended:

(1)　The various studies discussed above are curiously static (and they are also now somewhat dated). They identify a number of constraints on indigenous entrepreneurial development, they often make recommendations with respect to the policies that should be followed to encourage such development, but they do not get to grips with the dynamics of indigenous entrepreneurial development as such. This static quality is partly the result of:

(2)　the failure to analyse entrepreneurial development within its wider historical, economic and political setting. As noted already, Schatz in particular has emphasised 'environmental factors' as being an important constraint on indigenous entrepreneurial development, but his environmental factors are a rather random collection (in many cases, they will constrain entrepreneurial activity irrespective of its national or ethnic origin) and they do not appear to be derived from a coherent theoretical framework within which the analysis of the development process is located.

Such an approach was attempted by Swainson (1980) in her study of capitalist development in Kenya in the colonial and post-colonial period. Her research is an important contribution to the wider debate relating to the nature and characteristics of the development process in Kenya (for a summary of the debate see Godfrey, 1982), but, from the point of view of this discussion, it is her work on the emergence of an indigenous entrepreneurial class that is of relevance.

Swainson examined the origins of an African trading class in the 1940s and 1950s and noted that, even before political independence was gained in 1963, the larger African traders were beginning to move into small-scale manufacturing (saw mills, bakeries, motor mechanics). In the 1950s, foreign capital was active in encouraging the creation of an African trading class (for example, in the wholesaling and retailing of tobacco and cigarettes), but in the post-independence period it has been the state that has acted on behalf of the indigenous capitalist class, providing it with the advantages denied to it during the colonial period.

Swainson's central thesis was that the emerging African entrepreneurial class (bourgeoisie) is not subservient to or dependent on foreign capital, but is in fact consolidating its position both politically and economically and is capable of challenging foreign capital. As evidence to support this view she referred to: legislation that has enabled African traders to gain footholds in the commercial sector (including the procurement of businesses from both non-citizen and citizen Asians); the significant extension of credit facilities to African enterprises (the most powerful elements of which have been able to capture the largest proportion of state finance); the expansion in the number of African joint stock companies and the movement of African enterprises into the manufacturing sector since the mid-1970s; moves by the state to Africanise positions within TNC subsidiaries located in Kenya and to localise the ownership of these companies; the marked pattern of African managers using TNC subsidies to acquire their own capital for investment; the large numbers of Kenyan directors who have developed their own enterprises at the same time as holding down professional or executive occupations; the state control of certain productive sectors (for example, oil refining, power supply) and the state regulation of DFI in Kenya.

Swainson emphasised the high degree of interlinkage between foreign and domestic capital in Kenya and between positions within the state bureaucracy and private enterprise. A number of Kenyan capitalists have, however, developed independently of foreign capital and have developed links with foreign capital only once it was advantageous for them to do so.

Swainson concluded her analysis thus:

Two parallel and contradicting tendencies have been exhibited in post-colonial Kenya: the development of a domestic bourgeoisie and a rapid internationalisation of the global economy. In comparison with large multinational firms in Kenya, indigenous capital is small and insignificant. Nevertheless at the *present stage* of accumulation in Kenya it is still the case that value formation is *nationally* based and the state is able to support the interests of the internal bourgeoisie. During the independence period, within the limits set by Kenya's position in the global economy, the indigenous bourgeoisie have extended their control over the means of production. (Swainson, 1980, pp. 289–90.)[21]

OTHER STUDIES OF ENTREPRENEURSHIP

The extended family or extended kinship system remains an important form of social economic organisation in many LDCs, and a number of studies of entrepreneurship and industrial development have focused attention on the family firm or family-dominated enterprise (Khalaf and Shwayri, 1966; Nafziger, 1971; Papanek, 1971a; White, 1974a). Many economists have seen the family firm as being inimical to modern economic growth and industrialisation. The owner/managers of such firms, it has been argued, are prone to nepotism and paternalism, resistant to change and unable to delegate authority.

The Lebanon
This view was challenged in an early study of family firms in the Lebanon (Khalaf and Shwayri, 1966). In a detailed study of ten large family firms, Khalaf and Shwayri found that although the atmosphere in such firms was conducive to nepotism no evidence could in fact be found to support the charge. There was evidence of centralisation of authority and only limited delegation of responsibility, but these were not characteristics unique to the family firm and they did not appear to inhibit enterprise growth. Paternalism,

a legacy of feudal society, was much in evidence, but the authors argued (1966, p. 67) that even though

> the enterprises are still predominantly family-owned and family members may still hold the key positions ... they are subject, by and large, to rational and meritorious principles of control. Performance is slowly becoming the prevailing criterion for reward and promotion. Authority is no longer exclusively associated with property rights or ownership.

At a more general level, it was concluded that some traditional norms and practices need not retard industrial growth and that the socio-cultural environment in the Lebanon was in fact receptive to the changes or requirements of industrialisation. The fact that the owner/managers of the family firms studied seemed to be inconsistent in their attitudes and characteristics – an apparent receptivity to adaptive innovation combined with a conception of managerial functions that was authoritative and conservative in character – was merely a reflection of the transitional stage of industrialisation in the Lebanon.

Pakistan

Studies of industrial entrepreneurship in Pakistan (for example, White, 1974a) have tended to emphasise the family-firm dominated and highly concentrated nature of the industrial sector (see Chapter 3, section 3.2). White emphasised that the leading industrial families were not merely passive recipients of the benefits of government policies but were active in actually formulating and implementing those policies. Family members were often government ministers, ambassadors, members of special committees, etc., with the ability to exert direct influence on the administration of policy and the political power to offset or forestall government actions that would limit their economic power. He concluded (1974a, p. 297):

> ... the leading industrial families were actively involved and influential in the political and administrative processes that directly affected their industrial interests. From their economic power base, they were able to attain positions and influence which served to maintain and expand that base.

Papanek (1971a), too, referred to this aspect, but was more concerned with the background from which Pakistan's industrial entrepreneurs emerged. They came largely from the merchant capitalist class, with little formal education or sophisticated technical knowledge but with the ability to organise capital and obtain government permits. Specialised technical and managerial personnel were hired as necessary. The Pakistani industrial entrepreneur was thus a 'promoter' (Papanek, 1971a, p. 243) whose background in international trade and access to capital accumulated from trading profits, combined with close contacts in government and the wider business community, both encouraged and permitted him to take risks and move into new, more technologically advanced industrial ventures.

It is of interest to note that those entrepreneurs whose background was in small-scale industry and handicrafts and in retail trade were not as successful during post-independence industrialisation as the ex-traders. They lacked access to capital, technology and necessary contacts, and Papanek suggested that other LDCs, similar to Pakistan and wishing to encourage indigenous industrial enterprises, would be best advised to encourage and assist their large-scale traders to enter industry directly, rather than rely on the promotion of small-scale handicraft activities or the indigenisation of the modern manufacturing sector.

In the 1960s, the situation in Pakistan had begun to change. New industries were becoming more complex and required more advanced technical and managerial skills. The formal education of the descendants of the original industrial entrepreneurs was becoming of greater importance, with technically qualified family members being increasingly substituted for foreign personnel. Papanek recognised that these developments could lead to nepotism and inefficiency within the family firms but that competitive pressures could offset these adverse consequences.

India

India was one of the few countries in the developing world that had, at the time of political independence, a significant indigenous industrial entrepreneurial class. In 1914, European managing agencies had dominated the private corporate sector, but by the end of World War II (1945) this domination had been broken and Indian entrepreneurs were in a position to take over the businesses of departing aliens (Ray, 1979, p. 1).

The managing agency system has been the basic entrepreneurial unit in India (Nafziger, 1971, p. 309). The system originated in the first half of the nineteenth century (and was in theory legislated out of existence in the early 1960s) and, in the case of Indian managing agencies, was usually an extension of relationships in older family firms. The managing agency created a system within which the administration, finance and promotion of one or more legally separate companies was controlled by a single firm (Nafziger, 1971). The advantages claimed for the system related to the economies of large-scale organisation – economies in production, management, marketing, financial services, etc. The disadvantages of the system were that it not only increased the concentration of economic power both within and across industries (Nafziger, 1971, p. 310) but also placed control increasingly in the hands of financiers; thus financial manipulation rather than production performance became the dominant characteristic of the system (Byres, 1982). Byres quoted evidence that seems to suggest a decline in the share of reinvestible profits in output, a redistribution of income in favour of property and asset holders, and a tendency for members of higher-income groups to indulge increasingly in conspicuous consumption and/or non-productive investment (Byres, 1982, p. 155).

The Indian industrial sector is perhaps best known for its huge 'houses', variously referred to as financial groups (Bettelheim, 1968, pp. 68–70), investment companies or holding companies (Itō, 1978), of which Tata and Birla are the largest. The Tatas emerged in the industrial field in the late nineteenth century in cotton manufacturing. By 1914, Tata interests included trade, hotels, cotton manufacture, iron and steel, and hydroelectricity (Ray, 1979, p. 276). Tata suffered some setbacks during the inter-war slump, but by the end of World War II the group had diversified into chemicals, steel tubes, machine tools and locomotives. The Birla Group started off in trade and broke into the jute market after World War I. It subsequently diversified into cotton textiles, sugar, paper, newspaper publishing and insurance. Further expansion after World War II included the manufacture of textile machinery, automobiles, bicycles, ball-bearings, rayon, plastics, and take-overs of tea and coal interests, entry into aviation and banking and the flotation of investment and trading companies on a large scale (Ray, 1979, pp. 278–9).

The monopolistic structure of Indian industry and the potential and actual power wielded by the giant houses have been causes for concern in India (see Byres, 1982, p. 156). Some Indian economists have even gone so far as to argue that the very existence of monopoly capital is an obstacle to successful, private sector industrialisation in India. Chandra (1979, p. 1270), for example, argued that:

> ... monopolists in India have generally been able to retain or expand their market-power not so much by superior economic efficiency, but by controlling the supply of raw materials and intermediates through their intimate links with the State machinery at various levels, restrictive selling practices designed to shut out smaller firms, and an easy access to cheap institutional finance. On the other hand such credits, despite the nationalisation of banking and insurance, are effectively denied to the vast majority of small capitalists who have to fall back either on their own limited resources or on usurious money-lenders.

The question of the interrelationships between the state and private capital is discussed in section 4.19 below.

INDUSTRIAL ENTREPRENEURSHIP AND MANAGEMENT IN LDCs: SOME TENTATIVE CONCLUSIONS

A number of important points emerge from the survey of the growth and development of the industrial entrepreneur in LDCs.

(1) There appears to be an abundance of entrepreneurial spirits in all the LDCs studied. Indigenous businessmen are quick to perceive profitable opportunities and energetic in gaining command over the resources that will permit the exploitation of those opportunities. Pecuniary reasons generally underlie entrepreneurial activity, a general drive for wealth and status being especially noticeable in Nigeria. Considerations of economic nationalism are also of importance in certain countries at certain times (for example, India in the inter-war period).

(2) There is general agreement by outside observers that a shortage of capital is not a major problem, even though it is perceived to be so by indigenous businessmen themselves (see Akeredolu-Ale, 1972). Enterprises can be established with relatively limited capital and can expand rapidly through the reinvestment of profit. However, access to working capital

appears to be a problem for many smaller enterprises, especially in the early stages of their development.

(3)   Levels of efficiency in many enterprises appear to be very low, and a number of important managerial and technical deficiencies are highlighted, especially in the African studies – inability to delegate, low general levels of financial management and control, lack of attention to accounting and record keeping, the premature diversification of business interests, etc. With respect to Nigeria, Schatz (1977) argued that Nigerian entrepreneurial deficiencies were real enough but that their importance tended to be exaggerated. Kilby (1969, p. 338) concluded that

> . . . Nigerian businessmen are typically unaware that their managerial performance is any way wanting; they impute full responsibility for their difficulties to external factors over which they have no control, and they see their principal problem as lack of capital.

Page's (1980) study of the logging, saw-milling and furniture manufacturing sector in Ghana used a more formal, econometric approach to determine both levels of efficiency and variations in efficiency between different sectors. He found significant inter- and intra-industry differences in efficiency levels, and explained these results by reference to the quality and quantity of managerial inputs available to the firms. Low levels of education and experience on the part of management were reflected in lower levels of technical efficiency, but the nationality of management appeared as a significant explanatory variable in the regression analysis: higher proportions of expatriates in management increased the level of technical efficiency, which was also inversely related to the number of production workers per supervisor. Page (1980, pp. 335, 338) concluded:

> . . . variations in managerial effort and ability are significant factors in explaining a firm's position relative to the industry production frontier [the measure of technical efficiency] . . . efforts to increase the level of education of managers with regard to technical aspects of the production process, more intensive supervision of labor, and policies designed to increase the utilisation of installed capacity should yield benefits in terms of improved performance and reduced social costs.

(4)   Entrepreneurial performance is the result of the interaction between internal and external factors – entrepreneurial deficiencies on the one hand and an 'alien' or unhelpful environment on the other. It should be remembered, however, that both sets of factors are subject to rapid change, and that the gap between the actual and the potential effectiveness of indigenous entrepreneurs is likely to be closing over time. Both historical and structural factors are relevant to the analysis of the development of industrial entrepreneurship in LDCs.

(5)   In a number of countries (India, Pakistan, Nigeria, Kenya) the more successful, larger industrial entrepreneurs appear to have a background in trade (Harris, 1971; Papanek, 1971a; Sharma, 1973) rather than in

small-scale handicrafts and other manufacturing activities. It is perhaps because of this background that there is little evidence of innovation amongst industrial entrepreneurs in LDCs (but see Evans, 1976, on Brazil, and Fairchild, 1977, on Mexico, where contrary evidence is presented). Harris (1971) noted the imitation and adaptation of both processes and products and pointed to rapid responses to changing opportunities. However, in industries in which skill plays an important role (metal, wood, rubber and leather products, light engineering) the proportion of craftsmen who have founded small enterprises is larger than in industries in which organisational marketing or financial skills are of greater importance (Hoselitz, 1959, p. 209).

(6) Some of the limited evidence available (for Kenya, for example) suggests that indigenous businessmen are anxious to adopt the capitalist enterprise model. Evidence for the Philippines, however, does not support this view: Yoshihara (1971) argued that the low rate of return noted for Filipino enterprises resulted from unnecessary expenditure often lavished on family members occupying high positions in the corporations (foreign travel, expense accounts for automobiles, food, nightclubs, expenses for prestige items – helicopters, aeroplanes, large salaries for wives and other family members) and the under-reporting of earnings, which apparently is widespread. The ethic of hard work, frugal living and accumulation may not yet have implanted itself in all the emerging capitalist economies of the Third World!

(7) In virtually all LDCs, the role that the state plays has a very strong influence on entrepreneurial activity. It is the state that, in part at least, creates the economic and political environment within which indigenous enterprises develop, it is the state that provides many of the key inputs (for example, credit) that indigenous entrepreneurs most need and, last but not least, it is the state that determines the role of foreign capital in the economy (a topic that is considered in more detail in section 4.19 below). No study of indigenous entrepreneurial development is thus complete without a full consideration of the role of the state in that process.

4.17   THE DEVELOPMENT OF SMALL-SCALE ENTERPRISES[22]

The discussion of small-scale industrial enterprise development and the problems associated therewith obviously overlaps with the discussion of the informal sector (Chapter 3, section 3.2) and with the examination of the development of indigenous industrial entrepreneurship and management (section 4.16 above). Nevertheless, a number of new issues are raised and they require separate treatment.

The definition of a 'small enterprise' is not always straightforward as there are many different types of small-scale industrial enterprise activity, differing with respect to both size and nature and characteristics of operations. There are the traditional household or cottage enterprises; small factory enterprises, which have often developed from the former and retain some of their characteristics; and modern factory enterprises, where the absence of significant economies of scale makes small-scale production feasible

(Sutcliffe, 1971, ch. 6, section 6.7). Cottage or handicraft enterprises can themselves be subdivided between those that manufacture a high-quality product of artistic value, which can be sold to tourists and/or exported, and those that make a low-cost, low-quality product under primitive conditions serving low-income, local markets, and for which there is a minimal growth potential (Bryce, 1965, ch. 4).

A survey of the available empirical evidence noted a general tendency for small-scale enterprises to be relatively more important in the LDCs than in the developed industrialised economies, but pointed to the fact that, while the average size of enterprise was smaller in LDCs, the size distribution was such that a few large firms dominated the markets for particular products. In many LDCs, therefore, 'there is an enormous number of very small firms and a small number of very large firms . . . [but there is] . . . a lack of medium-sized factory industry which is common in more industrialised countries' (Sutcliffe, 1971, pp. 235–6).

This is not a static situation, however. Anderson (1982, p. 914), extending ideas first advanced by Hoselitz (1959), identified three phases through which manufacturing activities, classified according to scale, pass during the process of industrialisation:

(1)   a phase in which household manufacturing is predominant, accounting for one-half to three-quarters or more of total manufacturing employment;
(2)   a phase in which small workshops and factories emerge at a comparatively rapid rate, and act to displace household manufacturing in several sectors; and
(3)   a phase in which large-scale production becomes predominant, displacing the remaining household manufacturing activities and a large share – though not the whole – of workshop and small factory production.

These are not totally separate phases and there is some overlap between them. Furthermore, when the urban informal sector activities are sufficiently disaggregated, many of them are found to provide earnings opportunities over relatively long periods of time and are likely to thrive, rather than disappear, as industrialisation proceeds. King (1974), for example, likened the informal manufacturing sector to a 'moving frontier', taking over, year by year, a wider range of products.

These changes are in part the result of the varying relationships between small-scale and large-scale industrial plants in LDCs. Where both produce competitive products, large-scale (modern) plants will in time drive the small-scale out of business. Where, however, they are complementary to one another, as in the case of subcontracting for example, both size-categories of plant will tend to grow together (for a discussion of subcontracting, see Schmitz, 1982, pp. 435–7).

Small-scale industrial enterprise activities will also flourish when locational factors are such as to encourage the spatial dispersion or decentralisation of such activities, as for example is the case with factories processing dispersed raw materials or supplying local markets with a final product that is expensive to transport. Differentiated products having low scale economies and serving small total markets are likely to be produced in large numbers of small-scale establishments (Staley and Morse, 1965, ch. 5).[23]

In more advanced stages of industrialisation large firms tend to predominate for a variety of reasons: 'economies of scale with respect to plant; economies of scale with respect to management and marketing; possibly superior technical and management efficiency; preferential access to supporting infra-structure services and external finance, and concessionary finance along with investment incentives and tariff structures that in theory are neutral between large and small scale, but in practice favour large scale' (Anderson, 1982, p. 923). The available empirical evidence, inadequate though it is, suggests that a significant part of the growth of large-scale enterprises is rooted in the expansion of once small firms through the size distribution (Anderson, 1982, p. 926).

The potential of small-scale enterprise is not always realised, however. The problems faced by indigenous entrepreneurs have already been discussed in section 4.16, with the distinction being made between 'internal' constraints (relating to entrepreneurial competence) and 'external' or environmental constraints. The writers who emphasise the second type of constraint can be divided into two groups. One group argues that small producers are exploited by large firms through a variety of mechanisms and thus contribute to the accumulation of capital in large enterprises. This problem is beyond the scope of the present discussion and is summarised by Schmitz (1982, pp. 433–5). Another group of writers argues that the expansion of small-scale enterprises is prevented or retarded as a result of difficulties with respect to access to product markets, technology, raw materials and credit, and that government policies often reinforce, rather than release, these constraints. Access to production markets and to technology is not a 'static' problem but is in part related to the changing size distribution of industrial activities already referred to above. Difficulties of access to raw materials are perhaps more to size *per se* in so far as small-scale producers lack working capital, do not have a strong bargaining position *vis-à-vis* suppliers, and often face government discrimination in the allocation of raw materials (the evidence is surveyed by Schmitz, 1982, pp. 439–40). Access to credit is considered in section 4.18 below.

Both internal and external constraints can, in principle, be modified by suitable government policies, an issue dealt with in Chapter 6, section 6.6.

At this stage, two points can usefully be made by way of a conclusion to the above discussion:

(1) The real issue is not whether small enterprises have growth and employment potential but under what conditions such potential can be realised; the relative importance of the various factors working for and against small-scale enterprises needs to be identified and this can perhaps best be done through a case study approach (Schmitz, 1982, p. 445).

(2) Smallness of factory or plant size is not *in itself* a virtue; if small enterprises are to play a role in the long-run development process, it must be

because they are efficient enough to compete with large-scale producers (Sutcliffe, 1971, pp. 239–40). Small-scale enterprises exert a strong appeal to economists and development planners:

Properly defined and realistically approached, the small-industry field is important and can contribute much to the whole process of industrialisation. If confused by sentimentalism and approached emotionally with little regard for the costs and benefits involved, small industry development can easily become a missionary movement which accomplishes little but which diverts scarce resources of development funds and people away from other activities which, in most situations, could produce more industrial growth. (Bryce, 1965, p. 77)

4.18   FINANCE FOR INDUSTRIAL DEVELOPMENT

For the majority of LDCs, the greater part of the financial resources required for industrial development will continue to come from sources within the economy in the foreseeable future. Reference has already been made to the financing of transnational direct foreign investment (section 4.10); this section is concerned primarily with the financing of private indigenous enterprises from local sources, both private and public.

Little information is available on the share of gross fixed capital formation (GFCF) devoted to the manufacturing sector in LDCs. Sample evidence suggests that it varies greatly between different LDCs. On average, the manufacturing sector is estimated to absorb about one-fifth of gross fixed capital formation, that is, about 3–5 per cent of GDP (UNIDO, 1979a, ch. IX). Approximately 60 per cent of GFCF is for capacity expansion, the remaining 40 per cent representing amortisation and replacement.

There appears to be a positive relationship between per capita income and the share of national savings in total investible funds. For the very poorest countries, national savings account for approximately 40 per cent of gross domestic investment, whereas in higher-income LDCs national savings account for over 80 per cent of gross domestic investment. The relationship between external capital inflows and domestic savings is complex and ambiguous however, and it cannot be assumed that foreign capital inflows always lead to an increase in *total* capital availability (for a discussion of this issue see Newlyn, 1977b; for a case study of Brazil, see Sant'ana, 1983).

Foreign financial resources, other than DFI, are available for industrial development in LDCs. For example, UNIDO (1979a, ch. IX) has estimated that just over 5 per cent of Official Development Assistance (approximately US $1 billion) went to the manufacturing sector in the period 1975–6. LDCs also increasingly borrow in international capital markets, via the sale of foreign bonds (issued in a single national market), international bonds (underwritten and sold in more than one market simultaneously) and through Euro-currency or Euro-dollar borrowing. It is estimated that, in the mid-1970s, perhaps 15 per cent of the total public and private borrowing in international markets (approximately US $3.5 billion) went to the manufacturing sector (UNIDO, 1979a, pp. 297–8). The net contribution to domestic capital formation will of course be much lower than these figures suggest because of the reverse-flow cost of foreign resources, that is, the cost of servicing the foreign debt (interest and amortisation charges).

Reference has already been made (section 4.16 above) to the controversy over whether or not the availability of finance is a binding constraint on the growth of domestic enterprises. Sutcliffe (1971, ch. 4, section 4.7) argued that, in a capitalist economy, the demand for capital funds often creates its own supply, and that the level of savings in any economy cannot be judged to be adequate unless it is also known to what uses savings are to be put. Bryce (1965, p. 164) also argued that 'One of the greatest contradictions in the underdeveloped world is the remarkably large availability of local capital on the one hand and the relatively small use of such capital in industry on the other hand'. Governments in LDCs, however, appear to believe that there is an overall scarcity of capital funds, or that certain classes of borrowers do not have adequate access, or that the cost is too high. They have therefore attempted to pursue financial and fiscal policies aimed at improving the mobilisation, allocation and utilisation of domestic resources (not always successfully), and they have been active in establishing a variety of state-owned financial institutions to supply industrial credit.

In many LDCs, properly functioning capital markets are either non-existent or underdeveloped and, in the poorest LDCs, it is the banking system (the central bank and the commercial banks) that has the greatest potential for promoting investment. As economic growth occurs and financial development proceeds, a variety of non-banking financial institutions are created (insurance companies, pension funds, etc.), but the banking system usually remains the main source of finance for industrial development.

Commercial banking lending, however, is usually short term either because the banks lack the incentives, means and skills to advance long-term credits or because they are prevented from doing so by law or custom. Governments in LDCs have thus established industrial development banks or corporations that make funds available to industry on terms more favourable than those available from the private sector. In many cases these institutions serve as channels for the transmission of public funds for industrial investment or for the distribution of large foreign loans or grants to large numbers of individual borrowers. The World Bank, for example, has provided finance (almost US $3 billion) to sixty-eight development finance companies (a generic term used to describe any intermediary that provides medium- and long-term finance to assist the development of productive, non-agricultural enterprises) in forty-four countries to assist medium-scale productive enterprises (World Bank, 1976, 1978).

In addition to the provision of finance, specialised institutions often provide managerial, financial and accounting services and guidance to small-scale enterprises. Industrial credit need not only be restricted to the lending of money; it may also encompass the leasing of equipment, the rental of industrial estates and the mass purchase of supplies for distribution on credit terms to small-scale producers (UNIDO, 1979a, ch. IX). Some development finance companies even play an entrepreneurial role, generating new project ideas and taking the lead in their implementation (World Bank, 1976, p. 37).

There are a number of problems arising from the operations of such specialised agencies. There is often a high rate of default, there is some doubt about whether such loans can actually reach the smallest entrepreneurs (those on the fringe of, or just outside, the 'modern' sector) and there is a suspicion that it is often the stronger, larger firms that benefit at the expense of the smaller and perhaps more needy and deserving enterprises. It could also be argued that small firms become too dependent on state-provided finance, which perhaps stifles initiative and enterprise and encourages the mis-use of public funds. Swainson (1980, ch. 5) noted the initial heavy dependence of African firms on state finance, but saw it as bridging the gap that existed before African firms could begin to borrow more heavily from the commercial banking sector.

Appropriate financial policies and institutions are a necessary, but not a sufficient, condition for satisfactory industrial development (UNIDO, 1979a, p. 312). Savings must be mobilised and channelled into productive investment; but the availability of capital as such does not create profitable investment opportunities and it must therefore be regarded as a permissive, but not a leading factor in the industrialisation process.

From the viewpoint of the individual enterprise, finance for investment can be made available from internal or external sources, and the enterprise has to decide on the exact balance between alternative sources. Internal funds become available through retained profits, provisions made for depreciation, and tax provisions. External sources of finance (that is, external to the enterprise, not necessarily of foreign origin) include long-term or loan capital, and short- or medium-term capital (for example, bank credit, hire purchase or trade credit) (Devine *et al.*, 1979, ch. 7, section 7.6).

The actual method of finance adopted will depend, *inter alia*, on the size of the investment outlay, the type of firm involved (and, especially in the case of LDCs, its size and nationality) and the nature of the project to be financed. In general, evidence from the developed, industrialised economies indicates that firms have a preference for self-financing. Evidence from LDCs is limited, but a study of the savings behaviour of forty-three companies in the manufacturing sector in Kenya in the 1960s (Snowden, 1977) provided some interesting insights. Snowden concluded that the smaller and medium-sized enterprises tended to depend heavily on savings out of profits, but that the larger (and often foreign-owned) enterprises tended to use more loan capital and, as a consequence, made 'little net contribution to industrial financing in Kenya' (Snowden, 1977, p. 309).

Clearly, generalisations should not be made on the basis of such limited data. It is nevertheless worth pointing out that the dependence of individual firms on alternative sources of finance will vary between countries and over time, being influenced by the availability of funds from alternative sources, by government policy – both with respect to its attitudes towards private enterprise (domestic and foreign) and with respect to the provision of finance – and by the degree of political stability (or instability) in any country at any one time.

4.19 TRANSNATIONAL CORPORATIONS, DOMESTIC ENTERPRISES AND THE ROLE OF THE STATE IN LDCs

Reference has been made throughout this chapter to the strategic role that the state plays in the process of industrialisation in LDCs. The state participates, both directly and indirectly, in industrial development (see Chapter 5 for a fuller discussion), but it also performs a mediating role between its own interests and those of foreign and local capital, creating various and complex relationships. Such relationships differ both between countries and over time for individual countries, and this makes it hazardous, if not actually misleading, to generalise on the basis of the limited number of case studies available.

At the risk of over-simplification, three sets of relationships are of particular significance:

(i)   the relationships between TNC subsidiaries and domestic enterprises in the individual host LDCs;
(ii) the relationships between TNC subsidiaries and the host LDC state – this issue has been touched upon in section 4.15 and will not be referred to again here;
(iii) the relationship between domestic enterprises and the state in the individual LDC.

RELATIONSHIPS BETWEEN TNC SUBSIDIARIES AND DOMESTIC ENTERPRISES

Two questions can be posed in this context, although, given the existing state of empirical information, definitive answers cannot yet be given.

- Is it useful and/or necessary actually to distinguish between foreign and indigenous enterprises? That is, irrespective of what has been said above, is their behaviour sufficiently different to make the distinction between foreign and local capital meaningful?
- Can domestic enterprises survive TNC competition and coexist with TNCs in the longer run?

To question the distinction that is conventionally made between foreign and domestic enterprises is not as surprising as it at first seems. TNCs and domestic enterprises are increasingly coming together in joint ventures, the 'nationality' of which is not always immediately obvious, and some foreign firms in LDCs have become so well established that they have begun to take on 'national' characteristics. The evidence surveyed above suggests that both foreign and domestic enterprises are profit seekers, they appear to utilise similar technologies and, where differences in this respect do exist, it appears that they are being reduced over time.

Access to foreign technologies will differ between foreign and domestic firms and it may well be the case, as argued by Evans (1976) with respect to the pharmaceutical industry in Brazil, that domestic firms are more active in encouraging indigenous technological development (local product innovation in Evans' example) (see also Fairchild's 1977 study of Mexican industry). It is also probably the case that TNC subsidiaries will have greater opportunities for the manipulation of transfer prices and are likely to have a higher propensity to repatriate earnings of various kinds overseas.

The problems posed with respect to the possibilities of nationalising or otherwise 'controlling' an enterprise will clearly vary in magnitude between foreign and domestic firms, and this aspect highlights the essential difference between the TNC subsidiary and the domestic enterprise. It must always be remembered that the TNC subsidiary is a part of a wider global network and will always be responsive in some degree to the imperatives of a global strategy (Vernon, 1977, p. 203). However similar in behaviour foreign and domestic firms appear to be, the transnationality of the one and the 'simple' nationality of the other must never be overlooked.

The question of the coexistence of TNC subsidiaries and domestic enterprises in the same industry has been examined by Evans (1976, 1979). He analysed the progressive 'denationalisation' of the Brazilian pharmaceutical industry in the post World War II period, and concluded that:

> The effect of denationalisation is not the elimination of local participation in the market but the transformation of that participation. Local capital has gradually become relegated to smaller firms ... firms that survive on the basis of commercial acumen rather than industrial or technological innovation. Local capital no longer even vaguely threatens the most important source of the international firms' profits, that is, their monopoly of technological innovation, and the role of local capital becomes even more complementary to the role of foreign capital. (Evans, 1976, p. 126)[24]

Where denationalisation had occurred, Evans argued that it was the state itself, rather than the locally owned segment of the industry, that was most likely to 'challenge' the foreign-owned sector and exert political pressure on it. The relationship between the state and foreign capital is thus of crucial importance, as has already been pointed out, but the uniqueness and specificity of this relationship in individual LDCs make it dangerous to generalise on the basis of a limited number of case studies, valuable as they are.

RELATIONSHIPS BETWEEN DOMESTIC ENTERPRISES AND THE STATE

In many LDCs, although by no means all of them, a fundamental objective of public policy is to restrict or control foreign capital in order to encourage the growth of indigenous enterprises to enable them to compete with foreign capital or to develop in a complementary fashion (through forward and backward linkages). The state in the LDC thus interacts with foreign capital in a variety of ways – as a partner in joint ventures, as a competitor and as a controlling agency – in order to achieve this objective.

Policies to control foreign capital and promote indigenous industry are discussed in Chapter 6, sections 6.5 and 6.6. It is sufficient to note here that governments in LDCs restrict the sectors in which foreign capital can operate, buy out or otherwise disposses non-nationals who control key sectors of the economy (wholesaling, retailing, import–export) and pursue a variety of policies to encourage indigenous development (import restrictions, technical assistance, subsidised credit, etc.).

From the point of view of longer-run development therefore, the crucial issue is not the existing weakness or subservience of domestic to foreign capital, but rather the policies that the state may be pursuing to overcome the weakness and eliminate subservience. Over time, a combination of controls on foreign capital, active participation by the state in productive enterprises and the positive promotion of indigenous enterprise may well prove sufficient to create an environment within which indigenous enterprises can flourish and compete on an equal footing with TNCs in at least key sectors of the LDC economy. The impact of such policies on the wider economic and social development of the LDC cannot be predicted *a priori* (see section 4.15 above), and this is a powerful argument for the publication of further case studies of the kind considered in this chapter.

FURTHER READING

A number of books are available that review the theoretical and empirical literature relating to the TNC. Among the better books are Hood and Young (1979), Dunning (1981) and Caves (1982). The detailed empirical work of Vaitsos (1974) and Lall and Streeten (1977) is still of value, and the publications of the UN Centre on Transnational Corporations (United Nations, 1978, 1983) present the most up-to-date information and analysis available. From a radical perspective, the articles in Radice (1975) remain relevant and Lall's collected papers (1980a, 1981a), as well as his major survey article on linkages (Lall, 1978), are essential reading. Helleiner's 1975 article on technology transfer remains a seminal work. Similar textbooks and collections are not available for indigenous enterprises, but Staley and Morse (1965) remains the major text on small-scale enterprise development; Anderson (1982) and Schmitz (1982) are also very useful.

NOTES

1   The term 'transnational corporation' is used to indicate that such enterprises are usually owned and controlled by the citizens of the enterprise's home country. Multinational corporations (or enterprises) on this definition will be owned, or controlled, by the citizens, or governments, of several countries. In 1974, the Group of Eminent Persons (United Nations, 1974b) suggested that the definition of the TNC should be extended to include state-owned entities and co-operatives, on the grounds that such enterprises might well be profit seekers. There is as yet, however, no general agreement on this point. The 'home country' of the TNC is its country of origin; the 'host country' is the country where the direct foreign investment (DFI) is located or where the TNC otherwise conducts its operations. DFI involves the ownership of physical assets (mines, factories, plantations, sales offices, etc.) and is distinguished from portfolio investment, which involves the purchase of securities.

2   See also Baran and Sweezy (1968, ch. 2, p. 39) where it is argued that 'the search for

"maximum" profits can only be the search for the greatest *increase* in profits which is possible in the given situation, subject . . . to the elementary proviso that the exploitation of today's profit opportunities must not ruin tomorrow's'.

3   The *flow* of DFI to the LDCs is also highly concentrated. In the late 1970s, six LDCs – Argentina, Brazil, Hong Kong, Malaysia, Mexico and Singapore – consistently accounted for between one-half and three-quarters of total LDC inflows. It should be noted, however, that the People's Republic of China, which is not included in the aggregate data, is receiving large and growing amounts of direct foreign investment. OECD (1983, pp. 19–20) gave the following data: 1979, $200 million; 1980, $550 million; 1981, over $2 billion. The survey noted that 'China is likely to attract more direct investment in the future since its Foreign Investment Law of 1979 and subsequent regulations confirmed the importance China attaches to the participation of foreign capital in the modernisation of the country's economy'.

4   Nationally owned firms in Mexico are of importance in textiles, food and non-metallic mineral production; state firms play an important role in mining, printing, primary metal production and textiles (Newfarmer and Mueller, 1975, ch. III).

5   Brazilian corporations were of importance in non-metallic minerals, wood and paper products and food manufacturing; state enterprises were predominant in steel production and petroleum refining (Newfarmer and Mueller, 1975, ch. V).

6   In 1973, Mexico introduced the Law on Promotion of Mexican Investment and Regulation of Foreign Investment, which laid down the general rate of 49 per cent foreign capital ownership of manufacturing enterprises as a maximum. Exceptions have been made to this limit, however. The Mexican government is also promoting joint venture arrangements between public, domestic private and foreign capital. See World Bank (1979a), pp. 36–40.

7   In a more detailed analysis of TNC acquisitions of Brazilian firms in the electrical industry, Newfarmer (1979a) argued that TNC acquisitions were a function of the economic power of TNCs in the imperfect markets for finance and technology that surrounded the acquired Brazilian firms. Of forty-seven acquisitions in the electrical industry between 1960 and 1974, only one resulted in a Brazilian-controlled firm, and Newfarmer argued (p. 39) that these acquisitions had changed market structures – generally increasing concentration, raising barriers to entry and decreasing competition.

8   In general, automobile firms specialised in the manufacture of bodies, engines and transmissions and left technologically dissimilar areas, such as electrical, glass, rubber and paint production, to independent manufacturers. In addition, they left some highly innovative or specialised products (pistons, fasteners, fuel injection) to large independent producers, often transnationals, who were thus able to exploit economies of scale (Lall, 1980b, p. 211). Lall noted, however, that there were differences between individual firms, depending on their size and national industrial environment, and that producers of commercial vehicles (such as AL and TELCO) were often more specialised (that is, bought out more) than producers of volume passenger cars. For an analysis of the automobile industry in both developed and less developed countries, see Lall (1980c).

9   The K/L ratio and the K/O ratio will rank techniques in the same order only if efficient techniques are being considered (that is, techniques that are not inferior to any other techniques among those available). In this context, an inferior technique is taken to mean any technique that produces the same output as some other technique but uses more of at least one factor and no less of any other (Stewart, 1972, p. 99).

10 This argument appears to derive from the analytical framework developed by Stewart (1977, ch. 1). The actual technology in use in an LDC is constrained by (a) the nature of world technology, (b) the availability to the country of known techniques, and (c) the choice made among those available.

11 The eleven inputs are: unskilled labour; labour possessing a medium degree of skill; labour possessing a high degree of skill; labour and management with skills and knowhow giving capacity to maintain equipment; lower executive management; top decision-making management; capital embodied in machinery; capital embodied in buildings; working capital embodied in materials awaiting processing; working capital embodied in work in progress; and working capital embodied in stocks of finished goods.

12 It should be noted for the sake of completeness that the methodology used by Courtney and Leipziger has been seriously criticised by Lall (1978), Gaude (1975) and de Meza (1977).

13   $K/O = (K/L)/(O/L)$, where K = capital, L = labour and O = output. A low K/O thus requires either a low K/L or a high O/L (Willmore, 1976, p. 516).

14   Teece (1977, p. 259) has argued, however, that the resources required to transfer technology internationally are considerable and that '. . . it is quite inappropriate to regard existing technology as something that can be made available to all at zero social cost'. There are also significant variations in transfer costs, and it is equally inappropriate, therefore, 'to make sweeping generalisations about the process of technology transfer and the costs involved'.

15   For discussion of the various aspects and determinants of efficiency, see: White, 1976; Tyler, 1979; Page, 1980; and section 4.16 below. Little evidence exists that permits a comparison of the relative efficiency of TNCs and indigenous enterprises. Tyler (1979, p. 490) concluded tentatively that, in the Brazilian plastics and steel industries, foreign firms did not appear to be significantly more efficient than domestically owned private firms.

16   This is consistent with the great bulk of evidence, which suggests that import-substituting industrialisation does not in reality save foreign exchange. For a survey of the evidence, see Colman and Nixson (1978), ch. 8.

17   Vaitsos' work has not escaped criticism, however. Vernon (1977, pp. 154–5) argued that the results for Colombia were not typical, being based on the special circumstances ruling in Colombia at the time of the study (a ceiling on profits remission by foreign companies that allegedly made no allowance for the drug companies' investment in product development and trade names) and 'relatively uninhibited techniques of extrapolation'.

18   The owners of indigenous enterprises will also wish to minimise the taxes that they pay on profits and will no doubt attempt to manipulate transfer prices to their advantage whenever possible (or, more usually, over- or under-invoice to achieve the same result). Within the TNC, however, such flows are systematic and sustained, and both the rationale of, and the opportunities for, tax minimisation are different for the TNC subsidiary as compared to the indigenous enterprise. See Nixson (1983b) and section 4.19 below.

19   The four categories do not take account of possible differences in industrial composition of the sub-samples, and thus the comparision of rates of return may not be valid.

20   The contrast with Asian-owned businesses was significant. Over 80 per cent of jointly owned Asian firms were wholly family partnerships, compared with 13 per cent for African businesses; 60 per cent of Asian businessmen preferred relatives as business associates, compared with 8 per cent for Africans (Marris, 1971, p. 239).

21   As indicated earlier, the analysis of Kenyan development has generated much controversy. The more important contributions include: Leys, 1975a, 1978, 1980; Kaplinsky, 1980, 1982.

22   The literature usually refers to 'small-scale industry', even though it is the individual enterprise, establishment or factory that is being discussed. For the sake of clarity and consistency, the term 'enterprise' is used throughout this section and in Chapter 6, section 6.6.

23   A similar line of reasoning has been used to suggest that small-scale enterprises might well be able to export successfully. Bruch (1980) suggested that small-scale establishments engaged in the processing of spatially dispersed raw materials (especially where processing leads to a reduction in weight, bulk or perishability), in the manufacture of traditional products using labour-intensive indigenous technolgy, and in the manufacture of labour-intensive products using an internationally known technology not marked by economies of scale should have the potential to become competitive exporters. Tentative evidence from Malaysia lends support to this hypothesis. However, Bruch suggested that, in addition to the typical problems faced by small-scale producers, potential exporters face additional barriers: lack of information about international trading practices, insufficient knowledge of market conditions in foreign countries, quality deficiencies, difficulties in meeting delivery dates, and the need to cope with export formalities and documentation (Bruch, 1980, p. 431).

24   A study of the Argentinian pharmaceutical industry went even further than Evans and argued that domestic firms were reversing the process of denationalisation in the industry and were making some efforts to become technologically independent (see Chudnovsky, 1979).

5 Business Behaviour in the Public Sector

5.1 INTRODUCTION

State intervention in the industrialisation process is widespread in many LDCs. The role of government is evident both in its use of policy instruments intended to influence the private sector's activities and in its direct participation in the production of goods and services. While the impact of indirect policy measures on the growth and performance of the industrial sector as a whole has been the subject of extensive investigation (summarised in Cody *et al.*, 1980), much less attention has been given to the role of the public enterprises within that sector in developing countries.[1]

Within the constraints imposed by the limited research undertaken so far, this chapter examines the functions and behaviour of the public enterprise sector in LDCs. Section 5.2 begins by considering the problems of defining public enterprise sector. Section 5.4 discusses the financing of public and industrial activities of the sector in various developing countries. Section 5.3 examines the factors that have led to the establishment and growth of the public enterprises sector. Section 5.4 discusses the financing of public enterprises. Section 5.5 addresses the issue of evaluating public enterprise behaviour and performance, and section 5.6 reviews the available evidence on economic performance. The following section is concerned with the use of public enterprises as a means of achieving distributional objectives. Section 5.8 considers the conclusions to be drawn from the evidence of public enterprise performance. The final section provides a summary and conclusions to the chapter.

5.2 THE PUBLIC ENTERPRISE SECTOR IN LDCs

DEFINITION

Public enterprises (PEs) are normally defined in terms of two characteristics: they are owned and controlled by the government, and they produce a marketed output. It is often difficult, however, to give a precise meaning to these characteristics.

Majority ownership of an enterprise does not guarantee effective control over its operations. Where the number of public enterprises is large, the government may not have the administrative resources needed to exercise effective control. If the government acquires an existing enterprise through nationalisation, it may remain dependent upon the private sector to provide the necessary managerial, technical and marketing expertise. In joint ventures, the government's majority shareholding may be neutralised by a structure of voting procedures that preserves the private parties' control of key decision-making areas.

The identification of 'government' enterprises can also be problematic. In some instances, government ownership is transferred to an intermediate authority. In Zambia, for example, almost all government-owned concerns are controlled through a holding company, which in turn controls two further holding companies embracing more than 100 companies in which the central government has a majority shareholding (Turok, 1981). In some countries, for example Turkey and India, public enterprise statistics exclude all or some enterprises owned by regional and local authorities.

An output is 'marketed' if it is sold to final consumers or other producers, and revenue from sales accounts for a significant share of the enterprise's costs. In practice, differences in the level at which revenue becomes 'significant' and in the accounting practices used to calculate revenues and costs (see below) mean that the definition of marketed and non-marketed output produced by the public sector can vary between countries.

SIZE

None of the international organisations publishes comprehensive information on public enterprises on a regular basis, and the majority of countries do not identify public enterprises separately in their national statistics. The limited number that do so seldom provide information on the precise criteria used in defining the public enterprise sector (Abraham, 1975; Pathirane and Blades, 1982). The absence of a standard procedure for measuring the public enterprise sector makes cross-country comparisons difficult, since one is compelled to rely on data drawn from a variety of sources in which different criteria may have been used. These differences in coverage should be borne in mind when considering the figures in the following tables.

Tables 5.1 and 5.2 provide indicators of the size of the public enterprise

Table 5.1 *Share of public enterprise output in GDP, mid-1970s*

Africa	%	Asia	%	S. America	%
Benin	8	Bangladesh	6	Argentina	5
Ghana	38	India	10	Bolivia	12
Guinea	25	Rep. of Korea	7	Chile	13
Ivory Coast	10	Nepal	3	Paraguay	3
Kenya	9	Pakistan	6	Venezuela	28
Liberia	7	Philippines	4		
Mali	9				
Senegal	20				
Tanzania	14				
Togo	13				
Tunisia	26				
Zambia	38				

Source: World Bank (1983), Figure 5.6.

Table 5.2 *Share of public enterprise investment in gross fixed capital formation*

Country	Years	%
Algeria	1978–81	68
Burma	1978–80	61
Zambia	1979–80	61
Pakistan	1978–81	45
Ivory Coast	1979	40
Ethiopia	1978–80	37
Venezuela	1978–80	36
India	1978	33
Bangladesh	1974	31
Brazil	1980	23
Rep. of Korea	1978–80	23
Peru	1978–9	15

Source: World Bank (1983), Table 5.2.

sector in a sample of LDCs: the share of PE output in GDP, and the share of PE investment in gross fixed capital formation. The average contribution of public enterprises to GDP in LDCs rose from 7 per cent at the beginning of the 1970s to about 10 per cent at the end of the decade (World Bank, 1983, p. 49). Most countries fall in the 5–15 per cent range, but there is considerable variation, ranging from 3 per cent in Paraguay and Nepal to 38 per cent in Ghana and Zambia. In most LDCs, the share of public enterprise investment in total gross fixed capital formation exceeds 25 per cent, and in some cases accounts for more than 60 per cent of total investment.

Individual public enterprises are frequently among the largest concerns in LDCs. Of the fifty-two LDC firms included in *Fortune*'s 1979 list of the 500 largest non-US industrial concerns, thirty-four were public enterprises. In addition, these public enterprises accounted for 75 per cent of total sales by listed LDC firms, compared with less than 10 per cent for public enterprises among listed developed country firms (Jones and Mason, 1982, p. 41). In India, twenty-two of the largest twenty-five corporate enterprises were in public ownership in 1978 (Narain, 1979, p. 59); in South Korea, twelve of the largest sixteen enterprises were state owned in 1972 (Jones, 1976, p. 200); in Brazil, the ten largest firms are all public enterprises (Trebat, 1980); in Indonesia, the nine largest domestic firms are state owned (Gillis, 1980, p. 254).

SECTORAL DISTRIBUTION

Public enterprises are found in almost all types of economic activity in LDCs. Table 5.3 provides information on the relative importance of PEs in different sectors for a sample of developing countries. Public enterprises are still relatively more important in the traditional public utilities sector (electricity, gas, water) and also in the transport and communications industries. In many

Table 5.3 Public enterprise share of GDP by sector

Country	Agriculture	Commerce, services	Construction	Manufacturing	Mining	Transport, communication	Electricity, gas, water
				Percentage share of public enterprises in:			
Congo (1980)	*	*	**	**	*	***	*****
Ivory Coast (1979)	*	*	**	**	**	***	*****
Kenya (1980)	*	*	*	**	*	****	*****
Senegal (1980)	*	**	*	**	*****	***	*****
Sierra Leone (1979)	*	*	*	**	**	****	*****
Tanzania (1980–1)	*	***	**	***	*****	**	*****
Bangladesh (1980)	*	**	*	***	*****	**	*****
Burma (1980)	*	***	****	****	*****	***	*****
India (1978)	*	*	**	**	*****	***	*****
Rep. of Korea (1974–7)	*	*	*	**	**	***	*****
Nepal (1978–9)	*	**	N.A.	**	*	**	*****
Pakistan (1980)	*	**	*	**	**	***	*****
Sri Lanka (1974)	*	**	**	***	*	***	*****
Tunisia (1976)	*	*	N.A.	***	***	***	*****
Argentina (1980)	*	*	**	**	***	***	*****
Mexico (1980)	*	**	*	**	*****	****	*****
Nicaragua (1980)	**	**	*****	**	*****	****	*****
Uruguay (1979)	*	*	*	*	*	**	*****

Key: <5%   *
       <25%   **
       <50%   ***
       <75%   ****
       >75%   *****
       N.A.   not available

Source: World Bank (1983), Figure 5.4.

LDCs, public enterprises also account for a significant proportion of the natural resources sector's output. Rood (1976) estimated that by the mid-1970s more than 50 per cent, by value, of mineral extractive projects in sub-Saharan Africa were in government ownership. In many countries the petroleum and energy sectors are almost entirely in public ownership.

Public enterprises are much less significant in the agricultural and trading sectors, which in most LDCs are dominated by small-scale, privately owned enterprises. Public enterprises in these sectors often take the form of marketing agencies and can have a significant indirect effect on private sector activities through their purchasing and selling policies.

MANUFACTURING SECTOR

Public enterprise participation in the manufacturing sector varies widely between countries, from less than 10 per cent of value added in Argentina, Bolivia and Pakistan to more than 50 per cent in Syria, Tunisia, Egypt, Burma and Ethiopia (Table 5.4). Public enterprises appear to be more prominent in

Table 5.4   *Share of public enterprises in manufacturing value added and investment*

Country[a]	*Public enterprises' share of manufacturing value added %*		*Public enterprises' share of manufacturing investment %*	
Argentina	5.0	(1975)	N.A.	
Mexico	30.0	(1975)	65.0	(1975)
Brazil	19.4	(mid-1970s)	33.0	(1975)
Panama	4.0	(1977)	6.2	(1975)
Rep. of Korea	15.0	(1977)	N.A.	
Turkey	29.0	(1980)	47.8	(1972)
Syria	58.0	(1977)	97.7	(1977)
Tunisia	59.0	(1978–81)	53.7	(1977–81)
Ivory Coast	24.0[b]	(1979)	19.3	(1971–5)
Egypt	65.0	(1979)	81.4	(1979)
Zambia	51.0	(mid-1970s)	64.0	(1972)
Bolivia	8.0	(1973–5)	N.A.	
Senegal	20.0	(1974)	N.A.	
Pakistan	9.0	(1975)	42.6	(1975)
Sierra Leone	12.0	(1979)	N.A.	
Tanzania	38.0	(1974–7)	39.0	(1972)
India	15.0	(1978)	60.9	(1975–6)
Burma	56.0	(1980)	N.A.	
Ethiopia	61.0	(1979–80)	N.A.	
Bangladesh	40.0	(1978)	80.2	(1978–9)

Notes:
a   Countries are listed in descending order of GNP (1980) per capita.
b   Including mining.
N.A. = not available.

Sources: Col. 1: World Bank (1983), Figure 5.5, except Brazil and Zambia which are taken from UNIDO (1983c), Table I. Col. 2: UNIDO (1983c), Table I.

the manufacturing sector in LDCs than in DCs (using information on the numbers of public non-financial enterprises reported to the IMF in 1980, Pathirane and Blades, 1982, calculated that 34 per cent of public enterprises in LDCs were engaged in manufacturing, compared with 23 per cent in industrial countries), but there is no obvious pattern in the relative importance of manufacturing PEs in different LDCs. The ranking of the countries in Table 5.4 in descending order of GNP (1980) per capita fails to reveal any relationship between level of development and the share of public enterprises in manufacturing value added. A number of countries with a firm commitment to a socialist form of development (Tanzania, Burma, Ethiopia) appear to have succeeded in establishing a significant public manufacturing sector, but it is also the case that levels of public enterprise participation are at least as high in many capitalist LDCs.

Within the manufacturing sector, the relative importance of public enterprise participation varies between different branches of industry. As was pointed out in Chapter 3, section 3.2, public enterprises are most evident in the heavy goods industries (such as iron and steel), chemicals and transport equipment (see Table 3.3). In general, public enterprises are much less important in the production of consumer goods, apart from products such as tobacco, alcohol and sugar, where public ownership enables the government to operate a fiscal monopoly. The concentration of public enterprises in heavy, capital-intensive activities is reflected in Table 5.4, where, for those countries for which both output and investment data are available, the share of public enterprise investment in total manufacturing investment is almost always greater than the share in output.

In a number of the larger, more industrialised LDCs the public enterprise sector has emerged as a source of manufactured exports, in accordance with the shift in LDCs' export composition towards more capital-intensive products based on a standardised technology (Chapter 2, section 2.3). Ballance *et al.* (1982, pp. 284–5) detailed the variety of export markets and products supplied by Indian public enterprises: thermal sets, boiler equipment, transformers and compressors to the Middle East and the United States; radial drills, grinders, lathes, presses and tractors to the United States and Western and Eastern Europe; bicycle parts, hand tools, automobile parts and textile machinery to several African and Asian countries. Other Indian public enterprises have emerged as important international contractors and consultancy groups, particularly in the Middle East and Nigeria (p. 285). Indian Railways have undertaken major managerial and technical contracts in Nigeria and Sudan (UNIDO, 1982c, p. 30). By 1978, earnings from public enterprise exports of goods and services and marketing activities accounted for 29 per cent of India's total export receipts (UNIDO, 1982c, p. 26).

In the Republic of Korea, public enterprise exports accounted for less than 6 per cent of total exports in the mid-1970s, but, when the use of public enterprise inputs in private sector exports was allowed for, the share of the public enterprise sector in exports increased to 14 per cent (Jones and Wortzel, 1982, p. 219).

In Latin America, state-owned enterprises engaged in exporting are concentrated in the oil and mineral industries, and do not appear to make a significant contribution to manufactured exports (Vernon, 1981, p. 106). There are exceptions, however. For example, Brazilian public enterprises are important exporters of aircraft, armaments and military equipment, steel products, and the publicly owned Interbas enterprise markets a wide range of manufactured exports.

5.3   REASONS FOR THE ESTABLISHMENT AND GROWTH OF THE PUBLIC ENTERPRISE SECTOR

INTRODUCTION

What determines the size and structure of the public enterprise sector in LDCs? Common sense suggests that there will be no simple answer to this question. Indeed the wide variation in the share of the public enterprise sector that is evident in Tables 5.1 and 5.4 suggests, first, that many different factors – economic, social and political – are likely to influence the government's decision to undertake productive activities, and, second, that the importance of these factors will vary both between countries and within any given country over time.

The growth in the public enterprise sector can be analysed from two alternative, although not mutually exclusive, perspectives. The first approach views the establishment of public enterprises largely as the result of certain economic factors. Government ownership of the production process is seen as a non-ideological response to failures in the workings of the market mechanism. A second approach considers the public enterprise sector from a broader socio-political perspective, and sees its growth as being determined by the interplay of political and social forces within the developing countries.

THE ECONOMIC RATIONALE FOR PUBLIC ENTERPRISE

Economic theory traditionally has rationalised direct government participation in productive activities in terms of the imperfections in the market economy.[2] Welfare economics demonstrates that, in a perfectly competitive market economy, welfare-maximising behaviour by individuals, and profit-maximising behaviour by firms, result in a *Pareto optimum* equilibrium; that is, for a given distribution of income, the allocations of productive factors and outputs are such that it would be impossible to increase any person's welfare without reducing that of someone else. For this Pareto optimum to be achieved, it is necessary for certain *efficiency conditions* to be fulfilled in consumption and production decisions.[3]

The conditions necessary to guarantee a competitive Pareto optimum are not, however, met in the real world. Various sources of imperfection cause the economy to diverge from the perfectly competitive norm, and, from the welfare economics perspective, the establishment of public enterprises can be rationalised as a means of 'correcting' specific forms of market imperfections, thereby ensuring that the conditions necessary for the efficient operation of the market mechanism are met.

Indivisiblities in production and economies of scale

Where the minimum size of plant, or the output level required to yield minimum average production costs, is large relative to the level of demand, a monopolistic or oligopolistic market structure may emerge. This is typically the case in 'natural' monopolies such as are found in transportation, communications, and water and power utilities. Here public ownership is necessary to exploit economies of scale, while at the same time avoiding inefficient monopoly practices. Direct evidence on the correlation between public ownership and market concentration is lacking, however, with the exception of the study by Jones (1976) on South Korea, which reported that public enterprises operated overwhelmingly in markets with high concentration ratios, with no more than 10 per cent of public enterprise value added being sold in competitive markets (pp. 189–90).

Large size relative to factor supplies may also lead to public ownership. Where the investment requirements or entrepreneurial inputs are large, the private sector may be unable to mobilise the resources required to undertake the project, and state participation becomes necessary.

Large-scale investment projects requiring public sector participation are particularly evident in the minerals and basic industrial (chemical, iron and steel, petrochemical, fertiliser) sectors. In the case of the steel industry, for example, it is estimated that state enterprises produce more than 75 per cent of the total output in Argentina, Brazil, India, Turkey and Venezuela (Walter, 1979, p. 157). In the mining sector, there has been a marked trend towards larger mines, which, by facilitating mechanisation, has encouraged greater capital intensity. This has led to a rapid growth in the financial requirements of new developments, resulting in increased state participation, often in joint venture arrangements with foreign capital (Radetzki, 1980, p. 5). A similar pattern of rising financial requirements and increased state participation has been evident in the fertiliser and petrochemical industries in LDCs (UNIDO, 1981b, pp. 44–6).

Where private sector entrepreneurial activity is constrained by high risk aversion, poorly developed financial markets or a paucity of information, the state may undertake the entrepreneurial function. Jones (1976, pp. 148–9) indicated that 'entrepreneurial substitution' was the predominant developmental motive for the establishment of state manufacturing enterprises in South Korea. Walstedt (1980, p. 43) suggested that similar considerations motivated the early growth of the public manufacturing sector in Turkey. In Malaysia, the government established public enterprises with the intention of progressively increasing Malay managerial and equity participation to the point where public disinvestment became possible (Ling, 1980; Mallon, 1982). Similar policies of selling public enterprises to the private sector have been followed at various times in Pakistan, Brazil, the Philippines, South Korea and Singapore.

Externalities and linkages

The Pareto-optimum outcome assumes a coincidence between private and social benefits and costs. This condition is not met when one individual's consumption or production decision affects the welfare of other individuals and this external effect is not allowed for in the individual's private cost and benefit calculations. The presence of these externalities – which may be external benefits (where, for example, a firm's training of its labour force increases the quality of the nation's stock of human capital) or external costs (where, for example, environmental damage is caused by industrial activities) – is a further cause of market failure (see Little and Mirrlees, 1974, pp. 335–49, for a discussion of externalities in LDCs). Price and output decisions based on private costs will produce a non-optimal outcome, and the government may choose to take the activity into public ownership in order to ensure that price and output levels reflect social opportunity costs and benefits.[4]

In economies characterised by limited integration between different sectors, public investment can perform an important role in ensuring that the conditions necessary for industrial growth are met. Hirschman (1958) argued that the impact of public investment would be maximised if it was concentrated in industries with significant 'linkages' with other industries. These linkage effects might be in a backward direction to input suppliers, or forward to users of the industry's output. In some instances, investment would need to be made in anticipation of future needs, therefore creating the necessary conditions for growth ('development via excess capacity'); in other circumstances, investment would be intended to remove shortages or bottlenecks that were inhibiting further growth ('development via shortages').

In many LDCs, the desire to accelerate the process of industrialisation has led to public participation in sectors believed to have significant externalities or linkage effects. Basic industries such as iron and steel, chemicals, heavy engineering, fertilisers and petrochemicals are often seen as performing a catalytic function in the early stages of industrialisation by providing essential inputs to other manufacturing activities. Even when these products can be imported at lower resource cost, publicly owned domestic production in these 'commanding heights' activities may be rationalised in terms of their strategic economic importance. Emphasis on the development of the heavy industry sector was characteristic of Indian economic planning in the 1950s and 1960s. Programmes of industrial development in the public sector included the establishment of steel plants, coal mines, heavy machine building factories, fertiliser factories and the manufacture of heavy electrical equipment and oil exploration. In the Republic of Korea, the public sector was found to have much stronger forward linkages than the private sector (Jones, 1976, p. 94). In Brazil, Tyler (1976) found that the government-owned firms were concentrated in industries with strong forward linkages, particularly steel and chemicals.

THE LIMITATIONS OF WELFARE ECONOMICS ANALYSIS

Many of the important concerns that motivate public policy in LDCs cannot be accommodated easily within the neoclassical analytical framework, which therefore provides an incomplete explanation of public sector activities.

The neglect of distributional issues

There are an infinite number of Pareto optima, each corresponding to a particular initial distribution of income; since interpersonal comparisons of welfare are not possible on any objective basis, welfare economics cannot be used to determine the preferred Pareto optimum. For this purpose, it is necessary to rely on the normative judgement of the government about the desired distribution of income. The separation of efficiency from distributional issues has often resulted in an implicit assumption of optimality about the existing distribution of income. Attention is concentrated on the efficiency objective, with considerable effort and ingenuity being expended on the development of operational measures of economic efficiency that are then used as yardsticks of economic performance (these performance criteria are discussed in section 5.5).

There is, however, much concern in LDCs with distributional issues. Research has shown that the pattern of income and wealth distribution is frequently highly concentrated, with the structure of demand, and hence production, heavily influenced by high-income groups. Measures aimed at achieving a greater degree of income equality are important components of economic policy in many developing countries. However, many redistributive measures would be regarded as undesirable from a welfare economics perspective since they result in economic inefficiencies. Commenting on the limitations of the welfare economics treatment of distributional matters, Helleiner (1981a, p. 542) observed,

> Almost imperceptibly, prisoners of their own paradigm, students of economics risk beginning to regard all government policies as 'interventions', likely to impede the harmonious functioning of markets; and to regard the distribution of income (and power) as a matter wholly independent of market functioning, to be handled by separate policies (lump-sum transfers) that do not 'interfere' with markets.

In practice, public enterprises are often established and used as an instrument for the pursuit of distributional goals. This can take a variety of forms. The PE may be used to create employment or to preserve jobs where, for example, the state takes over unprofitable private sector concerns. In other instances, the location of public enterprises may be the means of reducing regional inequalities. Public enterprise output may be sold at subsidised prices to aid low-income consumers. The public enterprise sector may also be developed as a counterweight to the concentration of economic power among private indigenous interests. For example, the widespread nationalisation of domestic industrial enterprises in Pakistan in 1974 has been interpreted as an attempt to curb the economic influence of the forty-three 'leading families' who controlled much of the industrial and financial sectors (Sobhan, 1979b, p. 61). Similarly, Jones (1976, p. 139) argued that, in explaining the growth of public ownership in South Korea, '. . . an important role must also be assigned to conscious restraint of large concentrations of private economic power'.

Reliance on individual preferences and market demand

By relying on individual preferences, as revealed in the ability to pay for a good or service, the neoclassical framework excludes consideration both of the way in which individual preferences are formed and of the appropriateness of the consumption pattern. Many development economists would argue that commercial pressures such as advertising and product differentiation create a pattern of demand that is inappropriate to the needs of the mass of the population in LDCs. Lall (1976b, p. 189) suggested that:

> ... several 'characteristics' of products offered in world markets – determined by the product differentiation and marketing practices of large oligopolistic companies selling to rich markets rather than by any rational consideration of fulfilling the most urgent needs of poor countries – are costly, inappropriate and unnecessary in LDCs.

Considerations of this type have led to the establishment of public enterprises intended to replace 'inappropriate' imported or privately produced products. A well-documented example of this approach is the pharmaceutical industry, where growing concern over the excessive cost and product differentiation of the pharmaceutical TNCs' products has led a number of LDCs to establish publicly owned drug manufacturing capacity, which produces a limited range of generic drugs appropriate to the needs of the population (*World Development*, 1983).

A POLITICAL ECONOMY APPROACH TO THE ANALYSIS OF THE PUBLIC ENTERPRISE SECTOR

The preceding analysis of the economic determinants of the size and growth of the public enterprise sector in LDCs needs to be supplemented by a consideration of political and ideological factors.

It is conventional practice to distinguish between two types of state intervention: support and control (FitzGerald, 1977). In the first case, the function of public enterprises is confined mainly to performing a supportive role for the private sector, by undertaking investment in high-risk, low-return activities that provide the private sector with basic industrial inputs and infrastructural requirements. In the second case, the state assumes a more independent role, and public enterprises are used to pursue ends that may differ from, or be additional to, the market efficiency objective. In socialist economies, public ownership may be regarded as a necessary condition for the establishment of socialism and is therefore pursued as an end in itself.

These two approaches can be illustrated by contrasting the perceived role of the public and private enterprise sectors in the Republic of Korea and in Tanzania. In the Republic of Korea,

> private ownership of production should unconditionally be encouraged except in instances where it is necessary to control it to stimulate national development and protect the interests of the people. (President Park, 1970, quoted in Jones and Mason, 1982, p. 21)

Whereas in Tanzania,

> to build and maintain socialism it is essential that all the major means of production and exchange in the nation are controlled and owned by the peasants through the machinery of their Government and their co-operatives. (President Nyerere, The Arusha Declaration, 1967)

Differences in ideological orientation are likely, therefore, to be an important influence on the size and functions of the public enterprise sector in LDCs. This does not mean, however, that the public enterprise's role is static. Significant changes can and do occur over time within individual economies.

These changes may be associated with a sudden alteration in political régime. In Sri Lanka, the election of a socialist government in 1970 led to an expansion of public enterprise activities in the industrial, trading, plantation and agricultural sectors, which was subsequently reversed by the election of a new government in 1977 (UNIDO, 1982a). In Chile, the overthrow of the Allende government led to large-scale denationalisation: of the 465 firms in public ownership in 1973, only thirty-one remained in the public sector in 1978 (Foxley, 1980). In Bangladesh, the vacuum created by the departure of Pakistani industrialists in 1971 was filled by the state taking over the abandoned production units (Sobhan, 1983).

In other instances, the changes in the public enterprise sector's role have occurred more gradually, reflecting an evolving relationship between the state, the private domestic sector and foreign capital (see also Chapter 4, section 4.19). In most LDCs the effort to achieve economic independence by reducing the economy's dependence on foreign interests has been an important stimulus to the growth of the public enterprise sector. Table 5.5 shows the quickening pace of nationalisation over the period 1960–76 and indicates that nationalisation has occurred in each of the major industrial sectors, although the figures may distort the scale of nationalisation in some sectors as no account has been taken of the size of nationalised enterprises.

The existing relationship between the state and foreign interests may not be altered significantly by the transfer of ownership (although as Nixson, 1983b, argued, increased indigenous ownership may be a necessary, if not sufficient, condition for local control, and therefore should not be dismissed as mere 'window-dressing'). Since the operation of the nationalised production enterprises is often dependent upon foreign interests for technology, managerial skills and marketing and distributional outlets, the state has an interest in securing an accommodation with foreign capital. At the same time, the TNCs benefit from their association with the PEs by obtaining a secure source of raw materials, or by the access to the state bureaucracy and decision-making process that collaboration with the public enterprise sector may bring (Evans, 1979, ch. 5). This coincidence of interests gives rise to what has been described as a 'symbiotic relationship' between the state and the TNCs (Evans, 1977b; Langdon, 1977, 1979). This broad identity of interests does not eradicate conflict between foreign capital and the state, but it does mean that both parties' actions are constrained by the need to avoid destabilising the system of production of which both are a part and upon which

Table 5.5 Take-over of foreign enterprises in LDCs, by major industrial sector, 1960–76

	Total number	Mining and petroleum	Agriculture	Manufacturing	Trade	Public utility	Banking and insurance	Other
1960–9	455	72	98	76	28	31	133	17
1970–6	914	228	174	145	20	27	216	104

Source: United Nations (1978), Table III-29, p. 233.

both depend (see Chapter 4, section 4.15; also Kirkpatrick and Nixson, 1981).

In recent years there has been a significant growth in co-operative arrangements between the public enterprise and private sectors in the form of joint ventures. UNIDO (1983c, pp. 79–80) suggested that the growth in this form of arrangement was the result of the following reasons: first, government equity participation can stimulate local entrepreneurship by creating confidence among domestic investors; second, the involvement of private investment in public enterprises is a way of acquiring managerial, technological and marketing skills; third, the government may wish to spread its limited investment resources over a larger number of enterprises by subscribing to their equity on a partial basis; finally, the joint venture is seen as a means of controlling the activities of foreign investors (see United Nations, 1978, ch. IV and V).

The development of the Brazilian petrochemical industry is illustrative of this new form of relationship between the state, domestic private industry and transnationals. Government participation began in the 1960s as a result of local private industry's initiatives, which sought collaboration with the state and TNCs. Through time, however, local capital was 'squeezed out' of the industry by its inability to meet expansion needs, leading to a consolidation of relationships between the public enterprise component and the TNCs (Evans, 1977a, 1979). In Egypt, the 'open door' policy introduced in the 1970s increased the autonomy of the public enterprise sector and led to a significant number of joint ventures between public enterprises and private interests (UNIDO, 1983c, pp. 81–2). In a number of Latin American countries, collaboration with TNCs has facilitated the entry of manufacturing public enterprises into export markets (Vernon, 1981; Jones and Wortzel, 1982).

The discussion so far has emphasised how the public enterprise sector's role will be influenced by a government's political or ideological predilection, and has described the relationships that have evolved between the state-owned enterprises and the private industrial sector. It is evident, however, that the government represents a particular group, or coalition of interests, in the society, and control of the use of the state's resources and over the distribution of the benefits these resources generate can be used to advance the interests of certain groups in the economy while retarding others. A full understanding of a government's policy towards the public enterprise sector would require, therefore, a detailed study of the particular interest groups that have influence over, and are affected by, the publicly owned enterprises. Further consideration of these issues would extend the analysis beyond the terms of reference set for this chapter, but the interested reader will find this approach employed in the work of Petras (1977), Sobhan (1979a), Ahmad (1982) and Ansari (1983). Individual case studies using this analytical framework can be found in the work of Evans (1977b, 1979) on Brazil, Sobhan (1979b, 1983) on the South Asia economies and Bangladesh, respectively, and E. Jones (1981) on the Caribbean countries.

5.4   SOURCES OF PUBLIC ENTERPRISE FINANCE

The sources of public enterprise funding are as follows: external, governmental, domestic non-governmental, and internal.

Lending to the public enterprise sector in LDCs has been attractive to the international banking system, since such loans usually carry government guarantees against default. Flows of external commercial debt contracted by the LDC public enterprises in the Euro-currency market rose rapidly during the 1970s, increasing by almost 350 per cent over the period 1975–8. In 1978, new loan commitments to LDC state-owned firms amounted to almost one-third of total LDC commercial borrowing (Gillis *et al*., 1982, p. 263). The debts incurred by public enterprises have subsequently become a major element in the repayment difficulties encountered by countries such as Brazil, Zaire, Zambia and Indonesia.

Lending by international aid agencies has been an additional source of external funding for the public enterprise sector. Sobhan (1979b, p. 78) observed that '. . . for Pakistan, Bangladesh, Sri Lanka and Nepal and frequently for India, capital investment in public enterprise is closely tied to the availability of external resource inflows and the protracted process of aid negotiation and disbursement'. The use of aid funds for public enterprise financing can, by tying the project's design, technology and costs to the donor country's specifications, lead to the adoption of 'inappropriate' techniques of production.

Government funding of public enterprises combines equity capital, direct loans and operating subsidies. Gillis *et al*. (1982) observed that while most LDC governments have favoured loan-funding of public enterprises, government equity participation has been increasingly more important in recent years, particularly in the energy sector where, as noted already, joint ventures with private domestic and foreign capital are common. The public enterprise sector may also receive indirect government funding, from, for example, subsidised interest charges on loans, or special tax treatment. Floyd (1978) observed that in many LDCs public enterprises have partial or complete exemption from general income tax. It is also common practice to exempt public enterprises from customs duties on their imports. The earmarking of particular indirect tax revenues to public enterprises is particularly important in Colombia, Ghana and Brazil (Gillis *et al*., 1982, p. 266). Trebat (1980) estimated that in Brazil earmarked taxes accounted for 12 per cent of public enterprise investment finance in the mid-1970s.

Domestic non-government sources of PE finance are provided by the domestic banking system and specialised credit agencies. In fact, the separation of these sources from government funding may be more apparent than real, since in most LDCs the specialised credit agencies are predominantly under public control, and the banking system, if not owned by the state, will be subject to close government direction of its lending activities. This control over the financing system means that the PEs frequently receive preferential treatment in obtaining funds. The government will often specify the lending rate of interest, or require the credit agencies to give priority to PE lending. Specialised development banks may be required to buy long-term bonds or equity from the public enterprises. As a result of these financial controls, domestic non-government borrowing by PEs often contains a significant concessional component.

The final source of public enterprise funding, from internal operating surpluses (the difference between sales revenue and current expenditure on goods and services, excluding depreciation), is considered in section 5.6.

5.5   THE EVALUATION OF PUBLIC ENTERPRISE PERFORMANCE

INTRODUCTION

Because of their size and central position in many LDCs, the operations of public enterprises are of major importance to the performance of the economy as a whole. Performance can be defined in terms of success in achieving stated objectives, and in principle the process of performance evaluation would follow a step by step procedure of identifying the objectives set for the public enterprise sector, constructing performance indicators to measure the degree of attainment of these objectives, and measuring performance. In practice, however, there are considerable difficulties in implementing this sequential procedure.

First, the government's objectives for public enterprises are seldom stated clearly or unambiguously. Often the goals are expressed in such general terms ('maximise the contribution to society's well-being') that they can be used to justify almost any outcome. Where the objectives are stated explicitly, they may be inconsistent with each other or may frequently be altered in response to political circumstances.

Second, even if a set of objectives can be identified, it will be difficult to devise a satisfactory procedure for multiple-goals performance assessment. One response is simply to select a single objective as being of primary importance, and to concentrate on the estimation of performance indicators appropriate to this goal. As will be seen in section 5.6, this approach has been widely used in practice, with performance assessment being restricted to measures of economic efficiency. An alternative approach is to identify the relative importance attached by the government to each objective, and to use this information to establish 'equivalence values' or 'trade-offs' between each measure of performance. By selecting one objective as the general unit of account, the equivalence values can then, in principle, be used to express the other net benefits in terms of this numéraire and to calculate a total measure of performance as the weighted sum of different performance indicators.[5]

Third, there are serious difficulties in devising appropriate measures even of single-objective performance. The most widely used measures are based on a set of restrictive assumptions about market structure and behaviour. Since these assumptions are seldom fulfilled in practice, the interpretation of the performance measures is ambiguous, and different policy conclusions can be drawn from the findings.

Finally, there are frequently problems in obtaining the necessary data for the empirical estimation of the performance measures and in ensuring that the operating conditions and characteristics of different enterprises are sufficiently similar to allow meaningful comparisons of performance to be made.

MEASURES OF PERFORMANCE[6]

Section 5.3 pointed out that equilibrium in a perfectly competitive market is a state of economic, or Pareto, efficiency. This well-known result of the traditional welfare analysis has had an important influence on thinking about economic performance assessment, and forms the theoretical basis for three distinct, but related, approaches to performance measurement.

Profit measures

In the perfectly competitive model, profit-maximising behaviour leads to Pareto optimality. This result has frequently been interpreted to mean that an enterprise's financial profitability provides a satisfactory indicator of economic performance. However, the use of profitability has serious drawbacks as a measure of performance, particularly when applied to public enterprises.

Profit-maximising behaviour will ensure economic efficiency only in the context of perfectly competitive markets. Since most public enterprises are either monopolies or account for a large share of the market, an improvement in profit performance may represent the exercise of the enterprise's monopoly position in the market, rather than an improvement in efficiency. This can be seen in Figure 5.1, which compares the firm in perfect competition and in monopoly. In perfect competition, the firm faces a perfectly elastic demand curve (this is also the average revenue curve, AR,

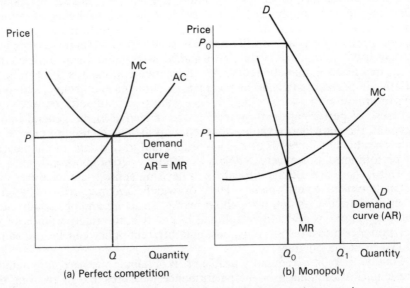

(a) Perfect competition   (b) Monopoly

Figure 5.1 Equilibrium in perfect competition and monopoly

and, in perfect competition, is the same as the marginal revenue, MR, curve). In equilibrium, the firm is earning normal profits and the average cost curve (AC) is tangential to the demand curve. Since the firm is assumed to be maximising profits, marginal revenue (MR) and marginal cost (MC) are equal. In perfect competition therefore, profit-maximising behaviour (MC = MR) results in a price (P) that coincides with the efficient price level (P = MC). In monopoly, however, the firm (which is also the industry) faces a downward-sloping demand curve. Profit-maximising behaviour (MC = MR) results in P_0Q_0, whereas efficiency pricing (P = MC) requires P_1Q_1.

As was argued earlier, public enterprise activities are often associated with significant externalities that do not enter into the estimates of financial profitability. This provides a further reason for believing that current profit performance will frequently be a poor indicator of the enterprise's efficiency performance. A related issue is that the market values used in calculating financial performance may not be equal to their efficiency values owing to market distortions, thus creating a further source of divergence between financial and efficiency performance (this point is discussed in greater detail in the sub-section on pricing criteria below).

Many public enterprises are engaged in large-scale activities, with major economies of scale. In Figure 5.2, with market demand DD, the application of efficiency pricing (P_2Q_2) will result in financial losses (price is below average costs), whereas profit-maximising behaviour will move price and quantity to P_1 and Q_1.

Finally, the calculation of total profit may differ between enterprises, with different accounting practices being followed in the treatment of asset valuation and depreciation allowances, interest payments on loan capital,

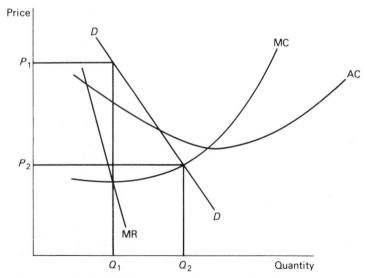

Figure 5.2 The effect of increasing returns to scale on profitability

managerial services, and the time period to which the calculations relate. These problems become particularly acute in the case of public enterprises, which often receive preferential terms on loans from the government-owned financial institutions and which may be partially or wholly exempt from taxation (Floyd, 1978).

Since many of the receipts and payments of public enterprises represent transfers within the public sector, the financial performance of PEs is frequently assessed in terms of their *operating surplus*. The operating surplus (or balance) is measured as the difference between sales revenue and expenditure on goods and services other than capital assets. It therefore excludes not only depreciation but also all receipts from government transfers and payments to the government in the form of interest, dividends and direct taxation. While the operating surplus measure eliminates the problems associated with the treatment of intra-public sector payments and receipts, care still needs to be taken in interpreting it as an absolute or relative measure of financial performance, since both revenue and current expenditure can be subject to government controls. An enterprise may be required to sell its output at a controlled price; it may obtain inputs at subsidised prices; or it may be obliged to purchase inputs produced by other public enterprises at prices above the market level.

Profitability (and, to an even greater extent, 'operating surplus'), therefore, is an unsatisfactory and ambiguous indicator of an enterprise's economic performance. Nevertheless, the financial record of public enterprises is widely used to judge performance. The argument that public enterprises should at least 'break even' by 'covering their costs' is often advanced, being justified in terms of either the incentive that such a requirement gives to efficient management, or the need to avoid the 'burden' of subsidisation from general tax revenue (see, for example, World Bank, 1983, Part II). However, while these arguments may have an intuitive, common sense appeal, they cannot be rationalised easily in terms of the efficiency analysis.

Productive efficiency and productivity growth measures
The perfect competition model postulates a state of productive efficiency in equilibrium, and this result provides an additional theoretical basis for deriving performance indicators.

Productive efficiency can be thought of as consisting of two components: technical efficiency, and allocative, or factor price, efficiency (Farrell, 1957). The former measures the degree of economy in resource inputs used to produce a given output. The latter measures the degree to which the best combination of different factors is achieved, having regard to their relative prices.

In Figure 5.3, *technical efficiency* is measured by the relative distance of the firm from the efficiency frontier, which represents the minimum combination of factor inputs needed, in the present state of technology, to produce a specified level of output. If a firm is actually using factor amounts represented by C, the relative technical efficiency is measured by $0A/0C$. *Allocative efficiency* is achieved when the ratio of factor prices is equal to the ratio of marginal products, as at B. The price line XX indicates the minimum cost of

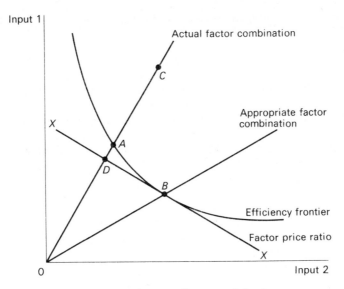

Figure 5.3 Productive efficiency of the firm

producing the level of output represented by the efficiency frontier. Since the total input costs at D are the same as at B, the relative allocative efficiency of the firm at C can be expressed as $0D/0A$. Over time, an improvement in productive efficiency occurs as the existing factor combination shifts towards A and/or B. At point B, production is both technical and allocative efficient.

When estimating productive efficiency (usually referred to as productivity), the relationship between output and inputs is represented by the production function. In Figure 5.3 it was assumed that output (O) could be produced by combining two factors of production, which are normally taken to be capital (K) and labour (L), with a given level of technical efficiency (T). In functional terms, in any time period (t),

$$O_t = f(K_t, L_t, T_t). \tag{5.1}$$

If an improvement in technical efficiency occurs within the firm (i.e. C moves towards A in Figure 5.3), the same output can be produced with fewer inputs of labour and capital, or, what is the same thing, a higher level of output can be produced with the same inputs. In terms of expression (5.1), if $O_{t+1} > O_t$, and $K_t = K_{t+1}$, and $L_t = L_{t+1}$, then the change in output is attributable to a change in T ($T_{t+1} > T_t$). This change in T is therefore a measure of *total productivity change*, and occurs whenever output changes relative to the inputs of capital and labour. Since the change in T measures the portion of the growth of output not attributable to increases in the factors of production, it is often referred to as the 'residual'.

In estimating total productivity changes, it is common practice to assume a particular production relationship, usually the Cobb–Douglas function, which has certain well-known properties (see Thirlwall, 1983, ch. 2). The function can be written as

$$O_t = T_t K_t^\alpha L_t^\beta, \tag{5.2}$$

where O_t is a measure of real output at time t, T_t is 'total' productivity, or technology, K_t is capital stock, L_t is labour input, α is the partial elasticity (responsiveness) of output with respect to a change in capital (holding labour constant) and β is the partial elasticity of output with respect to labour (holding capital constant). On the assumption of diminishing marginal productivity of factors, α and β will each be less than unity. The sum of the partial elasticities gives the scale of returns, and the Cobb–Douglas function is usually employed in a constrained form with the sum of α and β set equal to unity, i.e. constant returns to scale.

Equation (5.2) can now be used to estimate the separate influences of the sources of output growth. To do this, the equation is transformed into a rate of growth form by taking the logarithms of the variables and differentiating with respect to time,

$$\log O_t = \log T_t + \alpha \log K_t + \beta \log L_t$$

$$\frac{d \log O_t}{dt} = \frac{d \log T_t}{dt} + \alpha \frac{d \log K_t}{dt} + \beta \frac{d \log L_t}{dt} \tag{5.3}$$

Equation (5.3) can be rewritten in the equivalent form,

$$g_O = g_T + \alpha g_K + \beta g_L, \tag{5.4}$$

where g_O, g_T, g_K and g_L are the rates of growth of output, total productivity, capital and labour respectively, and α and β are the partial elasticities of output with respect to capital and labour.

Equation (5.4) can be rearranged as follows:

$$g_T = g_O - \alpha g_K - \beta g_L. \tag{5.5}$$

In other words, total factor productivity growth (g_T) is the difference between total output growth and the weighted growth of capital and labour inputs. Thus, with knowledge of the value of g_O, g_K, g_L, α and β, the growth in total factor productivity can be estimated.

A similar method of estimating total factor productivity change can be derived from the following equation:

$$T_t = \frac{O_t}{\alpha K_t + \beta L_t}, \tag{5.6}$$

where T_t, O_t, K_t and L_t are indices of total factor productivity, output, capital inputs and labour inputs, respectively, and α and β are the share of capital and labour in total income (i.e. weights) in the base period. A change in total factor productivity occurs, therefore, if O_t changes relative to $(\alpha K_t + \beta L_t)$ or vice versa.

It can be shown that, if markets are perfectly competitive, if production is subject to constant returns to scale and if factor payments are equal to their marginal product, then factor income shares will be equal to the elasticity of output with respect to each input.[7] The convenience of this result for empirical work has meant that, in estimating (5.5) or (5.6), most studies assign values to α and β according to each factor's share in total income.

The estimation of productivity change gives rise to many problems.[8] In particular, the estimate of total factor productivity (T) will measure technical efficiency only if the set of restrictive assumptions underlying the estimation procedure are met. If these conditions are not fulfilled, the interpretation of T becomes ambiguous. First, if markets are not competitive and the market prices of inputs differ from their marginal products, it becomes impossible to distinguish between the effects of changes in technical efficiency (shifts in the production frontier) and in allocative efficiency (movements along the frontier). For the same reason, the income shares used to estimate α and β may not be accurate measures of the partial elasticities. Second, if returns to scale are not constant, the effect of increasing or decreasing returns will be reflected in the total factor productivity estimate: increasing returns will bias the value of g_T upwards, and decreasing returns will bias it downwards.

Another major problem in measuring productivity changes is allowing for quality improvements in the output and inputs. If improvements in the quality of the output are neglected, the growth in productivity is understated. Conversely, if improvements in the quality of labour or capital inputs are ignored, the contribution of the inputs to output growth is understated, and the role of total factor productivity changes is exaggerated.

A further difficulty arises in combining the heterogeneous elements of labour and capital to form aggregate factor indices. If, for example, the labour input is measured in physical terms simply as the number of employees, then the effect of variations in part-time work, in number of hours worked, or in the balance between skilled and unskilled labour will be omitted from the calculation. If capital input is calculated on the basis of capital stock, difficulties arise in the determination of price deflators, the productive life of different assets, the degree of asset utilisation and changes in the composition of the capital stock.

An alternative to the use of total factor productivity measures is to calculate *partial productivity indices* for labour and capital. These are given by:

$$P_{L_t} = \frac{O_t}{L_t} \quad \text{and} \quad P_{K_t} = \frac{O_t}{K_t}$$

where P_{L_t} and P_{K_t} are indices of labour and capital productivity, respectively, and O_t, L_t and K_t are output, labour and capital indices, as before. A change in partial productivity occurs if O_t changes relative to L_t (or K_t) and vice versa.

The labour productivity measure has been widely used, largely because of comparative ease of calculation. However, there are difficulties in interpreting the measure that restrict its usefulness. Imperfections in product markets, rather than differences in technical requirements of factor inputs, may account for cross-firm differences in the output–labour ratio. Some enterprises are more monopolistic than others, enabling them to charge higher prices, which results in higher output value per employee. Differences in the nature of employment (part-time, seasonal, skill composition, etc.) may distort comparability of the output–labour ratio. If capital intensity and scale of output are correlated, variations in the firm's scale of operation will tend to affect the labour productivity measure. The fundamental weakness of the partial productivity measure is the assumption that the observed change in output is due entirely to the variation in the relevant single input (Bhalla, 1975b).

Pricing criteria

The perfect competition model implies that, in a situation of Pareto optimality, the firm's equilibrium output level will be set at the point where marginal cost and price are equal. This result provides the theoretical basis for the marginal cost pricing rule, which is often advocated as a means of improving the economic efficiency performance of public enterprises. Although the rule was originally developed in the context of the advanced countries' public utilities sectors, there has been a growing interest in recent years in applying the principle to public enterprise operations in LDCs.

The rationale for the marginal cost pricing rule can be clarified by referring to Figure 5.1(b). *DD* is the demand curve for the output of the enterprise's existing capital stock. The marginal cost curve (MC) represents the cost of supplying additional units of output. The total benefits to consumers is measured by their willingness to pay, that is, the area under the demand curve, and the total cost of supplying the output is given by the area under the supply curve. The objective is to maximise the net benefit, i.e. total benefit minus total cost. This is achieved with output level of Q_1 and price P_1, where the market clearing price is equal to marginal cost.

Figure 5.1(b) was presented in a deliberately simplified way to clarify the basic principles involved. In practice, the application of marginal cost pricing gives rise to various complications. First, there is the question of determining the correct concept of marginal cost. Marginal cost is defined with respect to a time period, and a distinction is usually drawn between short-run marginal costs (SRMC), measuring the addition to total costs incurred when output is increased by more intensive use of the existing capital stock, and long-run marginal costs (LRMC), measuring the extra costs of increasing output by expanding the plant size. If SRMC > LRMC, it indicates that it would be cheaper to increase output by increasing the plant size, rather than by using existing capacity more intensively. If capacity can be increased instantaneously and by marginal amounts, then, by following an optimal investment policy, SRMC and LRMC will always be equal. Thus, 'the argument about whether public enterprises should set prices equal to long-run or short-run marginal costs is only meaningful when capacity is not optimal' (Turvey, 1969, p. 283).

Although this argument provides a theoretical resolution of the 'SRMC versus LRMC' issue, it is of little practical value. The existence of capital indivisibilities, or 'lumpiness' in investment, means that adjustments to the capital stock are neither marginal nor instantaneous. Suppose that in Figure 5.4 the existing plant has a fixed maximum output of $\bar{q}_0$. Because of indivisibilities in investment, new investment increases the maximum capacity to $\bar{q}_1$. $SRMC_0$ is the short-run marginal cost curve associated with the initial capital stock – it rises steeply when the capacity constraint is reached. $SRMC_1$ is an equivalent curve associated with the new capital stock.

If demand is at level D_aD_a, price is set at p_0 and output is q_0. As demand increases to D_bD_b, the price must be increased to p_1 to ration the fixed output $\bar{q}_0$. At what point should capacity be increased to $\bar{q}_1$? Since investment can be undertaken only in 'lumpy' amounts, there cannot be an LRMC curve, so that the previous investment decision rule of comparing SRMC and LRMC values cannot be used. It becomes necessary, therefore, to compare the increase in total benefits from the new investment with the increase in total costs (the stream of future benefits and costs being discounted to present value terms). Since total benefits are measured by the area under the demand curve, we can envisage a further increase in demand to D_cD_c, where price has risen to p_2, which is just sufficient to yield an increase in benefits ($\bar{q}_0ABC$) sufficient to cover the additional investment costs (not shown in Figure 5.4), and the investment is therefore undertaken. Once installed, the fixed capacity costs become sunk costs ('bygones are bygones') and the appropriate pricing policy is SRMC, thereby ensuring efficient utilisation of existing capacity. Price therefore falls to p_0 again.

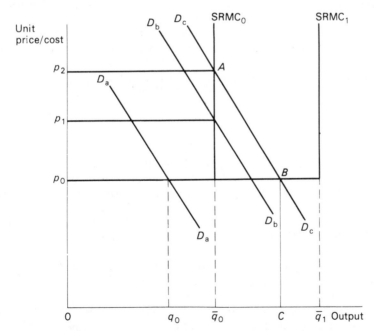

Figure 5.4 Marginal cost pricing with capacity indivisibilities

It is clear from Figure 5.4 that the SRMC rule results in large price fluctuations, which will create uncertainty and may therefore be unacceptable to consumers. To avoid this problem, it may be necessary to abandon a strict adherence to the short-run marginal cost pricing principle, and use a price based on an average of the different SRMC values.

A second issue of some importance is the relationship between marginal cost pricing and financial viability. Previously, it was shown that application of the MC price rule will result in financial deficits if there are increasing returns of scale in production (since the average cost curve is falling, marginal cost lies below average cost, and price is therefore less than average cost). Since these financial deficits cannot be financed in a way that is neutral as far as allocative efficiency is concerned, the problem in theory becomes one of weighting the inefficiencies resulting from pricing at above marginal cost in order to avoid financial losses, against the allocative inefficiencies created by financing the losses from distortionary taxes elsewhere in the economy. In reality, this type of general equilibrium calculation is impossible, and the issue is often resolved by requiring the public enterprise to adhere to the marginal cost pricing rule, while at the same time achieving a specified financial target.[9]

A further problem of particular importance in marginal cost pricing is the second-best issue. In deriving the marginal cost pricing rule, it was implicitly assumed that the efficiency-optimising conditions were met in the remaining sectors of the economy. The second-best theorem points out that if these optimum conditions are not met elsewhere in the economy, then one cannot assume that using marginal cost pricing in the remaining sector will improve the overall level of economic efficiency (Lipsey and Lancaster, 1957). Since there is no possibility of implementing the optimum solution, which would involve adjustments to taxes, prices and output levels throughout the economy, the choice is between devising approximations to the 'attainable best' marginal cost prices or 'standing by and sucking our thumbs under the sign of second best' (Mishan, 1962, quoted in Lintner, 1981). Not surprisingly, most observers have recommended the first of these responses. Lintner (1981, p. 33) argued that:

> The managements of state-owned and regulated industries cannot be held responsible for the operating policies of firms in other sectors of the economy, nor for deficiencies in tax structures and other aspects of government policy. All that can be expected of these managements is that they effectively use the best information available concerning demands, costs and technological substitutions and interdependencies to optimize their operations in the context of the existing economy.

If market values diverge significantly from their efficiency level, then one way in which the PEs can 'effectively use the best information available . . . to optimize their operations' will be to replace the 'distorted' market prices with shadow prices. The shadow price will reflect the economic cost (or value) of the input (or output) and can be thought of as being equivalent to the value that would have arisen if there had been no market distortions. In LDCs, market and efficiency values often differ (Balassa, 1982). For example, the wage paid to labour may exceed its marginal opportunity cost when there is widespread underemployment; import and export values will be understated if the foreign exchange rate is maintained at a level below equilibrium; controls on interest rates may result in undervaluation of the opportunity cost of capital; and so on. Adjustments for these types of market imperfection in the estimation of marginal cost prices will be necessary to ensure that decisions are based on economic costs and benefits rather than on market values.

Recent developments in the use of shadow prices for investment and pricing decisions have been concerned with assessing efficiency in the context of international trade.[10] For internationally traded goods and services, the efficient level of domestic production will be given when the marginal cost of production is equal to the world (import or export) price. These international prices, or, more generally, the equilibrium exchange rate, therefore provide a yardstick by which the efficiency of domestic production can be measured.

In the preceding paragraphs, a number of problems in using marginal cost pricing as a means of improving economic performance in the public enterprise sector have been discussed. It will be clear from the discussion that the marginal cost calculation will inevitably be difficult and will depend on the researcher's perception of the objectives of the pricing policy, the nature of market imperfections and the economic characteristics of the enterprise. At best, therefore, marginal cost estimates will serve as a benchmark, in terms of which current pricing policy can be assessed.

CONCLUSION

This section has discussed in some detail the three sets of performance indicators that can be derived from the welfare economics efficiency analysis. It has been shown that each of these approaches, and the specific measures derived from them, is subject to severe limitations in terms of interpretation and application. The assessment of public enterprise performance is complicated further by the fact that objectives other than economic efficiency often have a high priority in government policy towards the public enterprise sector. It should not be concluded, however, that the economist's concern with economic efficiency is misplaced. By calculating the efficiency costs of pursuing non-economic objectives, decision-makers are provided with a measure of the opportunity cost of their actions, which may in turn result in greater consistency in policy decision-making.

5.6   THE EMPIRICAL EVIDENCE ON PUBLIC ENTERPRISE PERFORMANCE

INTRODUCTION

This section reviews the empirical evidence on the performance of the public enterprise sector in LDCs, using the three market-based performance indicators discussed in the preceding section – namely, profitability and financial performance, productivity, and pricing policy. Before examining the evidence, however, it is worth re-emphasising the problems of measurement and interpretation associated with performance assessment. The real world rarely, if ever, conforms to the conditions specified by the economic theory underlying the performance measures, and studies differ significantly in the methodology employed to deal with these divergencies between theory and reality.

Further difficulties arise in comparative studies of performance, where it is important that the sectors or enterprises are assessed on a like-with-like basis. These conditions are seldom met. Private and public sector enterprises are often confronted with different factor prices, have differential access to production technology and know-how, and are subject to different operating criteria. In many cases, public enterprises occupy a monopoly position within an industry, and performance cannot be assessed on a comparative basis.

It is not surprising, therefore, that empirical evidence of public enterprise performance in LDCs is fragmentary, and, where available, needs to be interpreted with care.[11] With these reservations in mind, the following sections review the performance record of the public enterprise sector. For each of the performance measures, the studies are presented in descending order of aggregation, moving from the economy and sectoral level to individual enterprises.

PROFITABILITY AND FINANCIAL PERFORMANCE

Gantt and Dutto (1968). Although now somewhat out of date, this study provides the most comprehensive cross-country evidence on the financial performance of PEs in LDCs. The evidence was based on the performance of sixty-four government-owned corporations in twenty-six countries,[12] classified in six industry groups, and averaged over a seven-year period.

Estimates for operating surplus (revenue less expenditure, and excluding depreciation and intra-government transfers) show that the cross-industry average was positive in Latin America, Africa and Asia. On a cross-area basis, the transport (excluding railways), petroleum, electricity and communications industries all recorded a positive operating surplus, while the railway sector's operating surplus was negative. To facilitate comparisons of financial performance, operating surpluses were also expressed as a percentage of current activity, defined as the average of current revenue and expenditure. These results show that performance varied widely between areas and different types of industries. The Latin American enterprises averaged +2.1 per cent, barely covering their current operating costs, whereas the averages for Asia and Africa were +16.4 per cent and +19.5 per cent, respectively. The industry averages ranged from −13.5 per cent for railways to +43.3 per cent for petroleum (Latin America only).

When depreciation provision was added to current expenditure, none of the areas generated a surplus over current revenue. On an industry basis, only petroleum and electricity were able to generate sufficient current revenue to meet replacement investment needs.

World Bank (1983). On the basis of unpublished internal documents, the

World Bank reported that 'available data for SOEs [state-owned enterprises] in twenty-four developing countries showed a small operating surplus before depreciation in 1977. However, no account was taken of interest payments, subsidized input prices, taxes, or accumulated arrears. Proper provision for these items and depreciation would show SOEs in many of these countries to be in deficit' (p. 74).

Sobhan (1979b). This study provides information on the capacity of the public enterprise sector in several South Asian countries (Bangladesh, India, Nepal, Pakistan, Sri Lanka) to generate internal funds for the financing of capital replacement and expansion. Measuring gross savings as post-tax profits plus depreciation, the evidence indicates that public enterprises' gross savings as a share of gross fixed capital formation ranged from 31 per cent in India to over 100 per cent in Pakistan and Sri Lanka over the 1970–5 period.

United Nations (1981). In this report, the financial performance of publicly owned water supply authorities in seven Asian capital cities was examined, With the exception of Bombay, current charges were judged to be low compared to the costs of the water supply and the six remaining schemes had negative or marginal surplus revenue. It was estimated that in order to generate an adequate internal cash surplus to provide a substantial part of capital funds for system expansion, the rate of return to net fixed assets would need to be betweeen 6 and 8 per cent per annum, whereas the actual rate of return in the six city systems was found to be less than 1 per cent.

Trebat (1980). This study covered fifty of the largest public enterprises in Brazil during 1965–75, representing six industrial sectors (electricity, telecommunications, steel, petrochemicals, mining and railways). Estimated rates of return on physical capital investment (returns are calculated as value added less depreciation and wages) showed considerable variation across economic sectors, ranging from 41 per cent in petrochemicals to 6 per cent in communications in 1975. Although the data indicated a declining trend in profitability over the period, the Brazilian public enterprises examined had been generally profitable. The evidence also revealed that the selected public enterprises were able to finance 40–60 per cent of gross investment during 1966–75 using retained earnings and depreciation funds, a figure similar to the 50–60 per cent self-financing by Brazilian private firms.

UNIDO (1982d). In this study of Tanzania it appears that the industrial para-statal sector as a whole generated a positive operating surplus over the period 1967–78, that on average amounted to 66 per cent of the enterprises' fixed capital formation, although this average figure conceals large differences in the financial performance of individual enterprises.

Walstedt (1980). In Turkey, where state enterprises accounted for more than 30 per cent of manufacturing value added by the mid-1970s, rates of profit have been low, yielding negligible rates of return on capital. For the manufacturing PEs, the ratio of net profits (before interest and corporation tax) to total assets was 4–5 per cent over the 1967–71 period. Correcting for inadequate depreciation rates and for subsidised interest charges on borrowed funds would reduce the estimated rate profitability to zero or negative levels.

Kim (1981). This study compared, *inter alia*, the financial performance of publicly and privately owned enterprises within the manufacturing sector in Tanzania during the period 1970–5. Only those sub-sectors within manufacturing in which both public and private enterprises coexisted were examined. The results show that, in all years except 1971, government enterprises' receipts (excluding subsidies) were insufficient to cover current expenditure (excluding tax payments) and depreciation provision. In contrast, private sector firms recorded surpluses in five of the six years. These differences are partly attributable to the overmanning and higher wages per employee in public enterprises, reflecting the influence of objectives other than profit maximisation.

Funkhouser and MacAvoy (1979). This study compared the performance of a large number of private and public firms coexisting in a number of different industries in Indonesia, for the year 1971. Profit margins were calculated as sales revenue minus direct expenditures (excluding depreciation and interest), expressed as a percentage of sales revenue, and the performance of public and private enterprises in eleven industries was compared. These comparisons were made for four sub-samples: (i) all public and private firms; (ii) all public and private firms from those industries in which there were both types of company; (iii) public and private firms of comparable size only; and (iv) public and private firms 'paired' on the basis of comparable levels of sales of the same products. In each case, the average profit margin for public companies was found to be lower than for private firms, and the mean differences were statistically significant.

Summary
The preceding review of evidence on public enterprises' financial performance suggests a number of general conclusions. First, profitability does vary significantly between different industries. Rail transport and water utilities, for example, appear to perform less well than petrochemicals. These inter-industry differences reflect differences in the market conditions in each industry, and in the extent to which the charging of market prices is considered to be an appropriate method of allocating the public enterprise's output. Second, when comparisons are made between public and private concerns, profitability appears to be lower in the public enterprise sector. These findings need to be interpreted with care, however: the public and private firms may have different input costs, or be subject to different price controls. Finally, it should be remembered that financial performance is distinct from efficiency performance: a poor profitability record may be consistent with efficient operations, and vice versa.

PRODUCTIVITY PERFORMANCE

Public–private industry studies
Krueger and Tuncer (1982). This study estimated rates of growth in total factor productivity (TFP) and absolute levels of single-factor productivity for two-digit manufacturing industries in Turkey over the period 1963–76. Estimates are presented separately for public and private enterprises in each industry, and for the private and public manufacturing sectors as a whole. State-owned enterprises operated in almost all manufacturing sectors in Turkey, and competed with the outputs of private firms; by 1976, the PEs accounted for more than 30 per cent of manufacturing value added.

Total factor productivity growth was calculated as the difference between the trend growth rate of output and the weighted average rate of growth of capital, labour and other purchased inputs, where the weights were the shares of each factor in the value of total output. The results show that the public sector enterprises as a whole had a higher rate of total factor productivity growth (2.65 per cent) than their private sector counterparts (1.84 per cent). To test for a possible source of bias caused by the likelihood that PEs were constrained to hire more labour than was optimal from a viewpoint of productive efficiency, the rates of TFP growth were re-estimated for public sector industries using the shares of the private sector counterparts, on the grounds that these shares might more appropriately represent the outcome of cost-minimising behaviour. The result of this exercise was to raise the public sector's TFP growth rate to 2.85 per cent, increasing the gap between public and private sector performance.

The study also computed the capital and labour use per unit of output for private and public sectors in 1963 and 1976. For both years the estimates indicate a higher level of absolute factor productivity in almost all of the private sector enterprises; the only sectors where public enterprises showed greater efficiency were machinery, textiles, wearing apparel and footwear, and beverages and tobacco. In some activities, however, the public sector enterprises' productivity improved over time, relative to the private sector. For example, in chemicals, in 1963 the public sector achieved only about one-twelfth of the output per unit of input obtained by the private sector, but by 1976 it had increased its relative productivity to about one-third of the private sector.

The results of this study emphasise the importance of examining both the levels of, and the rates of growth in, factor productivity: it is not inconsistent for one sector to have a higher rate of productivity growth while at the same time being absolutely less efficient than the other sector.[13]

Dholakia (1978). This study compared the growth in total factor productivity in the public and private manufacturing sectors in India over the period 1960/1–1975/6. Estimates of net output and capital and labour inputs were made for both sectors over time, and the index of TFP was obtained as a residual. The results indicated a significantly higher rate of growth of TFP in the public enterprise sector (4.33 per cent per annum) than in the private sector (0.18 per cent per annum).

Perkins (1983). This study examined the types of technologies selected by private and public industrial enterprises in Tanzania. Using a sample of more than 300 industrial units in ten major industries, it establishes that small-scale, labour-intensive techniques were in use in each of the industries, and shows that the majority of these 'appropriate' techniques were technically (in terms of lower capital and labour to output ratios) and economically (in terms of lower unit production costs) superior to the more capital-intensive alternatives.

An examination of the technologies employed by the public enterprises (para-statals) shows that the more appropriate techniques were seldom used by them. In each industry, the para-statals' production techniques were found to be larger in scale, and more capital intensive, than those used by private concerns. Furthermore, a comparison of the average capital productivity of the para-statals with that of the most capital-productive firms in each industry found that in every industry the para-statals employed techniques that had considerably lower capital productivity than that achieved by private sector firms. In addition, despite their high capital intensity, only three para-statals employed techniques with the highest labour productivity in their respective industries. Consequently, only seven of the thirty-two para-statals studied were technically efficient; the remainder used both more capital and more labour to produce a unit of output than did privately owned firms in their industries.

The para-statals were also found to be high-cost producers, with unit production costs from 10 to 780 per cent higher than the lowest-cost firms in their industries. It was noted, however, that unit production costs were positively correlated with capital intensity, indicating that the choice of inappropriate capital-intensive techniques requiring imported raw materials, intermediate goods and capital equipment, as well as skilled (often expatriate) staff, may be an important cause of factor price, and hence productive, inefficiency in the para-statal sector.

Funkhouser and MacAvoy (1979). In addition to the evidence on financial performance reported above, this study of private and public industries in Indonesia also presents comparative data on costs of production. Comparing average unit production costs (excluding interest and depreciation) for the total sample of firms showed public enterprise costs to be above the overall sample average. However, when a restricted sample was constructed by pairing public and private firms of the same size in the same industry, the cost difference disappeared, suggesting, as noted by Millward and Parker (1983, p. 245), that 'there is no evidence that public firms are less cost efficient than private firms of the same size'.

Public–private enterprise studies
Tyler (1979). The objective of this study was to obtain firm-specific indices of technical efficiency for the Brazilian steel and plastics industries in 1971. Two different methods were used to define the technical efficiency frontier. The first followed Farrell's (1957) approach of using the most efficient firms' performance to define the efficiency frontier and comparing other firms with

the boundary ones. The second method used programming techniques to fit a Cobb–Douglas functional form to the data, which was then used to compute the maximum possible output for every observable input combination. The degree of technical efficiency was then calculated by comparing this maximum possible output with the observed level.

The results for the steel industry are of particular interest since government firms were prominent in this sector, accounting in 1971 for 54 per cent of production. The classification of the twenty-two firms in the industry into foreign (7), domestic (10) and government (5) owned allowed the average levels of technical efficiency to be compared. The results show that the averages of both technical efficiency indices were lower for public enterprises than for the domestic and foreign-owned firms. However, attempts to identify a statistically significant difference in technical efficiency levels according to firm ownership were unsuccessful. As a further qualification, it may be noted that there was substantial variance in the efficiency indices between firms, with the Farrell index of technical efficiency for government-owned firms ranging from 100 per cent to 20 per cent.

Hill (1982). In this study the economic performance of state-owned and privately owned mills in the Indonesian weaving industry in 1976 was compared. The study has two interesting features that make the comparison of productivity levels more meaningful than in many other studies: first, the firms in the industry were engaged in direct competition, and, second, only firms using the same production techniques were compared. Two different production techniques were considered, with government and private mills in each category. Comparing various performance indicators of the two groups of firms for each technique indicated that the state mills' performance was consistently inferior. Capital–output and labour–output ratios were significantly higher in the public enterprises, indicating a lower level of technical efficiency. However, since the state mills were considerably larger than private mills, possessing on average more than four times as many looms per factory, the observed differences in technical efficiency may in part reflect the influence of scale on average productivity levels. Detailed examination of the performance of individual state-owned mills – operating in an identical economic environment and subject to the same constraints and obligations resulting from public ownership – revealed major differences in performance, suggesting that internal management and organisation are an important determinant of performance.

Gupta (1982). This study compared the productivity performance of public and private enterprises in the Indian fertiliser industry. The analysis was made in terms of both total and single-factor productivity, and covered the period 1969/70–1976/7. The results indicated that productivity in the public sector firms had been lower than in the private sector, although over time the public sector's performance had improved relative to the private sector. The differences in performance were reduced considerably when allowance was made for higher input costs in the public enterprises, arising from their obligation to use indigenous feedstocks, and for the older, outmoded technology employed in the public sector (the government established the fertiliser industry as 'pioneer' enterprises in the 1950s, whereas the first private sector unit came into existence only in 1968). A comparison of performance at the individual unit level indicated that productivity performance in the most efficient public enterprises was comparable to that achieved by the more efficient private enterprises.

Summary

The available evidence on productivity performance is insufficient to allow a general conclusion about the relative performance of public and private enterprises. The results obtained for sectoral-level growth in total factor productivity in India and Turkey suggest that productivity growth has been more rapid in the public enterprise sector. This is nevertheless consistent with lower absolute productivity levels in public enterprises, and the various studies of performance at the industry and firm level appear to show higher productivity levels in private enterprises. However, closer examination of the evidence indicates that this conclusion needs to be qualified. In the studies by Gupta (1982) and Perkins (1983), government influence over the public enterprises' choice of production techniques was partly responsible for their lower productivity record; in Hill (1982) and Funkhouser and MacAvoy (1979), diseconomies of scale associated with differences in output levels may have contributed to different productivity levels in private and public firms; Tyler's (1979) study failed to find a statistically significant difference between public and private firms' performance. Thus, it appears that the studies undertaken so far have not compared firms that are sufficiently similar in their characteristics; when allowance is made for differences in output, factor prices and 'external' controls, the claims that public firms have lower productivity than private firms are not generally substantiated.[14]

PRICING PERFORMANCE

The earlier discussion of efficiency pricing drew attention to the conceptual problems associated with the marginal cost pricing principle. The problems are compounded by the practical difficulties that arise in the application of the principle – adjusting for market imperfections and factor price distortions, differentiating between the marginal costs of supplying different products produced by the same enterprise, identifying the relevant cost components to be included in marginal costs. Interpretation of the limited evidence that is available on the relationship between public enterprises' prices and marginal costs is therefore problematic.

In the case of manufactured goods that are internationally traded, a commodity's efficiency cost can be approximated by the marginal import price (this assumes, however, that the domestically produced and imported goods are substitutable). For Turkey, Waldstedt (1980) estimated the difference between domestic and international prices for a range of internationally traded outputs produced by state enterprises. After allowing for overvaluation of the exchange rate, and averaging over the period

1964–72, the results indicated that in most cases the domestic price exceeded the world price by an amount ranging from 11 (coal) to 81 (polyethylene) per cent. The only sectors in which domestic prices were lower than world prices were cotton yarn and cement (pp. 120–1). For the Sudan, Acharya (1979) obtained data on ex-factory prices set by the government for a group of products that were relatively homogeneous as product categories, and for which information on the price of comparable imports was also available. Comparing the domestic and c.i.f. import prices indicated that in the majority of cases domestic prices were higher. The commodities for which domestic prices were competitive were mainly based on local materials (cotton materials, leather goods, sugar).

An alternative means of evaluating the pricing policy of public enterprises is to compare price/marginal cost margins in private and public firms. It can be argued that if public enterprises and private firms face the same cost and demand conditions then, to the extent that the difference between price and marginal cost is lower in the public enterprises, pricing policy is closer to the efficency price level. The work of Funkhouser and MacAvoy (1979) analysed the prices of Indonesian public and private enterprises on this basis. They found consistently lower profit margins in the public enterprises, but attributed these to higher unit costs rather than to lower prices. However, since the analysis was based on average, rather than marginal, cost data, a more correct procedure would have been to compare price and cost margins with respect to the same output level. As pointed out earlier, in the sub-sample of results reported by Funkhouser and MacAvoy where output levels in the public and private were similar, the cost difference disappeared. This would appear to support the hypothesis that public enterprise pricing is based on criteria other than profit maximisation.

In the case of utilities, the public enterprise is usually a monopoly supplier, and the price/marginal cost relationship must be estimated directly. While the principles of public utility pricing in LDCs have been discussed at length (see, for example, Walters, 1968, on roads; Saunders and Warford, 1976, on water supply; Bennathan and Walters, 1979, on ports; Munasinghe and Warford, 1982, on electricity), there is only limited evidence on the pricing practices of these types of enterprises. Due (1980) and Churchill (1972) provided evidence for the rail sector in a number of African economies and for the road sector in Central America, respectively, that suggests that user prices have been below the marginal costs of supplying the infrastructural services. A study of municipal water supply in South Asian countries showed that the tariffs paid by consumers were generally low compared to the marginal cost of the water supply (United Nations, 1981). In a survey of irrigation water charges in nine Asian economies, the same study found (p. 44) that

only the Republic of Korea appears to have an effective system of water charges for public irrigation projects. . . . In the other countries, the water charges are assessed based on land productivity, area of irrigated land, season and kind of crop [related to the amount of water used], which has no bearing on the actual operation and maintenance costs or capital cost of the irrigation facilities.

The application of marginal cost pricing principles to electricity supply in LDCs was discussed in Munasinghe and Warford (1982). The study contained a series of case studies of the electric power supply sector in Indonesia, Pakistan, Philippines, Sri Lanka and Thailand. The long-run marginal cost of supplying different consumption categories was classified by time, voltage and geographical area. Comparing these cost estimates with the existing tariff structures indicated that in all cases the long-run marginal costs of capacity greatly exceeded the existing consumption charges.

The apparent absence of a strict adherence to marginal cost prices in the supply of public utilities' output may be due to a number of factors. First, as was pointed out in section 5.5, second-best deviations from strict marginal cost pricing may be justified, in efficiency terms, when there are significant market distortions. Second, there are major practical problems associated with the implementation of an effective system of marginal cost pricing, which often requires a complex tariff structure reflecting the variation in costs associated with different production units and with supplying different locations and time periods. A third reason may be the reluctance to allow essential services such as water, sanitation, electricity and public transport to be allocated on the basis of consumers' ability to pay. Distributional considerations are likely to be important in determining public utility tariffs, with prices being set at levels that are intended to make these basic goods and services accessible to low-income consumers.

Summary
The evidence on public enterprise pricing practice is fragmentary. The limited results that are available indicate that prices have generally not been closely related to marginal costs. However, the conceptual difficulties involved in determining the appropriate relationship between price and marginal cost when market imperfections are prevalent, and the ambiguous nature of the evidence, suggest that further research on this issue is required before any firm, overall conclusion can be reached.

5.7 PUBLIC ENTERPRISE AS A DISTRIBUTIONAL INSTRUMENT

So far, the performance of the public enterprise sector has been considered only in terms of the various economic efficiency criteria. It is obvious, however, that PEs cannot be regarded simply as commercial firms that happen to be owned by the state: in many cases the reason they are in the public sector is either that the private sector is unable or unwilling to establish the production activity, or that the enterprise is required to perform in a way that differs from the performance of the private sector. Thus, while acknowledging the relevance of efficiency performance assessment, consideration must also be given to the evidence on the 'non-economic', or social performance of the public enterprise sector.

Public enterprises can be used as an instrument for the redistribution of both wealth and income. The transfer of productive assets to the public sector will in itself affect the existing distribution of wealth by reducing the asset-holding of particular classes and interest groups. As was seen in section 5.3, a reduction in the concentration of economic power of domestic and/or foreign interests has been an important motivating factor in the establishment of public enterprises.[15] In the same way, the establishment of public enterprises in particular locations will affect the spatial distribution of productive assets. The prevailing pattern of wealth distribution in turn influences (and is influenced by) the distribution of the flow of income generated by society's assets.[16] In assessing the distributional impact of the public enterprise sector, it is also necessary to consider, therefore, how the income created by the enterprises is shared out between different interest groups in the economy.

The public enterprise sector is a major source of employment in many LDCs, and PEs are often used in an attempt to reduce unemployment and improve the wages and working conditions of labour. This can lead to overmanning and high wage costs in the public enterprise sector, compared to private firms, with adverse effects on productivity and profitability.[17]

The eventual impact of the public enterprise sector's employment and wage practices on income distribution is difficult to predict. Recent research on income inequality in LDCs has concentrated on identifying the contribution of various components to total inequality. This approach, known as decomposition analysis, provides an insight into the structure of inequality and the causes of inequality changes through time. If decomposition analysis is applied, for example, to data on the functional sources of household income, it can show how the contribution of each source of income to overall inequality depends positively on the degree of inequality within each income source, and on the importance of that income source in total income.[18] An increase in public enterprise employment and total wage payments will, *ceteris paribus*, increase the share of labour income *vis-à-vis* other sources of income (property, transfers, etc.). However, the effect on the overall inequality measure will depend also upon the changes in the labour income inequality index. If the public enterprises pay higher wages than other firms (for evidence on this for India and Tanzania, see Vermeulen and Sethi, 1982, and Knight and Sabot, 1983, respectively), and also draw their labour from the better-educated urban-based unemployed, rather than the poor households, then the intra-labour distribution of income may become more unequal.[19] The combined effect on the aggregate income distribution measure is therefore unpredictable.

Government controls over the pricing policy of public enterprises are used as an additional instrument to pursue distributional goals. Ceiling prices are frequently set for 'essential' goods in an effort to assist low-income consumers. Such policies may not have the desired effect, however, if the poorest households lack the purchasing capacity to buy the commodity even at the controlled price, or if the commodity is available for sale only in certain localities or regions. There is evidence to suggest that the distribution of basic public services (water, health, education) often fails to reach the lowest income groups and benefits mainly the well-to-do (Lamb and Schaffer, 1981).

The use of price controls may also create further undesirable side-effects. Setting the controlled price below the market level encourages a black market, with intermediary wholesalers, distributors and retailers sharing the scarcity premium as windfall gains. These effects will be reinforced if the government restricts the distribution of public enterprises' outputs to a limited number of private distributors. The evidence in Sobhan's (1983) study for Bangladesh illustrates this point. Excluding jute destined for the export market, some 75 per cent of the Bangladeshi public enterprise sector's manufacturing output was subject to price control. In almost all cases the administered ex-factory price was set at a level significantly lower than the market clearing price, giving rise to windfall gains at the distribution and retailing stages, with the scarcity premiums ranging from 80 to 400 per cent above the official controlled prices.

SUMMARY

Empirical studies of the distributional impact of public enterprise activities in LDCs are scarce, and there is an obvious need for further research in this area. The limited evidence that is available, however, does not indicate that the public enterprise sector has had a significant impact in reducing income inequalities. The conclusion reached in Sobhan's (1979b, p. 93) study on the use of the public enterprise sector in the South Asian economies as an instrument for achieving redistributional goals is probably applicable to most LDCs:

> The allocative regimes of public enterprises in the countries of South Asia appear to have in common the fact that there is no policy perspective within which public enterprise is used as an instrument of distribution. Public enterprise remains a means within the control of the government but the social purpose to which this means is applied continues to be permeated by confusion and conflict within the ranks of the policy-makers.

5.8   WHAT CONCLUSIONS CAN BE DRAWN FROM THE EVIDENCE ON PUBLIC ENTERPRISE PERFORMANCE?

At present, empirical studies of the performance of public enterprises in LDCs are limited. The interpretation of the evidence that is available is often complicated by the limitations of the data and by the conceptual ambiguities of the various measures of performance used.

The weight of evidence surveyed on financial performance appears to support the conclusion that public enterprise performance has been unsatisfactory. In most (but not all) cases, the public enterprise sector failed to generate sufficient revenue to cover current costs (including depreciation). The overall financial deficit (including new investment) was financed from a variety of sources (see section 5.4), but in many countries a significant share of the deficit was funded by central government. For example, in a sample of twenty-seven LDCs in 1976–9, the net budgetary payment (government subsidies, transfers and net lending to public enterprises, less dividends and interest payments by enterprises to government) to non-financial public enterprises averaged more than 3 per cent of GDP (World Bank, 1983, p. 74). In many individual countries the net claims of public enterprises on the government budget have grown rapidly in recent years – from less than 1 per cent of GDP in 1966–9 to 5 per cent in 1977 in Tanzania; from 4 per cent (1966–9) to 11 per cent (1978–80) in Sri Lanka; from 5 per cent (1966–9) to 10 per cent (1978–80) in Zambia (World Bank, 1983, Figure 8.1, p. 75). When compared with private enterprises, the profitability record of public enterprises appears to be consistently lower.

The productivity record of the public enterprises also seems, on balance, to have been unsatisfactory. With a number of important exceptions, the evidence indicates that productivity *levels* have been lower in the public sector than in the private sector, although productivity *growth* has often been higher in the public enterprises.

Evidence on the pricing practices of public enterprises is extremely limited, but from the results available it appears that efficiency pricing has not been adopted in the enterprises concerned.

Careful evaluation of the evidence on economic performance suggests, however, that an unqualified conclusion that public enterprise performance is 'unsatisfactory' would be injudicious. In many cases the poor performance of the public enterprise sector is attributable to factors over which the enterprise has no control. Low profitability is a characteristic of large-scale, declining-cost utilities that pursue marginal cost pricing. Performance is often affected adversely by the need to meet conditions and obligations imposed upon the enterprise by the government authorities. Labour productivity is reduced if the enterprise is required to retain more labour than is economically necessary. Capital productivity will be affected adversely if firms are required to install inappropriate machinery (this is often encouraged by the availability of imported turn-key projects under foreign aid programmes), or to invest in housing and social amenities for employees. Profitability is reduced when the government imposes administered, ceiling prices on the enterprise's output, or where the enterprise is required to supply goods to other state firms at subsidised prices.

The argument advanced in the preceding paragraph does not imply that 'poor' performance in the public enterprise sector can always be 'explained away' or ignored; rather it suggests that unsatisfactory performance is frequently caused by factors external to the enterprise, and an improvement in performance will be conditional upon a change in these conditions. The evaluation of economic performance helps to identify the opportunity cost (in efficiency terms) of pursuing non-efficiency goals, but it is a matter for government policy-makers to determine the appropriate 'trade-off' between conflicting objectives.

This consideration becomes most evident when the public enterprise is used as an instrument for pursuing distributional objectives. Requiring the public enterprise sector to increase its labour force beyond the optimum efficiency level, or to increase wage levels above the market rate, or to charge prices below the market level, may contribute to distributional goals (although, as pointed out in the previous section, such measures have not always had the desired impact), but will involve the enterprise in lower financial performance, lower economic efficiency performance and/or lower productivity performance.

It has been argued by some observers that, after allowance has been made for the effect of externally imposed constraints upon the public enterprise sector's economic performance, the characteristic features of large-scale enterprises may have an adverse effect upon the internal management and organisation of the firm. The absence of competitive market conditions, the divorce of ownership and control, and a failure to link individual financial rewards to performance may each contribute to a slackening in managerial effort to operate efficiently. Leibenstein (1966) introduced the concept of X-inefficiency to refer to situations where the firm's cost curves are above the minimum level possible, given the enterprise's current state of production knowledge:

> Even if all firms face the same prices for identical purchasable inputs and have equal access to knowledge of the state of the art, different organisational circumstances will normally lead to a variety of outputs. (Leibenstein, 1975, p. 580)

The concept of X-inefficiency has been referred to in a number of studies of public enterprise performance in LDCs (Gillis, 1982; Kim, 1981; Hill, 1982). The concept has proved difficult to apply, however, and there is little empirical evidence on the importance of X-inefficiencies. No attempt has been made to quantify the effect of public ownership, as distinct from large size, on X-inefficiency levels. As Gillis (1982, p. 21) pointed out,

> the next order of business for analysts working in the context of X-efficiency should perhaps be precisely that of devising empirical measures that can be used as tests for the presence or absence of X-efficiency.

The various factors that influence public enterprise performance will differ in importance between countries and will change in relative importance through time. Trebat (1980), for example, attributed the generally favourable financial performance of the Brazilian public enterprise sector during the mid-1960s–mid-1970s period to a number of factors specific to that period of Brazil's development. These factors included: the size of the Brazilian market, which allowed capital-intensive public enterprises to realise scale economies; an authoritarian government limiting the power of labour unions within public enterprises and removing the authority of Congress to oversee PE operations; a relatively large domestic supply of skilled technocrats and managers; a rapidly expanding market; the confidence of the international business community, which increased the flow of external financing to Brazilian state-owned firms.

Government policy, by shaping the general economic environment within which the enterprises operate and by setting the objectives to be pursued, has been seen to have a major influence on public enterprise performance. These goals in turn provide the basis for a normative judgement on the 'performance' of the public enterprise sector. The formulation of government policy towards the public enterprise sector and its translation into operational performance criteria are discussed further in Chapter 6, section 6.8.

5.9 CONCLUSIONS

It is only in recent years that the importance of the public enterprise sector in the industrialisation process in LDCs has been recognised. Although there is now a growing interest in the issues of public ownership and control over industry in the developing countries – the World Bank and the United Nations Industrial Development Organisation have both recently undertaken major research projects on this subject – empirical evidence is scarce, and there is a major imbalance between analytical material and applied research findings.

Within these constraints, this chapter has sought to achieve a number of objectives. The first purpose has been to draw attention to the importance of the public enterprise sector in many LDCs. The most obvious indications of this importance are the significant shares of the public enterprise sector in GDP and in total fixed capital formation. The share of public enterprises in the manufacturing sector shows much greater variation, ranging from less than 10 per cent of value added in some countries to more than 50 per cent in others.

The variation among LDCs in the degree of public ownership of industry reflects the varying economic, social and political factors that influence the role of the state in the industrialisation process. The 'market failure' argument provides an incomplete explanation of the size and structure of the public enterprise sector, and a more comprehensive analysis requires attention to be given to political and social influences. The relative importance of these different factors can change over time, and attention was drawn to evolving relationships between the state sector, private domestic interests, and foreign capital in developing countries.

The discussion of public enterprise performance emphasised the conceptual and practical difficulties that arise in attempting to evaluate performance. The interpretation of results obtained for each of the economic indicators (profitability, productivity, efficiency prices) was complicated by the theoretical ambiguity of the measures themselves and by the limitations of the data used. The evaluation of performance is complicated further by the conflict that often arises between the economic efficiency and distributional goals of public enterprises. Economic analysis can make an important contribution to performance assessment by identifying the quantitative importance of the conflict ('trade-off') associated with pursuing various objectives, but the choice of the relative weights to be attached to them is a political one, and a normative judgement on the performance of the public enterprise sector can be made only in relation to the objectives set for the enterprise. It follows that:

An overriding need, if the sector is to become an effective instrument of economic development, is for the formulation of ... a comprehensive strategy with objectives (economic and social), priorities, targets and implementation measures clearly defined at the global, sectoral and enterprise levels. This is a prerequisite not only for increasing the effectiveness of the sector, but also to establish a basis for measuring its performance in terms of capacity to produce industrial goods at an economic cost within clearly defined economic and social objectives. (UNIDO, 1979a, p. 328)

FURTHER READING

General introductions to the role of the public enterprise sector in LDCs can be found in Gillis (1980), Killick (1981, ch. 11), UNIDO (1979a, ch. X), and World Bank (1983, ch. 5). Much of the earlier literature is surveyed in Sheahan (1976). Millward and Parker (1983) and Devine *et al.* (1979, ch. 8) both provide a good theoretical discussion of performance measurement. Meier (1983) contains a collection of articles on pricing policy for public enterprises in LDCs. World Bank (1983, part II) is concerned with the efficiency aspects of public enterprise operations in LDCs. UNIDO (1983a) contains articles on performance evaluation and on government policy and control mechanisms for public enterprises in LDCs. Baumol (1980) and Jones (1982) contain articles relating to theoretical and empirical aspects of public enterprises in LDCs. Case studies of the public enterprise sector in a single country are found in Jones (1976) on the Republic of Korea, and Trebat (1983) on Brazil.

NOTES

1 In the opinion of one observer, 'in many countries, the influence of state-owned enterprises (SOEs) upon the course of development has for years been more significant than that of multinationals. . . . By whatever standard employed, SOEs now play a more critical role in the development process than do multinationals and [their] relative importance is likely to grow in the future' (Gillis, 1980, pp. 248–9).

2 For a good discussion of the market failure approach to explaining the size and function of the public enterprise sector in LDCs, see Lal (1980).

3 The efficiency conditions are as follows: (1) the marginal rate of substitution in consumption between any two goods should be the same for all consumers; (2) the marginal rate of substitution in production between any two resources (inputs) should be the same for all producers. If both these conditions are met, the Pareto-optimal composition of output will be that for which the marginal rate of substitution in consumption between any pair of goods (efficiency condition 1) is equal to the marginal rate of transformation in production (efficiency condition 2) between the same pair of goods. For a detailed exposition of the welfare economics analysis, see Lancaster (1974), ch. 10, or any intermediate level microeconomics textbook.

4 The alternative policy response is to 'internalise' the externalities, either by compelling the party responsible for external costs to compensate the affected parties or by subsidising the party responsible for external benefits.

5 This approach is discussed in UNIDO (1972), chs 11 and 18.

6 This section draws on Devine *et al.* (1979), ch. 8 and Killick (1981), ch. 11.

7 The elasticity of output with respect to labour, β, is $(dO/O)/(dL/L) = (dO . L)/(dL . O)$. If labour is paid its marginal product, then $dO/dL = w$, where w is the wage received by labour. Hence $\beta = w . (L/O)$, where $w . (L/O)$ is labour's share of total output.

8 See Kravis (1976), Nadiri (1970), Kennedy and Thirlwall (1972) for more detailed discussion of the methodology and problems of productivity measurement.

9 Most analysts have attempted to preserve the resource allocation advantages of marginal cost pricing while achieving satisfactory financial performance. The simplest approach is a two-part tariff with a variable charge equal to marginal cost, plus a lump sum to enable the financial target to be met. An alternative is to discriminate between consumers, charging a price according to 'what the traffic will bear', thereby attempting to appropriate the consumer's surplus. From the economic efficiency point of view, the most satisfactory adjustment is to apply the inverse elasticity rule where the greatest divergence from MC occurs for the consumers whose price elasticity is lowest, and vice versa (Baumol and Bradford, 1970). It is intuitively obvious that this will result in the smallest deviations from optimal levels of consumption consistent with the application of the MC pricing rule. For an excellent review of the literature on this issue, see Lintner (1981).

10 The current methodology of cost–benefit analysis as applied in LDCs extends the concept of shadow prices to take into account the effects of public sector investment and pricing decisions not only on economic efficiency but also on equity (both interpersonal and inter-temporal). A comprehensive treatment of this approach is given in Squire and van der Tak (1975) and Little and Mirrlees (1974).

11 In their excellent review of the comparative efficiency performance of the public enterprise sector in developed countries, Millward and Parker (1983) also pointed to 'the chasm between analytical work and empirical tests' (p. 200).

12 The study included a number of European countries.

13 If the public enterprise sector expanded over time by taking over private enterprises with a higher productivity level, it would bias the productivity growth rate upwards.

14 Millward and Parker (1983) reached a similar conclusion on the evidence from advanced country studies.

15 The distributional impact of these measures will be reduced, however, if the previous owners receive compensation.

16 The policy implications of the relationship between wealth and income redistribution have been widely debated in recent years. The 'redistribution with growth' approach favoured by the World Bank (Chenery *et al.*, 1973) argues that the incomes of the poor can be raised, without altering the existing distribution of wealth, by redistributing part of the additional income generated by this asset ownership pattern. Others have argued that the problem of poverty originates in the concentration of ownership and control of the means of production, and its alleviation requires a redistribution of wealth (Griffin, 1976; Leys, 1975b). The two approaches are compared in Stewart and Streeten (1976).

17 However, the 'efficiency wage' hypothesis argues that there may be a positive relationship between wages and productivity if, for example, higher wages improve the health, energy or morale of workers, or diminish labour turnover, attract the most productive members of the labour force, or reduce the likelihood of labour disputes.

18 The most widely used decomposition procedure, using the Gini coefficient, also includes the correlation between each income source and total income (Fields, 1980, pp. 101–3).

19 This emphasises the importance of labour market studies in LDCs, an area largely neglected by development economists. For an early contribution, see Arrighi (1970). The more recent literature on labour market segmentation was reviewed in Fields (1980), ch. 5. Stewart (1983) contains a collection of country studies on the relationship between labour market conditions, wages and income distribution.

6 Industrial Policies and Development

6.1 INTRODUCTION

The main purpose of this final chapter is to analyse a number of the specific industrial policy issues that have been raised in the preceding chapters. As a preliminary, this introduction provides an overview of industrial policy in LDCs, first by examining its relationship to development objectives in Third World countries and, second, by briefly reviewing the type and range of industrial measures that LDC governments have used to promote their development objectives.

DEVELOPMENT OBJECTIVES AND INDUSTRIAL POLICIES

The choice of industrial policy by an LDC government should reflect the development objectives it wishes to pursue and the constraints (political, institutional, administrative, etc.) on the means by which this may be achieved. Given the variation in both development objectives and constraints between Third World countries, there can be no single set of industrial policies that is 'best' for all of them. Variability in industrial policies between LDCs is not, of itself, a cause for concern. However, inconsistency between the industrial policies pursued and development objectives adopted within individual LDCs is a fairly widespread problem.

The *higher-order* development objectives adopted by LDC governments can be mainly grouped into two broadly defined categories: efficiency-related and distribution-related.[1] Efficiency-related objectives are concerned with maximising, over time, the total welfare accruing to the economy as a whole from the efficient use of the scarce resources at its disposal; distribution-related objectives are concerned with achieving the most satisfactory distribution of that total welfare between the different inhabitants of the economy. The means used to attain one type of objective do not necessarily promote the attainment of the other: for example, measures used to achieve greater equality of income within an economy may conflict with the efficient utilisation of resources. Therefore, where (as is commonly the case) a government adopts objectives drawn from more than one category, a trade-off between the attainment of these objectives is often required. For example, a government may sacrifice some opportunities to promote a more efficient allocation of resources in order to reduce differences in income levels within the economy. In practice, these kinds of trade-off will often be made in a fairly informal and non-explicit manner.

Higher-order objectives are usually defined in terms that are too broad to provide sufficiently precise guidance for the formulation of policy. In practice, therefore, they are often expressed in the form of much more specific *lower-order* objectives, such as an objective to stabilise the prices of certain public sector goods consumed by poorer sections of the community, or to promote the domestic production of commodities that were previously imported. Conflicts arise even more frequently in the pursuit of lower-order objectives because of the greater number of goals and the greater likelihood that policies designed to promote one lower-order objective will hamper the attainment of others. For example, measures to stabilise public sector prices may cause financial deficits to be incurred by public enterprises, which then reduce the public sector savings available to finance investment in import-substituting domestic industries.

In such ways as these, serious inconsistencies can arise between the sets of industrial policies that governments adopt and the higher-order development objectives that they hope to achieve. For this reason, a soundly based industrial development strategy should be formulated after careful determination of objectives (higher- and lower-order) and the selection of industrial policies that, taken as a whole, are broadly consistent with the attainment of those objectives. The nature of these objectives is examined further below.

Efficiency-related objectives
The objectives included within this category are concerned with increasing total social welfare over time, by such means as raising productive efficiency, allocative efficiency and dynamic efficiency.[2] Because these objectives cannot be directly expressed in quantitative terms, more specific, lower-order objectives are often adopted in their place. One such type of objective relates to the GNP growth rate and, more specifically, to the growth rate in manufacturing output. These, however, have a number of limitations. For example, changes in GNP may not be a good indicator of changes in social welfare (Juster, 1973); this is particularly the case in LDCs where the distinction between 'growth' and 'development' is considered to be particularly important (Nixson, 1984). In addition, overconcentration upon growth in the manufacturing sector can lead to undervaluing the potential contribution of growth and efficiency in the agricultural and service sectors to increased social welfare (World Bank, 1982; Baer and Samuelson, 1981). Thus, industrial growth objectives need to be carefully formulated, taking their broader resource use and social welfare implications fully into account.

Alternatively, attempts have been made to set efficiency objectives in terms of the decision rules (e.g. for pricing and investment) and types of market structure that are most likely to increase efficiency. The formulation of efficiency pricing and investment criteria has been most fully developed for public utility enterprises, but their practical application is still in its infancy in the industrial sectors of most LDCs (see Chapter 5, section 5.6). Market and overall concentration is typically high in the industrial sectors of most LDCs (see Chapter 3, sections 3.2 and 3.4) but their industrial policies rarely attempt, in any overall coherent manner, to modify market structures on efficiency grounds. The difficulties involved in formulating efficiency objectives in terms of pricing and investment criteria and more appropriate market structures in an LDC context are fairly formidable; nevertheless, there is scope for improvement on current practice in using this approach.

Distribution-related objectives

Typically, governments are not only concerned to increase the level of aggregate welfare within society; they are also concerned with how it is distributed among its members. The interpretation of what constitutes a 'satisfactory' distribution is a political matter and it may be expressed in a variety of ways. The most general form of the distribution objective is in terms of a desired distribution of income within society, but, in practice, this will usually be elaborated through the adoption of more specific, lower-order distributional objectives. These may identify specific basic needs to be satisfied, particular ethnic groups or regions that should receive favoured treatment, particular indigenous or foreign-owned groups whose economic power should be reduced, etc. (UNIDO, 1979a, ch. IV; Killick, 1981, chs 1–3). Alternatively, distributional objectives may be expressed as employment targets or be reflected in modified decision rules for pricing and investment.

In practice, difficulties can arise in defining precisely which target groups in society should receive favoured treatment, in devising measures that restrict benefits to these groups, and in avoiding significant, undesired side-effects occurring elsewhere in the economy. As in the case of efficiency objectives, great care is needed in the formulation of distribution-related objectives to ensure that they adequately reflect the higher-order goals being pursued and avoid, as far as possible, undesirable side-effects on other parts of the economy.

TYPES AND RANGES OF INDUSTRIAL POLICY MEASURES

The extent and form of government intervention in the industrial sector of a country is likely to be influenced by three sets of factors:

- the development objectives it pursues;
- the economic conditions it faces;
- its political commitment to, and administrative capability for, market intervention.

This combination of factors can result, at one extreme (e.g. Hong Kong), in a predominantly non-interventionist stance towards the industrial sector and, at the other (e.g. Tanzania and a number of socialist LDCs), in fairly extensive regulation of the structure, conduct and performance of the industrial sector. Over time, changes in economic and political conditions within a country may bring about major changes in the scope and form of its industrial policy as, for example, happened in Pakistan, Bangladesh and Chile during the 1970s.

For the most part, however, LDC governments intervene fairly extensively in the industrial sector and use a wide range of different policy measures for this purpose. This is illustrated in Table 6.1, which is based mainly upon a

Table 6.1 *Industrial policy measures in use in LDCs*

Area of intervention	Examples of policy measures used
Production and marketing	Industrial licensing, regulation of restrictive business practices, tax incentives to particular industries, creation of industrial estates, price controls, national planning, development and regulation of public enterprises and joint ventures
Employment and other factor markets	Minimum wage legislation, labour training schemes, restrictions on use of foreign labour, interest rate and credit controls, capital subsidies, tax benefits for business income
Foreign investment	Prohibition of private foreign investment, requirement for domestic majority ownership, constraints on profit remittances abroad and capital repatriation, exclusion of foreign investment from key industries, direct subsidies and tax incentives for foreign investment
Technology	Patent laws, research and development support, regulation of TNCs and technology agreements
Imports	Import licensing, quotas and prohibitions, import tariffs, multiple exchange rates
Exports	Export licensing, taxes and customs duties on exports, income tax concessions for export earnings, export credit, export processing zones, marketing assistance schemes

Source: Donges (1976).

survey of the policy measures applied by fifteen industrialising countries in the mid-1970s (Donges, 1976). Taking all of these measures together, virtually every important aspect of manufacturing activity appears to be potentially influenced by some form of government intervention: the level, composition and location of production; the methods and techniques of production; the prices of products and factor inputs; the type and concentration of ownership of production facilities; the nature and degree of market competition.

None of the policy measures listed in the table can be reliably evaluated except in the context of the country in which it is being applied and relative to the development objectives that its government is attempting to achieve. A number of the measures listed appear to be contradictory (for example, discouraging and encouraging foreign investment, discouraging and encouraging exports), but may simply reflect differences in economic circumstances or in the lower-order objectives that had been adopted when these measures were in force.

It is also apparent that many of the measures, although possibly devised with one set of objectives in view, could have repercussions on the attainment of other development objectives – and these repercussions are not necessarily favourable. For example,

- industrial licensing systems may be used to promote industrial growth in remote regions (to meet distributional objectives) but cause new establishments to be sited in high-cost locations (contrary to efficiency objectives);
- minimum wage legislation may promote a more equitable distribution of income but over-encourage capital-intensive methods of production;
- restrictions on TNCs may encourage the use of more 'appropriate' technologies and stimulate self-reliance and nation-building but deprive LDCs of entrepreneurial skills and capital resources;
- high import duties may stimulate the growth of output and employment in the indigenous manufacturing sector but the protection it receives may also lead to a fall in technical and productive efficiency.

This again underlines the importance of evaluating individual policy measures by reference to a country's overall development objectives and not simply referring to the individual lower-order objectives with which they are most closely associated.

In summary, a well-devised set of industrial policies should ideally be developed through a process involving:

- careful identification and definition of the development objectives that the industrial policies are intended to support;
- evaluation of proposed policies in terms of their likely contribution to the *full set* of development objectives;
- evaluation of likely problems in policy implementation to determine possible consequences of incomplete or inappropriate forms of implementation;
- revision of proposed policies, in the light of their evaluation, before they are finalised and implemented.

Where policies are already in operation, they should be submitted periodically to a similar review process to determine where there is scope for improvement.

In the remaining sections of this chapter, the analysis concentrates upon the following major areas of industrial policy and its implementation: trade strategies for industrialisation; industrial planning; the regulation of industrial concentration and competition (including separate sections on the regulation of TNCs and the promotion of small-scale enterprises); technological development; the control of public enterprises and the regulation of industrial location. In each case, consideration is given to the following types of question:

- What is the problem to which policy is addressed and what objectives is it attempting to promote?
- What are the policy measures taken?

- What are the effects of these policy measures?
- What policy changes, if any, may be desirable?

Inevitably, the analysis is at a broad level, but the approach that is adopted and the issues that are raised could be used in a more detailed examination of the industrial policies adopted in individual LDCs.

6.2   TRADE STRATEGIES FOR INDUSTRIALISATION

A distinction is normally drawn between two trade-related strategies of industrialisation: production for the domestic market of previously imported manufactured goods (import-substituting industrialisation – ISI); and the production of manufactured goods for external markets (export-oriented industrialisation – EOI). In the 1950s and 1960s, ISI dominated the industrialisation strategies of the larger Latin American economies (Brazil, Argentina and Mexico) and a number of large countries in South and South-East Asia (Pakistan, India, the Philippines). In the early to mid-1960s, ISI began to be adopted in a number of the more important sub-Saharan African economies (Nigeria, Kenya, Ghana, Zambia) and in the smaller Latin American and South-East Asian countries. Since the mid-1960s, an increasing number of LDCs have adopted EOI strategies. The earliest adherents of this approach – Republic of Korea, Taiwan, Singapore, Hong Kong – were joined subsequently by a number of larger semi-industrialised LDCs such as Brazil, Mexico and Argentina, which shifted from the earlier ISI strategy to policies aimed at encouraging EOI.[3]

THE EXPERIENCE OF IMPORT-SUBSTITUTING INDUSTRIALISATION

Criticism of the implementation and outcome of the ISI strategy has been widespread, and it is argued by many observers that ISI has 'failed' as an industrialisation strategy. The majority of LDCs have implemented the ISI strategy by the indiscriminate imposition of tariffs and quantitative restrictions on imports. There is considerable evidence to show that the industrial activities established under ISI often produce at higher cost than competing imports and are dependent upon protection from foreign competition for their survival. Market concentration is typically high, and productive capacity is frequently capital intensive and under-utilised. Furthermore preoccupation with import-substituting industrialisation has led to the neglect of other sectors, particularly agriculture, and has discouraged the export of both primary products and manufactured goods (Little, Scitovsky and Scott, 1970, chs 2 and 5).

Two broad approaches to explaining the ISI experience can be identified. The neoclassical critique argues that ISI has suffered from inefficient implementation, and that if protective structures were rationalised and lowered, and industrial development made more consistent with a country's comparative advantage, the inefficiency costs of ISI would be reduced and the transition to export-oriented industrialisation easier to achieve.[4] The second broad explanation is provided by the structuralist-dependency perspective, according to which the ISI strategy, when based on existing market structures, will inevitably result in the 'failure' of ISI to reduce the foreign exchange constraint and sustain a long-run growth of the economy.[5] From this perspective, the economic inefficiencies of ISI are explained by the pre-existing pattern of the ownership and control of the means of production and by the social relationships associated with these different ownership patterns.

The policy prescriptions that arise from these two interpretations of the ISI experience are very different. According to the neoclassical school, the appropriate policy recommendation is that trade restrictions should be relaxed and greater attention given to ensuring that producers face the 'correct' price signals. This should stimulate more efficient import substitution as well as encourage more production for export markets. This policy is not simply a crude *laissez-faire* free trade strategy, but can more accurately be described as one of export promotion. It requires active government involvement through the adoption of appropriate measures to provide equal economic incentives to production for domestic and foreign markets.[6]

The structuralists, in contrast, emphasise the need for significant changes in the economic structure of the economy (for example, land redistribution, income redistribution, greater 'national' control). Since the 'failure' of ISI is fundamentally due to its reliance upon existing market demands, greater government intervention through centralised industrial planning is seen as essential to its successful implementation (Nixson, 1981). A planned strategy of industrial development, in which import substitution is associated with, and complementary to, policies for agricultural development and the development of export opportunities, would avoid many of the problems that have emerged as a result of the largely unplanned, *ad hoc* government intervention under the market-based ISI strategy.

THE EXPERIENCE OF EXPORT-ORIENTED INDUSTRIALISATION

The alleged 'failure' of the ISI strategy has led to renewed interest in the EOI strategy, and has encouraged the resurgence of the neoclassical case for the adoption of outward-looking, export-based industrialisation policies. Advocates of this strategy point to the rapid growth in manufactured exports from certain LDCs during the 1960s and 1970s (see Chapter 2, section 2.3) and have attributed this growth to the adoption of EOI policies. It is argued that the pursuit of an EOI strategy will generate superior results, in terms of both allocative efficiency and economic growth, than ISI:

... export-oriented policies lead to better growth performance than policies favouring import substitution. This result is said to obtain because export-oriented policies, which provide similar incentives to sales in domestic and in foreign markets, lead to resource allocation according to comparative advantage, allow for greater capacity utilization, permit the exploitation of economies of scale, generate technological improvements in response to competition abroad and, in labour-surplus countries, contribute to increased employment. (Balassa, 1978, p. 181)

Although the rapid growth in manufactured exports from a limited number of LDCs has encouraged a belief in the merits of adopting EOI policies, a number of important qualifications can be made to the arguments used to support the case for export-based industrialisation.

First, the export success achieved by a limited group of newly industrialising countries (NICs) may not be possible for a large number of additional LDCs. Much of the expansion in the NICs' exports occurred during a period when world trade was growing rapidly and protectionism was minimal. With the slowdown in economic growth and heightening protectionism in the advanced countries, LDCs face increasing difficulties in expanding their manufactured exports (Chapter 2, section 2.5). The assumption that the NICs' export success can be replicated by other LDCs is also subject to a fallacy of composition. It has been calculated (using 1976 data) that if all LDCs had the same intensity of export production as the South-East Asian NICs (Republic of Korea, Taiwan, Singapore and Hong Kong), the share of all LDCs in the manufactured imports of the advanced countries would be more than 60 per cent (Cline, 1982).

Second, the evidence offered in support of the claim that EOI contributes more to economic growth than does ISI is often weak. Typically, the evidence is obtained from a comparison between export growth rates and either different trade regimes or the growth in GDP (Balassa, 1978; Tyler, 1981; Krueger, 1983). This type of analysis has several limitations. Since exports are part of total production, a positive correlation is likely to occur between the two. Correlation does not prove causality, and it is plausible that higher growth in domestic output has led to increased exports. Furthermore, if export performance is used as an index of commitment to export promotion policies, countries that have unsuccessfully pursued an EOI strategy are excluded from consideration.

Third, there has been little attempt to analyse the characteristics of export growth – its employment effects, the distribution of gains between foreign and domestic interests, the resource costs incurred in providing incentives (export subsidies, provision of infrastructural services, favourable tax treatment) to exporters.

Fourth, the experience of at least some of the major NIC exporters has been incorrectly interpreted. The detailed study of economic policy in the Republic of Korea and Taiwan, for example, shows that industrial development has been accompanied by a high degree of centralised planning and government regulation, with strict import and foreign exchange controls. The strategies that have been adopted in these cases have combined policies of selective import substitution and export promotion, with import substitution being used to develop local manufacturing capacity, which provides the basis for subsequent exporting activities. Singer's (1984, p. 11) comment on this 'purposeful interweaving of ISI and EOI' in the Republic of Korea's industrialisation strategy is worth quoting:

While this particular scheme suits Korean conditions, similar schemes could apply to most other LDCs, except perhaps the very smallest and the very largest. At any rate, such combinations and policy sequences seem a more promising approach to the industrialisation problems of developing countries today than to continue with doctrinal discussions of ISI and EOI and with the swings of fashion with changing circumstances from one to the other.

CONCLUSIONS

The review of LDCs' experience with trade-related industrialisation strategies suggests the following conclusions:

- It is simplistic to describe ISI as a 'failure' and/or EOI as a 'success'. Both strategies involve a complex set of economic relationships, each of which requires detailed evaluation. Furthermore, the neoclassical analysis of trade-related industrialisation strategies, on which such broad judgements are often based, is subject to various qualifications and limitations.
- ISI and EOI strategies should not be treated as mutually exclusive alternatives. In practice, elements of both strategies should be employed, and the relative importance of each strategy is likely to alter over time. The appropriate balance between ISI and EOI policy measures will be determined by, *inter alia*, an economy's level of industrialisation, its size and resource endowments, and its overall development objectives. Government involvement, through planning and other measures, in industrial sector activities is likely to be needed to ensure that the appropriate combination of EOI- and ISI-based industrial development is achieved.
- The choice of trade policies should be determined by the country's industrialisation objectives, and not vice versa.[7] Similarly, trade policies should not be seen as the only set of instruments with which to pursue the goals of industrialisation: the choice and use of trade-related measures should be made in conjunction with that of other governmental policy instruments that are appropriate to the attainment of those goals.

6.3   INDUSTRIAL PLANNING

The introduction to this chapter emphasised how industrial policies should ideally be chosen and evaluated in relation to a country's overall development objectives. In many LDCs, planning has been seen as providing the means of achieving this desired relationship between objectives and policies.

Economic planning can be defined as

a deliberate governmental attempt to coordinate economic decision making over the long run and to influence, direct and in some cases even control the level and growth of a nation's principal economic variables [income, consumption, employment, investment, saving, exports, imports, etc.] in order to achieve a predetermined set of development objectives. (Todaro, 1981, p. 430)

These planned targets are normally set out in a development plan, often, though not always, covering a five-year period. Ideally, the development plan will be comprehensive, covering the whole economy, and its construction will involve the use of a number of different planning techniques. The procedures used can be thought of as consisting of three stages, each associated with a different type of planning model. The first stage involves the use of macro models that treat the economy as a single entity and examine the functional relationships between the main macro aggregates (savings, investment, capital stock, export, imports) and the level of national output. Second, there are various inter-industry models in which the interrelationships between industries (or sectors) are considered. Input–output analysis is often used at this stage to show the transactions and interrelationships between different industries and to examine the feasibility of the planned output levels. A third stage involves the use of project appraisal and social cost–benefit analysis in deciding upon the allocation of resources between different projects within a particular industry.[8]

In principle, the results obtained at each level of the planning exercise should be consistent with each other: the macro model sets the aggregate targets, sectoral planning ensures an internally consistent set of sectoral targets, and project appraisal provides for the efficient selection of projects within each sector. The final set of plan targets will be arrived at after a circular process of checking the consistency between each level of planning (this process is known as 'iteration'). In practice, as discussed below, such consistency is often not fully realised.

Development planning is usually carried out in the context of the 'mixed' economy, where a part of the productive resources is privately owned while the other part is in public ownership. This means that the implementation of planning depends upon a mixture of direct government investment and production activities and indirect policy measures (taxation, licensing, tariffs, wages, subsidies, etc.) aimed at influencing the private sector's decisions so that they conform to the planned outcomes.

INDUSTRIAL PLANNING IN PRACTICE

Ideally, industrial planning should be an integral part of an overall planning exercise. In practice, however, the immense data and manpower resources needed to undertake a comprehensive planning exercise have meant that the plan is frequently partial in nature, concentrating on only one part of the national economy. The importance attached by many LDCs to rapid industrialisation has often resulted in priority being given to industrial planning, with a relative neglect of other sectors of the economy.

Industrial planning is concerned, *inter alia*, with the following decisions: the growth of the industrial sector as a whole; the choice and growth of separate industrial activities; the choice of projects within particular industries.[9]

Before reviewing the experience of industrial planning in LDCs, it is important to point out the conceptual and practical difficulties in devising and applying evaluation criteria (Killick, 1983, pp. 48–9). The ideal procedure would be to compare the results with what would have occurred in the absence of the plan. However, the difficulties in constructing this type of counterfactual, 'what would have been', test preclude its use in examining cross-country experiences. Most studies have instead measured the impact of planning in terms of the divergence between the actual outcomes and either (i) the plan target levels, or (ii) an implicit optimum situation (this is usually taken to be the Pareto-efficient outcome that was discussed in Chapter 5, section 5.5). Neither of these approaches is very satisfactory, however. Plan targets may have been set at deliberately unrealistic levels in order, for example, to attract foreign aid or to raise national aspirations. The usefulness of the efficiency-based criteria is limited by their inability to allow for dynamic efficiency gains.

Information on *industrial sector level planning* is contained in a UN study that compared the increases in manufacturing production recorded in LDCs during the first half of the 1970s with the targets set in national development plans (United Nations, 1977). Eleven of the thirty-two countries included in the study recorded an annual rate of increase in manufacturing output that exceeded the plan target, and in a further three countries the rate achieved was only slightly below target. In just over half the countries, therefore, the growth of the manufacturing sector fell substantially short of the target set.

There is also evidence to suggest that industrial planning has given insufficient attention to the growth of other complementary activities. In particular, the neglect of the agricultural sector has affected adversely the trend in agricultural production, which has in turn retarded industrial growth. In India, for example, agro-based industries suffered from stagnation in commercial crop production: shortages of textile fibres, especially jute, have been pronounced. The shortages of agricultural raw materials have also affected industrial production in such diverse countries as Argentina, Peru, the Philippines, Togo, Uganda and Tanzania (United Nations, 1977, pp. 33–5; also World Bank, 1982, Pt II).[10]

Planning at the *individual industry level* has been evaluated mainly in terms of the impact of the government's indirect policy measures on industrial activities. In an attempt to make private sector industrial investment and production decisions conform to the plan targets, many LDCs have made extensive use of industrial licensing schemes and systems of import quotas, tariffs and exchange controls. The economic consequences of these measures have been extensively studied by, among others, Little, Scitovsky and Scott (1970), Balassa *et al.* (1971), Bhagwati (1978) and Krueger (1978). These various studies have assessed the impact of industrial policy in terms of economic efficiency criteria. Since most industrial goods are traded internationally, the standard against which efficiency in domestic production is measured is the international price of an equivalent international good. The domestic resource cost (DRC) measure is a widely used technique for measuring the resource cost of production in terms of the domestic resources used (in domestic currency) relative to the foreign exchange gains through export or import replacement (in foreign currency). An activity is judged to be inefficient if the DRC is greater than the equilibrium exchange rate. A ranking of activities in terms of DRCs indicates the relative incentives for domestic resources to move into protected industries. This ranking of the resource-pull effects of the existing structure of protectionism can then be compared to the planned or intended pattern of incentives.[11]

The evidence that emerges from the large number of studies applying the DRC technique and other similar neoclassical measures is that industrial policy has encouraged high-cost, inefficient industrial production. (Much of this evidence is summarised in Balassa, 1982.) The conclusion drawn by neoclassical analysts is therefore that industrial planning has been a 'failure', and the policy recommendation is that trade policies should be 'liberalised' by removing protectionist measures and trade restrictions, thereby enabling the market to allocate resources to their most efficient uses. For other observers, however, the inefficiencies of industrial production are evidence of too little, rather than too much, industrial planning, and they would recommend the adoption of more effective forms of industrial planning in LDCs (Nixson, 1981). This important issue of the relationship between trade policies and industrial development was discussed in further detail in section 6.2 above.

Although the use of social cost–benefit analysis has been widely recommended for *project evaluation*, it appears that in practice these techniques have not had a significant influence on actual decision-making. Formal project evaluation is often undertaken to justify a decision already made rather than to provide a basis for making the decision. The uncertainty and subjectivity attached to the shadow values used in project evaluation will often enable the analyst to generate the net positive benefit needed to satisfy the funding agency. This situation is particularly common when projects are being funded by international aid agencies. The fact that social cost–benefit analysis is applied on a selective basis may also allow the decision-makers to protect or advance the interests of selected socio-economic groups in the country (Stewart, 1975).

Detailed studies of the industrial planning experience in individual LDCs, made largely from a neoclassical perspective, have concluded that it has been largely ineffectual (UNIDO, 1979b). In Brazil,

> setting priorities within the industrial sector was not co-ordinated. At no time did any person or institution attempt to set goals and to implement programmes to accomplish a specific pattern of industrial growth ... Formal economic analysis seems to have played a small part, if any, in setting priorities. (Bergsman, 1979, pp. 17–18)

In India,

> ... neither the desired nor the actual pattern of industrial investment in India can be said to have conformed to any sensible economic or technical criteria. Thus, it cannot be presumed that industrial planning succeeded in improving the social efficiency of industrial investment over what would have occurred as a result of purely market forces. ... (Lal, 1979, p. 36)

In the Republic of Korea,

> Top policy makers did not find comprehensive planning to be of material assistance either in reaching or carrying out policy decisions precisely because too few resources were devoted to planning. (Adelman and Westphal, 1979, p. 126)

In Turkey,

> If one evaluates the selection of industrial priorities according to the extent to which systematic use of the DRC, benefit-cost, or economic-rate-of-return (at shadow prices) criterion is relied on, the Turkish decision-making process fails the test. (Krueger and Tuncer, 1979, p. 176)

CONCLUSIONS

The record of industrial planning in LDCs suggests that the results have been disappointing. Measuring performance in relation to the targets set in the plans indicates that the majority of LDCs have failed to achieve the planned goals. When performance is assessed in terms of the 'efficiency norm', the evidence again points to widespread inefficiencies or resource misallocations in the industrial sector.

These shortcomings in industrial planning can be attributed to a variety of factors. In part, they may be the result of technical defects in the planning exercise – inadequate data, limitations of the models, unanticipated economic disturbances. Other observers have attributed poor planning performance to the lack of commitment and political will on the part of the decision-makers. Killick (1976, p. 177) argued that the planner's implicit assumption of a rational and consistent decision-making process is very different from what happens in practice:

> ... a behavioural view of politics and decision-making in developing countries conflicts at almost every point with the largely implicit 'rational actor' model of politics adopted by proponents of development planning ... Governments will not have clear and stable objectives, but the resolution and avoidance of social conflicts and the maintenance of their own authority are likely to be among their main preoccupations, with a consequential demotion of the development objective. The fragmentation of power, the implementation gap, and the large uncertainties surrounding many decisions seriously devalue the notion of optimization: the uncertainties and the fact of political instability also make for shorter time horizons than would be compatible with medium-term planning.

The fact that industrial planning has performed poorly need not lead to the conclusion that planning has 'failed'. It is extremely difficult to assess what would have happened in the absence of planning, or if planning practice was improved, and observers have drawn very different conclusions from the shortcomings of planning in individual LDCs. Lal (1979, p. 44), for example, recommended that for India

> . . . it is much better to let the private industrial structure evolve as a result of the private entrepreneurs' own forecasts, made in an environment where the actual prices they face are increasingly close to shadow prices.

whereas Adelman and Westphal (1979, p. 126) concluded that '. . . one possible lesson from the Republic of Korea's second five-year plan is not to despair of comprehensive planning too soon'.

It would be inappropriate, therefore, to reach the generalised conclusion that industrial planning in LDCs has been a failure. It does appear, however, that undue attention has often been given to public sector investment allocations, based on formal model-building exercises, while the planning of industrial policy towards the private sector has been largely neglected. The remaining topics in this chapter are concerned therefore with the formulation of more specific industrial policies.

6.4   INDUSTRIAL CONCENTRATION AND COMPETITION POLICY

INDUSTRIAL CONCENTRATION AND DEVELOPMENT

Industrial concentration is mainly measured in two ways:

- *seller concentration*: the proportion of an individual industry's production or sales that is controlled by the largest enterprises in that industry; and
- *overall concentration*: the proportion of the manufacturing sector as a whole that is controlled by the largest enterprises in that sector.

Although there is considerable variation in concentration levels both between LDCs and between their individual industries, the general situation is that these levels are high both absolutely and relative to the levels found in developed economies (see Chapter 3, sections 3.2 and 3.4 for details). The first question to consider, then, is what effects these high concentration levels might have on the attainment of efficiency-related and distribution-related objectives of development in LDCs.

High seller concentration, particularly if reinforced by high overall concentration, may have the following opposing effects on efficiency in individual markets (see Figures 3.2 and 3.3 in Chapter 3, section 3.4 for diagrammatic illustration):

- *loss* of welfare through causing increases in price–cost margins;
- *loss* of welfare through causing a decrease in X-efficiency;
- *gain* in welfare through securing economies of scale (technical, managerial, marketing, financial) that would otherwise be lost.

In the longer term, it may have additional, more uncertain, effects on efficiency:

- the financial incentive of higher price–cost margins may stimulate new entry and improvements in X-efficiency, or it may result in further restrictive practices by existing producers to protect their higher profits, which results in a greater wastage of resources;
- higher price–cost margins enable more financial resources to be made available for research, development and innovation, but the lower competition in concentrated markets may reduce the pressure to innovate.

Where high concentration leads to high profit margins, there will also be a transfer of welfare from consumers to producers. If the producers are large indigenous groups or TNCs, this transfer of welfare is often regarded as unfavourable because the beneficiaries tend to be relatively affluent. Where the producers are publicly owned enterprises, the distributional impact is less certain since it depends upon the final use to which their surpluses are put (see Chapter 5, section 5.7). Alternatively, high concentration levels may enable large-scale enterprises (particularly in the public sector) to finance the employment of more low-wage workers than can be justified on efficiency grounds. This may have a favourable distributional impact, although it also results in a fall in X-efficiency. Thus, at the theoretical level, the economic impacts of high concentration levels are ambiguous: depending upon the circumstances of the particular case, both the overall efficiency and distributional effects may be favourable or unfavourable.

Empirical studies of the effects of high concentration levels in LDCs are fairly limited but they provide some support for the view that high seller concentration is associated with above-average price–cost margins and with lower X-efficiency (see Chapter 3, section 3.4). At the same time, high levels of seller concentration tend to exist in those industries in which technical economies of scale are important (see Chapter 3, section 3.4). Similarly, although large-scale public enterprises may achieve lower X-efficiency than their privately owned counterparts, this may, as mentioned above, partially reflect their employment of additional labour in support of distributional objectives (see Chapter 5, section 5.7). Thus the ambiguous nature of the net economic impact of high concentration levels at the theoretical level also tends to be borne out in practice. The policy implications of this situation are examined below.

COMPETITION POLICY: THEORY AND PRACTICE

The main implication of the above analysis is that high concentration levels *per se* are not necessarily inconsistent with LDCs' development objectives and therefore it would be inappropriate, *as a general policy*, to prohibit them. At the same time, in particular cases, large-scale enterprises in highly concentrated industries may exercise their market power in a way that has adverse efficiency and distributional consequences. Therefore, some form of flexible but effective competition policy is desirable, which can minimise the likelihood of adverse impacts in particular cases without losing the benefits accruing from large-scale activity.

In practice, however, it is rare for LDCs to have an explicit, operational competition policy of any form. In a survey carried out by UNCTAD in 1977, the only LDCs that were identified as possessing legislative or constitutional provision relating to the control of restrictive business practices (RBP)[12] were the Caribbean Community, India, Pakistan, Malaysia and certain Latin American countries (Argentina, Brazil, Chile, Colombia and Mexico) (UNCTAD, 1978b).[13] In certain of these cases, the provision made was fairly limited (in a number of countries it applied only to foreign-owned enterprises) and in many cases the legislation was weakly applied or largely non-operative (Long, 1981). For example, in India (which is one of the few LDCs with fairly comprehensive legislation in this area), the Monopolies and Restrictive Trade Practices Act (1969) made provision for the regulation of a wide range of restrictive business practices (covering all of the main types of situation listed in note 12), but the combined effects of drafting deficiencies in the initial legislation, subsequent liberalising of the law and slow application of its provisions have seriously limited its impact (Chandra, 1977; Paranjape, 1982). This dilution in impact is partly a consequence of more difficult economic conditions, but it also reflects the successful lobbying of industrial, trading and other interests (Paranjape, 1982).

Any evaluation of competition policy should ideally be undertaken within a wider policy framework that includes not only RBP controls but other types of frequently used development policy instruments that may indirectly influence concentration levels and business practices within highly concentrated markets. These include:

• foreign trade restrictions;
• price controls;
• industrial licensing;
• restructuring of existing enterprises into larger units;
• reservation of particular economic activities of national importance to government;
• financial and other controls over public enterprises;
• regulation of foreign investment in host LDCs;
• patent legislation and regulation of the transfer of technology.

Certain of these measures may reduce the adverse consequences of high concentration but others have the opposite effect. In some cases, also, the effects on concentration levels have been the opposite to what was intended. For example, the industrial licensing policy in India has, from time to time, worked to the advantage of the large industrial houses, although the intention had been to reduce their power and influence (Ghose, 1974).

IMPROVEMENTS TO COMPETITION POLICY

If the adverse impacts of high concentration on the attainment of development objectives are to be minimised, two kinds of improvement in competition policy may be desirable:

● more careful review and formulation of those other development policies that indirectly affect concentration levels and business practice, in order to avoid the more seriously damaging efficiency and distributional impacts that they may be causing at the present;
● more widespread application of soundly based RBP policies in LDCs to limit the adverse efficiency and distributional impacts of high concentration but without, at the same time, losing the benefits of large-scale operations.

UNCTAD has elaborated a 'model law' to provide guidance to developing countries for such policies and its main features are summarised below (UNCTAD, 1979):

● The broad objectives of RBP legislation should be to: control the concentration of economic power, promote competition, encourage innovation, create conditions favourable to employment, help to control inflation, encourage balanced economic development, promote social welfare (particularly in the interests of consumers).
● It should establish a new investigative authority, the RBP Commission: its members should have no prejudicial financial interest; they should combine experience in legal and economic matters, and have reasonable security of tenure and not be removable except by special procedure; the Commission should be empowered to make investigations, publish reports and make recommendations for implementation, subject to the approval of the appropriate authority.
● The Commission's powers of investigation and recommendation should cover (subject to certain exemptions): restrictive agreements between enterprises, restrictive acts by firms possessing dominant power, acts leading to a concentration of economic power, and the natural expansion of enterprises beyond a threshold size.

In the final analysis, the practical impact of such RBP policies as these, assuming political commitment to their adoption and implementation, would largely depend upon the degree of independence and competence of the Commission, the scope of its investigative powers, the resources placed at its disposal and the 'publicness' of its activities and reports.

6.5   REGULATION OF TRANSNATIONAL CORPORATIONS

The TNC subsidiary is a part of a wider global network, and it will always be responsive, in some degree, to the demands of the parent company's global strategy. On the other hand, the government of the host LDC within which the subsidiary is located will be pursuing its own objectives with respect to economic development in general, and industrialisation in particular, within its own country. It is highly likely, therefore, that there will be conflict between these competing sets of objectives (Oyelabi, 1974, p. 106).

The main areas of actual or potential conflict include:

- *the balance of payments*: the LDC government may wish to maximise the earning, and minimise the expenditure, of foreign exchange, whereas the TNC may be reluctant to export, may establish highly import-intensive operations within the LDC, and may wish to repatriate as high a proportion of its earnings as possible (and use the manipulation of transfer prices to secure that objective);
- *employment creation*: the LDC government may wish to encourage job creation, whereas the TNC may use more capital-intensive technologies than domestic firms (or at least raise the overall level of capital intensity within the manufacturing sector); TNC production may well destroy jobs in the informal or handicraft sectors of the economy (although the TNC is not unique in this respect); and the limited linkages established with other firms in the economy will reduce the creation of indirect employment opportunities;
- *technology transfer*: the LDC government may wish to encourage the effective transfer and anchorage of useful and/or 'appropriate' technology by TNCs and stimulate the development of an indigenous technological capacity; the interests of the TNC, however, may work in the opposite direction.

These examples clearly do not exhaust all the areas of potential or actual conflict, but they illustrate the importance of the problem and the need for the creation of a framework, at both the national and international level, within which the interests of both TNCs and LDCs can best be accommodated.

NATIONAL POLICIES

The UN (United Nations, 1983, ch. III) classified LDCs into three groups according to their policies towards TNCs.

First, there are LDCs (the smaller countries in the African, Caribbean and Pacific regions) that have been unable to attract substantial amounts of direct foreign investment (DFI) despite their 'open-door', liberal policies towards it. The investment laws and policies of these countries are largely concerned with regulating the entry of DFI, and with the provision of substantial incentives to DFI.

Second, there are countries that originally excluded, or severely limited, the participation of TNCs in their economies but that have modified their policies significantly in the past few years, and now encourage TNC participation in joint ventures with local enterprises. This group of LDCs includes both those attempting to develop along socialist lines (People's Republic of China, Cuba, Vietnam) and others following alternative development paths (Egypt) or pursuing the socialist path less vigorously (Tanzania). In the case of China, for example, it has been argued (OECD, 1983, pp. 19–20) that the

Foreign Investment Law of 1979 and subsequent regulations confirmed the importance attached to the participation of foreign capital in the modernisation of the Chinese economy. Furthermore, 'China is ready to accept, and will even require, a certain degree of equity participation by its foreign partners in order to ensure their identification with the joint ventures' (p. 20).

Third, there are LDCs with sizeable domestic markets that have attracted the bulk of DFI flows to the developing world (Argentina, Brazil, Chile, Mexico, India, Indonesia, Republic of Korea, Venezuela). In the early 1970s most of these countries introduced rigorous regulatory regimes for foreign investment and technology inflows, aimed not at diminishing or discouraging inflows of DFI but at controlling them. Such regulations included:

- the screening and registration of foreign investment;
- the prohibition or restriction of foreign participation in specified sectors;
- the control of take-overs;
- the restriction of foreign capital to minority holdings in certain sectors;
- the specific regulation of technology agreements;
- the control of restrictive business practices (see section 6.4 above);
- performance requirements for the subsidiaries of TNCs.

(United Nations, 1983, pp. 56–7)

Since the mid-1970s, however, many of these countries have modified their policies and have adopted a more flexible and pragmatic approach to facilitate and accelerate DFI inflows. This liberalisation is the result of two opposing forces: (i) balance of payments and growth problems, which have necessitated the creation of a more attractive investment climate to encourage foreign capital inflows; (ii) the growing expertise and experience of certain LDCs in dealing with TNCs, which has strengthened the former's bargaining position.

The United Nations (1983, p. 58) has highlighted the key features of recent developments:

First, within the framework of basic objectives and regulatory mechanisms, there is a growing emphasis on planning for and promoting the inflow of desired foreign investment and technology into specified priority sectors. Secondly, there is increasing emphasis on performance requirements for foreign enterprises, particularly the increase of local content, export commitments and the transfer of technology. Thirdly, policies and programmes have been adopted with a view to building up national technological and managerial capabilities.

Performance requirements, in particular, are becoming of greater importance in many LDCs, especially the full and effective transfer of technology, and the training of nationals. There is a growing awareness that the benefits accruing to the national economy depend on the building up of national industrial entrepreneurial and technological capabilities and that such objectives can best be achieved by regulation rather than, for example, nationalisation (United Nations, 1983, p. 11).

INTERNATIONAL POLICIES

National action on its own is clearly inadequate to deal effectively with the global strategies of the TNCs, and the international regulation of TNCs has become 'one of the major endeavours of the world community within the past decade' (United Nations 1983, p. 105). The objective is to create an international framework that will maximise the positive contributions of TNCs to development and minimise their negative effects and at the same time contribute to the security of foreign investment through the establishment of clear and stable 'rules of the game'.

There are a number of different codes of conduct (both general and issue-specific) in operation or under discussion at the present time. They include: the International Labour Office (ILO) Tripartite Declaration of Principles Concerning Multinational Enterprises and Social Policy (adopted 1977); the Draft International Code of Conduct on the Transfer of Technology, being negotiated under the auspices of UNCTAD; and the United Nations Code of Conduct on Transnational Corporations, being negotiated under the auspices of the Commission on Transnational Corporations.

The negotiations concerning the proposed UN Code in particular have encountered many fundamental problems, including, for example, definition of a TNC, the treatment of TNC affiliates *vis-à-vis* local enterprises, and the relations between LDC governments and TNCs. If adopted, the UN Code is likely to be voluntary in nature and implemented largely through national action, although the UN Centre on Transnational Corporations will have an important role to play in collecting, analysing and disseminating information to assist in the implementation of the Code. (For further details, see United Nations, 1983, pp. 105–24; Nixson, 1983a.)

CONCLUSIONS

All TNC regulatory mechanisms, both national and international, have a common objective and face a common problem. The objective is to regulate DFI inflows or TNC activities so as to maximise the benefits and minimise the costs associated with them, assessed from the standpoint of the regulator. The problem is that regulation by a potential host government may reduce the inflow or scare away the TNC, with a loss of potential benefits greater than the reduction in costs. A balance must thus be struck between the creation of a favourable investment climate and the judicious use of incentives on the one hand, and the use of regulations to ensure that DFI is in accord with development priorities on the other hand.

It could be argued that LDCs have been too generous in the investment regimes offered to TNCs. On the other hand, it has been argued that in the mineral sector of LDCs, for example, an inadequate investment climate has discouraged necessary transnational DFI (see, for example, Brandt

Commission, 1980, ch. 9). Empirical evidence by itself can neither prove nor disprove these propositions but overall, given LDC competition for TNC investment, it seems more likely that LDCs have been unintentionally generous in the past and that some redressing of that balance is to be expected in the future.

6.6   DEVELOPMENT OF SMALL-SCALE ENTERPRISES

The encouragement of small-scale enterprises is an intergral part of the industrialisation programmes of most LDCs. The advantages claimed for such enterprises are:

- they both encourage entrepreneurship and economise in its use (see Chapter 4, section 4.16);
- they are more likely to utilise labour-intensive technologies than large-scale enterprises and are thus more effective creators of direct employment opportunities (although there is some evidence that small-scale enterprises are occasionally more capital intensive than large-scale ones – Sutcliffe, 1971, pp. 237–8, cites evidence from India);
- they can usually be rapidly established and put into operation to produce quick returns (Bryce, 1960, ch. 2);
- small-scale enterprise development can encourage the process of both inter- and intra-regional decentralisation – small-scale enterprises can be located both in smaller urban centres and in rural areas; in India, for example, the establishment of small-scale village enterprises is seen as an essential element in rural development via expanding employment opportunities, raising incomes and living standards and bringing about a more balanced and integrated rural economy;
- small-scale industrialisation permits the achievement of wider economic and socio-political objectives – such a strategy of industrialisation was clearly an essential element in Gandhi's economic philosophy and played an important role in Maoist thought on economic development in the People's Republic of China.

Staley and Morse (1965, ch. 12) have identified three types of policy towards small enterprise development: passive, protective and developmental. A passive policy is simply one of neglect, resulting from indifference, lack of information or lack of leadership. A protective policy is, as the name implies, designed to defend existing small enterprises against competition from larger and/or more modern enterprises (both indigenous and foreign). The example they quoted is of the protective measures taken to help large numbers of handloom weavers and their families in India – reserved markets for handloom products, quotas on mill cloth, etc. (Staley and Morse, 1965, p. 317). The developmental approach to small enterprise promotion has as its objective the creation of 'economically viable enterprises which can stand on their own feet without perpetual subsidy and can make a positive contribution to the growth of real income and therefore to better living levels' (p. 318). This approach emphasises the importance of efficiency in new small-scale enterprises. Small producers must be encouraged to adopt new methods and move into new lines of production and, in the longer run, they should be encouraged, wherever possible, to become medium- or even large-scale producers.

Staley and Morse (1965, pp. 320–1) suggested the following policy maxims:

- promotion of modernisation (of products, technology, business and management methods);
- promotion of selective growth (to help worthy small industry to grow);
- promotion of management improvement;
- promotion of technological improvement and adaptation of technology to local conditions (see section 6.7 below);
- promotion of complementarity among different types and sizes of industry (creation of inter-industry linkages, subcontracting, etc.).

The ten major policy areas or measures that they identified as being necessary to achieve these objectives are:

(1) the provision of industrial advisory services (extension or counselling services);
(2) the training of entrepreneur managers and supervisory personnel;
(3) the provision of industrial research services;
(4) the provision of developmental finance;
(5) the provision of factory sites and buildings (industrial estates);
(6) the provision of common facility services;
(7) facilitating the procurement of materials and equipment;
(8) the provision of marketing aids (the supply of market information, joint market promotion efforts, help in exporting marketing, etc.);
(9) provision of labour relations services;
(10) stimulation of inter-firm contacts and assistance.

(Staley and Morse, 1965, ch. 13)

The small enterprise development programme must be geared to the resources and requirements of each individual country, but clearly the experiences of other countries may be relevant in formulating policies. For example, Livingstone (1982) compared the 'workshop cluster' approach of Tanzania with the 'extension approach' of Kenya. In Tanzania, promotional efforts centred on the establishment of industrial estates provided with certain common facilities. Tenants on the estates, when questioned, attached great importance to the provision of premises and the greater ease in selling their product from an estate location (although little assistance was given in marketing). Likewise training by the management of the estate was not provided on a significant scale although there was evidence of managerial and technical skill upgrading. Livingstone saw the main advantage of the estate arrangement lying in the injection of capital into craft industry and in the possibility of increasing the managerial contribution to small enterprise development (Livingstone, 1982, p. 357).

In Kenya, on the other hand, the extension approach was used in the hope of reaching a larger number of entrepreneurs and spreading the benefits of the programme more widely. The strategy adopted was to establish Rural Industrial Development Centres in the smaller townships located in the main agricultural areas, consisting of central workshops, offices and classrooms, to serve as the base for the provision of extension services (for example, bookkeeping advice, the introduction of clients to profitable new product lines) to scattered local artisans. However, the costs of the programme were high and the benefits of limited value. Livingstone (1982, p. 364) argued that the extension approach failed to recognise that the artisan's greatest need was capital rather than advice, and he advocated the workshop estate approach, concentrating on appropriate standards and technologies and being used to upgrade informal sector artisan enterprises in both rural and urban areas.[14]

SMALL-SCALE ENTERPRISE DEVELOPMENT AND EMPLOYMENT CREATION

There is general agreement amongst economists concerned with the problems of LDCs that the modern or 'formal' sector is not likely to provide sufficient jobs both to absorb new entrants to the labour force and to eliminate the existing pool of unemployed or underemployed workers (Sen, 1980, p. 145; for a discussion of employment policy, see Squire, 1981). Much depends, therefore, on the ability of the informal/small-scale enterprise sector to create employment opportunities if it is allowed, and encouraged, to do so.

The World Employment Programme of the International Labour Office (ILO) in particular has focused attention on the labour intensity of the technologies used in this sector, the 'appropriateness' of its products, its flexibility and its dynamism (Plant, 1983). The ILO recommends that governments in LDCs should attempt to encourage, rather than restrict, the development of small-scale, informal sector enterprises through the types of policies listed above, but that they should also at the same time attempt to improve the working conditions within the sector. Clearly there is a conflict between the 'informality' of this sector and its ability to supply low-priced goods and services on the one hand, and the desire to improve working conditions and average incomes within this sector, on the other hand. The reconciliation of these opposing forces is a problem that governments in LDCs must face if the potential benefits of informal sector/small-scale enterprise development are to be fully realised in practice. This is not to suggest that this sector can provide a complete solution to the problems of industrialisation and employment in LDCs, but rather to emphasise that it has an important role to play in the creation of immediate employment opportunities and the production of 'appropriate' goods and services (Sen, 1980, p. 152).

6.7   TECHNOLOGICAL DEVELOPMENT[15]

The LDCs are often described as technologically dependent economies. The concept of technological dependence is imprecise and difficult to define rigorously, but in general it refers to a situation where 'the *major source* of a country's technology comes from abroad' (Stewart, 1977, p. 116; emphasis in original). It originates, at least initially, in the lack of a capacity within the LDC to produce modern technology and in the limited flexibility and substitutability of domestic for foreign resources.

Stewart (1977, p. 123) highlighted the following undesirable consequences of technological dependence:

- the high cost of importing foreign technologies (see Chapter 4, section 4.8);
- the loss of national control over decisions regarding technology;
- the inappropriateness of the technology received; and,
- the lack of an effective domestic scientific and innovative capacity.

In order to reduce their technological dependence, the LDCs must (i) control their technology imports to offset or modify the undesirable consequences of imported technologies, and (ii) reduce the extent of technology imports. Obviously these are not, in principle, mutually exclusive policies but in many cases they may well be, in that LDCs may find that they have to increase their imports of technology in order to develop their own technological capacity (that is, their ability to generate new technologies). What seems to be of importance, therefore, is not the simple fact of importing technology as such, but rather the terms and conditions under which technology is imported and the use to which that technology is put within the importing country (that is, its exchange, adaptation, modification and diffusion within the LDC).

With respect to control of technology imports, there is an increasing awareness among many LDCs that the technology component is the most important part of the DFI 'package', and that the more efficient acquisition of technology should be an important objective of policies towards foreign investment and participation. There is also a growing realisation that

> . . . an indigenous technological capability is a necessary condition for the evaluation of technology to be obtained from abroad, for the effective utilisation of the transferred technology, for its adaptation to local conditions, for getting better terms for the transfer in negotiation with foreign enterprises and for the generation of 'appropriate' indigenous technologies. *In other words, indigenous technological capability is not an alternative to transfer but a necessary condition for it*. (United Nations 1983, p. 67; emphasis added)

The implication of the latter point is that, even if LDCs are merely to modify or adapt imported technologies (obtained via direct foreign investment, or licensing, or from any other source), they will require a fairly well-developed and sophisticated domestic technological capacity that few of them at present possess. LDCs are thus beginning to formulate technology policy strategies that include:

- – identification of technological needs;
- – selection of suitable technology and technology suppliers;
- – strengthening the capacity of national enterprises in acquiring foreign technology;
- – regulation of the terms and conditions of technology transfer arrangements;
- – facilitating the absorption of imported technologies and the promotion of indigenous technological capabilities.

(United Nations, 1983, p. 68)

Technology policy needs to be implemented through the adoption of technology plans that should be integral parts of national development plans:

The technology plans should embrace essential responsibilities, such as budgeting, management, co-ordination, stimulation and execution of technological activities and cover specific requirements at the sectoral and intersectoral levels for the assessment, transfer, acquisition, adaptation and development of technology. They should reflect short-term, medium-term and long-term strategies, including determination of technological priorities, mobilisation of natural resources, dissemination of the existing national stock of technology, identification of sectors in which imported technology would be required and determination of R and D priorities for the development and improvement of indigenous technologies. Particularly important in this connection is to initiate now the process of substitution of imported technologies by domestic ones. (UNCTAD, 1981b, p. 60)

THE DEVELOPMENT OF 'APPROPRIATE' TECHNOLOGY[16]

The criticism is often made that modern, capital-intensive, imported technologies are 'inappropriate' and irrelevant to the needs of the relatively capital-scarce, labour-abundant LDCs. It is therefore recommended that LDCs should select and utilise more 'appropriate' technologies. 'Appropriate' in this context is variously defined as 'the set of techniques which makes optimum use of available resources in a given environment' (Morawetz, 1974, pp. 517–18) or, less formally, as the technology 'appropriate to a country's factors of production in that it maximises the use of those factors which are locally plentiful ... such as labour and raw materials, while minimising the use of those which are locally scarce, such as capital and skilled management' (Harper and Soon, 1979, pp. 101–2).

The advantages usually claimed for appropriate technology are as follows:

- reduced investment requirements per job created (lower K/L ratio);
- smaller scale of operation and higher level of capacity utilisation;
- utilisation of local raw materials and locally available skills;

- simplicity: simple to make, operate, repair and maintain (Stewart, 1977, p. 104);
- creation of linkages with other sectors of the economy, especially through purchase of local inputs, the manufacture of spare parts and the local production of the machinery itself (the promotion of a local capital goods sector – see below);
- compatibility with existing social structures – the introduction of an 'appropriate' technology should cause the least possible disruption to the lives of those most affected by it (see Harper and Soon, 1979, p. 103);
- suitability for location in rural areas.

Two important issues are raised by this discussion. First, where are 'appropriate' technologies to come from? As Stewart (1977, ch. 4) has argued, a more 'appropriate' choice may be made from among existing techniques, or new, more 'appropriate' techniques may be developed as a matter of deliberate policy. This latter alternative in turn raises the second question: who is to develop the new techniques – TNCs, indigenous enterprises, aid agencies (public and private), or the LDC government? TNCs are unlikely to be in the forefront of the development of either 'appropriate' processes or products (Griffin, 1977) and, although there have been a number of calls for international action (see, for example, the contributions to Bhalla, 1979, and Robinson 1979a), ultimate responsibility must be with national governments and the various institutions they have created for this purpose.

The question of the 'appropriateness' of products raises a number of further issues at both the theoretical and policy level. What is an 'appropriate' product? How can, or should, people be persuaded to consume such products? What is the relationship between 'appropriate' products and 'appropriate' technology (it cannot simply be assumed that the former will be produced using the latter – many products, both final consumer goods and intermediate goods, may be vital to the development effort yet be produced by large-scale, capital-intensive, imported technologies)? These fundamental issues, and the related policy implicaitons, have yet to be considered by the great majority of LDCs.

THE ESTABLISHMENT OF A CAPITAL GOODS SECTOR

The central role of the capital goods (machine-making) sector in the process of growth and development is now generally recognised. When the limited availability of foreign exchange restricts the import of capital goods, the expansion of the domestic capital goods sector provides the means for overcoming the problem of transforming savings into investment, thus accelerating economic growth (Mitra, 1979). In addition, not only do new products and processes generally require new machines but the capital goods sector itself is a major initiator of change, and those changes transmit themselves rapidly within and across sectors. As Stewart (1977, pp. 152–3) observed:

> ... innovation is likely to be concentrated in the capital goods sector ... economies without a capital goods sector are more than proportionately weakened when it comes to innovatory activity ... lacking such sectors, underdeveloped countries have to import not only their machinery, but also their technical progress. The nature and direction of technical progress is thus determined from the outside.

Two sets of policy implications are suggested by this discussion. For those LDCs with significant capital goods sectors already established (India, Brazil, Republic of Korea), policies need to focus on raising both static and dynamic efficiency.[17] For those LDCs wishing to establish or encourage the development of a capital goods sector, selective and effective state intervention is necessary in order (i) to ensure the creation of external economies of scale, (ii) to protect the infant capital goods industries, and (iii) to reduce uncertainty through economic planning (Mitra, 1979).

6.8   CONTROL AND ACCOUNTABILITY OF PUBLIC ENTERPRISES

The fundamental aim of policy towards the public enterprise sector is to ensure that the decisions taken by the enterprises are consistent with the objectives of the government. The problem is therefore one of developing an effective system of control. The difficulty that confronts the policy-maker is to devise a control system that avoids, on the one hand, the costs associated with complete decentralisation and, on the other hand, the disadvantages of centralisation. Too little control will mean that the performance is determined by the independent decisions of each enterprise's management, whereas too much interference in the day-to-day decision-making of the enterprise can lead to what Killick (1981, p. 289) described as 'the trivialisation of political control'. What is needed, therefore, is a control system in which management is accountable for its results, but at the same time has the necessary autonomy to achieve the objectives that have been set for it.

The form that public enterprise control systems take in practice, and the extent to which they successfully reconcile the requirements for control and autonomy, will be influenced by:

- the legal and institutional form of public enterprises;
- the extent to which quantitative operational 'rules' and 'controls' are established for the public enterprises;
- the extent to which the government's objectives are clearly stated and consistently followed.

LEGAL AND INSTITUTIONAL STRUCTURE

Public enterprises can take a number of different forms, of which the most common are departmental enterprises, statutory corporations and limited companies. A departmental enterprise is not a legal entity, and is part of an existing government ministry; it has no separate budget, and is managed by civil servants. The statutory corporation is legally separate from the government, and is normally administered by a board appointed by the government. The public corporation structure is often modelled on the British system, and is intended to fulfil the 'need for a high degree of freedom, boldness and enterprise in management' in contrast to the 'caution and circumspection . . . typical of Government departments' (Robson, 1960, p. 47, quoted in Rees, 1976). The limited company form is established under company law, with government contributing to the equity capital. Government control is exercised either through its membership of the managing board, or indirectly through a government holding company, the board of which supervises the individual companies in the public sector.

Recalling the earlier discussion on the need to achieve a balance between the extremes of decentralisation and complete control, it might be thought that the public corporation form provides the most appropriate institutional structure for public enterprises. The experience of both developed and developing countries that have adopted this institutional structure does not suggest, however, that it has been entirely satisfactory. Rees's judgement (1976, p. 21) on the UK experience is that:[18]

> It cannot be claimed that the system has worked especially well. Because of the degree of centralization, it is relatively costly in resources and time . . . It is also possible to argue that there are many instances in which ministerial intervention has worsened the performance of public enterprise without any apparent gains to the 'national interest' and in so far as the degree of centralization of the control system facilitates such intervention, this is a contributory factor.

The significance of institutional structure and legal status for the performance of the public enterprise should not be exaggerated, however. More significant influences on performance are likely to be the rules and conditions governing their operations, the ability and motivation of management, and the general economic environment within which they operate.

RULES AND CRITERIA FOR PUBLIC ENTERPRISE OPERATIONS

There have been many attempts to devise criteria that will induce public enterprises to meet the objectives of economic (i.e. allocative) efficiency and/or profitability. Marginal cost pricing is widely advocated as a means of achieving allocative efficiency. However, as was pointed out in Chapter 5, sections 5.5 and 5.6, there are important practical and theoretical difficulties associated with this pricing rule. Financial targets may be set to reflect the government's concern with profitability. In principle, separate financial targets should be set for each enterprise, with allowance for, *inter alia*, the age of its capital stock, the possible existence of increasing returns to scale (see Figure 5.2), and the degree of price restraint imposed upon the enterprise by the government. In practice, however, financial targets are often set independently of the cost conditions within particular enterprises, and may therefore be inconsistent with the use of marginal cost pricing.

Public enterprises are frequently required to pursue objectives additional to those of profitability and economic efficiency. There are a number of practical policy measures that can be used to 'operationalise' these additional 'non-economic' objectives. One such approach is for the government to provide financial support for specified loss-making activities that the public enterprise is required to undertake in pursuit of other objectives of government policy (these are frequently related to income distribution goals). The public enterprise is then required to meet a specified financial target. In Senegal, for example, the government has negotiated formal agreements with the public enterprises operating in the transport sector. Under these agreements, the government makes a three-year commitment to meet the enterprises' costs of operating unprofitable 'social' services to remote areas and to give the enterprises greater autonomy in its day-to-day decision-making. In return the enterprises agree to specific targets for financial and productivity performance (World Bank, 1983, p. 79).

A more complex method of incorporating different objectives into an operational performance indicator is to assess public enterprises in terms of their 'public profitability' record. 'Public profit' can be thought of as financial (private) profits, adjusted for efficiency and other social objectives. Inputs and outputs are revalued at shadow prices to allow for the divergence between market and efficiency values; the costs of non-commercial objectives are deducted before public profit is calculated and treated as implicit subsidies to the enterprise. Enterprises are then judged on the basis of their trend in public profitability. This approach was implemented in Pakistan in 1981, with the monitoring and evaluation being undertaken by a semi-autonomous agency responsible to the Minstry of Production. The government rewards good performance with a salary bonus to the enterprise's management. Similar procedures of 'public profitability' evaluation have been established in the Republic of Korea and Venezuela (World Bank, 1983, p. 82).

The adoption of procedures for setting specific operating criteria and performance targets is likely to help make explicit the costs and benefits of pursuing various objectives, and can contribute to a more rational and informed evaluation of public enterprise performance.

It was suggested in Chapter 5 that managerial motivation may be a further influence upon the performance of the public enterprise. The level of X-efficiency may be raised by the adoption of appropriate policy measures. Greater emphasis on the professional capabilities of managerial appointments could contribute to improved performance – in many LDCs, senior staff are drawn from the civil service or political parties and have limited experience in managing an industrial enterprise. In some countries, there is a serious shortage of national managerial personnel, and this has contributed to a high rate of turnover. A study of nine sub-Saharan African countries, for example, found that the average tenure of public enterprise general managers in the 1970s was less than two years (World Bank, 1983, p. 84). In these circumstances, it may be necessary to utilise managerial contracts with foreign firms and to establish managerial training schemes. The performance of public enterprise personnel may be raised by linking results to rewards. These rewards may be pecuniary, in the form of performance bonuses or profit sharing, or they may be non-pecuniary – prestige, increased responsibility, national recognition.

Finally, the competitive environment within which the public enterprise operates may influence its performance. In some cases it may be possible to expose the enterprise to greater competition, for example by requiring publicly owned industries to compete with imports, or by splitting large public monopolies into smaller, autonomous units. In other instances, where the public enterprise is a natural monopoly or produces goods and services that are not traded internationally, government legislation on monopoly control and practices can be an instrument for improving public enterprise performance (see section 6.4 above).

THE PUBLIC ENTERPRISE SECTOR'S OBJECTIVES

The discussion so far has been about the design of appropriate policies as the *means* of meeting given *ends*, represented by the government's objectives. Assuming that the government has a well-defined and identifiable set of objectives that it wishes the public enterprise to pursue, the role of the economist is to identify policies that are not contributing to the achievement of these objectives, and to propose alternative measures that would facilitate the achievement of the government's goals. The determination of the 'correct' objectives for the public enterprise sector is part of the political process, however, and the economist must be careful to avoid condemning political decisions as 'irrational' or 'interference' simply because they conflict with the profitability or efficiency performance criteria.

In practice, the political process seldom gives the analyst a clearly defined set of objectives in which the relative importance of each objective is specified. The discussion of industrial planning (section 6.3 above) indicated the complexity of the government decision-making process, and the influence of inter-group interests and tensions within it. This suggests that improving economic performance in the public enterprise sector may not always have a high priority among the government's objectives, and explains why 'often there are strong political motives for keeping objectives fuzzy and not analyzing trade-offs' (World Bank, 1983, p. 77). The dilemma that confronts the analyst is that without clear objectives there is no basis on which to judge public enterprise performance.

6.9 SPATIAL IMBALANCES AND INDUSTRIAL LOCATION POLICIES

During recent years there has been increasing concern over the spatial imbalances in development (between regions, rural and urban areas and cities of different sizes) that are being experienced in most LDCs. Such imbalances, it is felt, could be both economically wasteful and inequitable; they could also lead to intolerable social and environmental pressures where growth is most rapid, and political resentment and unrest where it is most sluggish. Among the different factors to which such imbalances have been attributed is the pattern of industrial development adopted in many LDCs. The implication sometimes drawn is that if this development pattern were to be modified (most obviously, through government policies towards industrial location), these imbalances could be reduced and the higher-order objectives described in the opening section of this chapter could be more fully realised.

However, the relationships between industrial development policy, spatial imbalances and the attainment of higher-order objectives are considerably more complex than implied above. These relationships are explored further below, when considering the following questions:

- To what extent do spatial imbalances exist in LDCs?
- What is the relationship between industrial development and spatial imbalances?
- Do spatial imbalances conflict with the attainment of higher-order objectives?
- What is the appropriate role and form of industrial location policy in reducing these imbalances?

SPATIAL IMBALANCES, INDUSTRIAL DEVELOPMENT AND HIGHER-ORDER OBJECTIVES

Spatial imbalances

There are three types of spatial imbalance in LDCs that commonly give rise to concern:

- *Regional imbalance* is associated with the presence within a country of large regional differences in average per capita incomes, in economic growth and in migration rates. Such measures as exist indicate that regional disparities within LDCs are typically very great and are substantially larger, in relative terms, than in most DCs. For example, the ratio between the average per capita income in the richest and poorest region in a DC is typically in the order of two or less; in an LDC it may range between three and ten (or even higher)[19] (Renaud, 1981; Gilbert and Goodman, 1976; Williamson, 1965).
- *Rural/urban imbalance* is primarily associated with rural/urban migration, which contributes between one-third and one-half of the urban population growth in LDCs (United Nations, 1980). This, if continued and combined with the current high rate of natural increase in urban areas, means that the urban population of Africa, Asia and Latin America is expected to increase by 166 per cent between 1975 and the year 2000 (United Nations, 1980).
- *Intra-urban sector imbalance* is particularly associated with the above-average growth of the existing largest cities in LDCs at the relative expense of their smaller urban communities. In 1950 there was only one LDC city with a population in excess of 5 million; by 1975 this number had increased to ten and by the year 2000 it is expected to be

forty-three (United Nations, 1975a). The twelve fastest-growing large cities are all located in LDCs and are believed to have more than doubled their population over the last fifteen years (Todaro, 1981, p. 228).

Industrial development and spatial imbalance

Radically different interpretations are placed upon the nature of the spatial imbalances described above and their relationship to the industrial development process occurring within LDCs; and the policy implications of each are correspondingly different (Gilbert and Goodman, 1976).

One school of thought takes the view that spatial imbalances in the form of disparities in factor prices, per capita incomes, etc. are to be expected during the early stages of development in an economy because the economic activities at different locations are not closely integrated within the same market system. Further, the major restructuring of an economy that takes place during the early stages of industrialisation is bound to result in different growth rates at different locations within the economy and in short-term disparities in per capita incomes owing to the existence of market imperfections. However, according to this viewpoint,

> these 'imperfections' will disappear during the process of economic growth due to the unification of factor markets and the greater interdependence of regional economies. In short, market forces can be relied upon to equalise regional *per capita* incomes as the economy proceeds from 'under-development' through 'take-off' to 'economic maturity'. (Gilbert and Goodman, 1976, p. 120)

The tendency for regional disparities in per capita incomes to be less in DCs than in LDCs has been used in support of this explanation (Williamson, 1965), but others have questioned whether the DC experience can be safely transposed into the Third World context (Gilbert and Goodman, 1976). To the extent that it can, however, it supports the case for a 'non-meddlesome' government policy towards the spatial distribution of industrial activities in LDCs other than possibly expediting the removal of market imperfections that is expected to occur eventually, in any case, as an indirect result of economic growth.

An alternative school of thought takes the view that the existing imbalances in an LDC (which may have been inherited from an entirely different, e.g. colonial political and economic regime) may be self-perpetuating rather than self-correcting. If, for example, an LDC's development strategy is based upon the promotion of import-substituting industries, using modern, large-scale production techniques, the locational pull of any existing large city (or region) for new industrial plants will be particularly strong because of its accessibility to the major domestic market, existing infrastructure facilities, a better-qualified supply of labour and (usually) better government contacts. If sufficient numbers of new industrial establishments are established in the large city/region, they will tend to reinforce its initial locational advantages. For example, agglomeration economies will accrue and the size of the major domestic market will grow as its population expands and its spending power increases. At the same time, the political power of the major city/region will increase, which may lead to a big-city and industrial bias in the development policies and investment activities that are approved by national government (Gilbert and Goodman, 1976; Gugler, 1982). The corollary to this is that insufficient attention is paid to increasing the efficiency of the agricultural sector and stimulating material-processing activities in rural areas. Small-scale industrial enterprises using more traditional methods of production and located in smaller urban areas become progressively less competitive and lose their local markets to the more modern, larger-scale plants. The resulting migration to the large city deprives rural and smaller urban communities in other regions of their younger and more innovative workers.

To the extent that this alternative analysis is accepted (and some supporting evidence is available – United Nations, 1980; Fuentes, 1983), it implies that a much stronger and more comprehensive interventionist role in the development process may be justified. Development policies that are not directly concerned with industrial location as such (for example, trade or infrastructure policies) would need to be corrected for spatial bias. Also, if the inherited spatial pattern of economic activity is felt to be inappropriate, industrial location policies could not rely on the removal of market imperfections necessarily to produce a more appropriate spatial pattern. They may also need to contain a package of investment and other measures to promote viable and economically efficient industrial centres in other regions and smaller cities in the country. Devising a sound package of such measures is not an easy task, as will be explained shortly; securing political support for the implementation of such measures may be even more difficult unless they can be shown to be in the long-term interests of the big city.

Spatial imbalances and higher-order objectives

So far it has been implicitly assumed that spatial balance, in some sense, is a desirable goal – but is it necessarily consistent with the higher-order development objectives of efficiency and equity? Unless 'spatial balance' is very carefully and restrictively defined, this is unlikely to be the case, for the following reasons:

First, in any dynamic economy, resource reallocation must take place and this will have a spatial dimension such that spatially balanced development is unlikely to be resource efficient. Over the shorter term (which may be prolonged where serious market imperfections exist), this adjustment process will be associated with differences in factor payments and per capita income levels between different locations. In these kinds of circumstances, resistance to spatial imbalance, *irrespective of its nature and cause*, is likely to conflict at some point with the attainment of efficiency objectives.

Secondly, *spatial equity* (that is, spatial equality in average per capita incomes) is not necessarily consistent with *person equity* (reductions in income inequalities between persons). Measures to achieve the former may not promote the latter objective. For example, Brazil's regional policy during the 1960s, which aimed to promote the development of its relatively deprived north-east region, appears to have been associated with an increasingly unequal income distribution among inhabitants in that region (Gilbert and Goodman, 1976).

This suggests that industrial location policy should be formulated with the attainment of efficiency and interpersonal equity objectives primarily in view rather than some predetermined notion of spatial balance. Almost certainly this will imply neither spatial stability in the simplistic sense (i.e. zero change in the spatial distribution of activities) in which it has been described above, nor uncritical acceptance of existing spatial imbalances and trends (given possible market imperfections, inherited spatial patterns, development policy bias, and the self-reinforcing mechanisms in operation).

INDUSTRIAL LOCATION POLICY IN A WIDER CONTEXT

The main conclusions to be drawn from the foregoing analysis are:

- industrial location policy should be formulated to meet efficiency and equity objectives rather than some preconceived notion of spatial balance;
- location policy should not be narrowly conceived, since the overall development strategy that is adopted (and superimposed upon an inherited spatial pattern of settlements and economic activities) will itself also have a major influence upon whether development occurs efficiently and equitably over space.

A carefully targeted, but broadly based, industrial location strategy should be formulated and implemented. What follows is an outline of some of the more specific features that might be contained within such a strategy.

Political commitment and appropriate structures

Renaud, writing in the context of national urban policy, stated, 'The most crucial prerequisites for an effective national urbanisation strategy are political commitment at the highest level and appropriate adjustments of the governmental structure and modes of operation' (Renaud, 1981, p. 129). One of the most difficult tasks is to obtain political commitment from the most powerful interests in the dominant city and region to promote development for the less powerful in other regions and smaller cities with whom they feel no immediate affinity of interest. Devolution of power and decentralisation of decision-making, either to existing regional or city administrations or to newly created development authorities, are often desirable to inject an element of local participation into the decision-taking and implementation process (Stohr, 1975). Again, however, some degree of resistance from the central authorities is to be expected.

Correction, at source, of spatial bias in development policies

The areas of development policy (in addition to those directly related to industrial location) that may be a source of spatial bias are numerous and only the most important can be indicated here. In a number of cases, they include policies that have been discussed in a slightly different context earlier in this chapter.

National economic planning priorities. Three areas of particular concern, because of their possible spatial effects, are: (a) insufficient attention to the structural reorganisation and more efficient development of the agricultural sector; (b) locational bias in infrastructure investment and social capital; and (c) bias towards large-scale industry in selecting industrial development priorities. More careful and objective application of efficiency and equity criteria in the planning process is required to try to counteract these biases.

Trade policies. Overdependence on an import-substituting policy of industrial development is likely to encourage the overconcentration of economic activity in the dominant city and region. A less restrictive trade policy, which provides for some export promotion, may facilitate other forms of manufacturing production, geared to overseas markets, in other cities.

Monopoly control and technology policies. The regulation of industrial concentration, both overall and at the individual market level, is often relatively weak in most LDCs, as are the controls exercised over capital-intensive, imported technologies. In the absence of effective regulation, much of the industrial development has been achieved through large-scale, capital-intensive enterprises, for which the locational pull of the dominant city or region is particularly strong. This might be counterbalanced through a stricter application of monopoly control policy, combined with measures to promote smaller-scale, less capital-intensive enterprises, which may be more economically viable in smaller cities located in other regions (see sections 6.6 and 6.7 above).

Urban management policies. Particularly in the larger cities, inefficient and inequitable resource allocation results from the absence of a satisfactory mechanism to handle the substantial externalities arising from road congestion, environmental pollution, etc. Whether or not this results in big cities being larger than they should be is open to dispute (Tolley, 1974; Gugler, 1982), but there is little doubt that the presence of uncontrolled externalities distorts the spatial distribution of industrial activity, both within and between different urban areas. Remedies lie in the direction of appropriately designed land-use controls, and urban utility pricing and investment policies (Renaud, 1981).

Industrial location policy measures
The extent to which industrial location policies, narrowly defined, are used in LDCs is very variable, but in most countries they are not particularly well developed or very effective in promoting higher-order development objectives. Such policies may contain provisions to discourage or prevent new industrial development in certain areas (described as 'stick' policies) and various financial or other inducements to encourage development in particular alternative areas ('carrot' policies).

Where 'stick' policies have been used (for example, as part of an industrial licensing system), the instrument has often been applied in an over-simplistic manner. Nor only may industrial production have been forced away from its least social cost location, but it may also have been fragmented between different locations, causing the further loss of economies of large-scale production. If administrative controls are to be used in this way, then those who apply them should be aware of the likely costs and benefits for each category of industrial development so that they are not applied in a way that is economically wasteful.

Financial inducements typically take the form of tax concessions, capital investment subsidies, subsidised industrial buildings or subsidised public utility services. These tend to encourage a capital-intensive bias in the types of enterprise that are attracted, which may be the least suitable for the areas concerned. Labour subsidies are far less frequently used as a tool of industrial location policy even though they may be more justified on efficiency grounds (see Chapter 5, section 5.5 for the 'shadow price' arguments that support this conclusion).

On a more ambitious scale, attempts have been made to establish new industrial growth centres, either in existing medium-sized cities, or by creating entirely new cities. The underlying logic is described by Gilbert and Gugler (1982, pp. 173–4).

At its simplest, the growth-centre notion conceives of an urban complex containing a series of industrial enterprises focused on a dynamic growth industry. The growth industry stimulates the emergence of ancillary companies whose presence lowers its own operation costs. Specialised services and a skilled labour force emerge which help to maintain inter-regional competitiveness and generate new activities.

The reasons why LDC governments may choose to make non-marginal adjustments to the spatial pattern of their industrial development have been explained earlier in this section and, in theory at least, the practice can be entirely consistent with a government's higher-order efficiency and equity objectives. To date, however, the practical success that has been achieved with growth centre schemes (in DCs as well as in LDCs) has been very limited (Renaud, 1981; Gilbert and Gugler, 1982). As a result, although the growth centre concept has not been abandoned, it is now applied in a much more selective and cautious manner. This is reflected in the following 'basic lessons learned from past-experience' drawn by Renaud (1981, pp. 130–1):

- In most cases, new towns are wasteful and inefficient ways of approaching the problems of rapid urban growth.
- A spatial strategy that can emphasize intermediate-size cities . . . and major transport corridors will be building from a position of strength.
- Planning for any area cannot be done effectively in isolation. It must be part of a national strategy and based upon the comparative advantage of the region as well as a realistic appraisal of national resource constraints.

The spatial changes taking place in settlement and economic activity patterns within LDCs are very extensive. While there is no special reason why imbalances, broadly defined, should not occur, there is equally no reason to believe that the actual spatial changes that are now being experienced are optimal from either efficiency or equity viewpoints. The industrial location policies in operation in LDCs are, taken as a whole, not well developed or sufficiently clearly targeted on high-level development objectives. This, however, is only one source of deficiency in spatial policies. At a more fundamental level, the spatial bias in the overall development strategies being pursued in LDCs will need to be addressed before a total solution can be devised (Lipton, 1977).

6.10   CONCLUSIONS

Most Third World countries look to industrialisation as a major contributor to their economic development and try to devise policies in order to make more rapid industrialisation possible. Over the past twenty-five years, a number of LDCs have achieved an impressive rate of industrial expansion (although others have not, see Table 1.1) and the Third World as a whole has set its sights on the ambitious target of producing 25 per cent of world manufacturing value added by the year 2000 (see Chapter 2, section 2.5). This target looks increasingly difficult to attain in the current world economic climate, as Third World export markets for manufactures fail to expand at the necessary rate, owing to economic stagnation and increased protectionism. There is, then, a need to reappraise both the overall industrial growth that may be realistically achieved in the Third World by the turn of the century and, of equal importance, the particular development objectives that this industrial expansion should serve and the detailed policies by which it might be most satisfactorily accomplished.

DEVELOPMENT OBJECTIVES AND INDUSTRIAL POLICIES

An underlying theme of this final chapter has been the danger of over-generalisation and over-simplification in the formulation of development objectives and policy instruments for the industrial sector. LDCs differ greatly in their social and political systems, and in their existing economic and industrial structures; it should therefore be expected that there will be a corresponding variation in the development objectives and industrialisation strategies that they choose to adopt (Chapter 1, section 1.4). Development objectives need to be carefully formulated in the context of the particular country in which they are to be applied, they should be made consistent with each other and be capable of implementation, and they should provide the criteria by which particular industrial development policies can be adequately evaluated (section 6.1 above).

The process of selecting appropriate development policies is considerably more complex than many of the more simplistic statements on industrial policy sometimes suggest. As the preceding sections of this chapter have shown, it *cannot* be safely assumed, in all circumstances and conditions, that:

- import-substituting industrialisation has 'failed' and should be abandoned, and that export-oriented industrialisation has been 'successful' and should be generally adopted (section 6.2);

- industrial planning has been unsuccessful, and therefore should be terminated (section 6.3);
- industrial concentration levels are high and therefore more competition should be stimulated through stricter monopoly power controls (section 6.4);
- the activities of TNCs harm LDC economies and therefore their involvement in these economies should be terminated or severely controlled (section 6.5);
- small-scale enterprises should be promoted at the expense of large-scale enterprises (section 6.6);
- more labour-intensive technologies should always be preferred to capital-intensive ones (section 6.7);
- public enterprises should be submitted to stricter regulation and control (section 6.8);
- spatial imbalances in industrial development should be eliminated (section 6.9).

Each of these generalised policy statements would need to be heavily qualified before it could be accepted. These qualifications (for example, relating to the circumstances in which each of these statements would apply, the detailed content of the policy, the type and range of exceptions and their appropriate treatment) would vary both in nature and extent from one LDC to another. In practice, the scope for 'large design' general solutions to the industrial problems of the Third World appears to be fairly limited.

POLICY EVALUATION AND RESEARCH NEEDS

In these circumstances, the careful formulation and evaluation of industrial polices appropriate to particular LDCs (including evaluation of the likelihood of their implementation) is liable to be of greater practical assistance to industrial development in the Third World than the search for 'golden rules' of general applicability.[20] If so, the quality of these evaluations becomes of critical importance.

Such evaluations should depend heavily, if they are to be satisfactory, upon a good understanding of the economic mechanisms through which industrial policies transmit their effects. In this book, the forms of analysis used in both development economics and industrial economics have been drawn upon to review what is known about the relevant mechanisms at three levels of aggregation. These are:

- the sectoral level (Chapter 2);
- the individual industry and market level (Chapter 3); and
- the individual enterprise level (Chapters 4 and 5).

From the review, it is apparent that the level of understanding of how these mechanisms operate in LDCs is very uneven. Some aspects have been studied fairly fully, although not completely; others have been relatively neglected. The areas of analysis that have been most fully explored include:

- patterns of change in industrial structure at different stages of development (Chapter 2, sections 2.2 and 2.4);
- the behaviour and performance of TNCs (Chapter 4, sections 4.2–4.15).

Relative to these, the following areas of analysis are under-researched:

- the influence of market structure and overall levels of industrial concentration on market performance (Chapter 3, sections 3.3 and 3.4);
- the behaviour and performance of large, indigenous industrial groups and of small-scale domestic enterprises (Chapter 4, sections 4.16 and 4.17);
- the behaviour and overall performance of publicly owned industrial enterprises and joint ventures (Chapter 5, sections 5.5–5.8).

The existence of these deficiencies points to the need for a more balanced programme of research into the behaviour and performance of the industrial sector in LDCs that draws upon the combined approaches of development economics and industrial economics. The research methods that are used will need to vary according to the level of aggregation at which the analysis takes place. At the sectoral level, the formal statistical analysis of mainly published data will continue to be necessary, although it is important that the limitations in the quality of the data are fully appreciated. These limitations should be reduced as better-quality data become available.[21] At other levels, for example the market and enterprise levels, the case study approach (although more time consuming) will often yield richer and more usable data than can be obtained from published sources alone.

FURTHER READING

The following references are grouped according to the main policy issues that have been analysed in this chapter. The literature on ISI and EOI strategies is reviewed in Kirkpatrick and Nixson (1983), parts III–IV. The neoclassical approach to trade policy and industrialisation is presented in Corden (1980); and Nixson (1981, 1982) discusses the structuralist-dependency interpretation of ISI. Killick (1976) presents a perceptive view of the economic planner's role in the political decision-making process, while UNIDO (1979b) contains a number of individual country studies of industrial planning and selection procedures. Long (1981) provides a useful general introduction to the international regulation of restrictive business practices, which may be up-dated by reference to UNCTAD (annual). United Nations (1983), ch. III, summarises the status of international negotiations on various proposed codes of conduct relating to the control of TNCs.

Staley and Morse (1965) remains the classic text on the development of small-scale enterprises, which may be supplemented by Schmitz (1982) and Anderson (1982). Robinson (1979a) contains an extensive discussion of 'appropriate' technology, and UNCTAD (1981b) should be consulted on the planning of technological development. A useful introduction to the subject of public enterprise policy is provided by World Bank (1983), part II. Jones (1983) examines the relationship between objectives and control mechanisms for public enterprises, and Ansari (1983) compares the economic efficiency and political economy approaches to this subject. Gilbert and Gugler (1982) and Renaud (1981) both survey spatial imbalances within the development process in the Third World, paying particular attention to the problem of rapid urbanisation.

NOTES

1 Some writers add a third category, 'self-reliance and nation building'. For a further discussion of development objectives, consult UNIDO (1979a), ch. IV; Cody *et al.* (1980), ch. 1; Killick (1981), chs 1–3.

2 *Productive efficiency* comprises technical and factor price efficiency. The former measures the degree of economy in resource inputs used to produce a given output; the latter measures the degree to which the best combination of resource inputs is used, having regard to their relative opportunity costs (see Chapter 5, section 5.5 for further details). Where changes in productive efficiency occur in the absence of technical change, they may be referred to as changes in X-efficiency (Devine *et al.*, 1979, ch. 8). *Allocative efficiency* (which includes factor price efficiency) refers to the extent to which the allocation of resources within the economy meets the efficiency conditions for Pareto optimality. *Dynamic efficiency* both encompasses and extends the concepts of productive efficiency and allocative efficiency. It also includes the longer-term, indirect increases in total welfare that may result from structural and technical changes in the economy, which might otherwise be neglected when using more traditional forms of welfare analysis. These longer-term impacts are believed by a number of development economists to be the major kinds of benefit accruing during the development process (Nixson, 1984).

3 On the basis of cross-section data, Chenery (1979) observed that ISI has typically been preferred by large economies, and in general it has been the smaller countries that have followed outward-looking, export-oriented strategies of industrialisation. If the natural resource base and size of the domestic market are limited, continued industrial expansion will require production for export markets at an early stage.

4 Neoclassical evaluations of the ISI experience are found in Little, Scitovsky and Scott (1970), Balassa *et al.* (1971), Krueger (1978) and Bhagwati (1978).

5 The structuralist-dependency perspective is discussed in detail in Nixson (1981, 1982).

6 For examples of neoclassical recommendations for LDCs' trade and industrialisation strategies, see Keesing (1979b) and Balassa (1980).

7 This point is emphasised by ul Haq (1973, p. 101):

> Trade should not be regarded as a pace-setter in any relevant development strategy for the developing world but merely as a derivative. The developing countries should first define a viable strategy for attacking their problems of unemployment and mass poverty. Trade policies should be geared to meeting the objectives.

The so-called 'basic-industry' strategy of industrialisation (Rweyemamu, 1973; Thomas 1974; Singh, 1979; Roemer, 1981), with its emphasis on the domestic establishment of strategic producer goods industries, argued that the choice of trade policies should be based on an evaluation of their contribution to the development of inter-sectoral linkages within the domestic economy.

8 These different approaches are discussed in Todaro (1981), ch. 15, and in Kuyuenhoven (1980). A more technical discussion of planning methodology and techniques is contained in Blitzer *et al.* (1975).

9 Industrial planning may also be concerned with: choice of industrial location (see section 6.9 below), the proportion of production to be exported, the choice of techniques of production, the relative shares of the private and public sectors – see Sutcliffe (1971, p. 303).

10 The poor performance of the agricultural sector may have been due, however, to factors other than government planning and policy.

11 The DRC measure and other efficiency performance criteria are discussed in detail in Pearson (1976).

12   'Competition policy' is often referred to as 'RBP policy' by international organisations such as UNCTAD. Depending upon its scope in a given country, it may cover the control of overall concentration and of concentration in particular markets; it may also regulate restrictive trade practices by a dominant firm or by a group of firms participating in a restrictive trading agreement. The instruments of control may include legal prohibitions, administrative regulation by governmental officials and the establishment of special regulatory commissions or courts.

13   The competition policies operated by DCs, as well as LDCs, vary considerably in their scope and content (UNCTAD, annual). A comparison of the competition policies operated in the UK, USA and EEC is contained in George and Joll (1981), chs 13 and 14.

14   The question of whether or not the availability of capital is a major constraint on the establishment and expansion of small-scale enterprises has been discussed in Chapter 4, section 4.16 and reference has also been made (Chapter 4, section 4.18) to the institutions established by governments in LDCs to channel credit to small-scale enterprises.

15   The definition of technology utilised in this section is given at the beginning of Chapter 4, section 4.8. Dunning (1982, p. 9) reproduced an UNCTAD definition and classification of technology that is also relevant to this discusion:

> Technology is an essential input to production, and as such it is bought and sold in the world market as a 'commodity' embodied in one of the following forms:
>
> (i)   in capital goods and sometimes intermediary goods which are bought and sold in markets, particularly in connection with investment decisions;
>
> (ii)   in human labour, usually qualified and sometimes highly qualified and specialised manpower, with capacity to make correct use of the equipments and techniques and to master the problem solving and information producing apparati;
>
> (iii) in information whether of a technical or of a commercial nature, which is provided in markets, or kept secret as part of monopolistic practices.

16   A number of different terms have been used to describe the type of technology that LDCs are thought to need: appropriate, intermediate, labour-intensive, alternative, progressive (see Stewart, 1977, p. 96). This variety often leads to confusion: 'appropriate' technologies, for example, are not necessarily labour intensive, and the term 'appropriate' is often used without raising the essential question – 'appropriate' with respect to what or to whom?

17   Static efficiency considerations relate to improved labour skills, plant layout, quality of materials and parts inputs, operating and maintenance practices, scheduling, etc. (Mitra, 1979, p.v); dynamic efficiency considerations relate to continuous cost reductions achieved through changes in the manufacturing process and major design innovations (Mitra, 1979, p. vi; Pack, 1981). See also note 2 above.

18   Studies of the UK-type public corporation structure in LDCs are contained in Pozen (1976) and Ahmad (1983).

19   These ratios are normally based upon *money* income data; ideally, if the information were available, they should be based upon *real* income data.

20   This is not to deny, however, the value of more general comparative studies of industrialisation experience in LDCs.

21   One such project, which has been undertaken by the World Bank, aims to develop an industrial data base of internationally consistent data, classified at the four-digit level of the ISIC (*World Bank Research News*, 1983).

Bibliography

Abraham, W. I. (1975), 'Accounting for the public sector in development planning', *Review of Income and Wealth*, series 21, pp. 371–390.

Acharya, S. N. (1979), 'Incentives for resource allocation: a case study of Sudan', *World Bank Staff Working Paper no. 367* (Washington, DC: The World Bank).

Adejugbe, A. (1979), 'Manufacturing', in F. A. Olaoku (ed.), *Structure of the Nigerian Economy* (London: Macmillan), pp. 34–50.

Adelman, I. and Westphal, L. (1979), 'Industrial priorities in the Republic of Korea', in UNIDO, *Industrial Priorities in Developing Countries* (New York: United Nations), pp. 113–128.

Adikibi, O. T. (1983), 'The transfer of technology to Nigeria: the case of tyre production', C. H. Kirkpatrick and F. I. Nixson (eds), *The Industrialisation of Less Developed Countries* (Manchester: Manchester University Press), pp. 81–110.

Agarwal, J. P. (1976), 'Factor proportions in foreign and domestic firms in Indian manufacturing', *Economic Journal*, vol. 86, no. 343, September, pp. 589–594.

Agarwala, A. N. and Singh, S. P. (eds) (1958), *The Economics of Underdevelopment* (Bombay: Oxford University Press).

Agmon, T. and Kindleberger, C. P. (eds) (1977), *Multinationals from Small Countries* (Cambridge, Mass: The MIT Press).

Ahmad, M. (1982), 'Political economy of public enterprise', in L. P. Jones (ed), *Public Enterprise in Less-Developed Countries* (Cambridge: Cambridge University Press), pp. 49–64.

Ahmad, M. (1983), 'Organizational framework, institutional relationships, and management of public industrial enterprises', in *The Changing Role of the Public Industrial Sector in Development*, UNIDO/IS.386, mimeo.

Ahmad, Q. K. (1978), 'The manufacturing sector of Bangladesh: an overview', *Bangladesh Development Studies*, vol. 6, no. 4, pp. 387–416.

Akeredolu-Ale, E. O. (1972), 'Environmental, organizational and group factors in the evolution of private indigenous entrepreneurship in Nigeria', *Nigerian Journal of Economic and Social Studies*, vol. 14, no. 2, July, pp. 237–256.

Akpakpan, E. B. (1983), 'Foreign firms and indigenous firms in economic development: a case study of the brewing industry in Nigeria', Ph.D. thesis (Manchester: University of Manchester), mimeo.

Amjad, R. (1977), 'Profitability and industrial concentration in Pakistan', *Journal of Development Studies*, vol. 13, no. 3, pp 181–198.

Anderson, D. (1982), 'Small industry in developing countries: a discussion of issues', *World Development*, vol. 10, no. 11, November, pp. 913–948.

Ansari, J. A. (1983), 'Conflicting paradigms: the evaluation of public industrial enterprises as agents of national development', *Industry and Development*, no. 7 (New York: United Nations), pp. 37–51.

Arrighi, G. (1970), 'International corporations, labor aristocracies and economic development in tropical Africa', in R. Rhodes (ed.), *Imperialism and Underdevelopment* (New York: Monthly Review Press), pp. 220–267.

Baer, W. (1974), 'The role of government enterprises in Latin America's industrialisation', in D. Geithman (ed.), *Fiscal Policy for Industrialization and Development in Latin America* (Gainsville: University Presses of Florida), pp. 263–292.

Baer, W. (1976), 'Technology, employment and development: empirical findings', *World Development*, vol. 4, no. 2, pp. 121–130.

Baer, W., Kerstenetzky, I. and Villela, A. V. (1973), 'The changing role of the state in the Brazilian economy', *World Development*, vol. 1, no. 11, pp. 23–34.

Baer, W. and Samuelson, L. (1981), 'Toward a service-oriented growth strategy', *World Development*, vol. 9, no. 6, June, pp. 499–514.

Bain, J. S. (1966), *International Differences in Industrial Structure* (New Haven, Conn.: Yale University Press).

Balassa, B. (1978), 'Exports and economic growth', *Journal of Development Economics*, vol. 5, no. 2, June, pp. 181–189.

Balassa, B. (1980), 'The process of industrial development and alternative development strategies', *World Bank Staff Working Paper no. 438* (Washington, DC: World Bank).

Balassa, B. (1982), 'Disequilibrium analysis in developing economies: an overview', *World Development*, vol. 10, no. 12, December, pp. 1027–1038.

Balassa, B. *et al.* (1971), *The Structure of Protection in Developing Countries* (Baltimore, Md.: The Johns Hopkins University Press).

Ballance, R., Ansari, J. A. and Singer, H. (1982), *The International Economy and Industrial Development: The Impact of Trade and Investment on the Third World* (Brighton, Sussex: Wheatsheaf Books).

Ballance, R. and Sinclair, S. (1983), *Collapse and Survival: Industry Strategies in a Changing World* (London: Allen & Unwin).

Banerji, R. (1978), 'Average size of plants in manufacturing and capital intensity: a cross-country analysis by industry', *Journal of Development Economics*, vol. 5, pp. 155–166.

Baran, P. and Sweezy, P. (1968), *Monopoly Capital* (Harmondsworth, Middx: Penguin Books).

Barnett, R. J. and Müller, R. E. (1974), *Global Reach: The Power of the Multinational Corporation* (New York: Simon and Schuster).

Batchelor, R. A., Major, R. L. and Morgan, A. D. (1980a), *Industrialisation and the Basis for Trade* (Cambridge: Cambridge University Press).

Batchelor, R. A., Major, R. L. and Morgan, A. D. (1980b), 'Industrialisation and the basis for trade', *National Institute Economic Review*, no. 93, August, pp. 55–58.

Baumol, W. J. (ed.) (1980), *Public and Private Enterprises in a Mixed Economy* (New York: St Martin's Press).

Baumol, W. J. and Bradford, D. F. (1970), 'Optimal departures from marginal cost pricing', *American Economic Review*, vol. 60, June, pp. 265–283.

Bennathan, E. and Walters, A. A. (1979), *Port Pricing and Investment Policy for Developing Countries* (Oxford: Oxford University Press for the World Bank).

Bergsman, J. (1979), 'Industrial priorities in Brazil', in UNIDO, *Industrial Priorities in Developing Countries* (New York: United Nations), pp. 12–23.

Bernstein, H. (ed.) (1973), *Underdevelopment and Development* (Harmondsworth, Middx: Penguin Books).

Bettelheim, C. (1968), *India Independent* (New York: Monthly Review Press).

Bhagwati, J. (1978), *Anatomy and Consequences of Exchange Control Regimes* (Cambridge, Mass.: Ballinger for the National Institute of Economic Research).

Bhalla, A. S. (ed.) (1975a), *Technology and Employment in Industry: A Case Study Approach* (Geneva: International Labour Office).

Bhalla, A. S. (1975b), 'The concept and measurement of labour intensity', in A. S.

Bhalla (ed.), *Technology and Employment in Industry: A Case Study Approach* (Geneva: International Labour Office), pp. 11–33.

Bhalla, A. S. (ed.) (1979), *Towards Global Action for Appropriate Technology* (Oxford: Pergamon Press).

Bienefeld, M. and Godfrey, M. (eds) (1982), *The Struggle for Development: National Strategies in an International Context* (Chichester, Sussex: John Wiley & Sons).

Biersteker, T. J. (1978), *Distortion or Development? Contending Perspectives on the Multinational Corporation* (Cambridge, Mass.: MIT Press).

Blitzer, C. R. *et al.* (1975), *Economy-Wide Models and Development Planning* (Oxford: Oxford University Press for the World Bank).

Bornschier, V. (1980), 'Multinational corporations and economic growth: a cross-national test of the decapitalization thesis', *Journal of Development Economics*, vol. 7, pp. 191–210.

Brandt Commission (1980), *North–South: A Programme for Survival* (London: Pan Books).

Braun, D. (1983), 'Transnational corporations and development: the pharmaceutical industry in Colombia', in C. H. Kirkpatrick and F. I. Nixson (eds), *The Industrialisation of Less Developed Countries* (Manchester: Manchester University Press), pp. 111–137.

Bromley, R. (1978), 'The urban informal sector: why is it worth discussing?', *World Development*, vol. 6, no. 9/10, pp. 1033–1040.

Bruch, M. (1980), 'Small establishments as exporters of manufactures: tentative evidence from Malaysia', *World Development*, vol. 8, no. 5/6, May/June, pp. 429–442.

Bryce, M. D. (1960), *Industrial Development: A Guide for Accelerating Economic Growth* (Tokyo: McGraw-Hill).

Bryce, M. D. (1965), *Policies and Methods for Industrial Development* (New York: McGraw-Hill).

Byres, T. J. (1982), 'India: capitalist industrialisation or structural stasis? in M. Bienefeld and M. Godfrey (eds), *The Struggle for Development: National Strategies in an Internatinal Context* (Chichester, Sussex: John Wiley & Sons), pp. 135–164.

Cable, J. (1983), 'Economics and politics of protection: some case studies of industries', *World Bank Staff Working Paper no. 569* (Washington, DC: The World Bank).

Caves, R. E. (1971), 'International corporations: the industrial economics of foreign investment', *Economica*, vol. 38, pp. 1–27; reprinted in J. H. Dunning (ed.), *International Investment* (Harmondsworth, Middx: Penguin Books, 1972), pp. 265–301.

Caves, R. E. (1982), *Multinational Enterprise and Economic Analysis* (Cambridge: Cambridge University Press).

Chandra, N. K. (1977), 'Monopoly legislation and policy in India', *Economic and Political Weekly*, vol. 12, no. 33/34, pp. 1405–1418.

Chandra, N. K. (1979), 'Monopoly capital, private corporate sector and the Indian economy: a study in relative growth, 1931–76', *Economic and Political Weekly*, Special no. 14, nos 30–32, August, pp. 1243–1271.

Chenery, H. B. (1960), 'Patterns of industrial growth', *American Economic Review*, vol. 50, no. 4, September, pp. 624–654.

Chenery, H. B. (1979), *Structural Change and Development Policy* (Oxford: Oxford University Press for the World Bank).

Chenery, H. B. (1980), 'Interactions between industrialisation and exports', *American Economic Review*, Papers and Proceedings, vol. 70, pp. 281–287.

Chenery, H. B. (1983), 'Interaction between theory and observation in development', *World Development*, vol. 11, no. 10, October, pp. 853–861.
Chenery, H. and Keesing, D. B. (1979), 'World trade and output of manufactures: structural trends and developing countries' exports', *World Bank Staff Working Paper no. 316* (Washington, DC: The World Bank).
Chenery, H. B. and Syrquin, M. (1975), *Patterns of Development 1950–1970* (Oxford: Oxford University Press for the World Bank).
Chenery, H. B. and Taylor, L. (1968), 'Development patterns: among countries and over time', *The Review of Economics and Statistics*, vol. 50, no. 4, November, pp. 391–416.
Chenery, H. B. *et al.* (1973), *Redistribution with Growth* (Baltimore, Md.: Johns Hopkins University Press).
Chudnovsky, D. (1979), 'The challenge by domestic enterprises to the transnational corporations' domination: a case study of the Argentine pharmaceutical industry', *World Development*, vol. 7, no. 1, January, pp. 45–58.
Chung, B. S. and Lee, C. H. (1980), 'The choice of production techniques by foreign and local firms in Korea', *Economic Development and Cultural Change*, vol. 29, no. 1, October, pp. 135–140.
Churchill, A. (1972), *Road User Charges in Central America*, World Bank Staff Occasional Paper 15 (Washington, DC: The World Bank).
Clark, C. G. (1957), *The Conditions of Economic Progress*, 3rd edn (London: Macmillan).
Clark, N. (1975), 'The multi-national corporation: the transfer of technology and dependence', *Development and Change*, vol. 6, no. 1, January, pp. 5–21.
Cline, W. R. (1982), 'Can the East Asian model of development be generalised?', *World Development*, vol. 10, no. 2, February, pp. 81–90.
Cody, J., Hughes, H. and Wall, D. (eds) (1980), *Policies for Industrial Progress in Developing Countries* (Oxford: Oxford University Press for the World Bank).
Cohen, B. I. (1975), *Multinational Firms and Asian Exports* (New Haven, Conn., and London: Yale University Press).
Colman, D. and Nixson, F. (1978), *Economics of Change in Less Developed Countries* (Oxford: Philip Allan).
Connor, J. M. and Mueller, W. F. (1982), 'Market structure and performance of US multinationals in Brazil and Mexico', *Journal of Development Studies*, vol. 18, no. 3, April, pp. 329–353.
Corden, W. M. (1980), 'Trade policies', in J. Cody, H. Hughes and D. Wall (eds), *Policies for Industrial Progress in Developing Countries* (Oxford: Oxford University Press for the World Bank), pp. 39–92.
Courtney, W. H. and Leipziger, D. M. (1975), 'Multinational corporations in LDCs: the choice of technology', *Oxford Bulletin of Economics and Statistics*, vol. 37, no. 4, November, pp. 297–304.
Cukor, G. (1974), *Strategies for Industrialisation in Developing Countries* (London: C. Hurst).

de la Torre, J. (1974), 'Foreign investment and export dependency', *Economic Development and Cultural Change*, vol. 23, no. 1, October, pp. 133–150.
de Meza, D. E. (1977), 'Multinational corporations in LDCs: a comment', *Oxford Bulletin of Economics and Statistics*, vol. 39, no. 3, August, pp. 237–244.
Derossi, F. (1972), *The Mexican Entrepreneur* (Paris: OECD Development Centre).
Devine, P. J., Lee, N., Jones, R. M. and Tyson, W. J. (1979), *An Introduction to Industrial Economics*, 3rd edn (London: Allen & Unwin).
Dholakia, B. H. (1978), 'Relative performance of public and private manufacturing enterprises in India: total factor productivity approach', *Economic and Political*

Weekly, Review of Management, vol. 13, no. 2, pp. M4–M11.

Diaz-Alejandro, C. F. (1974), 'Some characteristics of recent export expansion in Latin America', in H. Giersch (ed.), *The International Division of Labour: Problems and Perspectives* (Tübingen: J. C. Mohr).

Diaz-Alejandro, C. F. (1977), 'Foreign direct investment by Latin Americans', in T. Agmon and C. P. Kindleberger (eds), *Multinationals from Small Countries* (Cambridge, Mass.: The MIT Press), pp. 167–195.

Donges, J. B. (1976), 'A comparative survey of industrialisation policies in fifteen semi-industrial countries', *Weltwirtschaftliches Archiv*, vol. 112, no. 4, pp. 626–659.

Donges, J. B. and Reidel, J. (1977), 'The expansion of manufactured exports in developing countries: an empirical assessment of demand and supply issues', *Weltwirtschaftliches Archiv*, vol. 113, no. 2, pp. 250–267.

Due, J. F. (1980), 'The economic viability of the railways of tropical Africa', *Journal of Development Economics*, vol. 7, pp. 263–272.

Dunning, J. H. (ed.) (1972), *International Investment* (Harmondsworth, Middx: Penguin Books).

Dunning, J. H. (1981), *International Production and the Multinational Enterprise* (London: Allen & Unwin).

Dunning, J. H. (1982), 'Towards a taxonomy of technology transfer and possible impacts on OECD countries', in *North/South Technology Transfer: The Adjustments Ahead* (Paris: Organisation for Economic Co-operation and Development), pp. 8–24.

Eckaus, R. (1955), 'The factor-proportions problem in underdeveloped areas', *American Economic Review*, vol. 45, no. 4, September, pp. 539–565; reprinted in A. N. Agarawala and S. P. Singh (eds), *The Economics of Underdevelopment* (Bombay: Oxford University Press, 1958), pp. 348–378.

ECLA (1971), 'Public enterprises: their present significance and their potential in development', *Economic Bulletin for Latin America*, vol. 16, no. 1, pp. 1–70.

Evans, P. B. (1976), 'Foreign investment and industrial transformation: a Brazilian case study', *Journal of Development Economics*, vol. 3, pp. 119–139.

Evans, P. B. (1977a), 'Direct investment and industrial concentration', *Journal of Development Studies*, vol. 13, no. 4, July, pp. 373–386.

Evans, P. (1977b), 'Multinationals, state-owned corporations, and the transformation of imperialism: a Brazilian case study', *Economic Development and Cultural Change*, vol. 26, no. 1, October, pp. 43–64.

Evans, P. (1979), *Dependent Development: The Alliance of Multinational, State and Local Capital in Brazil* (Princeton, NJ: Princeton University Press).

Fairchild, L. G. (1977), 'Performance and technology of United States and national firms in Mexico', *Journal of Development Studies*, vol. 14, no. 1, October, pp. 14–34.

Falcon, W. P. and Papanek, G. F. (eds) (1971), *Development Policy II – The Pakistan Experience* (Cambridge, Mass.: Harvard University Press).

Farrell, M. J. (1957), 'The measurement of productive efficiency', *Journal of the Royal Statistical Society*, Series A, vol. 120, part III, pp. 253–290.

Feder, E. (1977), 'Capitalism's last-ditch effort to save underdeveloped agricultures: international agribusiness, the World Bank and the rural poor', *Journal of Contemporary Asia*, vol. 7, no. 1, pp. 56–78.

Fessey, M. C. (1981), 'Business censuses and surveys in developing countries', *The Statistician*, vol. 30, no. 2, pp. 97–106.

Fields, G. (1980), *Poverty, Inequality and Development* (Cambridge: Cambridge University Press).

Finger, J. M. (1975), 'Tariff provisions for offshore assembly and the exports of developing countries', *Economic Journal*, vol. 85, no. 338, June, pp. 365–371.

FitzGerald, E. V. K. (1977), 'The public investment criterion and the role of the state', *Journal of Development Studies*, vol. 13, no. 4, July, pp. 365–372.

Floyd, R. H. (1978), 'Some aspects of income taxation of public enterprises', *IMF Staff Papers*, vol. 25, no. 4, pp. 310–342.

Foreign and Commonwealth Office (1979), *The Newly Industrialising Countries and the Adjustment Problem*, Government Economic Service Working Paper no. 18 (London: HMSO), January.

Forsyth, D. J. C. and Solomon, R. F. (1977), 'Choice of technology and nationality of ownership in manufacturing in a developing country', *Oxford Economic Papers*, vol. 29, no. 2, July, pp. 258–282.

Forsyth, D. J. C., McBain, N. S. and Solomon, R. F. (1980), 'Technical rigidity and appropriate technology in less developed countries', *World Development*, vol. 8, no. 5/6, May/June, pp. 371–398.

Foxley, A. (1980), 'Stabilization policies and stagflation: the cases of Brazil and Chile', *World Development*, vol. 8, No. 11, November, pp. 887–912.

Franko, L. G. (1981), 'Adjusting to export thrusts of newly industrialising countries: an advanced country perspective', *Economic Journal*, vol. 91, no. 362, June, pp. 486–506.

Fransman, M. (ed.) (1982), *Industry and Accumulation in Africa* (London: Heinemann).

Fuentes, P. E. (1983), 'The spatial distribution of industrial production in Brazil, 1960–1970', Ph.D. thesis (Manchester: University of Manchester), mimeo.

Funkhouser, R. and MacAvoy, P. W. (1979), 'A sample of observations on comparative prices in public and private enterprise', *Journal of Public Economics*, vol. 11, pp. 353–368.

Gan, W. B. (1978), 'The relationship between market concentration and profitability in Malaysian manufacturing industries', *Malayan Economic Review*, vol. 23, no. 1, pp. 1–13.

Gan, W. B. and Tham, S. Y. (1977), 'Market structure and price-cost margins in Malaysian manufacturing industries', *The Developing Economies*, vol. 15, no. 3, pp. 280–292.

Gantt, A. H. and Dutto, G. (1968), 'Financial performance of government-owned corporations in less developed countries', *IMF Staff Papers*, vol. 15, pp. 102–142.

Gaude, J. (1975), 'Capital–labour substitution possibilities: a review of empirical evidence', in A. S. Bhalla (ed.) *Technology and Employment in Industry: A Case Study Approach* (Geneva: International Labour Office), pp. 35–38.

Gemmell, N. (1982), 'Economic development and structural change: the role of the service sector', *Journal of Development Studies*, vol. 19, no. 1, October, pp. 37–66.

George K. D. and Joll, C. (1981), *Industrial Organisation: Competition, Growth and Structural Change*, 3rd edn (London: Allen & Unwin).

Gershenberg, I. and Ryan, T. C. I. (1978), 'Does parentage matter? An analysis of transnational and other firms: an East African case', *Journal of Developing Areas*, vol. 13, October, pp. 3–10.

Gersovitz, M. *et al.* (1982), *The Theory and Experience of Economic Development: Essays in Honor of Sir W. Arthur Lewis* (London: Allen & Unwin).

Ghose, A. (1974), 'Investment behaviour of monopoly houses', *Economic and Political Weekly*, vol. 9, nos 43, 44, 45/46, pp. 1813–1824, 1868–1876, 1911–1915.

Ghosh, A. (1975), 'Concentration and growth of Indian industries, 1948–68' *Journal of Industrial Economics*, vol. 23, no. 3, pp. 203–222.

Gilbert, A. and Gugler, J. (1982), *Cities, Poverty and Development: Urbanisation in the Third World* (Oxford: Oxford University Press).

Gilbert, A. G. and Goodman, D. E. (1976), 'Regional income disparities and economic development: a critique', in A. Gilbert (ed.) *Development Planning and Spatial Structure* (London: John Wiley).

Gillis, M. (1980), 'The role of state enterprises in economic development', *Social Research*, Summer, pp. 248–289.

Gillis, M. (1982), 'Allocative and X-efficiency in state-owned mining enterprises: comparisons between Bolivia and Indonesia', *Journal of Comparative Economics*, vol. 6, no. 1, pp. 1–23.

Gillis, M., Jenkins, G. P. and Lessard, D. R. (1982), 'Public-enterprise finance: towards a synthesis', in L. P. Jones (ed.), *Public Enterprise in Less Developed Countries* (Cambridge: Cambridge University Press), pp. 257–280.

Godfrey, M. (1982), 'Kenya: African capitalism or simple dependency?', in M. Bienefeld and M. Godfrey (eds), *The Struggle for Development: National Strategies in an International Context* (Chichester, Sussex: John Wiley & Sons), pp. 265–291.

Griffin, K. (1976), *Land Concentration and Rural Poverty* (London: Macmillan).

Griffin, K. (1977), 'Multinational corporations and basic needs development', *Development and Change*, vol. 8, pp. 61–76.

Gugler, J. (1982), 'Overurbanisation reconsidered', *Economic Development and Cultural Change*, vol. 31, no. 1, pp. 173–190.

Gupta, M. (1982), 'Productivity performance of the public and the private sectors in India: a case study of the fertiliser industry', *Indian Economic Review*, vol. 17, pp. 165–186.

Gupta, V. E. (1968), 'Cost-functions, concentration and barriers to entry in twenty-nine manufacturing industries in India', *Journal of Industrial Economics*, vol. 26, no. 1, pp. 57–72.

Hanson, J. S. (1975), 'Transfer pricing in the multinational corporation: a critical appraisal', *World Development*, vol. 3, nos 11 & 12, pp. 857–865.

Harper, M. and Soon, Tan Thiam (1979), *Small Enterprises in Developing Countries: Case Studies and Conclusions* (London: Intermediate Technology Publications).

Harris, J. R. (1971), 'Nigerian entrepreneurship in industry', in P. Kilby (ed.), *Entrepreneurship and Economic Development* (New York: The Free Press), pp. 331–356.

Harris, J. R. (1972), 'On the concept of entrepreneurship, with an application to Nigeria', in S. P. Schatz (ed.), *South of the Sahara: Development in African Economies* (London: Macmillan), pp. 5–27.

Harris, J. R. and Rowe, M. P. (1966), 'Entrepreneurial patterns in the Nigerian sawmilling industry', *Nigerian Journal of Economic and Social Studies*, vol. 8, no. 1, March, pp. 67–95.

Havrylyshyn, O. and Alikhani, I. (1982), 'Is there a case for export optimism? An inquiry into the existence of a second generation of successful exporters', *Weltwirtschaftliches Archiv*, vol. 118, no. 4, pp. 651–663.

Hay, D. A. and Morris, D. J. (1979), *Industrial Economics: Theory and Evidence* (Oxford: Oxford University Press).

Hazari, R. K. (1966), *The Structure of the Corporate Private Sector: A Study of Concentration, Ownership and Control* (London: Asian Publishing House).

Helleiner, G. K. (1973), 'Manufactured exports from less developed countries and multinational firms', *Economic Journal*, vol. 83, no. 329, March, pp. 21–47.

Helleiner, G. K. (1975), 'The role of multinational corporations in the less developed countries' trade in technology', *World Development*, vol. 3, no. 4, April, pp. 161–189.

Helleiner, G. K. (1981a), 'The Refsnes seminar: economic theory and north–south negotiations', *World Development*, vol. 9, no. 6, June, pp. 539–556.

Helleiner, G. K. (1981b), *Intra-Firm Trade and the Developing Countries* (London: Macmillan).

Hill, H. (1982), 'State enterprises in a competitive industry: an Indonesian case study', *World Development*, vol. 10, no. 11, November, pp. 1015–1023.

Hirsch, S. (1974), 'Hypotheses regarding trade between developing and industrial countries', in H. Giersch (ed.), *The International Division of Labour: Problems and Perspectives* (Tübingen: Mohr).

Hirschman, A. (1958), *The Strategy of Economic Development* (New Haven, Conn.: Yale University Press).

Hoffman, W. G. (1958), *The Growth of Industrial Economies* (Manchester: Manchester University Press).

Hone, A. (1974), 'Multinational corporations and multinational buying groups: their impact on the growth of Asia's exports of manufactures – myths and realities', *World Development*, vol. 2, no. 2, February, pp. 145–149.

Hood, N. and Young, S. (1979), *The Economics of Multinational Enterprise* (London: Longman).

Hoselitz, B. F. (1959), 'Small industry in underdeveloped countries', *Journal of Economic History*, vol. 19, no. 4, pp. 600–618; reprinted in I. Livingstone (ed.), *Development Economics and Policy: Readings* (London: Allen & Unwin, 1981), pp. 203–211.

House, W. J. (1973), 'Market structure and industry performance: the case of Kenya', *Oxford Economic Papers*, vol. 25, no. 3, pp. 405–419.

House, W. J. (1976), 'Market structure and industry performance: the case of Kenya revisited', *Journal of Economic Studies*, vol. 3, no. 2, pp. 117–132.

Hughes, H. (1980), 'Achievements and objectives of industrialisation', in J. Cody, H. Hughes and D. Wall (eds), *Policies for Industrial Progress in Developing Countries* (Oxford: Oxford University Press for the World Bank).

Industrial Research Unit (1975), *Small-Scale Industries* (Nsukka: University of Nigeria).

International Labour Office (1972), *Employment, Incomes and Equality: A Strategy for Increasing Productive Employment in Kenya* (Geneva: ILO).

Itō, S. (1978), 'On the basic nature of the investment company in India', *The Developing Economies*, vol. 16, no. 3, September, pp. 223–238.

James, J. and Lister, S. (1980), 'Galbraith revisited: advertising in non-affluent societies', *World Development*, vol. 8, no. 1, January, pp. 87–96.

Jameson, K. P. (1982), 'A critical examination of "The Patterns of Development"', *Journal of Development Studies*, vol. 18, no. 4, July, pp. 431–446.

Jenkins, R. (1979),'The export performance of multinational corporations in Mexican industry', *Journal of Development Studies*, vol. 15, no. 3, April, pp. 89–107.

Jones, E. (1981), 'Role of the state in public enterprise', in *Public Sector issues in the Commonwealth Caribbean*, special issue of *Social and Economic Studies*, vol. 30, no. 1, March, pp. 17–45.

Jones, L. P. (1976), *Public Enterprise and Economic Development* (Seoul: Korean Development Institute).

Jones, L. P. (ed.) (1982), *Public Enterprise in Less Developed Countries* (Cambridge: Cambridge University Press).

Jones, L. P. (1983), 'The linkage between objectives and control mechanisms in the public manufacturing sector', *Industry and Development* (New York: United Nations), no. 7, pp. 1–12.

Jones, L. P. and Mason, E. S. (1982), 'Role of economic factors in determining the size and structure of the public-enterprise sector in less-developed countries with mixed economies', in L. P. Jones (ed.), *Public Enterprise in Less Developed Countries* (Cambridge: Cambridge University Press), pp. 17–48.

Jones, L. P. and Wortzel, L. H. (1982), 'Public enterprise and manufactured exports in less developed countries: institutional and market factors determining comparative advantage', in L. P. Jones (ed.), *Public Enterprise in Less Developed Countries* (Cambridge: Cambridge University Press), pp. 217–244.

Juster, T. (1973), 'A framework for the measurement of economic and social performance', in M. Moss (ed.), *The Measurement of Economic and Social Performance* (New York: National Bureau of Economic Research).

Kaplinsky, R. (ed.) (1978a), *Readings on the Multinational Corporation in Kenya* (Nairobi: Oxford University Press).

Kaplinsky, R. (1978b), 'Technical change and the multinational corporation: some British multinationals in Kenya', in R. Kaplinsky (ed.), *Readings on the Multinational Corporation in Kenya* (Nairobi: Oxford University Press), pp. 201–260.

Kaplinsky, R. (1979), 'Export-oriented growth: a large international firm in a small developing country', *World Development*, vol. 7, no. 8/9, August–September, pp. 825–834.

Kaplinsky, R. (1980), 'Capitalist accumulation in the periphery – the Kenyan case re-examined', *Review of African Political Economy*, no. 17, January–April, pp. 83–105.

Kaplinsky, R. (1982), 'Capitalist accumulation in the periphery: Kenya', in M. Fransman (ed.), *Industry and Accumulation in Africa* (London: Heinemann), pp. 193–221.

Katrak, H. (1980), 'Industrial structure, foreign trade and price-cost margins in Indian manufacturing industries', *Journal of Development Studies*, vol. 17, no. 1, pp. 62–79.

Keesing, D. B. (1979a), 'World trade and output of manufactures: structural trends and developing countries' exports', *World Bank Staff Working Paper no. 316* (Washington, DC: The World Bank).

Keesing, D. (1979b), 'Trade policy for developing countries', *World Bank Staff Working Paper no. 353* (Washington, DC: The World Bank).

Kemal, A. R. (1978), 'An analysis of industrial efficiency in Pakistan, 1959/60–69/70' Ph.D. thesis (Manchester: University of Manchester), mimeo.

Kennedy, C. and Thirlwall, A. P. (1972), 'Surveys in applied economics: technical progress', *Economic Journal*, vol. 82, no. 1, March, pp. 11–72.

Khalaf, S. and Shwayri, E. (1966), 'Family firms and industrial development: the Lebanese case', *Economic Development and Cultural Change*, vol. 15, no. 1, October, pp. 59–69.

Kilby, P. (1965), *African Enterprise: The Nigerian Bread Industry*, Hoover Institution Studies 8 (Stanford, Calif.: The Hoover Institution on War, Revolution and Peace, Stanford University).

Kilby, P. (1969), *Industrialization in an Open Economy: Nigeria 1945–1966* (Cambridge: Cambridge University Press).

Kilby, P. (ed.) (1971), *Entrepreneurship and Economic Development* (New York: The Free Press).

Killick, T. (1976), 'The possibilities of development planning', *Oxford Economic Papers*, vol. 41, no. 3, November, pp. 161–184.

Killick, T. (1981), *Policy Economics: A Textbook of Applied Economics for Developing Countries* (London: Heinemann).

Killick, T. (1983), 'Development planning in Africa: experiences, weaknesses and prescriptions', *Development Policy Review*, vol. 1, no. 1, pp. 47–76.

Kim, K. S. (1981), 'Enterprise performance in the public and private sectors: Tanzanian experience, 1970–75', *Journal of Developing Areas*, vol. 15, April, pp. 471–484.

King, K. J. (1974), 'Kenya's informal machine-makers: a study of small-scale industry in Kenya's emergent artisan society', *World Development*, vol. 2, no. 4 and 5, April–May, pp. 9–28.

Kirkpatrick, C. H. and Nixson, F. I. (1981). 'Transnational corporations and economic development', *Journal of Modern African Studies*, vol. 19, no. 3, pp. 367–399.

Kirkpatrick, C. H. and Nixson, F. I. (eds) (1983), *The Industrialisation of Less Developed Countries* (Manchester: Manchester University Press).

Kirkpatrick, C. H. and Yamin, M. (1981), 'The determinants of export subsidiary formation by US transnationals in developing countries: an inter-industry analysis', *World Development*, vol. 9, no. 4, April, pp. 373–82.

Knight, J. B. and Sabot, R. H. (1983), 'The role of the firm in wage determination: an African case study', *Oxford Economic Papers*, vol. 35, no. 1, March, pp. 45–66.

Kravis, I. B. (1976), 'A survey of international comparisons of productivity', *Economic Journal*, vol. 86, no. 1, March, pp. 1–44.

Krueger, A. (1978), *Liberalization Attempts and Consequences* (Cambridge, Mass.: Ballinger, for the National Institute of Economic Research).

Krueger, A. (1980), 'Impact of foreign trade on employment in United States industry', in J. Black and B. Hindley (eds), *Current Issues in Commercial Policy and Diplomacy* (London: Macmillan for the Trade Policy Research Centre).

Krueger, A. (1983), 'The effects of trade strategies on growth', *Finance and Development*, vol. 20, no. 2, June, pp. 6–8.

Krueger, A. and Tuncer, B. (1979), 'Industrial priorities in Turkey', in UNIDO, *Industrial Priorities in Developing Countries* (New York: United Nations), pp. 129–169.

Krueger, A. O. and Tuncer, B. (1982), 'Growth of factor productivity in Turkish manufacturing industries', *Journal of Development Economics*, vol. 11, pp. 307–325.

Kumar, N. (1982), 'Regulating multi-national monopolies in India', *Economic and Political Weekly*, vol. 17, no. 22, pp. 909–917.

Kuyvenhoven, A. (1980), 'New industrial planning techniques: macro, sectoral and project linkages', *Industry and Development* (New York: United Nations), no. 5, pp. 18–40.

Kuznets, S. (1965), *Economic Growth and Structure: Selected Essays* (New York: W. W. Norton).

Kuznets, S. (1966), *Modern Economic Growth: Rate, Structure and Spread* (New Haven and London: Yale University Press).

Kuznets, S. (1971), *Economic Growth of Nations: Total Output and Production Structure* (Cambridge Mass.: The Belknap Press of Harvard University Press).

Kuznets, S. (1982), 'The pattern of shift of labor force from agriculture, 1950–70', in M. Gersovitz *et al.* (eds), *The Theory and Experience of Economic Development: Essays in Honor of Sir W. Arthur Lewis* (London: Allen & Unwin). pp. 43–59.

Laird, S. (1981), 'Intra-industry trade and the expansion, diversification and integration of the trade of the developing countries', *Trade and Development, an UNCTAD Review*, no. 3, Winter.

Lal, D. (1979), 'Industrial priorities in India', in UNIDO *Industrial Priorities in Developing Countries* (New York: United Nations), pp. 24–47.

Lal, D. (1980), 'Public enterprises', in J. Cody, H. Hughes and D. Wall (eds) *Policies for Industrial Progress in Developing Countries* (Oxford: Oxford University Press for the World Bank).

Lall, S. (1973), 'Transfer-pricing by multinational manufacturing firms', *Oxford Bulletin of Economics and Statistics*, vol. 35, no. 3, August, pp. 173–193.

Lall, S. (1976a), 'Financial and profit performance of MNCs in developing countries: some evidence from an Indian and Colombian sample', *World Development*, vol, 4, no. 9, pp. 713–724.

Lall, S. (1976b), 'Conflicts of concepts: welfare economics and developing countries', *World Development*, vol. 4, no. 3, March, pp. 181–195.

Lall, S. (1978), 'Transnationals, domestic enterprises and industrial structure in host LDCs: a survey', *Oxford Economic Papers*, vol. 30, no. 2, July, pp. 217–248; reprinted in I. Livingstone (ed.), *Development Economics and Policy: Readings* (London: Allen & Unwin, 1981), pp. 148–163.

Lall, S. (1979a), 'Transfer pricing and developing countries: some problems of investigation', *World Development*, vol. 7, no. 1, January, pp. 59–71.

Lall, S. (1979b), 'Multinationals and market structure in an open developing economy: the case of Malaysia', *Weltwirtschaftliches Archiv*, vol. 115, June, pp. 325–350; reprinted in S. Lall, *The Multinational Corporation: Nine Essays* (London: Macmillan), pp. 65–90.

Lall, S. (1980a), *The Multinational Corporation: Nine Essays* (London: Macmillan).

Lall, S. (1980b), 'Vertical inter-firm linkages in LDCs: an empirical study', *Oxford Bulletin of Economics and Statistics*, vol. 42, no. 3, August, pp. 203–226.

Lall, S. (1980c), 'The international automotive industry and the developing world', *World Development*, vol. 8, no. 10, October, pp. 789–812.

Lall, S. (1981a), *Developing Countries in the International Economy: Selected Papers* (London: Macmillan).

Lall, S. (1981b), 'Recent trends in exports of manufactures by newly-industrialising countries', in S. Lall, *Developing Countries in the International Economy: Selected Papers* (London: Macmillan), pp. 173–227.

Lall, S. (1982), 'The emergence of third world multinationals: Indian joint ventures overseas', *World Development*, vol. 10, no. 2, February, pp. 127–146.

Lall, S. and Streeten, P. (1977), *Foreign Investment, Transnationals and Developing Countries* (London: Macmillan).

Lamb, G. B. and Schaffer, B. B. (1981), *Can Equity be Organised?* (Farnborough, Hampshire: Gower Press).

Lancaster, K. (1974), *Introduction to Modern Micro Economics*, 2nd edn (Chicago: Rand McNally).

Langdon, S. (1975), 'Multinational corporations, taste transfer and underdevelopment: a case study from Kenya', *Review of African Political Economy*, no. 2, January–April, pp. 12–35.

Langdon, S. (1977), 'The state and capitalism in Kenya', *Review of African Political Economy*, no. 8, January–April, pp. 90–98.

Langdon, S. (1979), 'Multinational corporations and the state in Africa', in J. J. Villamil (ed.), *Transnational Capitalism and National Dependence: New Perspectives on Dependence* (Brighton, Sussex: Harvester Press), pp. 223–240.

Lecraw, D. (1977), 'Direct investment by firms from less developed countries', *Oxford Economic Papers*, vol. 29, no. 3, November, pp. 442–457.

Lee Sheng Yi (1976), 'Public enterprise and economic development in Singapore', *The Malayan Economic Review*, vol. 21, no. 2, October, pp. 49–73.

Leff, N. H. (1978), 'Industrial organisation and entrepreneurship in the developing countries: the economic groups', *Economic Development and Cultural Change*, vol. 26, no. 4, pp. 661–675.

Leff, N. H. (1979a), 'Entrepreneurship and economic development: the problem revisited', *Journal of Economic Literature*, vol. 17, no. 1, pp. 46–64.

Leff, N. H. (1979b), 'Monopoly capitalism and public policy in developing countries', *Kyklos*, vol. 32, no. 4, pp. 718–738.

Leibenstein, H. (1966), 'Allocative efficiency vs. X-efficiency', *American Economic Review*, vol. 56, June, pp. 392–415.

Leibenstein, H. (1975), 'Aspects of the X-efficiency theory of the firm', *Bell Journal of Economics*, vol. 6, no. 21, Autumn, pp. 580–606.

Leibenstein, H. (1977), 'X-efficiency theory. Conventional entrepreneurship and excess capacity creation in the LDCs', *Economic Development and Cultural Change*, vol. 25, supplement, pp. 288–299.

Leipziger, D. M. (1976), 'Production characteristics in foreign enclave and domestic manufacturing: the case of India', *World Development*, vol. 4, no. 4, pp. 321–325.

Leys, C. (1975a), *Underdevelopment in Kenya: The Political Economy of Neo-Colonialism* (London: Heinemann).

Leys, C. (1975b), 'The politics of redistribution with growth', *IDS Bulletin*, vol. 7, no. 2, August, pp. 4–9.

Leys, C. (1978), 'Capital accumulation, class formation and dependency – the significance of the Kenyan case', *The Socialist Register 1978* (London: Merlin Press), pp. 241–266; reprinted in M. Fransman (ed.), *Industry and Accumulation in Africa* (London: Heinemann, 1982), pp. 170–192.

Leys, C. (1980), 'Kenya: what does "dependency" mean?', *Review of African Political Economy*, no. 17, January–April, pp. 108–113.

Lindsey, C. W. (1977), 'Market concentration in Philippine manufacturing, 1970', *Philippine Economic Journal*, vol. 16, no. 3, pp. 289–312.

Lindsey, C. W. (1979), 'Size, structure, turnover and mobility of the largest manufacturing firms in a developing country: the case of the Philippines', *Journal of Industrial Economics*, vol. 28, no. 2, pp. 189–200.

Ling, S. L. M. (1979), 'Effects of type of industry on shareholding distribution in Malaysian manufacturing industries', *Malayan Economic Review*, vol. 24, no. 1, pp. 63–84.

Ling, S. L. M. (1980), 'Shareholdings of non-personal investors in manufacturing companies of Malaysia', *Review of Income and Wealth*, vol. 26, no. 1, pp. 115–131.

Linter, J. (1981), 'Economic theory and financial management', in R. Vernon and Y. Aharoni (eds), *State Owned Enterprise in the Western Economies* (London: Croom Helm).

Lipsey, R. and Lancaster, K. (1957), 'The general theory of second best', *Review of Economic Studies*, vol. 24, no. 1, pp. 11–32.

Lipton, M. (1977), *Why Poor People Stay Poor. Urban Bias in World Development* (London: Maurice Temple Smith).

Little, I. M. D. and Mirrlees, J. (1974), *Project Appraisal and Planning for Developing Countries* (London: Heinemann).

Little, I. M. D., Scitovsky, T. and Scott, M. (1970), *Industry and Trade in Some Developing Countries* (London: Oxford University Press).

Livingstone, I. (ed.) (1981), *Development Economics and Policy: Readings* (London: Allen & Unwin).

Livingstone, I. (1982), 'Alternative approaches to small industry promotion', in M. Fransman (ed.), *Industry and Accumulation in Africa* (London: Heinemann), pp. 354–371.

Long, F. (1981), *Restrictive Business Practices, Transnational Corporations and*

Development: A Survey (Boston, The Hague, London: Martinus Nijhoff Publishing).

Mallon, R. D. (1982), 'Public enterprise versus other methods of state intervention as instruments of redistribution policy: the Malaysian experience', in L. P. Jones (ed.), *Public Enterprise in Less Developed Countries* (Cambridge: Cambridge University Press), pp. 313–326.

Marris, P. (1971), 'African businessmen in a dual economy', *Journal of Industrial Economics*, vol. 19, no. 3, July, pp. 231–245.

Marris, P. and Somerset, A. (1971), *African Businessmen: A Study of Entrepreneurship and Development in Kenya* (London: Routledge & Kegan Paul; Nairobi: East African Publishing House).

Mason, R. H. (1973), 'Some observations on the choice of technology by multinational firms in developing countries', *The Review of Economics and Statistics*, vol. 55, pp. 349–355.

Meier, G. M. (ed.) (1983), *Pricing Policy for Development Management* (Baltimore, Md.: The Johns Hopkins University Press for the Economic Development Institute of the World Bank).

Meller, P. (1978), 'The pattern of industrial concentration in Latin America', *Journal of Industrial Economics*, vol. 27, no. 1, pp. 41–47.

Merhav, M. (1969), *Technological Dependence, Monopoly and Growth* (Oxford: Pergamon Press).

Millward, R. and Parker, D. M. (1983), 'Public and private enterprise: comparative behaviour and relative efficiency', in R. Millward, D. Parker, L. Rosenthal, M. T. Sumner and N. Topham, *Public Sector Economics* (London: Longman), pp. 199–274.

Mishan, E. J. (1962), 'Second thoughts on second best', *Oxford Economic Papers*, vol. 14, October, pp. 205–217.

Mitra, J. D. (1979), 'The capital goods sector in LDCs: a case for state intervention?', *World Bank Staff Working Paper no. 343* (Washington, DC: The World Bank).

Morawetz, D. (1974), 'Employment implications of industrialisation in developing countries: a survey', *Economic Journal*, vol. 84, no. 335, September, pp. 491–542.

Morawetz, D. (1976), 'Elasticities of substitution in industry: what do we learn from eonometric estimates?', *World Development*, vol. 4, no. 1, pp. 11–15.

Morley, S. A. and Smith, G. W. (1977a), 'The choice of technology: multinational firms in Brazil', *Economic Development and Cultural Change*, vol. 24, January, pp. 239–264.

Morley, S. A. and Smith, G. W. (1977b), 'Limited search and the technology choices of multinational firms in Brazil', *Quarterly Journal of Economics*, vol. 91, no. 2, May, pp. 263–287.

Munasinghe, M. and Warford, J. J. (1982), *Electricity Pricing* (Baltimore, Md.: The Johns Hopkins University Press for the World Bank).

Nadiri, M. I. (1970), 'Some approaches to the theory and measurement of total factor productivity: a survey', *Journal of Economic Literature*, vol. 8, no. 4, December, pp. 1137–1177.

Nafziger, E. W. (1971), 'Indian entrepreneurship: a survey', in P. Kilby (ed.), *Entrepreneurship and Economic Development* (New York: The Free Press), pp. 287–316.

Nam, W. H. (1975), 'The determinants of industrial concentration: the case of Korea', *Malayan Economic Review*, vol. 20, no 1, pp. 37–48.

Narain, L. (1979), 'Public enterprise in India: an overview', *Annals of Public Cooperative Economy*, vol. 50, no. 4, pp. 59–79.

Nayyar, D. (1978), 'Transnational corporations and manufactured exports from poor countries', *Economic Journal*, vol. 88, no. 349, March, pp. 59–84.

Newfarmer, R. S. (1979a), 'TNC takeovers in Brazil: the uneven distribution of benefits in the market for firms', *World Development*, vol. 7, no. 1, January, pp. 25–43.

Newfarmer, R. S. (1979b), 'Oligopolistic tactics to control markets and the growth of TNCs in Brazil's electrical industry', *Journal of Development Studies*, vol. 15, no. 3, April, pp. 108–140.

Newfarmer, R. S. and Mueller, W. F. (1975), *Multinational Corporations in Brazil and Mexico: Structural Sources of Economic and Non-Economic Power* (Washington, DC: US Senate Subcommittee on Multinational Corporations).

Newlyn, W. T. (1977a), *The Financing of Economic Development* (Oxford: Clarendon Press).

Newlyn, W. T. (1977b), 'Foreign finance', in W. T. Newlyn, *The Financing of Economic Development* (Oxford: Clarendon Press), pp. 93–145.

Nixson, F. I. (1973), *Economic Integration and Industrial Location: An East African Case Study* (London: Longman).

Nixson, F. I. (1981), 'State intervention, economic planning and import-substituting industrialisation: the experience of the LDCs', *METU Studies in Development*, special issue (Ankara, Turkey).

Nixson, F. I. (1982) 'Import-substituting industrialisation', in M. Fransman (ed.), *Industry and Accumulation in Africa* (London: Heinemann).

Nixson, F. I. (1983a), 'Controlling the transnationals? Political economy and the U.N. code of conduct', *International Journal of the Sociology of Law*, vol. 11, no. 1, February, pp. 83–103.

Nixson, F. I. (1983b), 'Transnational corporations and Third World industrialisation', paper presented to *Socialist Economic Review*, Annual Conference, London. Also: *Manchester Discussion Paper in Development Studies*, 8305, mimeo.

Nixson, F. I. (1984), '"Economic development": a suitable case for treatment?' in B. Ingham and C. Simmons (eds), *The Historical Dimensions of Economic Development* (London: Frank Cass), forthcoming.

Nixson, F. and Yamin, M. (1980), 'The United Nations on transnational corporations: a summary and a critique', *British Journal of International Studies*, vol. 6, April, pp. 16–31.

Nyerere, J. K. (1967), 'The Arusha Declaration', in *Freedom and Socialism* (Nairobi: Oxford University Press), pp. 231–250.

OECD (1979a), *The Case for Positive Adjustment Policies, a Compendium of OECD Documents* (Paris: Organisation for Economic Co-operation and Development).

OECD (1979b), *Transfer Pricing and Multinational Enterprises* (Paris: Organisation for Economic Co-operation and Development).

OECD (1979c), *The Impact of the Newly Industrialising Countries on Production and Trade in Manufactures* (Paris: Organisation for Economic Co-operation and Development).

OECD (1982a), *Development Co-operation, 1982 Review* (Paris: Organisation for Economic Co-operation and Development).

OECD (1982b), *North/South Technology Transfer: The Adjustments Ahead* (Paris: Organisation for Economic Co-operation and Development).

OECD (1983), *Investing in Developing Countries*, 5th revised edn (Paris: Organisation for Economic Co-operation and Development).

OECD (various issues), *Development Co-operation Review* (Paris: Organisation for Economic Co-operation and Development).

Oyelabi, J. Ade (1974), 'The developing countries' point of view: 1', in D. Wallace, Jr (ed.), *International Control of Investment: The Düsseldorf Conference on Multinational Corporations* (New York: Praeger), pp. 101–109.

Ozawa, T. (1979), 'International investment and industrial structure: new theoretical implications from the Japanese experience', *Oxford Economic Papers*, vol. 31, no. 1, March, pp. 72–92.

Pack, H. (1976), 'The substitution of labour for capital in Kenyan manufacturing', *Economic Journal*, vol. 86, no. 341, March, pp. 45–58.

Pack, H. (1981), 'Fostering the capital-goods sector in LDCs', *World Development*, vol. 9, no. 3, March, pp. 227–250.

Packard, P. C. (1969), 'A note on concentration and profit rates within the manufacturing sector 1963 and 1965', *Nigerian Journal of Economic and Social Studies*, vol. 2, no. 3, pp. 379–397.

Page, Jr, J. M. (1980), 'Technical efficiency and economic performance: some evidence from Ghana', *Oxford Economic Papers*, vol. 32, no. 2, July, pp. 319–339.

Papanek, G. F. (1971a), 'Pakistan's industrial entrepreneurs – education, occupational background, and finance', in W. P. Falcon and G. F. Papanek (eds), *Development Policy II — The Pakistan Experience* (Cambridge, Mass.: Harvard University Press), pp. 237–261.

Papanek, G. F. (1971b), 'The development of entrepreneurship', in P. Kilby (ed.) *Entrepreneurship and Economic Development* (New York: The Free Press), pp. 317–330.

Paranjape, H. K. (1980), 'New statement on industrial policy', *Economic and Political Weekly*, vol. 15, no. 38, pp. 1592–1597.

Paranjape, H. K. (1982), 'The vanishing MRTP act', *Economic and Political Weekly*, vol. 17, no. 23, pp. 955–961.

Pathirane, L. and Blades, D. (1982), 'Defining and measuring the public sector: some international comparisons', *Review of Income and Wealth*, Series 28, no. 3, September, pp. 261–289.

Pearson, S. R. (1976), 'Net social profitability, domestic resource costs and effective rate of protection', *Journal of Development Studies*, vol. 12, no. 4, July, pp. 320–333.

Perkins, F. C. (1983), 'Technology choice, industrialisation and development experiences in Tanzania', *The Journal of Development Studies*, vol. 19, no. 2, January, pp. 213–243.

Petras, J. (1977), 'State capitalism and the third world', *Development and Change*, vol. 8, no. 1, pp. 1–17.

Phillips, D. A. (1980), 'Choice of technology and industrial transformation: the case of the United Republic of Tanzania', *Industry and Development* (New York: United Nations Industrial Development Organisation), no. 5, pp. 85–106.

Plant, R. (1983), *A Short Guide to the ILO World Employment Programme* (Geneva: International Labour Office).

Pozen, R. (1976), *Legal Choices for State Enterprise in the Third World* (New York: New York University Press).

Primeaux, W. J. (1977), 'An assessment of X-efficiency gained through competition', *Review of Economics and Statistics*, vol. 59, no. 1, pp. 105–108.

Radetzki, M. (1980), 'Changing structures in the financing of the minerals industry in LDCs', *Development and Change*, vol. 11, no. 1, pp. 1–15.

Radice, H. (ed.) (1975), *International Firms and Modern Imperialism* Harmondsworth, Middx: Penguin Books).

Ray, R. K. (1979), *Industrialization in India: Growth and Conflict in the Private Corporate Sector 1914–47* (Delhi: Oxford University Press).

Rees, R. (1976), *Public Enterprise Economics* (London: Weidenfeld & Nicolson).

Renaud, B. (1981), *National Urbanisation Policy in Developing Countries* (New York: Oxford University Press).

Reuber, G. L. (1973), *Private Foreign Investment in Development* (Oxford: Clarendon Press).

Rhodes, R. (ed.) (1970), *Imperialism and Underdevelopment* (New York: Monthly Review Press).

Robinson, A. (ed.) (1979a), *Appropriate Technologies for Third World Development* (London: Macmillan).

Robinson, A. (1979b), 'The availability of appropriate technologies', in A. Robinson (ed.), *Appropriate Technologies for Third World Development* (London: Macmillan), pp. 26–51.

Robson, W. A. (1960), *Nationalized Industry and Public Ownership* (London: Allen & Unwin).

Roemer, M. (1981), 'Dependence and industrialisation strategies', *World Development*, vol. 9, no. 5, May, pp. 429–434.

Rood, L. L. (1976), 'Nationalisation and indigenisation in Africa', *Journal of Modern African Studies*, vol. 14, no. 3, September, pp. 427–447.

Rweyemamu, J. (1973), *Underdevelopment and Industrialisation in Tanzania: A Study of Perverse Capitalist Industrial Development* (Nairobi: Oxford University Press).

Sampson, G. P. (1980), 'Contemporary protectionism and the exports of developing countries', *World Development*, vol. 8, no. 2, February, pp. 113–128.

Sant'ana, J. A. (1983), 'The role of foreign capital in recent Brazilian development', in C. H. Kirkpatrick and F. I. Nixson (eds), *The Industrialisation of Less Developed Countries* (Manchester: Manchester University Press), pp. 172–195.

Saunders, R. J. and Warford, J. J. (1976), *Village Water Supply* (Baltimore, Md: The Johns Hopkins University Press for the World Bank).

Sawhney, P. K. and Sawhney, B. L. (1973), 'Capacity-utilisation, concentration and price-cost margins: results of Indian industries', *Journal of Industrial Economics*, vol. 21, no. 2, pp. 145–153.

Sawyer, M. C. (1981), *The Economics of Industries and Firms* (London: Macmillan).

Schatz, S. P. (1963), 'Economic environment and private enterprise in West Africa', *The Economic Bulletin (Ghana)*, vol. 7, no. 4, December.

Schatz, S. P. (ed.) (1972a), *South of the Sahara: Development in African Economies* (London: Macmillan).

Schatz, S. P. (1972b), 'Development in an adverse economic environment', in S. P. Schatz (ed.) *South of the Sahara: Development in African Economies* (London: Macmillan), pp. 28–60.

Schatz, S. P. (1977), *Nigerian Capitalism* (Berkeley, Los Angeles, London: University of California Press).

Scherer, F. M. (1980), *Industrial Market Structure and Economic Performance*, 2nd edn (Chicago: Rand McNally).

Schmitz, H. (1982), 'Growth constraints on small-scale manufacturing in developing countries: a critical review', *World Development*, vol. 10, no. 6, pp. 429–450.

Schumpeter, J. A. (1934), *The Theory of Economic Development* (Cambridge, Mass.: Harvard University Press).

Sen, A. (1980), 'Labor and technology', in J. Cody, H. Hughes and D. Wall (eds), *Policies for Industrial Progress in Developing Countries* (Oxford: Oxford University Press for the World Bank), pp. 121–158.

Sharma, R. A. (1973), 'Emerging patterns of industrial entrepreneurship in India', *The Developing Economies*, vol. 11, no. 1, March, pp. 39–61.

Sharpston, M. (1975), 'International sub-contracting', *Oxford Economic Papers*, vol. 27, no. 1, March, pp. 94–135.

Sharwani, K. (1976), 'Some new evidence on concentration and profitability in Pakistan's large-scale manufacturing industries', *Pakistan Development Review*, vol. 15, no. 3, pp. 272–289.

Sheahan, J. B. (1976), 'Public enterprise in developing countries', in W. G. Shepherd (ed.). *Public Enterprise: Economic Analysis of Theory and Practice* (Lexington, Mass.: D. C. Heath).

Sicat, G. P. and Villarroel, A. M. (1974), 'Industrial concentration in the Philippines', *Philippine Economic Journal*, vol. 13, no. 2, pp. 85–129.

Singer, H. W. (1979), 'Policy implications of the Lima target', *Industry and Development*, no. 3, Special Issue for the Third General Conference of the United Nations Industrial Development Organisation (New York: United Nations).

Singer, H. W. (1983), 'North–South multipliers', *World Development*, vol. 11, no. 5, May, pp. 451–455.

Singer, H. (1984), 'Industrialisation: where do we stand? where are we going?' (Brighton, Sussex: The Institute of Development Studies), mimeo.

Singh, A. (1979), 'The "basic needs" approach to development vs. the new international economic order: the significance of Third World industrialisation', *World Development*, vol. 7, no. 6, June, pp. 585–606.

Snowden, N. (1977), 'Company savings in Kenya's manufacturing sector', in W. T. Newlyn (ed.), *The Financing of Economic Development* (Oxford: Clarendon Press), pp. 287–310.

Sobhan, R. (1979a), 'Public enterprises and the nature of the state', *Development and Change*, vol. 10, no. 1, pp. 23–40.

Sobhan, R. (1979b), 'Public enterprise as an instrument of policy in anti-poverty strategies in South Asia', *Economic Bulletin for Asia and the Pacific* (published by the Economic and Social Commission for Asia and the Pacific), vol. 30, no. 1, June, pp. 56–97.

Sobhan, R. (1983), 'Distributive regimes under public enterprise: a case study of the Bangladesh experience', in F. Stewart (ed.), *Work, Income and Inequality: Payments Systems in the Third World* (London: Macmillan), pp. 138–167.

Solomon, R. F. and Forsyth, D. J. C. (1977), 'Substitution of labour for capital in the foreign sector: some further evidence', *Economic Journal*, vol. 87, no. 346, June, pp. 283–289.

Squire, L. (1981), *Employment Policy in Developing Countries, A Survey of Issues and Evidence* (Oxford: Oxford University Press for the World Bank).

Squire, L. and van der Tak, H. (1975), *Economic Analysis of Projects* (Baltimore, Md: The Johns Hopkins University Press for the World Bank).

Staley, E. and Morse, R. (1965), *Modern Small Industry for Developing Countries* (New York: McGraw-Hill).

Stern, R. (1975), 'Testing trade theories', in P. Kenen (ed.), *International Trade and Finance* (Cambridge: Cambridge University Press).

Steuer, M. D. and Voivodas, C. (1965), 'Import substitution and Chenery's patterns of industrial growth – a further study', *Economia Internazionale*, vol. 18, no. 1, February, pp. 47–82.

Stewart, F. (1972), 'Choice of technique in developing countries', *Journal of Development Studies*, vol. 9, no. 1, October, pp. 99–121.

Stewart, F. (1975), 'A note on social cost benefit analysis and class conflict in LDCs', *World Development*, vol. 3, no. 1, January, pp. 31–39.

Stewart, F. (1977), *Technology and Underdevelopment* (London: Macmillan).

Stewart, F. (ed.) (1983), *Work, Income and Inequality: Payment Systems in the Third World* (London: Macmillan).

Stewart, F. and Streeten, P. (1976), 'New strategies for development: poverty, income distribution and growth', *Oxford Economic Papers*, vol. 28, no. 3, November, pp. 381–405.

Stohr, W. (1975), *Regional Development: Experiences and Prospects in Latin America* (Paris: Mouton).

Streeten, P. (1972), 'The multinational corporation and the nation state', in *The Frontiers of Development Studies* (London: Macmillan), pp. 233–238.

Sunkel, O. (1973), 'Transnational capitalism and national disintegration in Latin America', *Social and Economic Studies*, vol. 22, no. 1, March, pp. 132–176.

Sunkel, O. and Fuenzalida, E. F. (1979), 'Transnationalisation and its national consequences', in J. J. Villamil (ed.), *Transnational Capitalism and National Development: New Perspectives on Dependence* (Hassocks, Sussex: Harvester Press), pp. 67–93.

Sutcliffe, R. B. (1971), *Industry and Underdevelopment* (London: Addison-Wesley).

Swainson, N. (1980), *The Development of Corporate Capitalism in Kenya 1918–1977* (London: Heinemann).

Teece, D. J. (1977), 'Technology transfer by multinational firms: the resource cost of transferring technological know-how', *Economic Journal*, vol. 87, no. 346, June, pp. 242–261.

Teitel, S. (1975), 'Economies of scale and size of plant: the evidence and implications for the developing countries', *Journal of Common Market Studies*, vol. 13, no. 1, pp. 92–115.

Temin, P. (1967), 'A time series test of patterns of industrial growth', *Economic Development and Cultural Change*, vol. 15, no. 2, pp. 174–182.

Teriba, O., Edozien, E. C. and Kayode, M. O. (1972), 'Some aspects of ownership and control structure of business enterprise in a developing country: the Nigerian case', *Nigerian Journal of Economic and Social Studies*, vol. 14, no. 1, pp. 3–26.

Thirwall, A. P. (1983), *Growth and Development*, 3rd edn (London: Macmillan).

Thomas, C. Y. (1974), *Dependence and Transformation* (New York: Monthly Review Press).

Todaro, M. (1981), *Economic Development in the Third World*, 2nd edn (London: Longman).

Tokman, V. E. (1978), 'An exploration into the nature of informal–formal sector relationships', *World Development*, vol. 6, no. 9/10, pp. 1065–1075.

Tolley, G. S. (1974), 'Welfare economics of city bigness', *Journal of Urban Economics*, vol. 1, pp. 324–345.

Trebat, T. J. (1980), 'An evaluation of the economic performance of large public enterprises in Brazil 1965–75', Technical Paper Series no. 24 (Austin: The University of Texas Institute of Latin American Studies).

Trebat, T. J. (1983), *Brazil's State Owned Enterprises* (Cambridge: Cambridge University Press).

Turok, B. (1981), 'Control in the parastatal sector of Zambia', *Journal of Modern African Studies*, vol. 19, no. 3, pp. 421–446.

Turvey, R. (1969), 'Marginal cost', *Economic Journal*, vol. 79, no. 2, June, pp. 282–299.

Tyler, W. G. (1976), 'Brazilian industrialization and industrial policies: a survey', *World Development*, vol. 4, no. 10/11, October/November, pp. 863–882.

Tyler, W. G. (1979), 'Technical efficiency in production in a developing country: an empirical examination of the Brazilian plastics and steel industries', *Oxford Economic Papers*, vol. 31, no. 3, November, pp. 477–495.

Tyler, W. G. (1981), 'Growth and export expansion in developing countries', *Journal of Development Economics*, vol. 9, pp. 121–130.

ul Haq, M. (1973), 'Industrialisation and trade strategies in the 1970s: developing country alternatives', in P. Streeten (ed.), *Trade Strategies for Development* (London: Macmillan).

United Nations (1971), *Indexes to the International Industrial Classification of All Economic Activities*, UN Statistical Papers, Series M, no. 4, rev. 2, add. 1.

United Nations (1974a), *The Acquisition of Technology from Multinational Corporations by Developing Countries*, ST/ESA/12 (New York: United Nations).

United Nations (1974b), *The Impact of Multinational Corporations on Development and on International Relations (Report of the Group of Eminent Persons)*, E/5500/rev. 1; ST/ESA/6 (New York: United Nations).

United Nations (1975a), *Trends and Prospects in the Population of Urban Agglomeration, 1950–2000* (New York: United Nations).

United Nations (1975b), 'Industrialisation and development: progress and problems in developing countries', *Journal of Development Planning* (Centre for Development Planning, Projections and Policies), no. 8, pp. 1–60.

United Nations (1977), 'Implementation of development plans: the experience of developing countries in the first half of the 1970s', *Journal of Development Planning* (Centre for Development Planning, Projections and Policies), no. 12, pp. 1–65.

United Nations (1978), *Transnational Corporations in World Development: A Re-examination*, E/C.10/38 (New York: United Nations).

United Nations (1979), *Supplementary Material on the Issue of Defining Transnational Corporations*, E/C.10/58 (New York: United Nations).

United Nations (1980), *Patterns of Urban and Rural Population Growth* (New York: United Nations).

United Nations (1981), 'Proceedings of the expert group on water pricing', *Water Resources Series No. 55* (New York: United Nations).

United Nations (1983), *Transnational Corporations in World Development: Third Survey*, ST/CTC/46 (New York: United Nations).

United Nations (annual), *Yearbook of Industrial Statistics* (New York: United Nations).

UNCTAD (1977), *Dominant Positions of Market Power of Transnational Corporations: Use of the Transfer Pricing Mechanism*, TD/B/C.2/167 (Geneva: United Nations Conference on Trade and Development).

UNCTAD (1978a), *Dynamic Products in the Exports of Manufactured Goods from Developing Countries to Developed Market-Economy Countries, 1970 to 1976*, ST/MD/18 (Geneva: United Nations Conference on Trade and Development).

UNCTAD (1978b), *Annual Report on Legislative and Other Developments in Developed and Developing Countries in the Control of Restrictive Business Practices 1977* (New York: United Nations).

UNCTAD (1979), *First Draft of a Model Law or Laws on Restrictive Business Practices to Assist Developing Countries in Devising Appropriate Legislation* (New York: United Nations).

UNCTAD (1981a), *Trade and Development Report, 1981* (New York: United Nations).

UNCTAD (1981b), *Planning the Technological Transformation of Developing Countries*, TD/B/C.6/50 (New York: United Nations).

UNCTAD (1982), *Trade and Development Report 1982*, 3 vols (Geneva: United Nations Conference on Trade and Development).

UNCTAD (1983), *Protectionism, Trade Relations and Structural Adjustment*, TD/274, UNCTAD VI (Belgrade).

UNCTAD (annual), *Annual Report on Legislative and Other Developments in Developed and Developing Countries in the Control of Restrictive Business Practices* (New York: United Nations).

UNIDO (1972), *Guidelines for Project Evaluation* (New York: United Nations).

UNIDO (1979a), *World Industry Since 1960: Progress and Prospects* (New York: United Nations).

UNIDO (1979b), *Industrial Priorities in Developing Countries: The Selection Process in Brazil, India, Mexico, Republic of Korea and Turkey* (New York: United Nations).

UNIDO (1981a), *World Industry in 1980* (New York: United Nations).

UNIDO (1981b), *Structural Changes in Industry* (New York: United Nations).

UNIDO (1982a), *The Role of the Public Industrial Enterprise Sector in Sri Lanka*, UNIDO/IS.349.

UNIDO (1982b), *The Role of the Public Industrial Sector in Brazil*, UNIDO/IS.357.

UNIDO (1982c), *Role of the Public Industrial Enterprises in India*, UNIDO/IS.367.

UNIDO (1982d), *The Role of the Public Sector in the Industrialisation of the United Republic of Tanzania*, UNIDO/IS.358.

UNIDO (1983a), *Industry and Development*, no. 7, special issue on public enterprises (New York: United Nations).

UNIDO (1983b), *Selected Statistical Indicators*, ID/WD.391/1.

UNIDO (1983c), *The Changing Role of the Public Industrial Sector in Development*, UNIDO/IS.386.

Vaitsos, C. V. (1973), 'Bargaining and the distribution of returns in the purchase of technology by developing countries', in H. Bernstein (ed.), *Underdevelopment and Development* (Harmondsworth, Middx: Penguin Books), pp. 315–322.

Vaitsos, C. V. (1974), *Intercountry Income Distribution and Transnational Enterprises* (Oxford: Clarendon Press).

Vanlommel, E., de Brabander, B. and Liebaers, D. (1977), 'Industrial concentration in Belgium: empirical comparisons of alternative sector concentration measures', *Journal of Industrial Economics*, vol. 26, no. 1, pp. 1–20.

Vermeulen, B. and Sethi, R. (1982), 'Labour–management conflict resolution in state-owned enterprises: a comparison of public- and private-sector practices in India', in L. P. Jones (ed.), *Public Enterprise in Less Developed Countries* (Cambridge: Cambridge University Press), pp. 141–168.

Vernon, R. (1966), 'International investment and international trade in the product cycle', *Quarterly Journal of Economics*, vol. 80, pp. 190–207; reprinted in J. H. Dunning (ed.), *International Investment* (Harmondsworth, Middx: Penguin Books, 1972), pp. 305–325.

Vernon, R. (1971), *Sovereignty at Bay: The Multinational Spread of U.S. Enterprises* (Harmondsworth, Middx: Penguin Books).

Vernon, R. (1977), *Storm Over the Multinationals: The Real Issues* (London: Macmillan).

Vernon, R. (1979), 'The product cycle hypothesis in a new international environment', *Oxford Bulletin of Economics and Statistics*, vol. 41, no. 4, November, pp. 255–267.

Vernon, R. (1981), 'The state-owned enterprise in Latin American exports', *Quarterly Review of Economics and Business*, vol. 21, no. 2, Summer, pp. 98–114.

Villamil, J. J. (ed.) (1979), *Transnational Capitalism and National Development: New Perspectives on Dependence* (Hassocks, Sussex: Harvester Press).

Walgreen, J. A. (1971), 'Cost functions, concentration and barriers to entry in twenty-nine manufacturing industries in India: a comment and reinterpretation', *Journal of Industrial Economics*, vol. 20, no. 1, pp. 90–95.

Wallace, D. Jr (1974), *International Control of Investment: The Düsseldorf Conference on Multinational Corporations* (New York: Praeger).

Walstedt, B. (1980), *State Manufacturing Enterprise in a Mixed Economy: The Turkish Case* (Baltimore, Md: The Johns Hopkins University Press, for the World Bank).

Walter, I. (1979), 'Protection of industries in trouble – the case of iron and steel', *The World Economy*, vol. 2, no. 2, pp. 155–188.

Walters, A. A. (1968), *The Economics of Road User Charges* (Baltimore, Md: The Johns Hopkins Press, for the World Bank).

Wells, L. T., Jr (1972), 'International trade: the product cycle approach', in L. T. Wells (ed.), *The Product Life Cycle and International Trade* (Cambridge, Mass.: Graduate School of Business Administration, Harvard University).

Wells, L. T. (1973), 'Economic man and engineering man: choice of technology in a low wage country', *Public Policy*, Summer.

Wells, L. T. (1977), 'The internationalisation of firms from developing countries', in T. Agmon and C. P. Kindleberger (eds), *Multinationals from Small Countries* (Cambridge, Mass.: The MIT Press), pp. 133–156.

White, L. J. (1974a), 'Pakistan's industrial families: the extent, causes and effects of their economic power', *Journal of Development Studies*, vol. 10, nos 3 & 4, April/July, pp. 273–304.

White, L. J. (1974b), *Industrial Concentration and Economic Power in Pakistan* (Princeton, NJ: Princeton University Press).

White, L. J. (1976), 'Appropriate technology, X-efficiency, and a competitive environment: some evidence from Pakistan', *Quarterly Journal of Economics*, vol. 90, no. 4, November, pp. 575–589.

White, L. J. (1978), 'The evidence on appropriate factor proportions for manufacturing in less developed countries: a survey', *Economic Development and Cultural Change*, vol. 27, no. 1, October, pp. 27–59.

White, L. J. (1979), 'Appropriate factor proportions for manufacturing in less developed countries: a survey of the evidence', in A. Robinson (ed.), *Appropriate Technologies for Third World Development* (London: Macmillan), pp. 300–341.

Williamson, J. G. (1965), 'Regional inequality and the process of national development: a description of the patterns', *Economic Development and Cultural Change*, vol. 13, no. 4, pp. 3–43.

Willmore, L. (1976), 'Direct foreign investment in Central American manufacturing', *World Development*, vol. 4, no. 6, pp. 499–517.

Winston, G. C. (1979), 'The appeal of inappropriate technologies: self-inflicted wages, ethnic pride and corruption', *World Development*, vol. 7, no. 8/9, August–September, pp. 835–845.

World Bank (1976), *Development Finance Companies* (Washington, DC: Sector Policy Paper).

World Bank (1978), *Employment and Development of Small Enterprises* (Washington, DC: Sector Policy Paper).

World Bank (1979a), *Mexico: Manufacturing Sector: Situation, Prospects and Policies* (Washington, DC: World Bank).

World Bank (1979b), *World Development Report, 1979* (Washington, DC: International Bank for Reconstruction and Development).

World Bank (1980), *World Development Report, 1980* (Washington, DC: International Bank for Reconstruction and Development).

World Bank (1981), *World Development Report, 1981* (Washington, DC: International Bank for Reconstruction and Development).

World Bank (1982), *World Development Report, 1982* (London: Oxford University Press for the World Bank).

World Bank (1983), *World Development Report, 1983* (London: Oxford University Press for the World Bank).

World Bank (annual), *World Development Report* (London: Oxford University Press for the World Bank).

World Bank Research News (1983), vol. 4, no. 2, pp. 23–24.

World Development (1983), *Pharmaceuticals and Health in the Third World*, special issue, vol. 11, pp. 165–328.

Yamin, M. (1983), 'Direct foreign investment as an instrument of corporate rivalry: theory and evidence from the LDCs', in C. H. Kirkpatrick and F. I. Nixson (eds), *The Industrialisation of Less Developed Countries* (Manchester: Manchester University Press), pp. 196–225.

Yoshihara, K. (1971), 'A study of Philippine manufacturing corporations', *The Developing Economies*, vol. 9, pp. 268–289.

Author Index

Subject Index

and individual preferences 160
and Pareto conditions 156, 190

Yugoslavia 94

Zaire 164
Zambia 6, 9, 151, 152, 154, 164, 187, 197
Zimbabwe 6